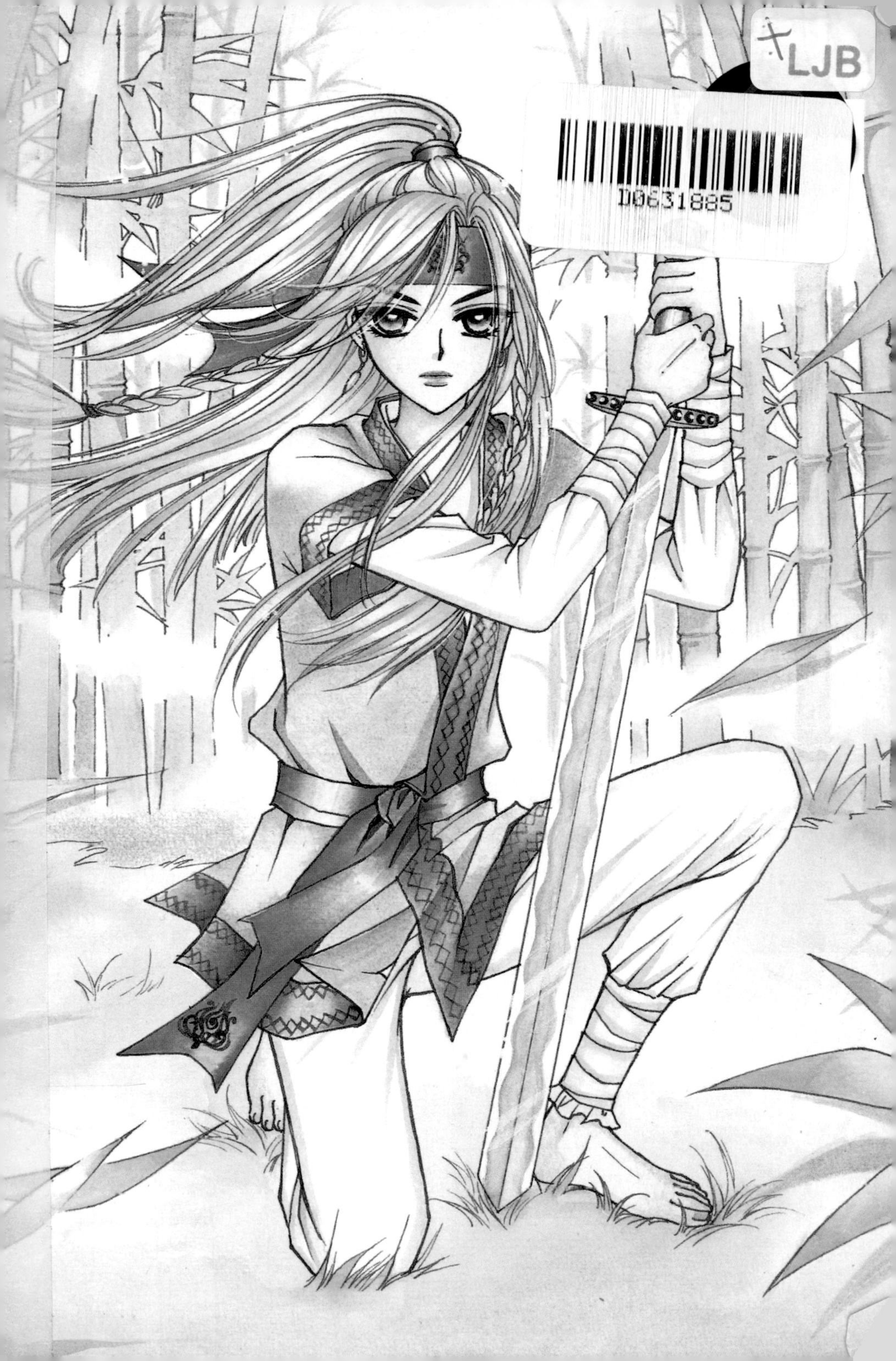

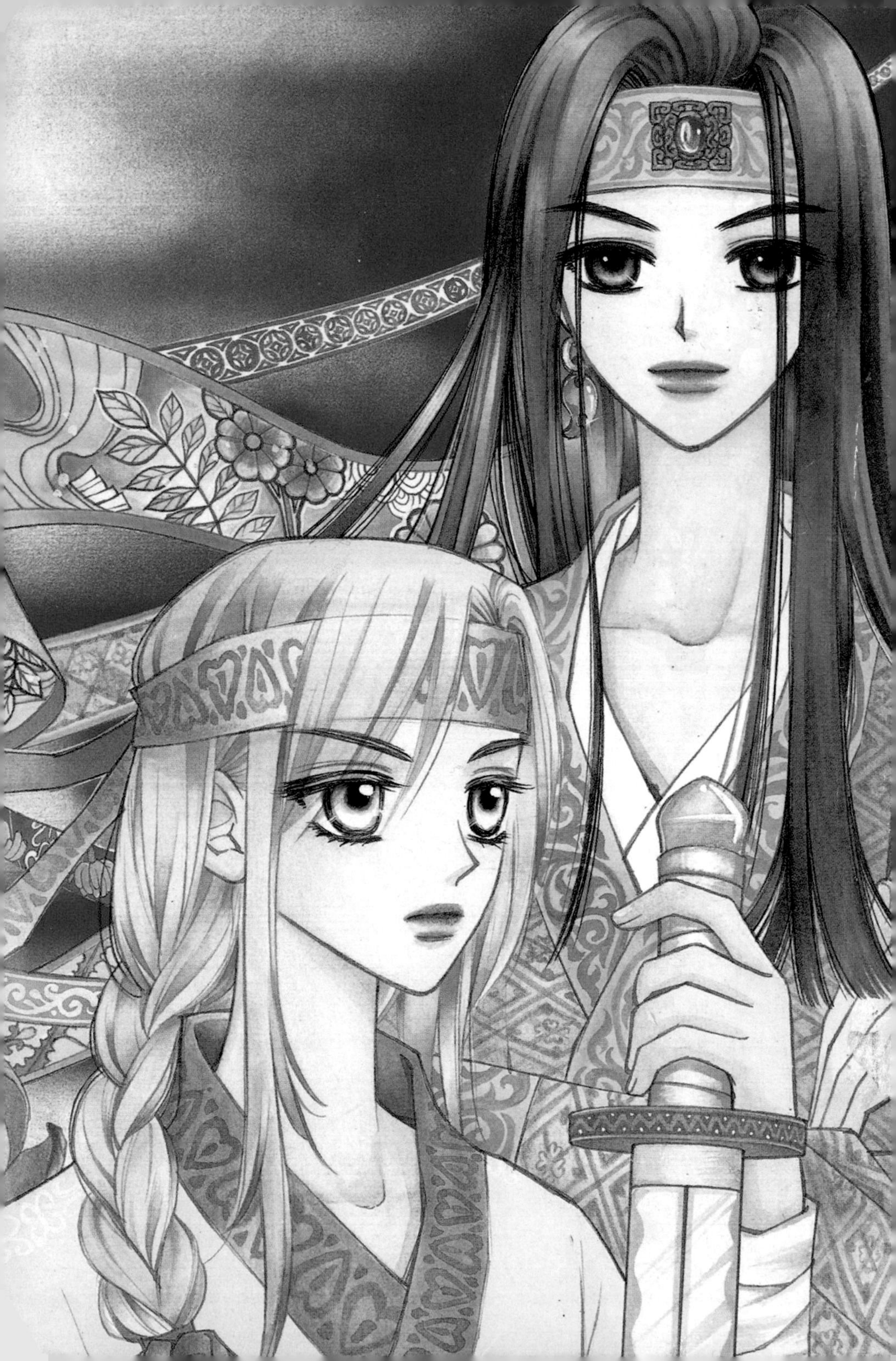

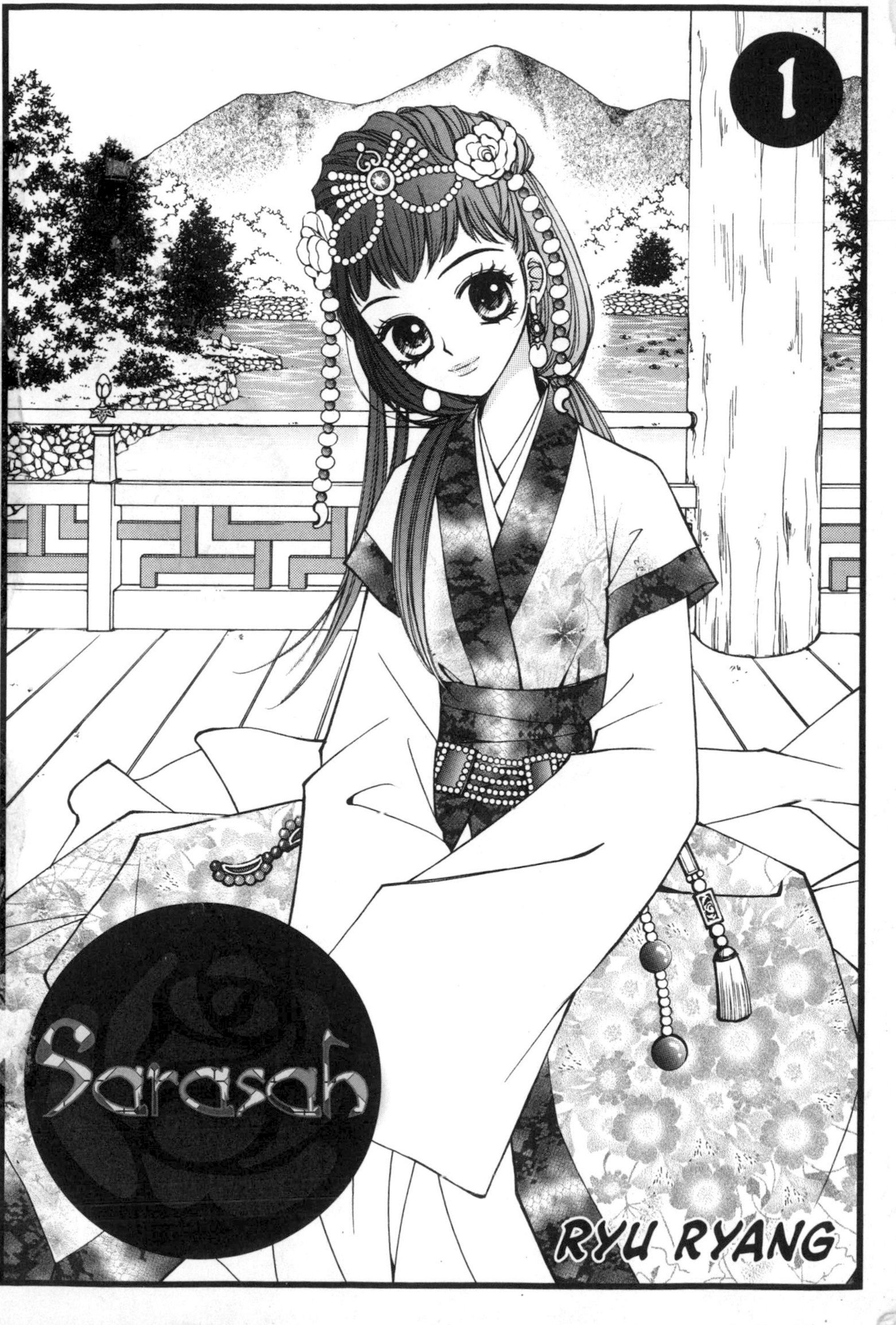
1
Sarasah
RYU RYANG

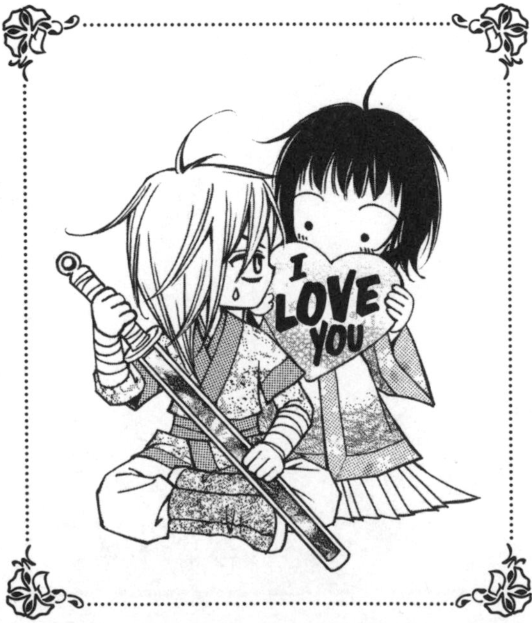
I LOVE YOU

"THE MOST DIFFICULT THING TO EXPLAIN IN LIFE IS THE SIMPLEST TRUTH CALLED LOVE."

—RAMANATHAN SRINIVASAN

"LOVE HAS ALWAYS BEEN THE MOST IMPORTANT BUSINESS IN MY LIFE, I SHOULD SAY THE ONLY ONE."

—STENDHAL

"LOVE IS LIKE THE MEASLES; WE ALL HAVE TO GO THROUGH IT."

—JEROME K. JEROME

"TO LIVE WITHOUT LOVING IS NOT REALLY TO LIVE."

—MOLIÈRE

"THE SWEETEST JOY, THE WILDEST WOE IS LOVE."

—PHILIP JAMES BAILEY

"THAT IS THE TRUE MEASURE OF LOVE, WHEN WE BELIEVE THAT WE ALONE CAN LOVE, THAT NO ONE COULD EVER HAVE LOVED SO BEFORE US, AND THAT NO ONE WILL LOVE IN THE SAME WAY AFTER US."

—GOETHE

"YOU KNOW QUITE WELL, DEEP WITHIN YOU, THAT THERE IS ONLY A SINGLE MAGIC, A SINGLE POWER, A SINGLE SALVATION...AND THAT IS CALLED LOVING."

—HESSE

"THERE IS ONLY ONE HAPPINESS IN LIFE, TO LOVE AND BE LOVED."

—GEORGE SAND

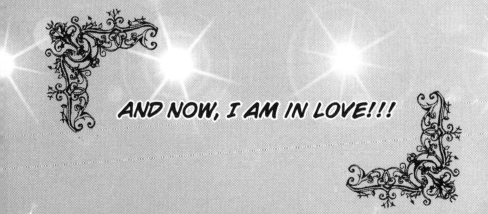

AND NOW, I AM IN LOVE!!!

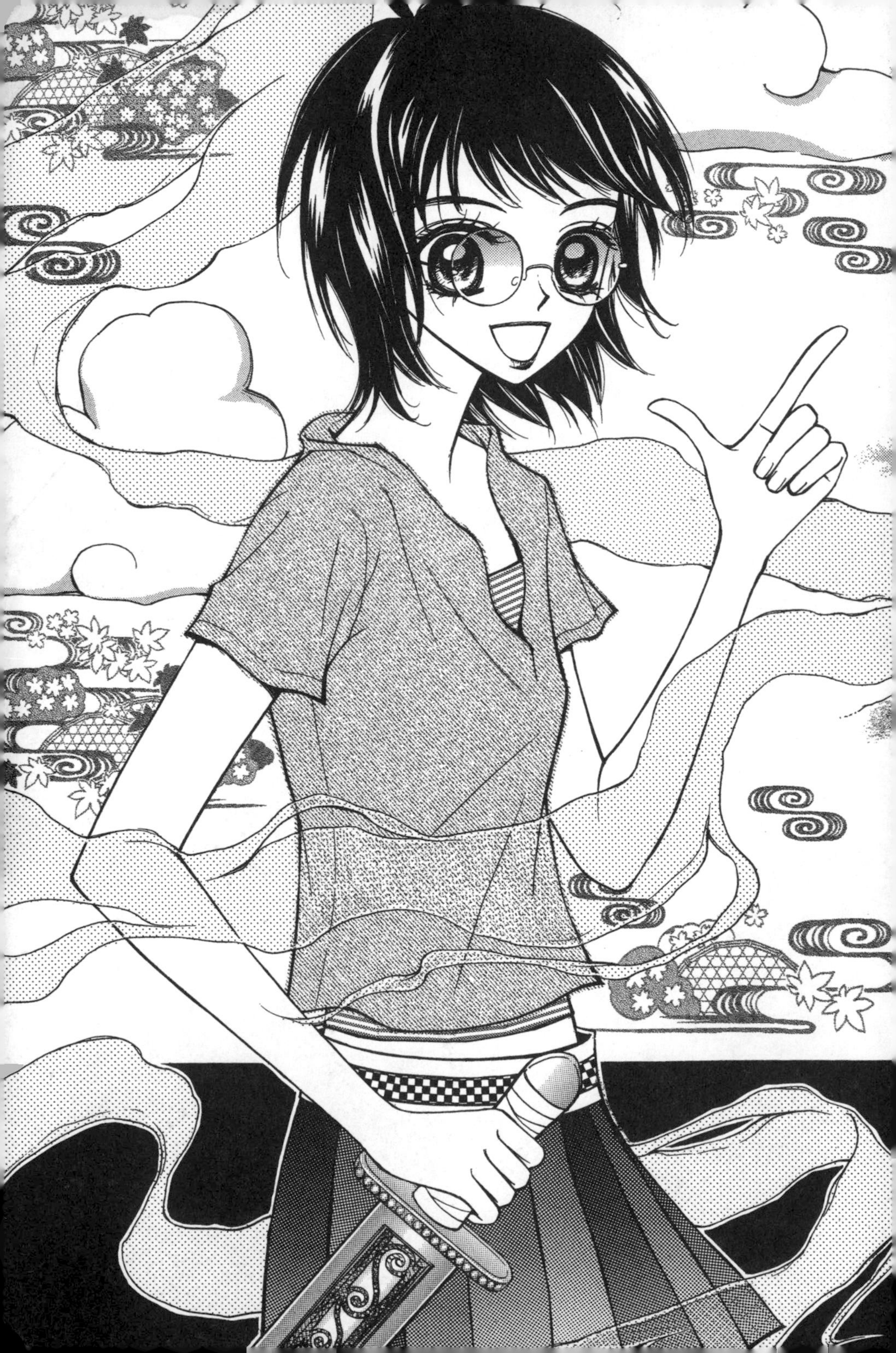

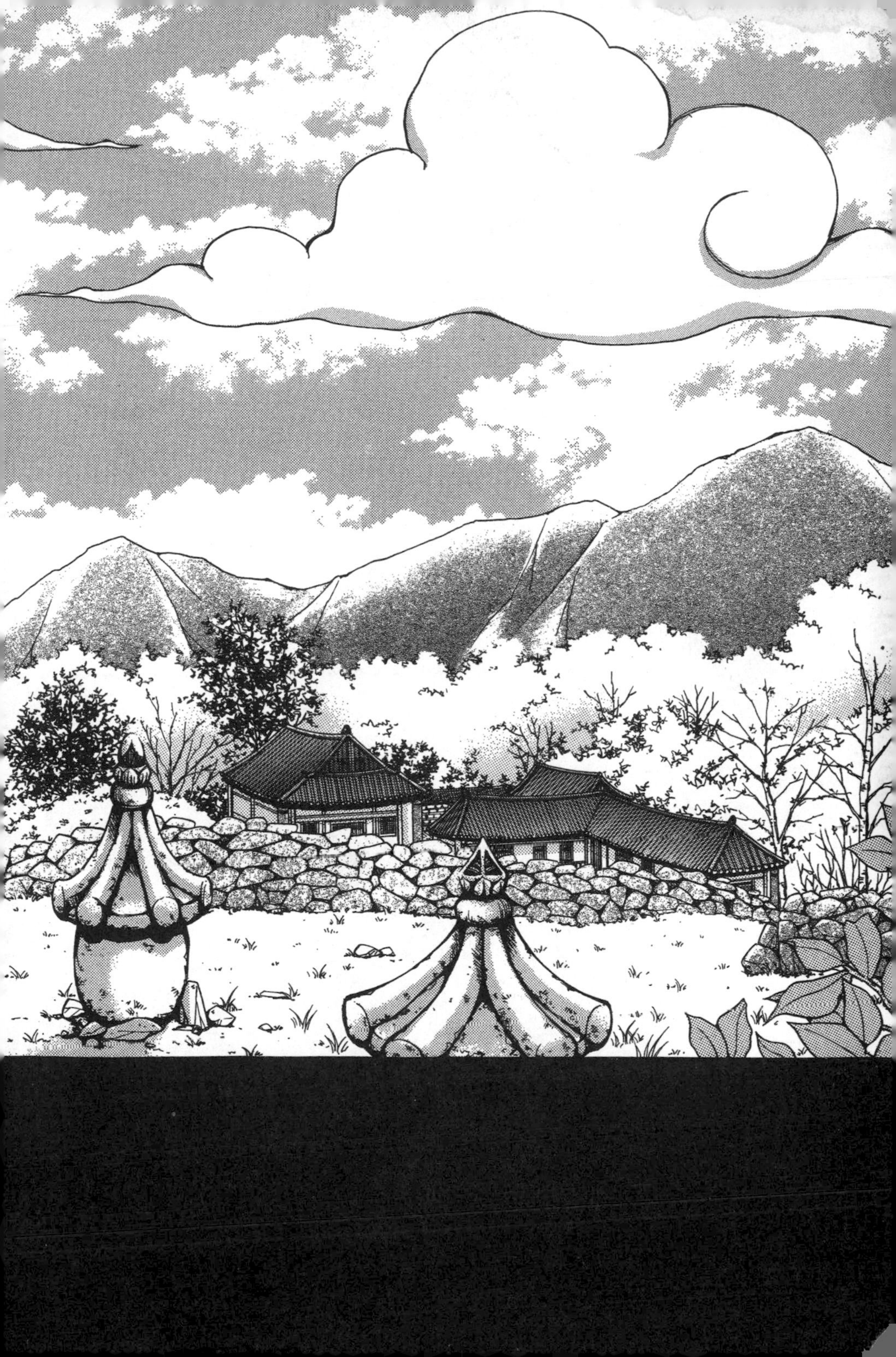

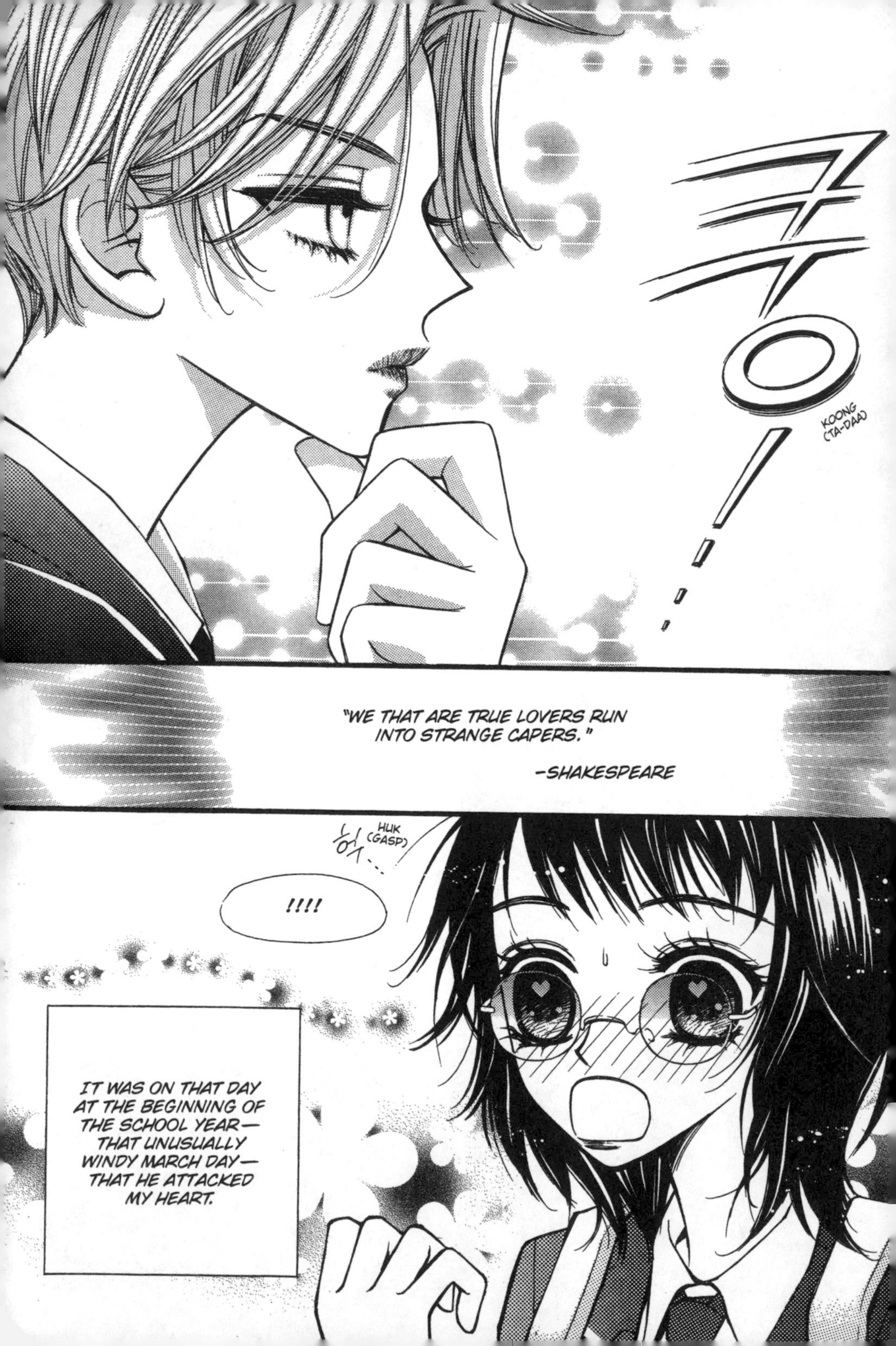
KOONG (TA-DAA)
"WE THAT ARE TRUE LOVERS RUN INTO STRANGE CAPERS."
-SHAKESPEARE
헉...
HUK (GASP)
!!!!
IT WAS ON THAT DAY AT THE BEGINNING OF THE SCHOOL YEAR—THAT UNUSUALLY WINDY MARCH DAY—THAT HE ATTACKED MY HEART.

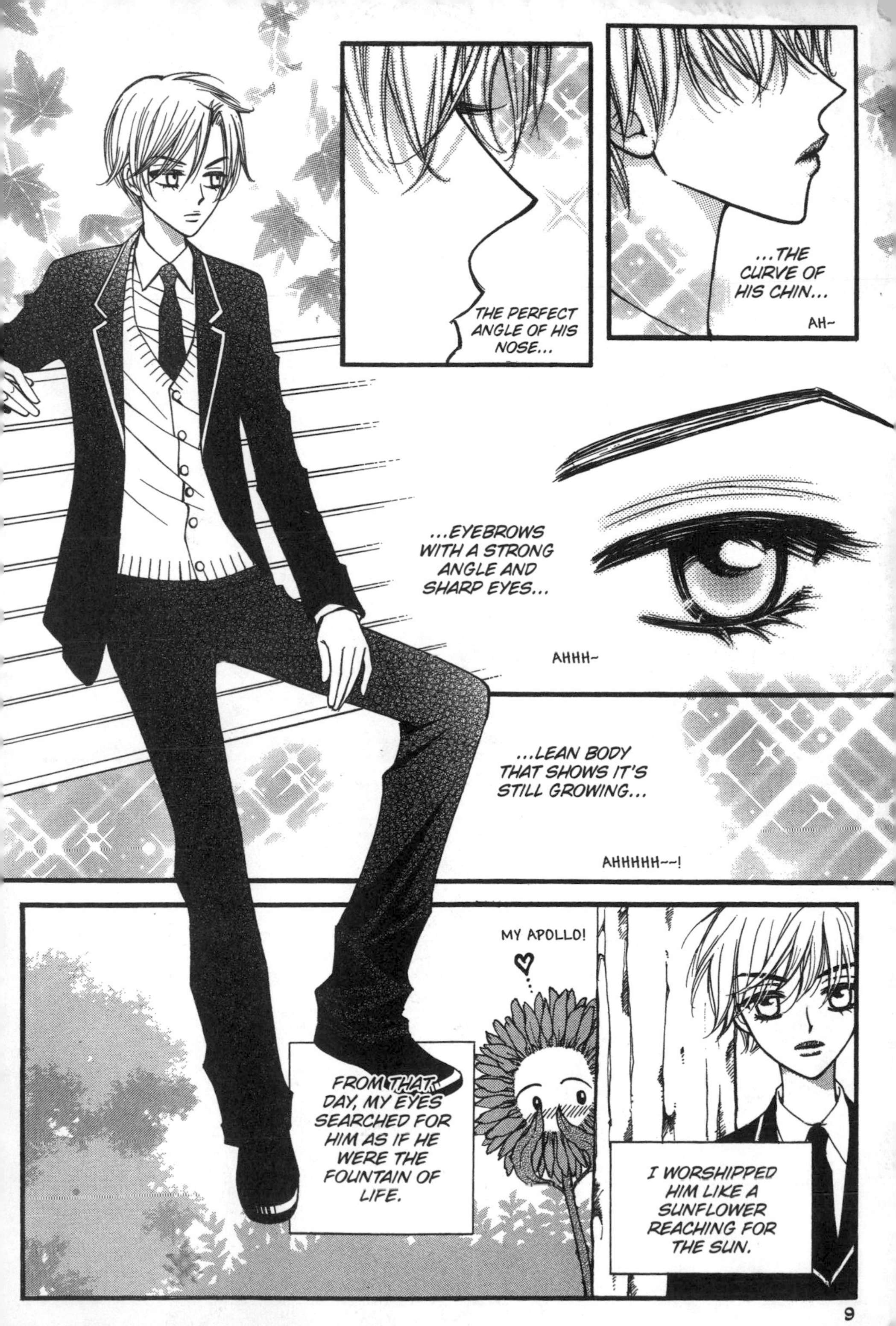
THE PERFECT ANGLE OF HIS NOSE...
...THE CURVE OF HIS CHIN...
AH~
...EYEBROWS WITH A STRONG ANGLE AND SHARP EYES...
AHHH~
...LEAN BODY THAT SHOWS IT'S STILL GROWING...
AHHHHH~~!
FROM THAT DAY, MY EYES SEARCHED FOR HIM AS IF HE WERE THE FOUNTAIN OF LIFE.
MY APOLLO!
I WORSHIPPED HIM LIKE A SUNFLOWER REACHING FOR THE SUN.

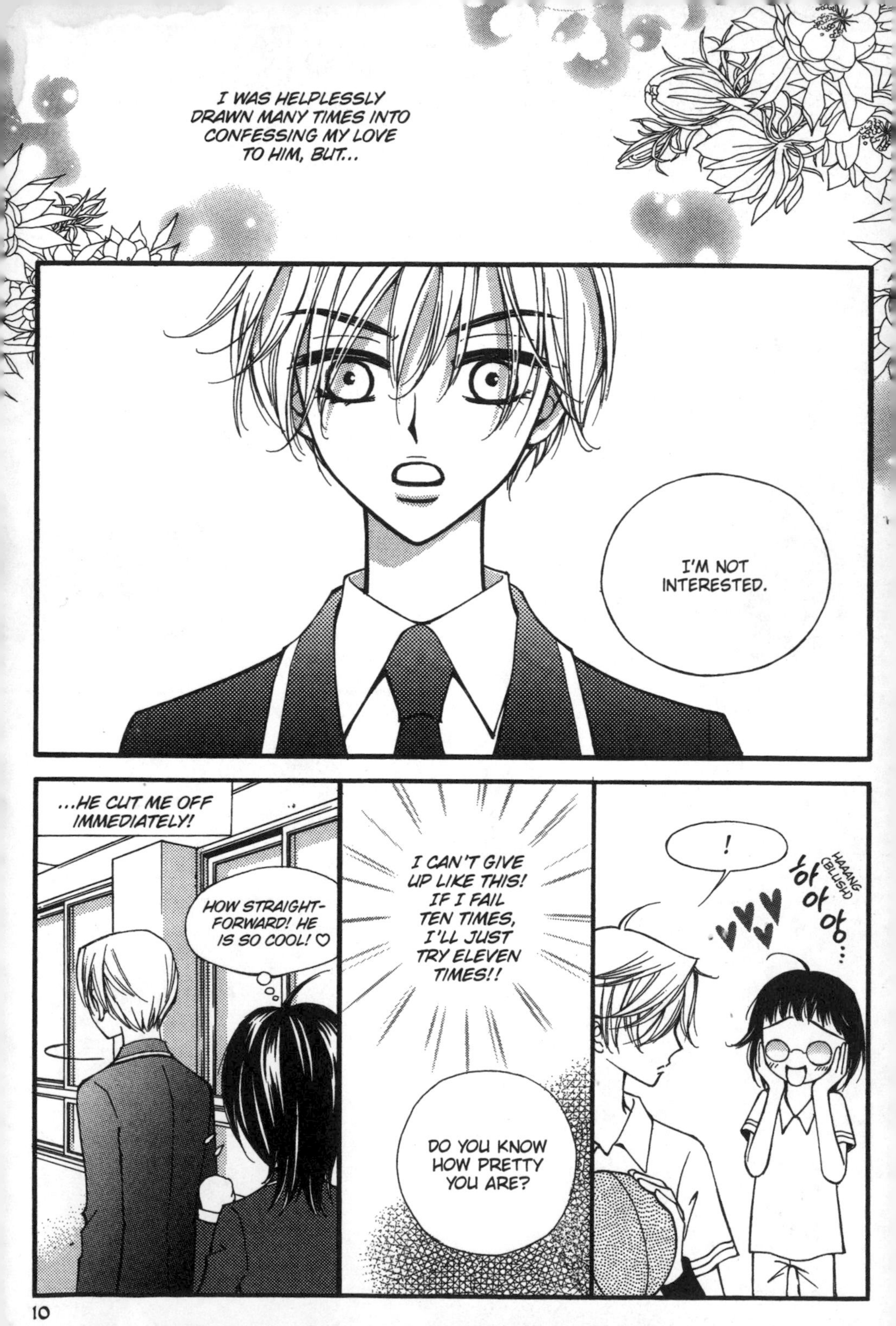
I WAS HELPLESSLY DRAWN MANY TIMES INTO CONFESSING MY LOVE TO HIM, BUT...
I'M NOT INTERESTED.
...HE CUT ME OFF IMMEDIATELY!
HOW STRAIGHT-FORWARD! HE IS SO COOL! ♡
I CAN'T GIVE UP LIKE THIS! IF I FAIL TEN TIMES, I'LL JUST TRY ELEVEN TIMES!!
DO YOU KNOW HOW PRETTY YOU ARE?
!
하아앙...
HAAAANG (BLUSH)

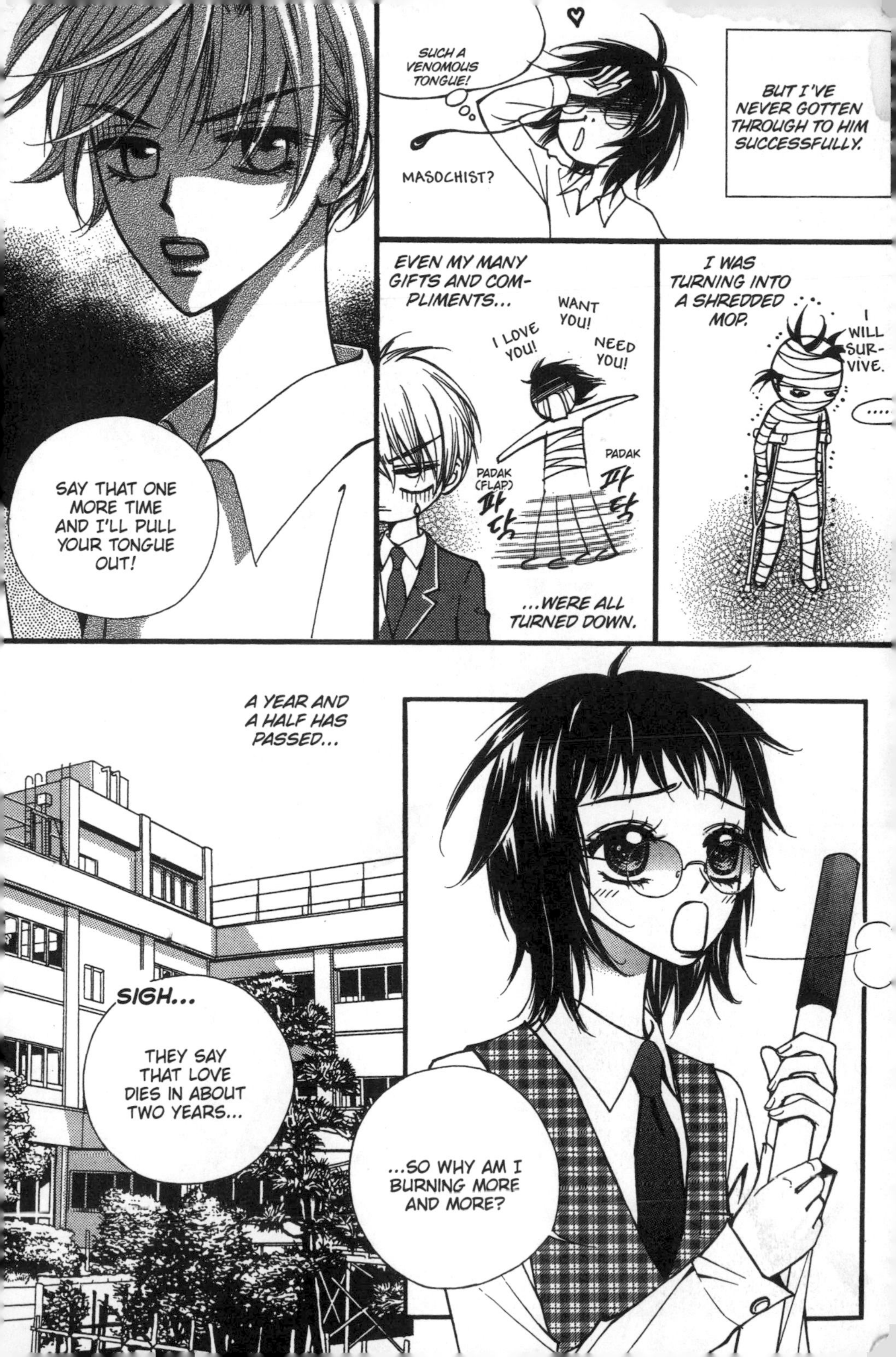
SAY THAT ONE MORE TIME AND I'LL PULL YOUR TONGUE OUT!
SUCH A VENOMOUS TONGUE!
MASOCHIST?
BUT I'VE NEVER GOTTEN THROUGH TO HIM SUCCESSFULLY.
EVEN MY MANY GIFTS AND COMPLIMENTS...
I LOVE YOU!
WANT YOU!
NEED YOU!
PADAK (FLAP)
파닥
PADAK
파닥
...WERE ALL TURNED DOWN.
I WAS TURNING INTO A SHREDDED MOP.
I WILL SURVIVE.
.....
A YEAR AND A HALF HAS PASSED...
SIGH...
THEY SAY THAT LOVE DIES IN ABOUT TWO YEARS...
...SO WHY AM I BURNING MORE AND MORE?

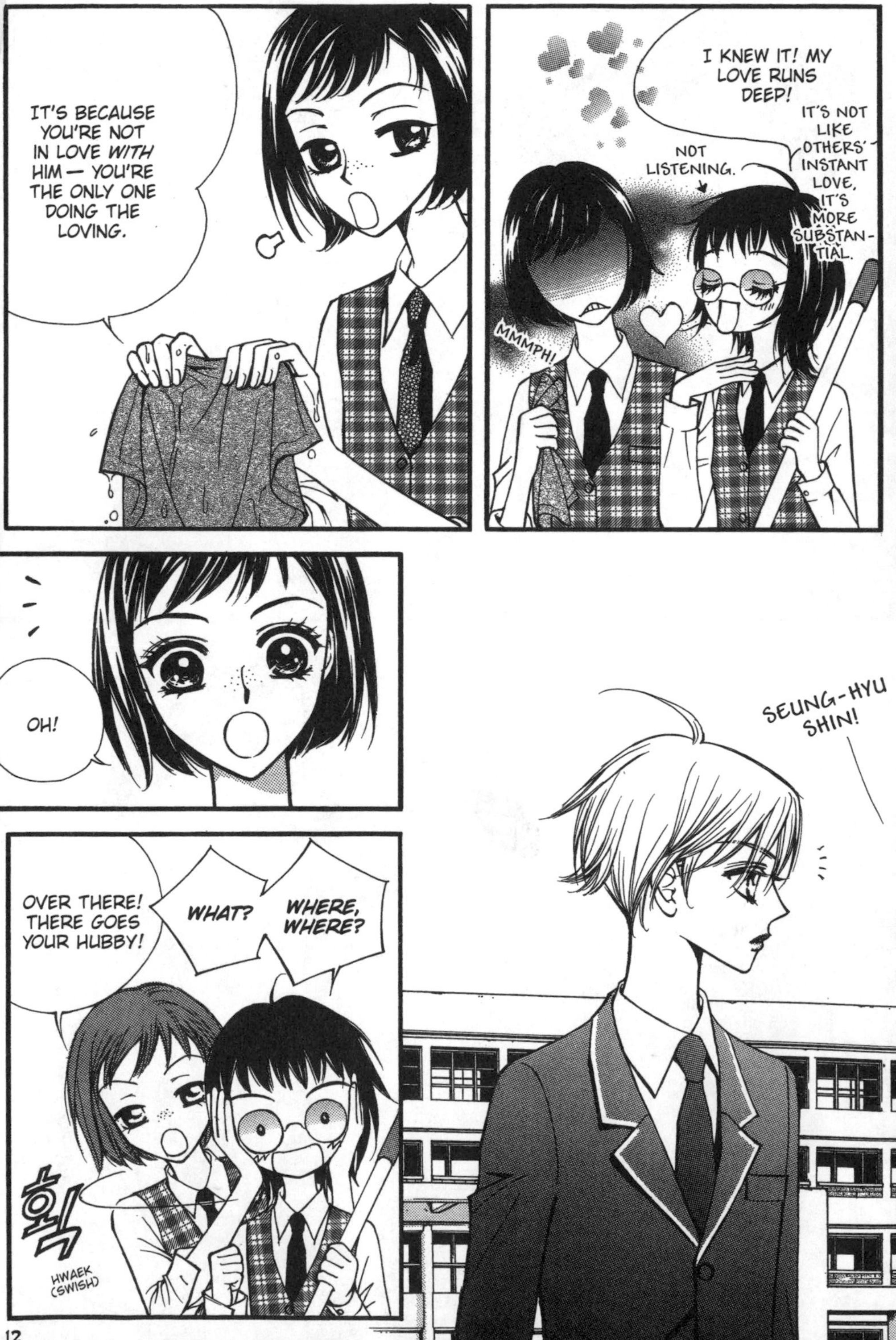
IT'S BECAUSE YOU'RE NOT IN LOVE *WITH* HIM — YOU'RE THE ONLY ONE DOING THE LOVING.
I KNEW IT! MY LOVE RUNS DEEP!
IT'S NOT LIKE OTHERS' INSTANT LOVE, IT'S MORE SUBSTAN-TIAL.
NOT LISTENING.
MMMPH!
OH!
OVER THERE! THERE GOES YOUR HUBBY!
WHAT?
WHERE, WHERE?
홱
HWAEK (SWISH)
SEUNG-HYU SHIN!

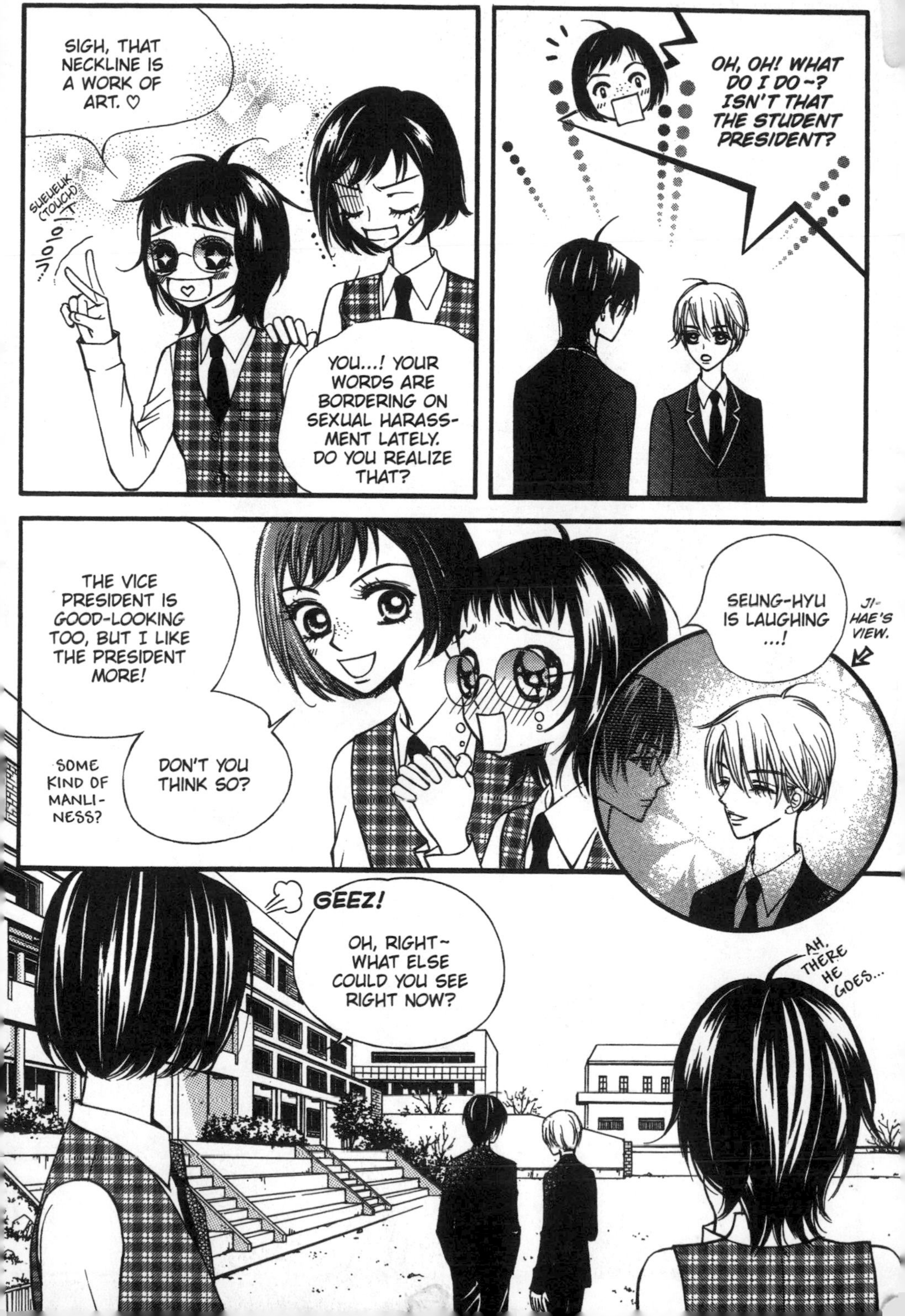
SIGH, THAT NECKLINE IS A WORK OF ART. ♡
SUEUEUK (TOUCH)
...HIHI
YOU...! YOUR WORDS ARE BORDERING ON SEXUAL HARASS-MENT LATELY. DO YOU REALIZE THAT?
OH, OH! WHAT DO I DO~? ISN'T THAT THE STUDENT PRESIDENT?
THE VICE PRESIDENT IS GOOD-LOOKING TOO, BUT I LIKE THE PRESIDENT MORE!
DON'T YOU THINK SO?
SOME KIND OF MANLI-NESS?
SEUNG-HYU IS LAUGHING ...!
JI-HAE'S VIEW.
GEEZ!
OH, RIGHT~ WHAT ELSE COULD YOU SEE RIGHT NOW?
AH, THERE HE GOES...

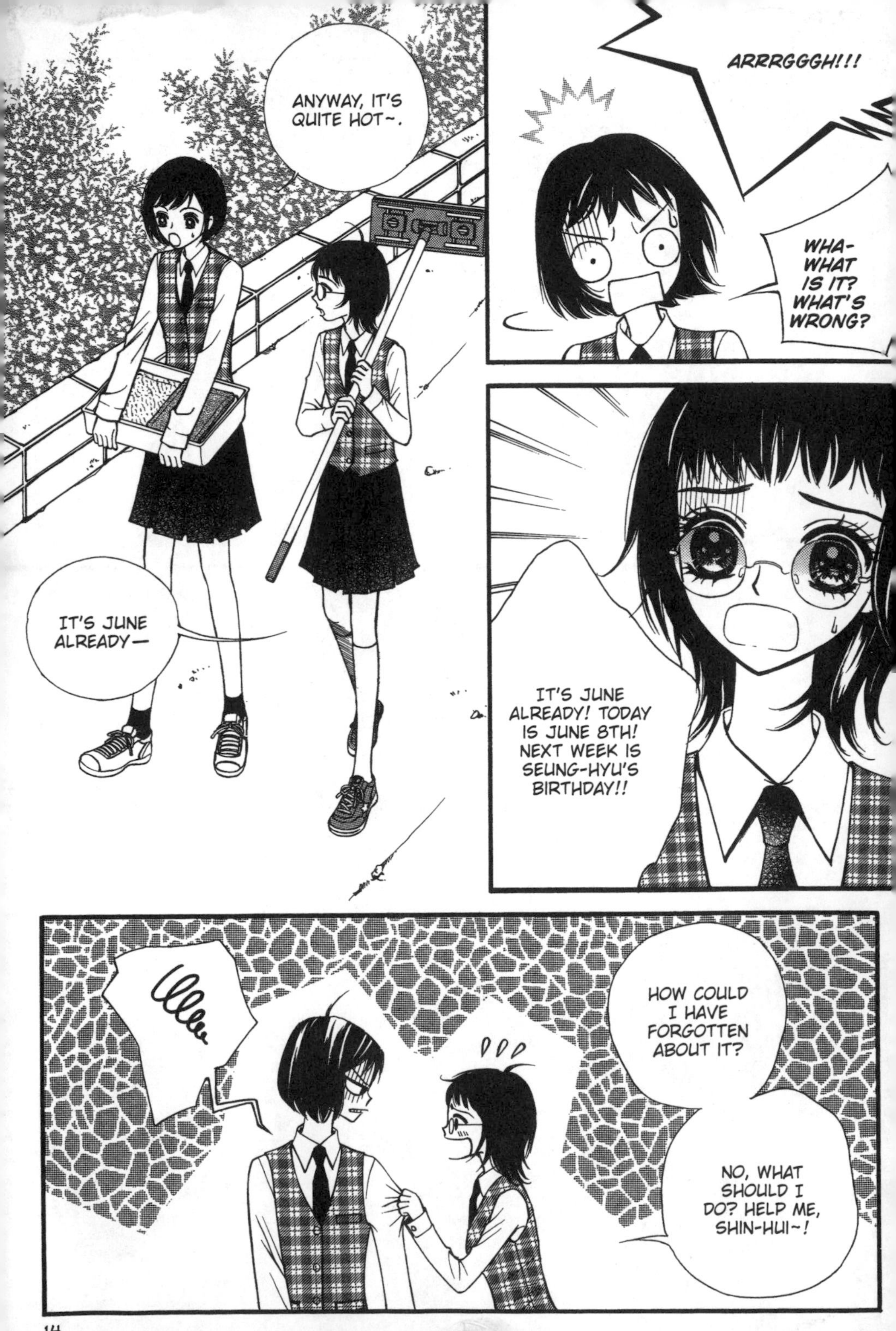
ANYWAY, IT'S QUITE HOT~.
IT'S JUNE ALREADY—
ARRRGGGH!!!
WHA-WHAT IS IT? WHAT'S WRONG?
IT'S JUNE ALREADY! TODAY IS JUNE 8TH! NEXT WEEK IS SEUNG-HYU'S BIRTHDAY!!
HOW COULD I HAVE FORGOTTEN ABOUT IT?
NO, WHAT SHOULD I DO? HELP ME, SHIN-HUI~!

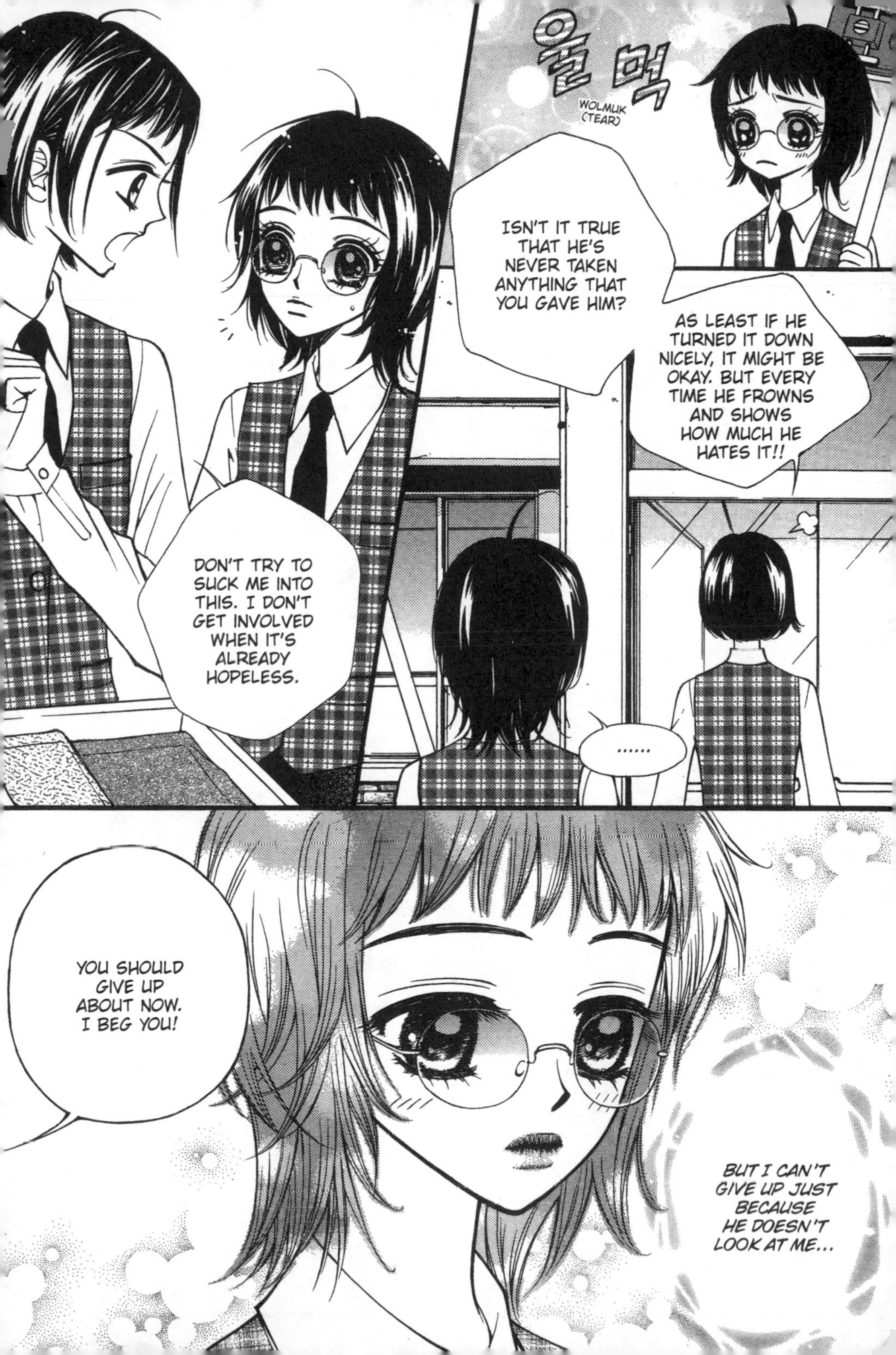
DON'T TRY TO SUCK ME INTO THIS. I DON'T GET INVOLVED WHEN IT'S ALREADY HOPELESS.
울먹
WOLMUK (TEAR)
ISN'T IT TRUE THAT HE'S NEVER TAKEN ANYTHING THAT YOU GAVE HIM?
AS LEAST IF HE TURNED IT DOWN NICELY, IT MIGHT BE OKAY. BUT EVERY TIME HE FROWNS AND SHOWS HOW MUCH HE HATES IT!!
......
YOU SHOULD GIVE UP ABOUT NOW. I BEG YOU!
BUT I CAN'T GIVE UP JUST BECAUSE HE DOESN'T LOOK AT ME...

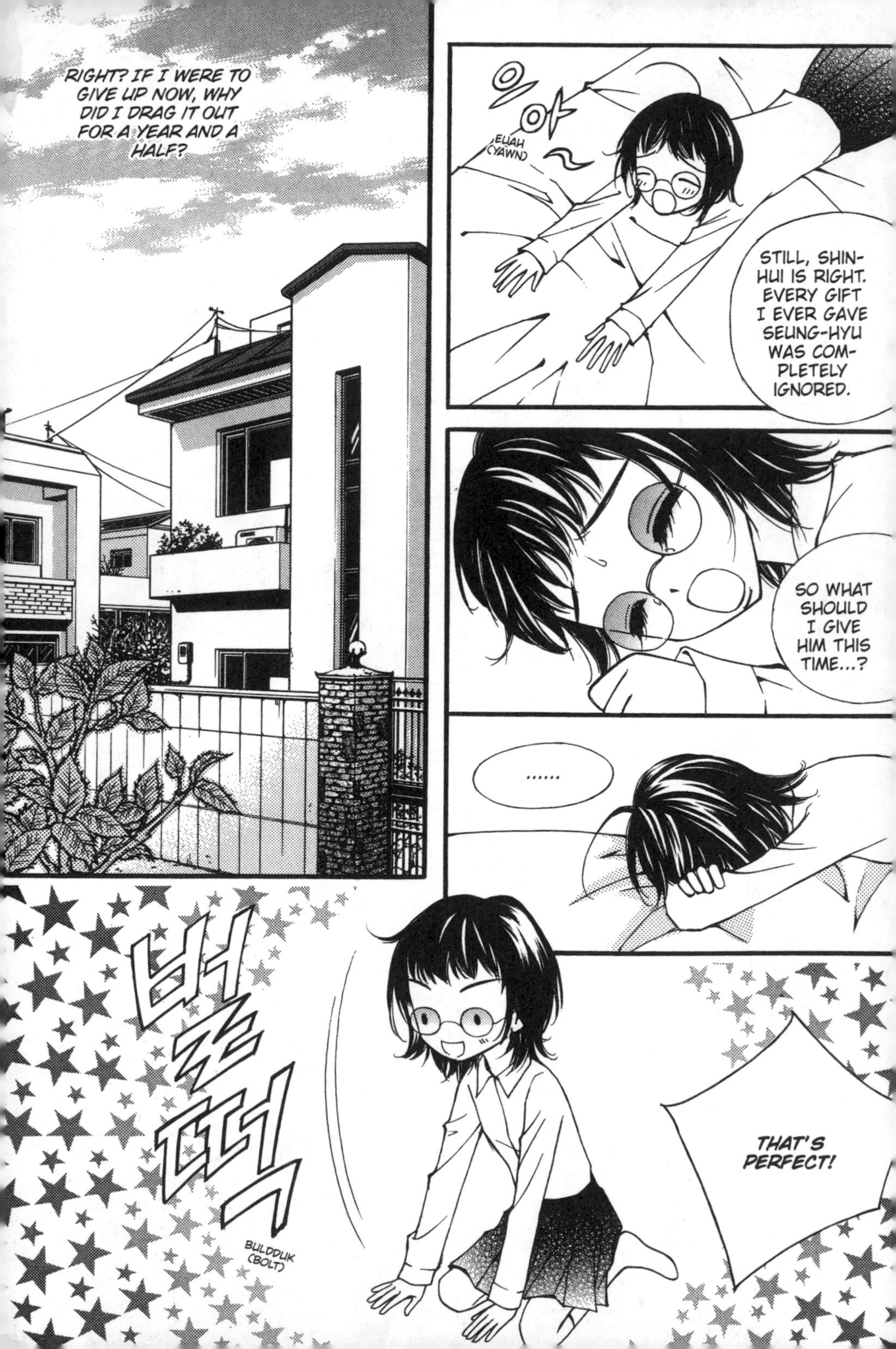
RIGHT? IF I WERE TO GIVE UP NOW, WHY DID I DRAG IT OUT FOR A YEAR AND A HALF?
으아
EUAH (YAWN)
STILL, SHIN-HUI IS RIGHT. EVERY GIFT I EVER GAVE SEUNG-HYU WAS COMPLETELY IGNORED.
SO WHAT SHOULD I GIVE HIM THIS TIME...?
......
벌떡
BULDDUK (BOLT)
THAT'S PERFECT!

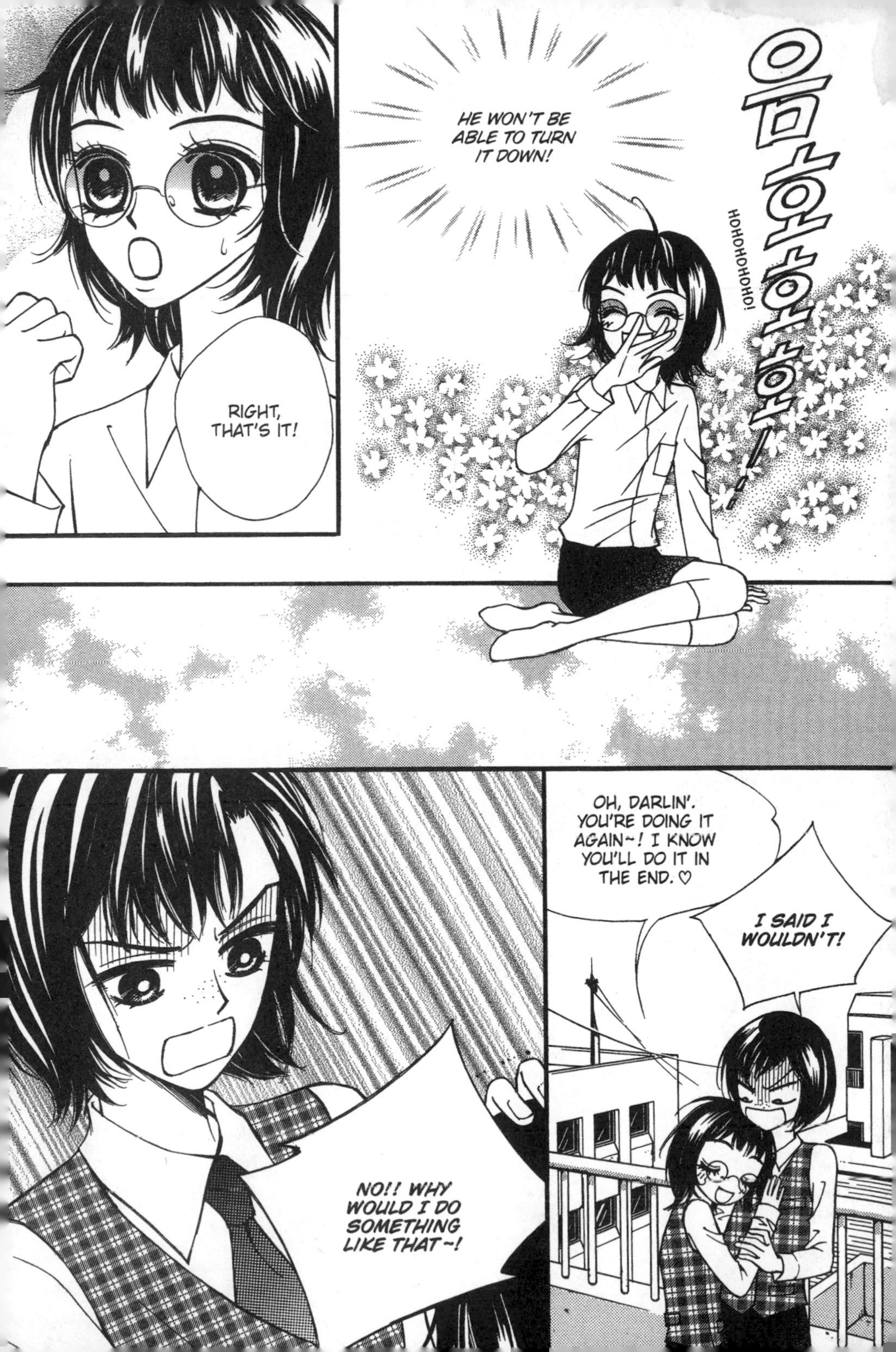
RIGHT, THAT'S IT!
HE WON'T BE ABLE TO TURN IT DOWN!
음호호호호
HOHOHOHOHO!
NO!! WHY WOULD I DO SOMETHING LIKE THAT~!
OH, DARLIN'. YOU'RE DOING IT AGAIN~! I KNOW YOU'LL DO IT IN THE END. ♡
I SAID I WOULDN'T!

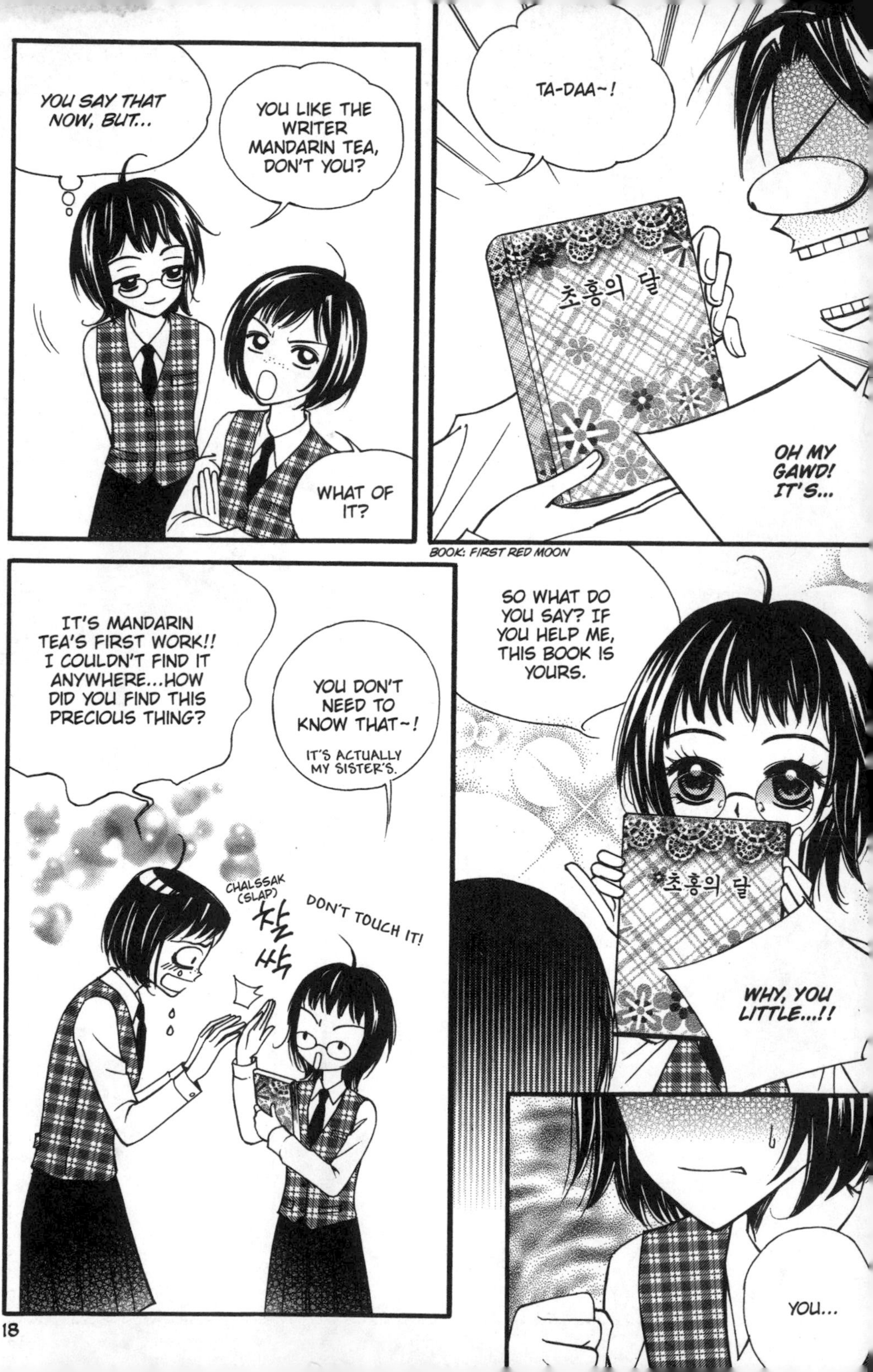
YOU SAY THAT NOW, BUT...
YOU LIKE THE WRITER MANDARIN TEA, DON'T YOU?
WHAT OF IT?
TA-DAA~!
초홍의 달
OH MY GAWD! IT'S...
BOOK: FIRST RED MOON
IT'S MANDARIN TEA'S FIRST WORK!! I COULDN'T FIND IT ANYWHERE...HOW DID YOU FIND THIS PRECIOUS THING?
YOU DON'T NEED TO KNOW THAT~!
IT'S ACTUALLY MY SISTER'S.
CHALSSAK (SLAP)
찰싹
DON'T TOUCH IT!
SO WHAT DO YOU SAY? IF YOU HELP ME, THIS BOOK IS YOURS.
초홍의 달
WHY, YOU LITTLE...!!
YOU...

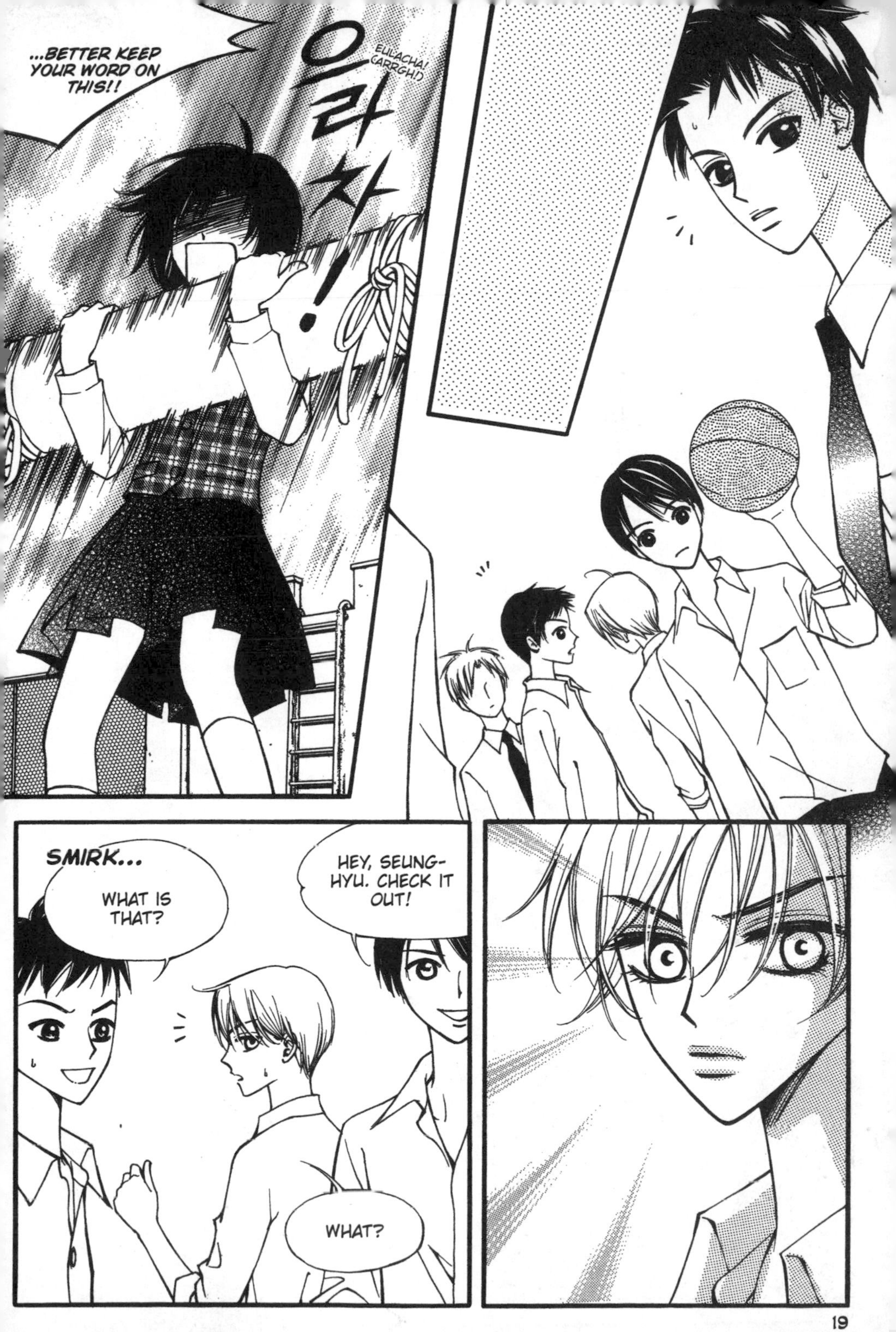
...BETTER KEEP YOUR WORD ON THIS!!
으라차!
EULACHA! (ARRGH!)
SMIRK...
WHAT IS THAT?
HEY, SEUNG-HYU. CHECK IT OUT!
WHAT?

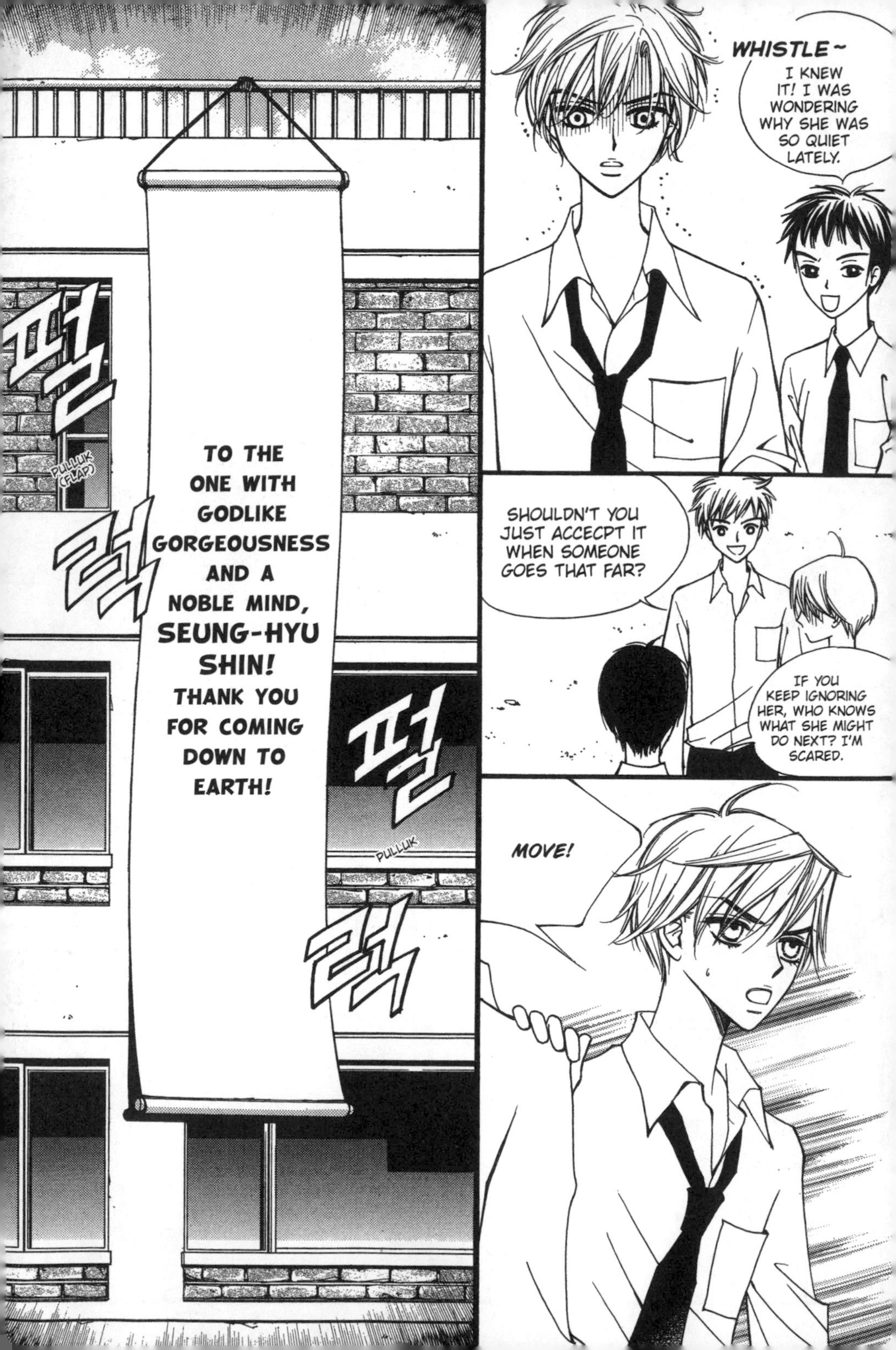

펄럭
PULLUK (FLAP)
TO THE ONE WITH GODLIKE GORGEOUSNESS AND A NOBLE MIND, SEUNG-HYU SHIN! THANK YOU FOR COMING DOWN TO EARTH!
펄럭
PULLUK
WHISTLE ~
I KNEW IT! I WAS WONDERING WHY SHE WAS SO QUIET LATELY.
SHOULDN'T YOU JUST ACCECPT IT WHEN SOMEONE GOES THAT FAR?
IF YOU KEEP IGNORING HER, WHO KNOWS WHAT SHE MIGHT DO NEXT? I'M SCARED.
MOVE!

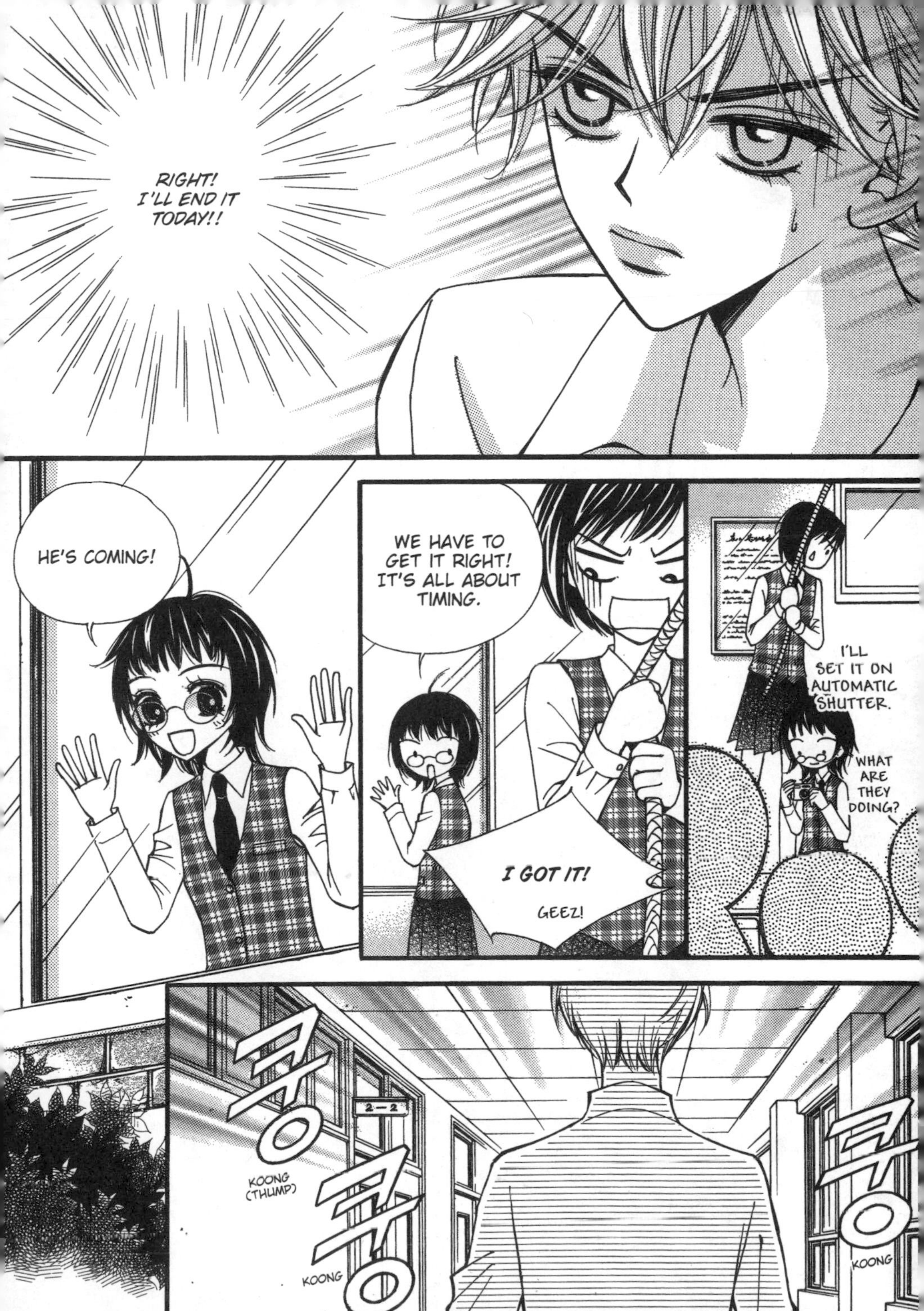
RIGHT! I'LL END IT TODAY!!
HE'S COMING!
WE HAVE TO GET IT RIGHT! IT'S ALL ABOUT TIMING.
I GOT IT!
GEEZ!
I'LL SET IT ON AUTOMATIC SHUTTER.
WHAT ARE THEY DOING?
2-2
KOONG (THUMP)
KOONG
KOONG

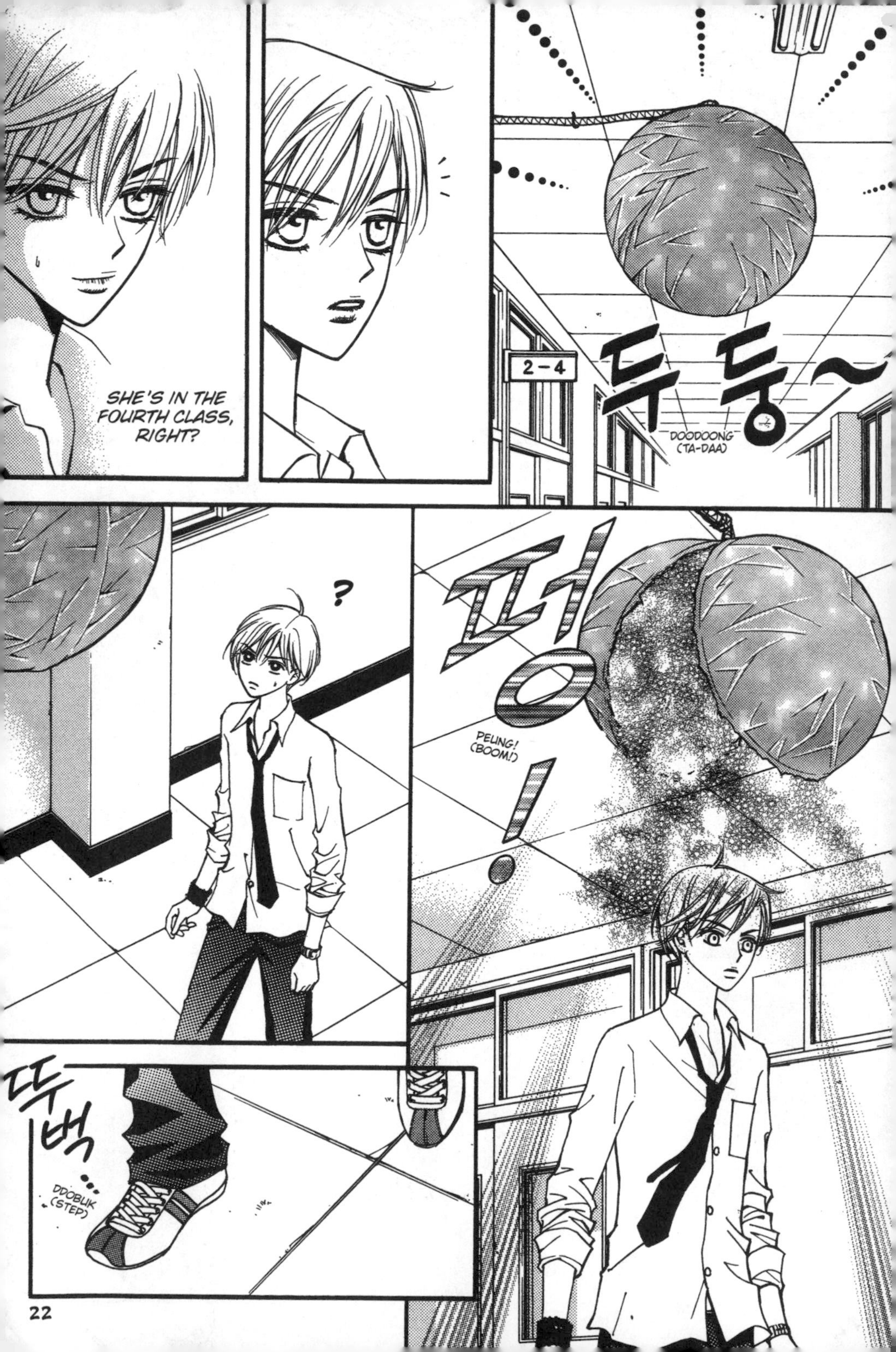
SHE'S IN THE FOURTH CLASS, RIGHT?
2-4
두둥~
DOODOONG (TA-DAA)
?
뚜벅
DDOBUK (STEP)
펑!
PEUNG! (BOOM!)

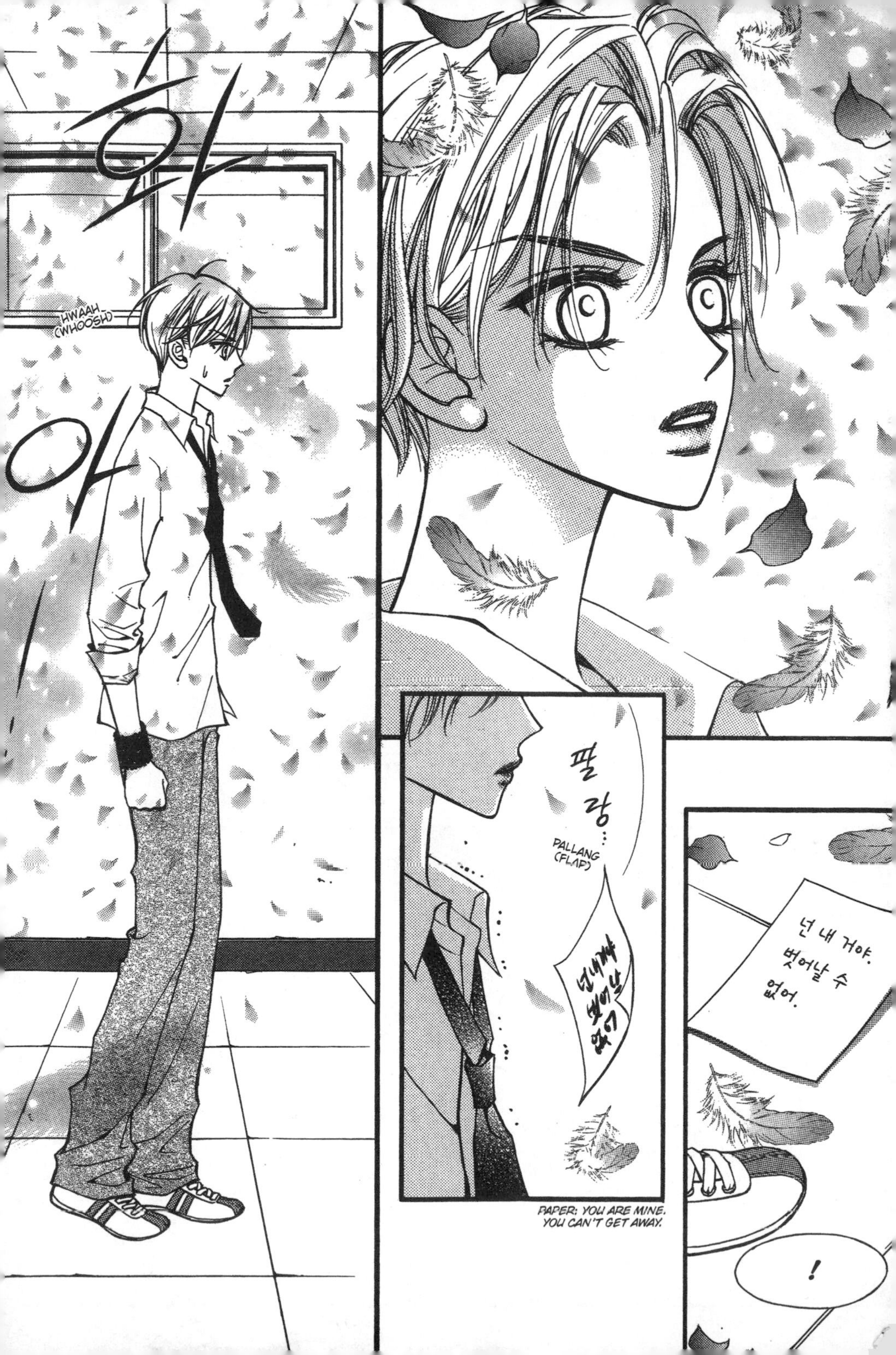
화아
HWAAH (WHOOSH)
팔랑…
PALLANG (FLAP)
넌 내 거야.
벗어날 수
없어.
PAPER: YOU ARE MINE.
YOU CAN'T GET AWAY.
!

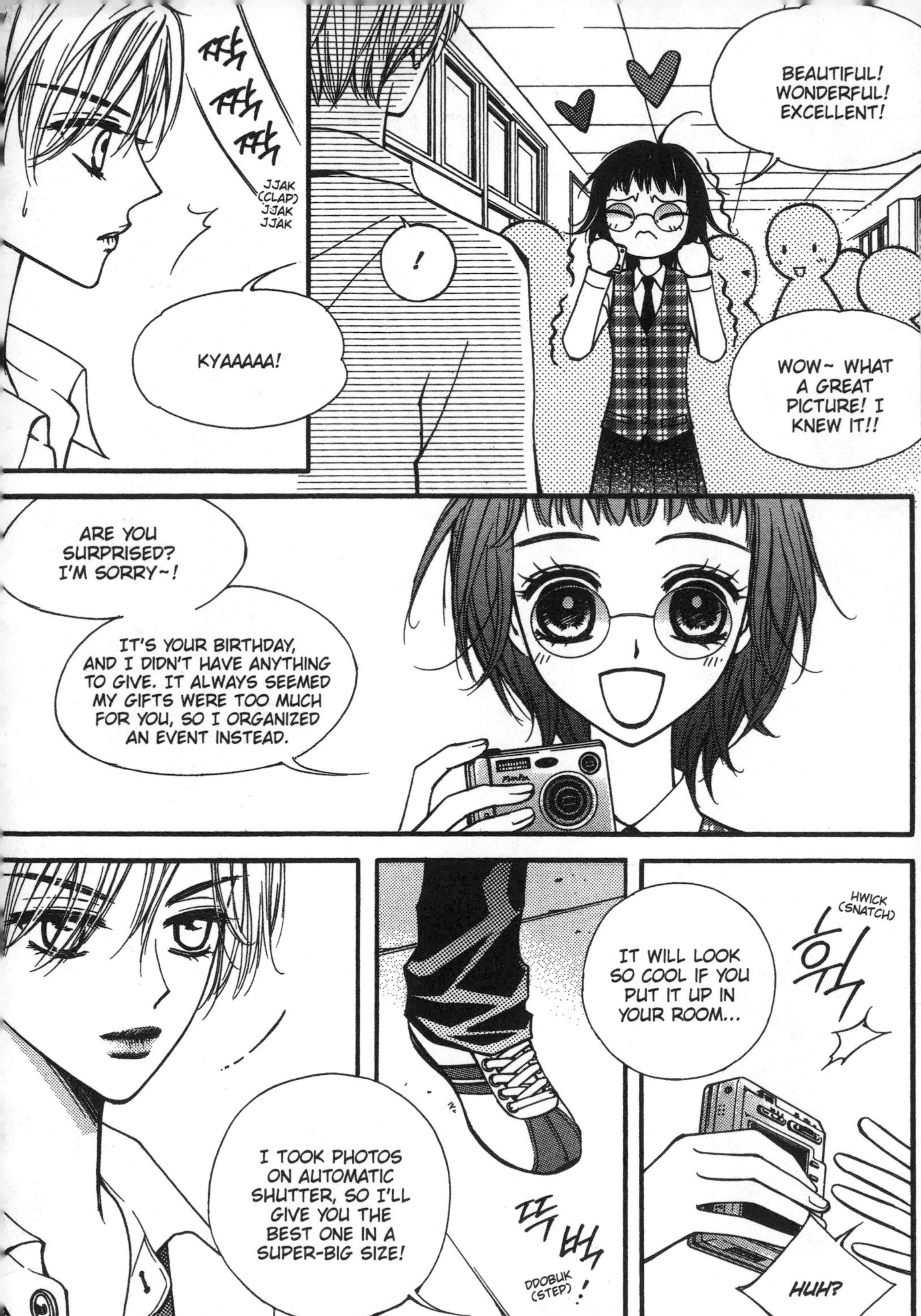

짝
짝
짝
JJAK (CLAP) JJAK JJAK
KYAAAAA!
!
BEAUTIFUL! WONDERFUL! EXCELLENT!
WOW~ WHAT A GREAT PICTURE! I KNEW IT!!
ARE YOU SURPRISED? I'M SORRY~!
IT'S YOUR BIRTHDAY, AND I DIDN'T HAVE ANYTHING TO GIVE. IT ALWAYS SEEMED MY GIFTS WERE TOO MUCH FOR YOU, SO I ORGANIZED AN EVENT INSTEAD.
...
I TOOK PHOTOS ON AUTOMATIC SHUTTER, SO I'LL GIVE YOU THE BEST ONE IN A SUPER-BIG SIZE!
뚜벅
DDOBUK (STEP)
IT WILL LOOK SO COOL IF YOU PUT IT UP IN YOUR ROOM...
휙
HWICK (SNATCH)
HUH?

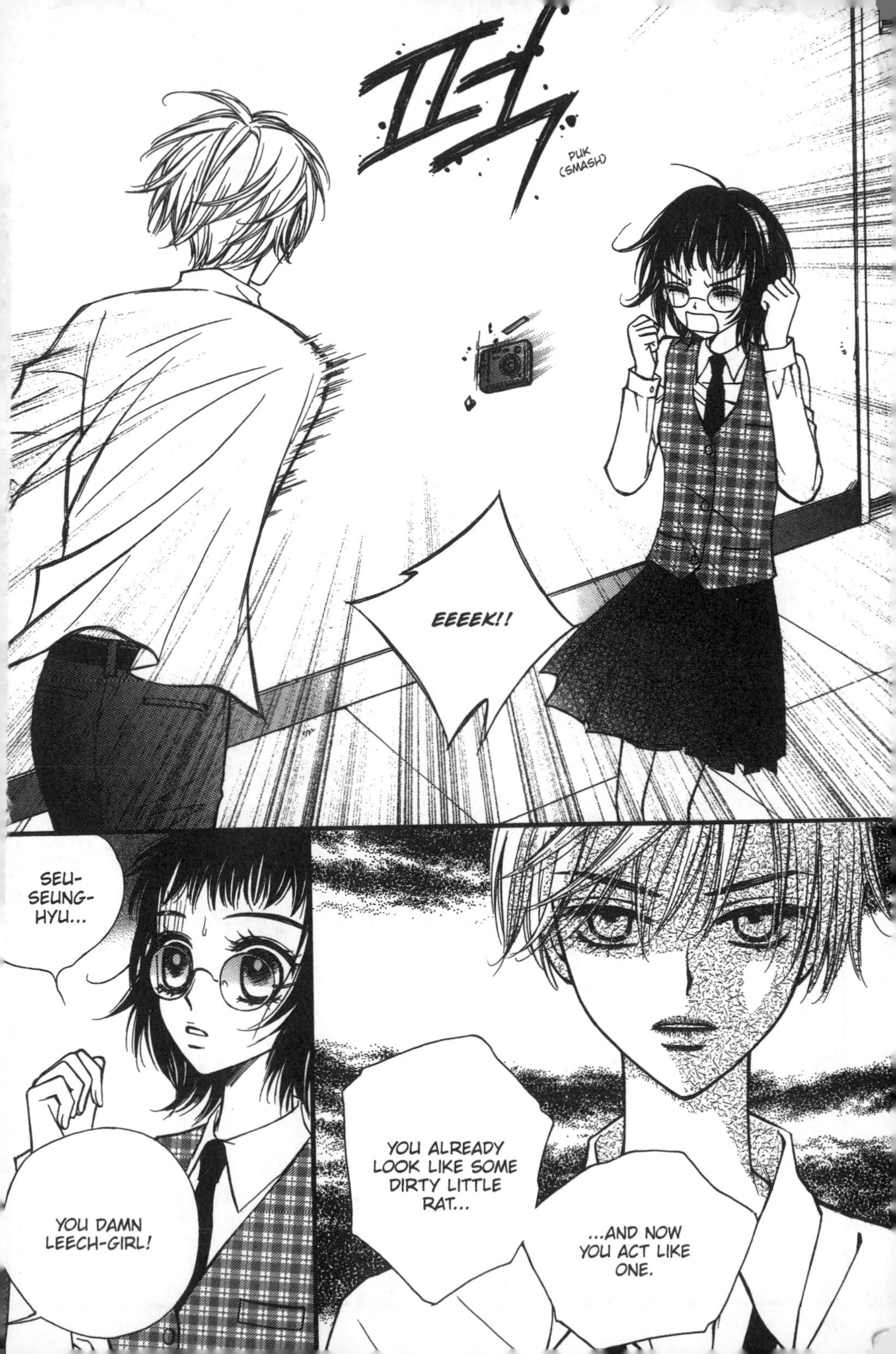
PUK
(SMASH)
EEEEK!!
SEU-
SEUNG-
HYU...
YOU DAMN
LEECH-GIRL!
YOU ALREADY
LOOK LIKE SOME
DIRTY LITTLE
RAT...
...AND NOW
YOU ACT LIKE
ONE.

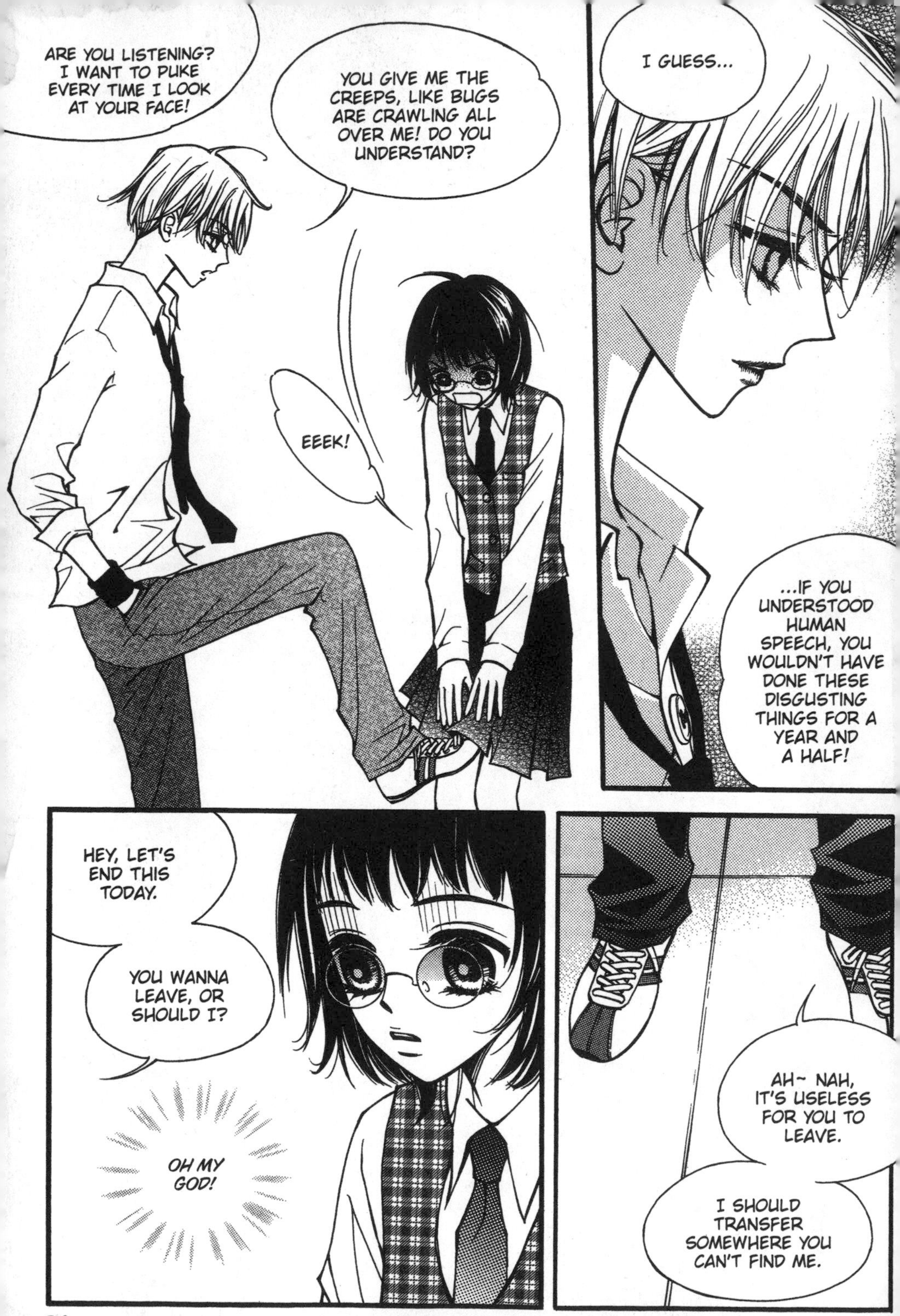
ARE YOU LISTENING? I WANT TO PUKE EVERY TIME I LOOK AT YOUR FACE!
YOU GIVE ME THE CREEPS, LIKE BUGS ARE CRAWLING ALL OVER ME! DO YOU UNDERSTAND?
EEEK!
I GUESS...
...IF YOU UNDERSTOOD HUMAN SPEECH, YOU WOULDN'T HAVE DONE THESE DISGUSTING THINGS FOR A YEAR AND A HALF!
HEY, LET'S END THIS TODAY.
YOU WANNA LEAVE, OR SHOULD I?
OH MY GOD!
AH~ NAH, IT'S USELESS FOR YOU TO LEAVE.
I SHOULD TRANSFER SOMEWHERE YOU CAN'T FIND ME.

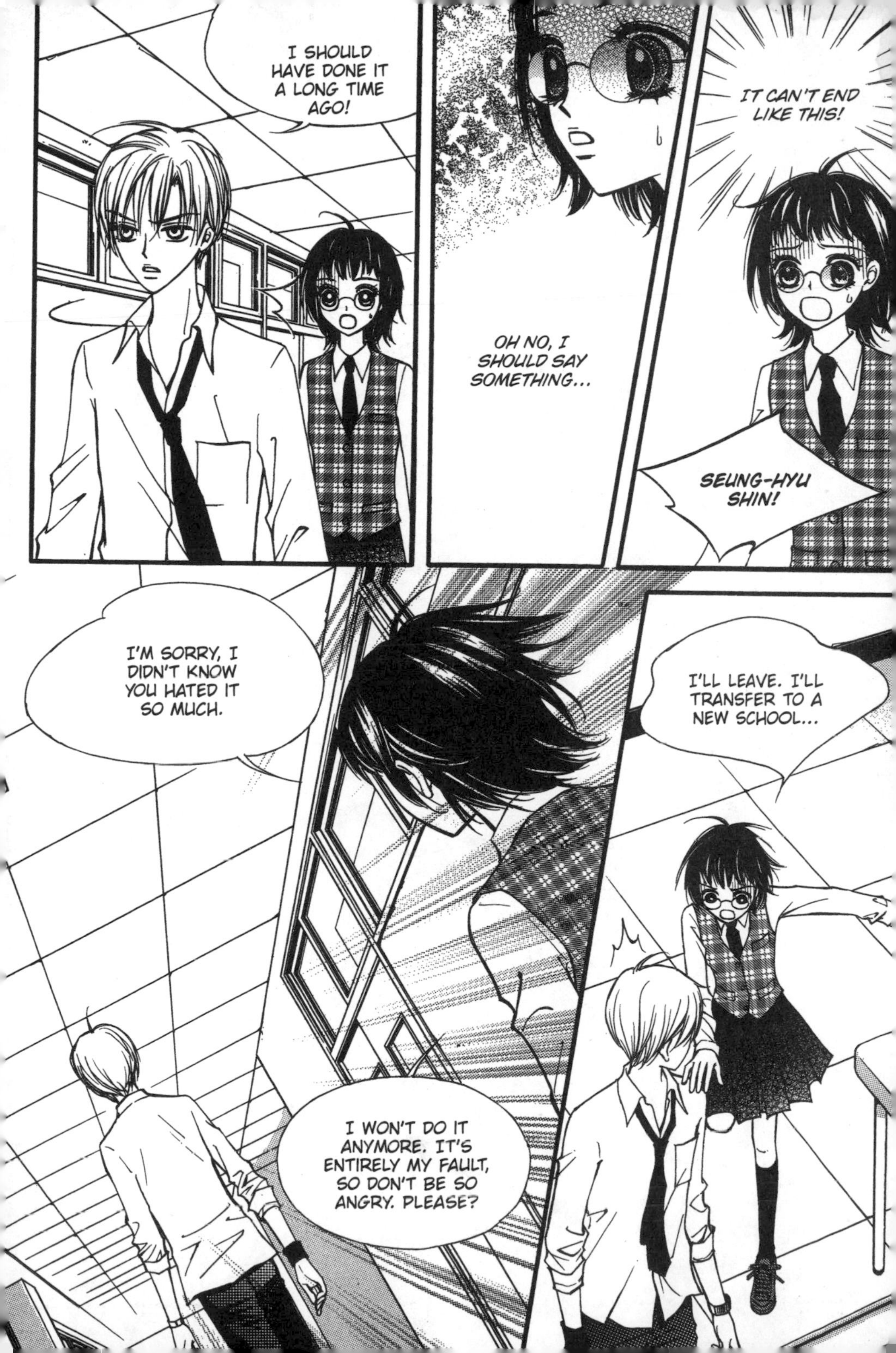
I SHOULD HAVE DONE IT A LONG TIME AGO!
OH NO, I SHOULD SAY SOMETHING...
IT CAN'T END LIKE THIS!
SEUNG-HYU SHIN!
I'M SORRY, I DIDN'T KNOW YOU HATED IT SO MUCH.
I WON'T DO IT ANYMORE. IT'S ENTIRELY MY FAULT, SO DON'T BE SO ANGRY. PLEASE?
I'LL LEAVE. I'LL TRANSFER TO A NEW SCHOOL...

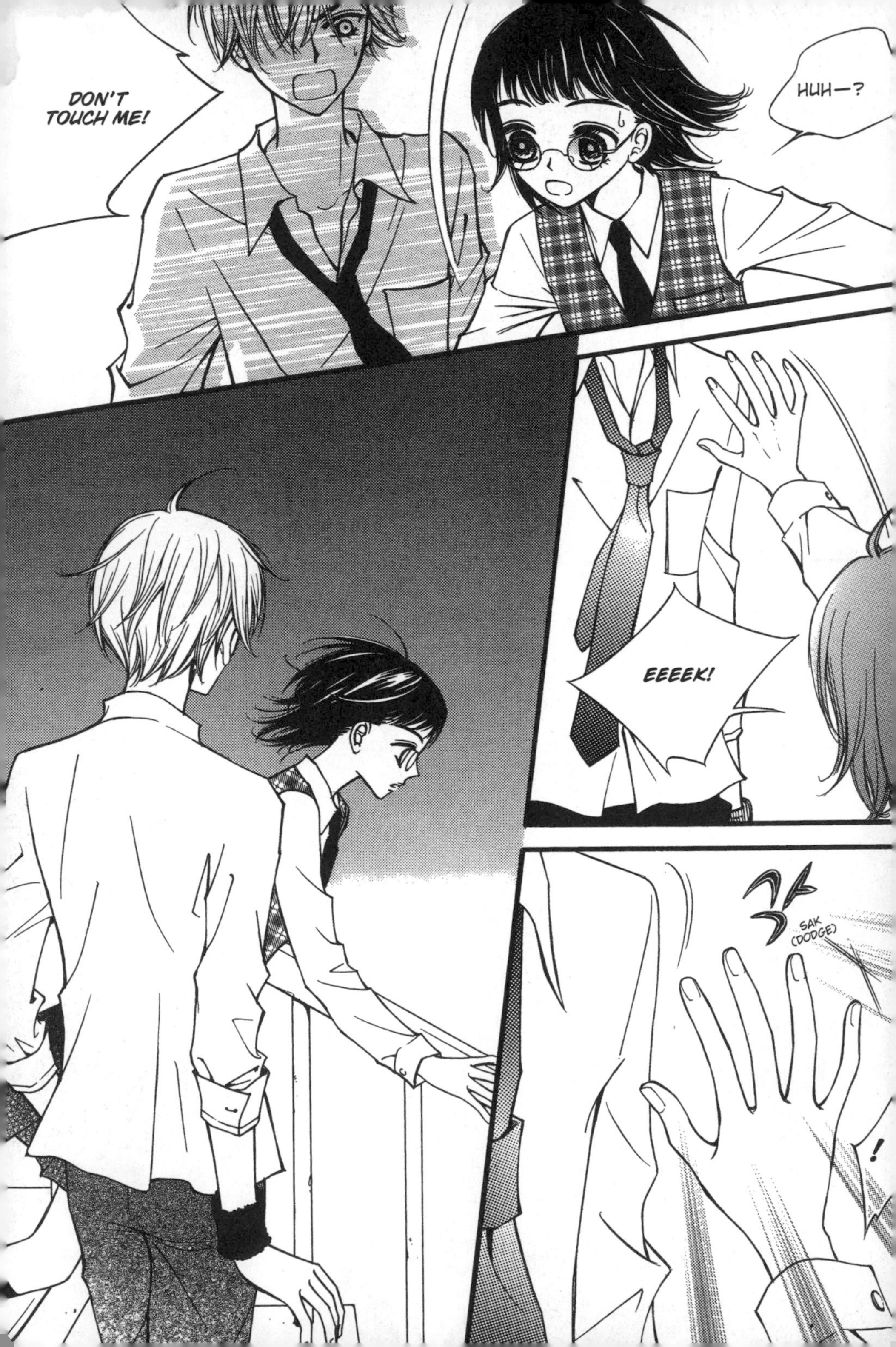
DON'T TOUCH ME!
HUH—?
EEEEK!
SAK (DODGE)
!

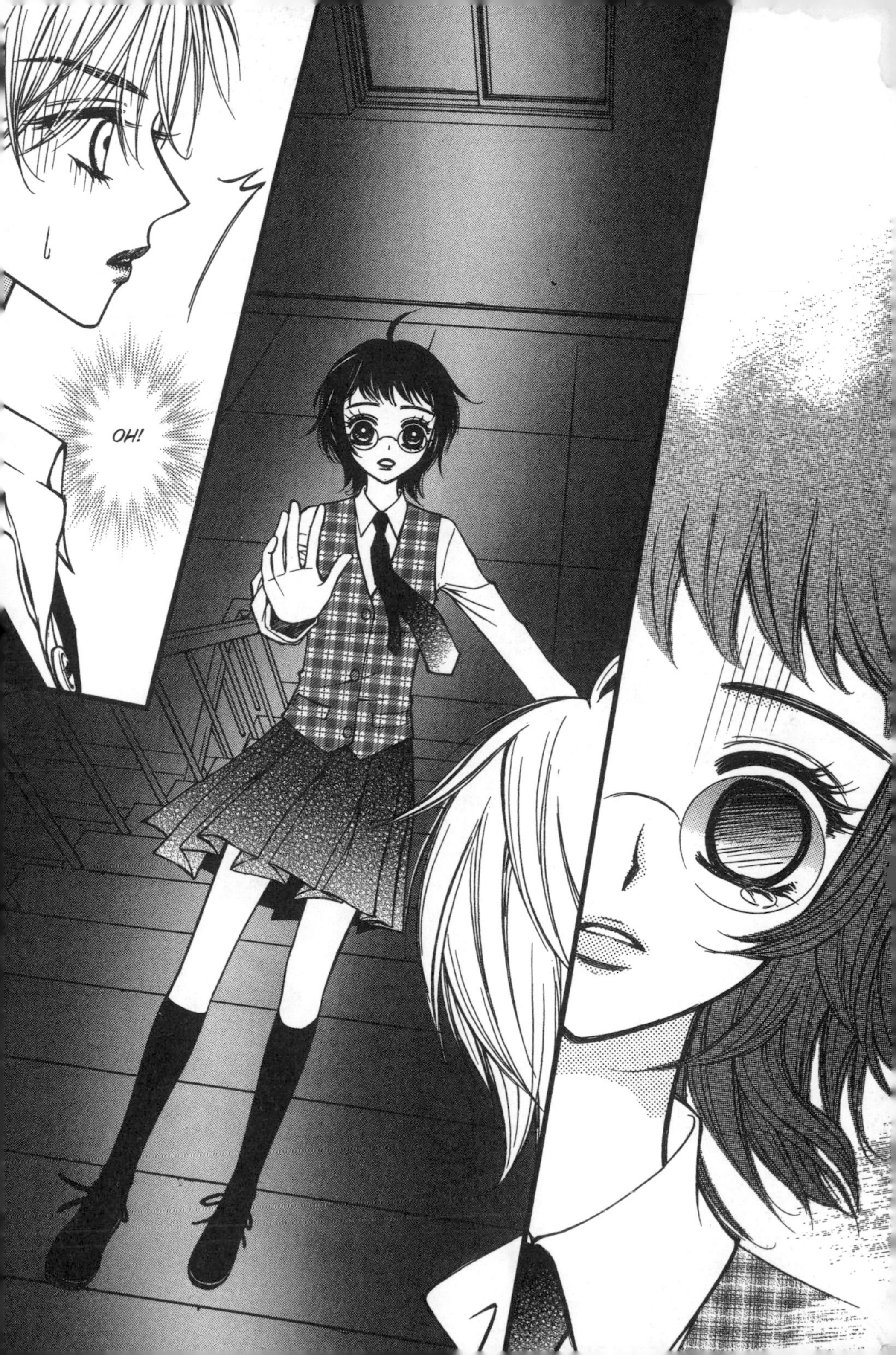
OH!

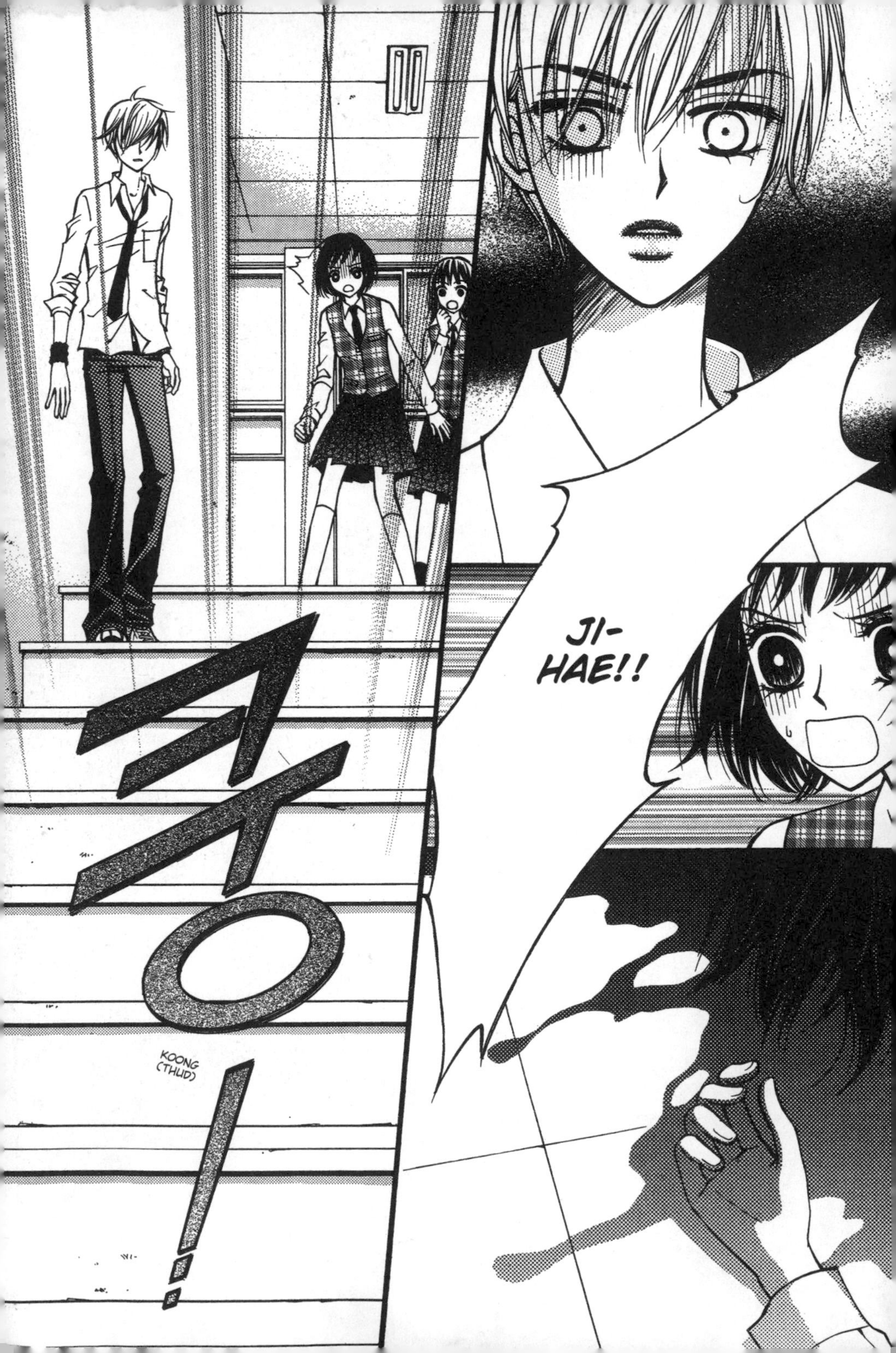

쿵—!
KOONG (THUD)
JI-HAE!!

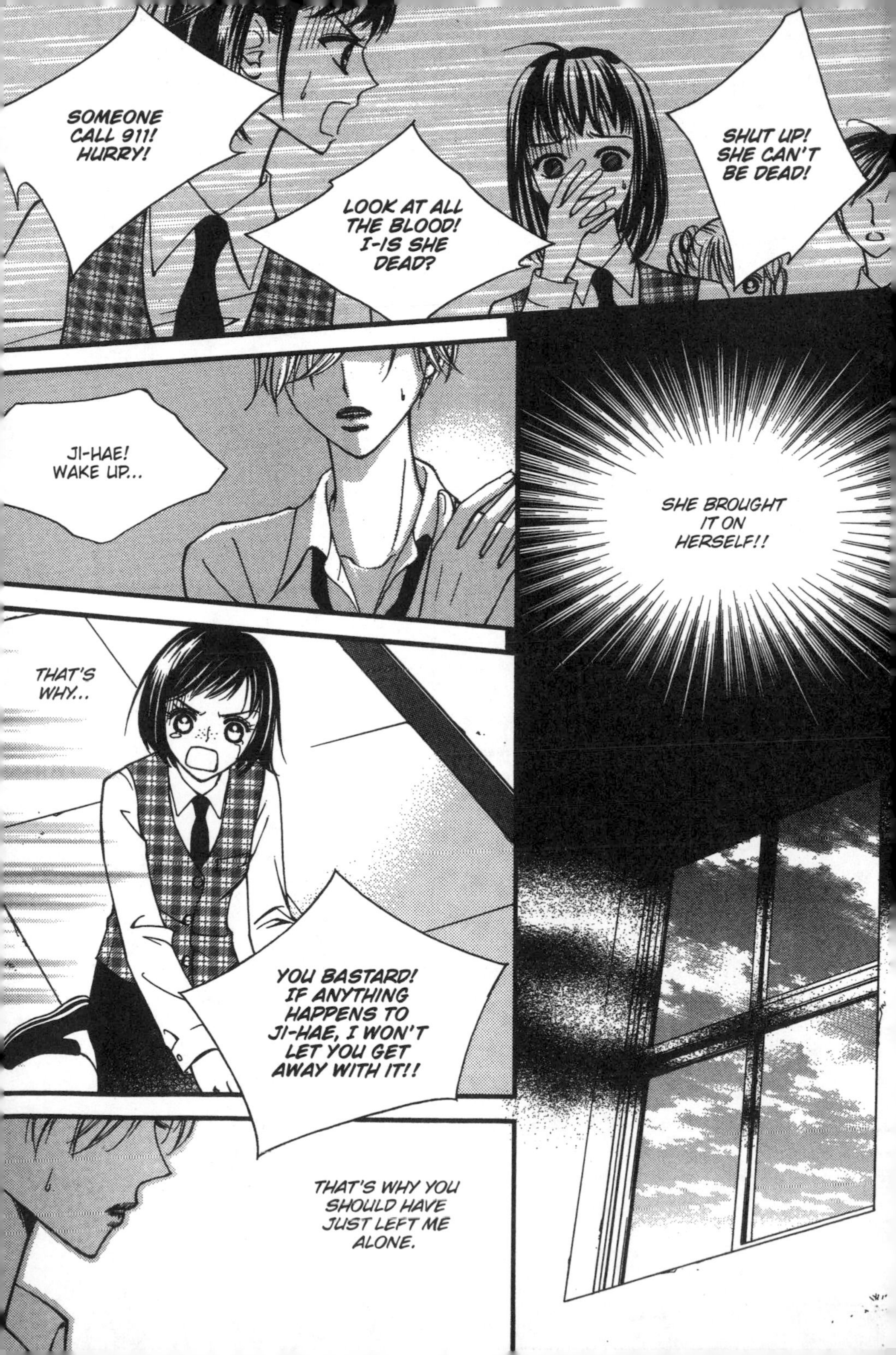
SOMEONE CALL 911! HURRY!
LOOK AT ALL THE BLOOD! I-IS SHE DEAD?
SHUT UP! SHE CAN'T BE DEAD!
JI-HAE! WAKE UP...
THAT'S WHY...
YOU BASTARD! IF ANYTHING HAPPENS TO JI-HAE, I WON'T LET YOU GET AWAY WITH IT!!
THAT'S WHY YOU SHOULD HAVE JUST LEFT ME ALONE.
SHE BROUGHT IT ON HERSELF!!

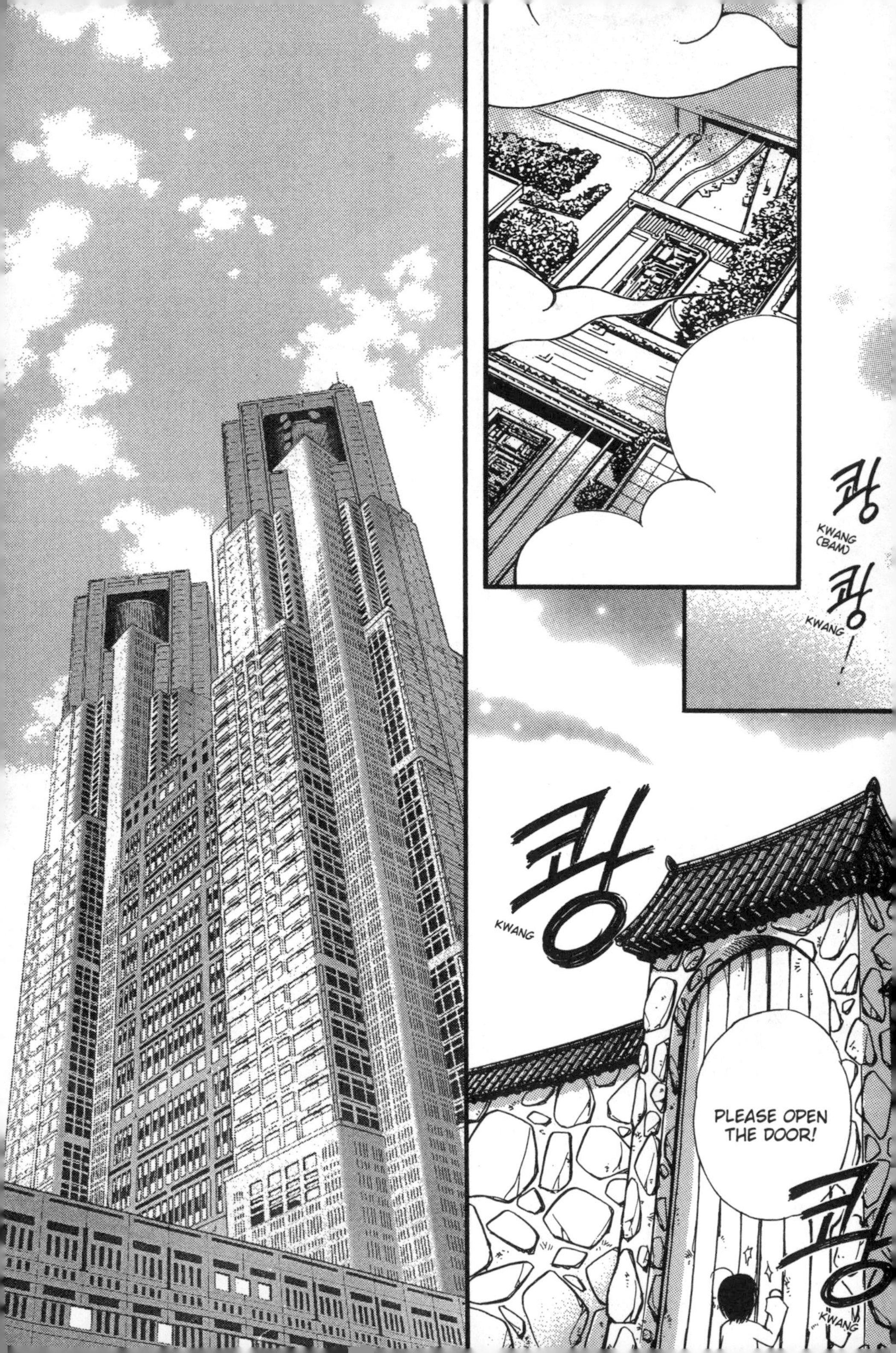

쾅
KWANG (BAM)
쾅
KWANG
쾅
KWANG
PLEASE OPEN THE DOOR!
쾅
KWANG

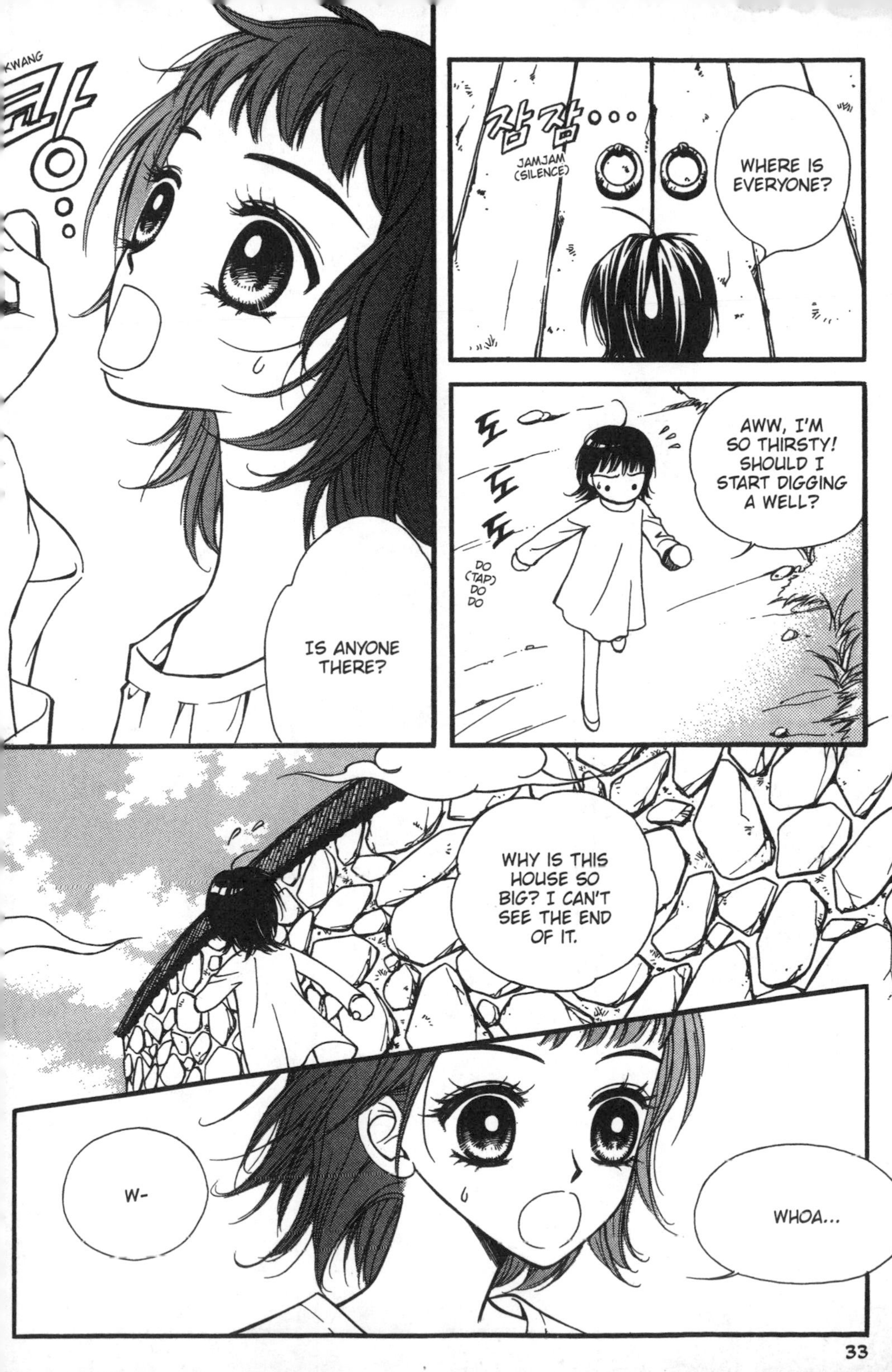
KWANG
IS ANYONE THERE?
잠잠...
JAMJAM (SILENCE)
WHERE IS EVERYONE?
도 도 도
DO (TAP) DO DO
AWW, I'M SO THIRSTY! SHOULD I START DIGGING A WELL?
WHY IS THIS HOUSE SO BIG? I CAN'T SEE THE END OF IT.
W-
WHOA...

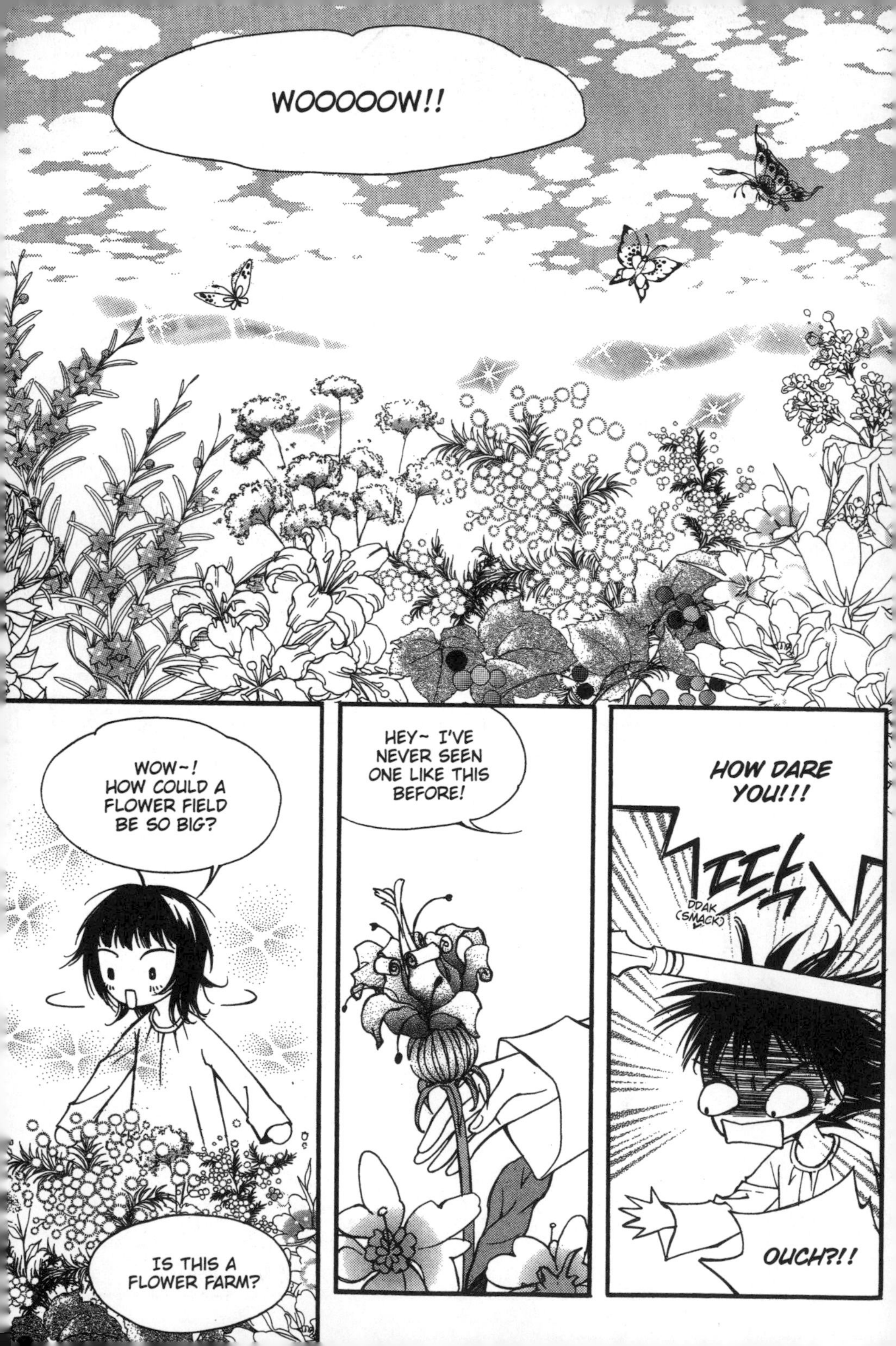

WOOOOOW!!
WOW~! HOW COULD A FLOWER FIELD BE SO BIG?
IS THIS A FLOWER FARM?
HEY~ I'VE NEVER SEEN ONE LIKE THIS BEFORE!
HOW DARE YOU!!!
DDAK (SMACK)
OUCH?!!

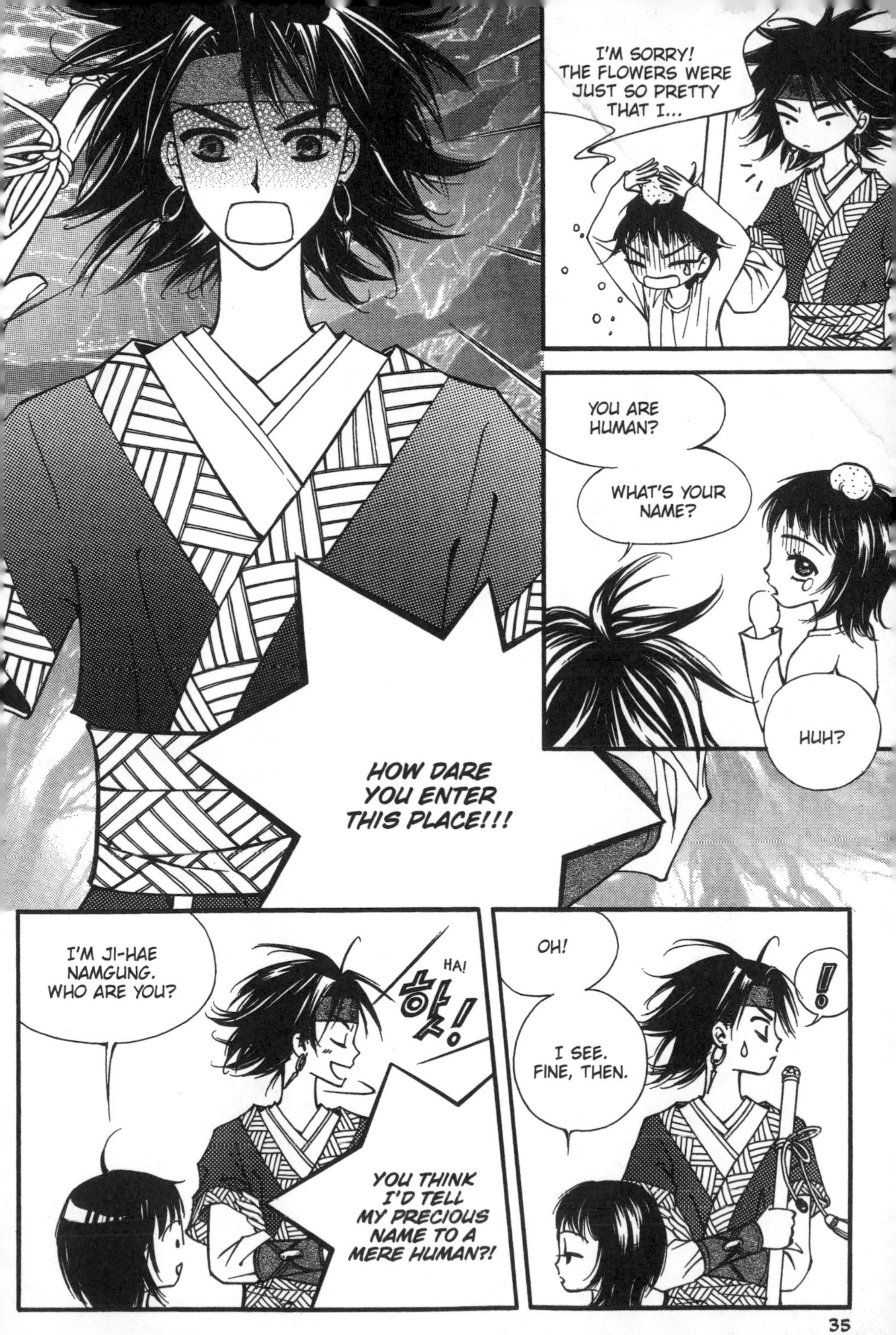
HOW DARE YOU ENTER THIS PLACE!!!
I'M SORRY! THE FLOWERS WERE JUST SO PRETTY THAT I...
YOU ARE HUMAN?
WHAT'S YOUR NAME?
HUH?
I'M JI-HAE NAMGUNG. WHO ARE YOU?
HA!
핫!
YOU THINK I'D TELL MY PRECIOUS NAME TO A MERE HUMAN?!
OH!
I SEE. FINE, THEN.
!

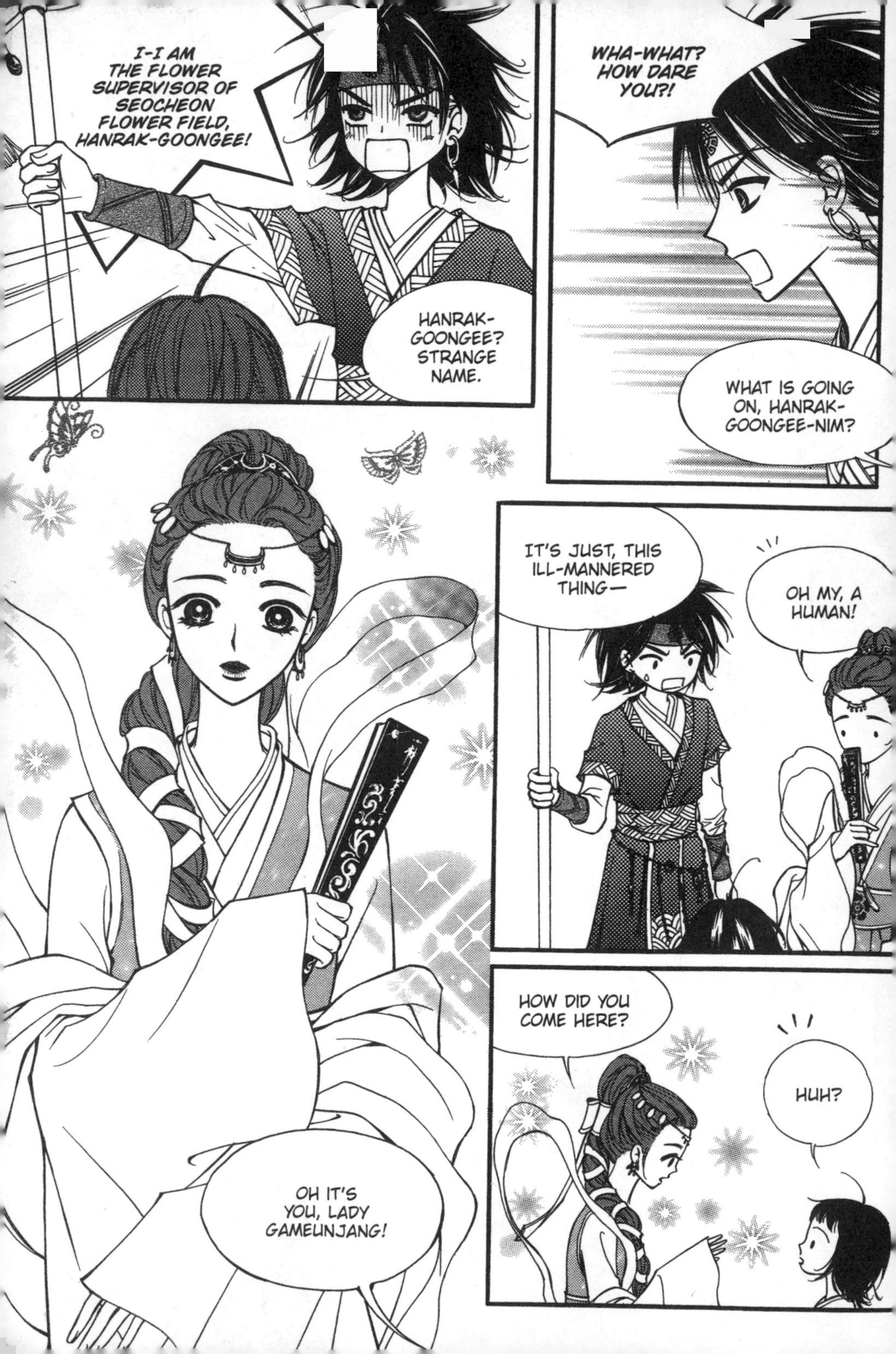
I-I AM THE FLOWER SUPERVISOR OF SEOCHEON FLOWER FIELD, HANRAK-GOONGEE!
HANRAK-GOONGEE? STRANGE NAME.
WHA-WHAT? HOW DARE YOU?!
WHAT IS GOING ON, HANRAK-GOONGEE-NIM?
OH IT'S YOU, LADY GAMEUNJANG!
IT'S JUST, THIS ILL-MANNERED THING—
OH MY, A HUMAN!
HOW DID YOU COME HERE?
HUH?

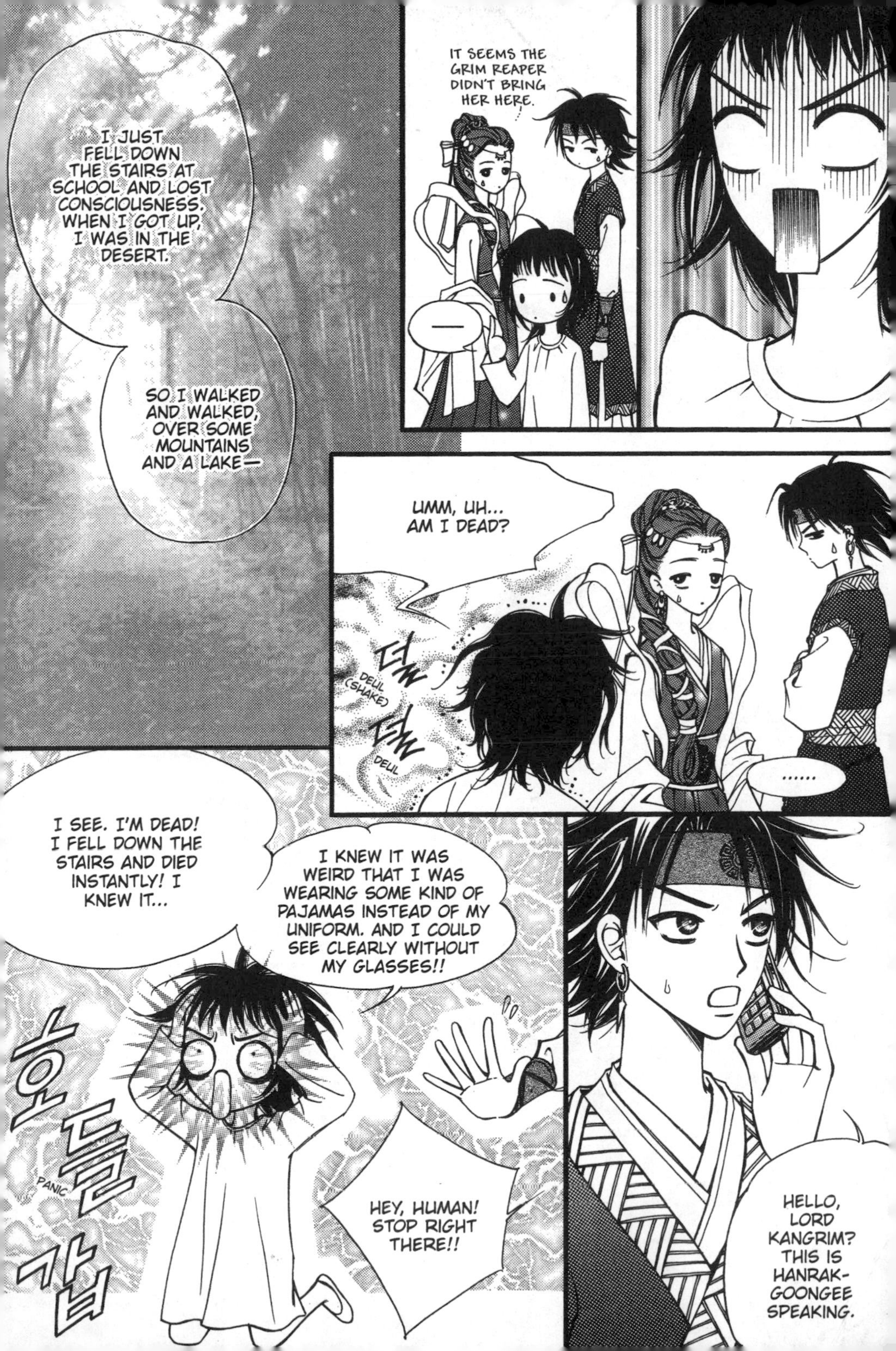

I JUST FELL DOWN THE STAIRS AT SCHOOL AND LOST CONSCIOUSNESS. WHEN I GOT UP, I WAS IN THE DESERT.
SO I WALKED AND WALKED, OVER SOME MOUNTAINS AND A LAKE—
IT SEEMS THE GRIM REAPER DIDN'T BRING HER HERE.
—
UMM, UH... AM I DEAD?
덜덜
DEUL (SHAKE)
덜덜
DEUL
......
I SEE. I'M DEAD! I FELL DOWN THE STAIRS AND DIED INSTANTLY! I KNEW IT...
I KNEW IT WAS WEIRD THAT I WAS WEARING SOME KIND OF PAJAMAS INSTEAD OF MY UNIFORM. AND I COULD SEE CLEARLY WITHOUT MY GLASSES!!
호들갑
PANIC
HEY, HUMAN! STOP RIGHT THERE!!
HELLO, LORD KANGRIM? THIS IS HANRAK-GOONGEE SPEAKING.

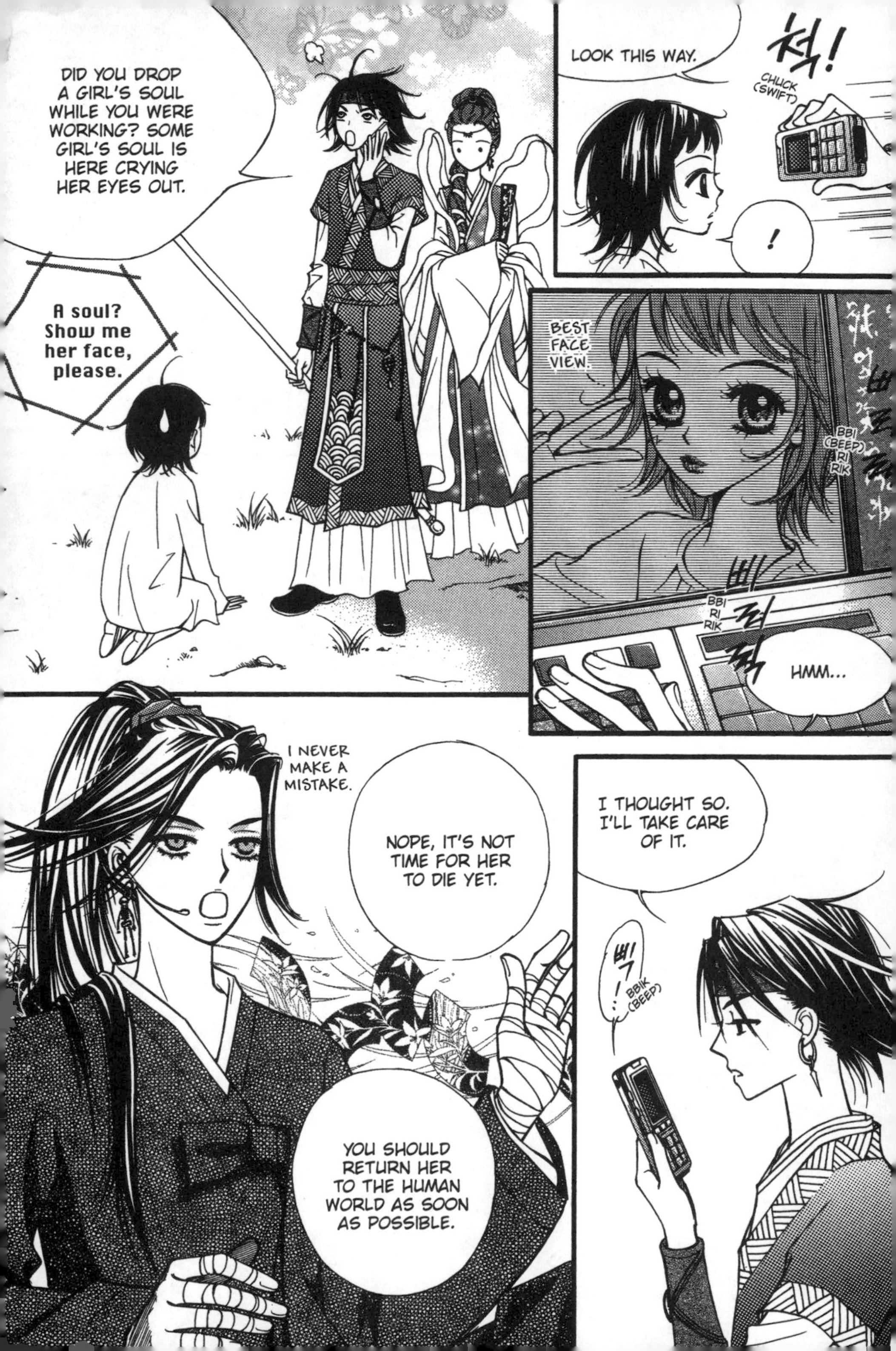
DID YOU DROP A GIRL'S SOUL WHILE YOU WERE WORKING? SOME GIRL'S SOUL IS HERE CRYING HER EYES OUT.
A soul? Show me her face, please.
LOOK THIS WAY.
척!
CHUCK (SWIFT)
!
BEST FACE VIEW.
BBI (BEEP) RI RIK
삐리릭
BBI RI RIK
HMM...
I NEVER MAKE A MISTAKE.
NOPE, IT'S NOT TIME FOR HER TO DIE YET.
YOU SHOULD RETURN HER TO THE HUMAN WORLD AS SOON AS POSSIBLE.
I THOUGHT SO. I'LL TAKE CARE OF IT.
삑!
BBIK (BEEP)

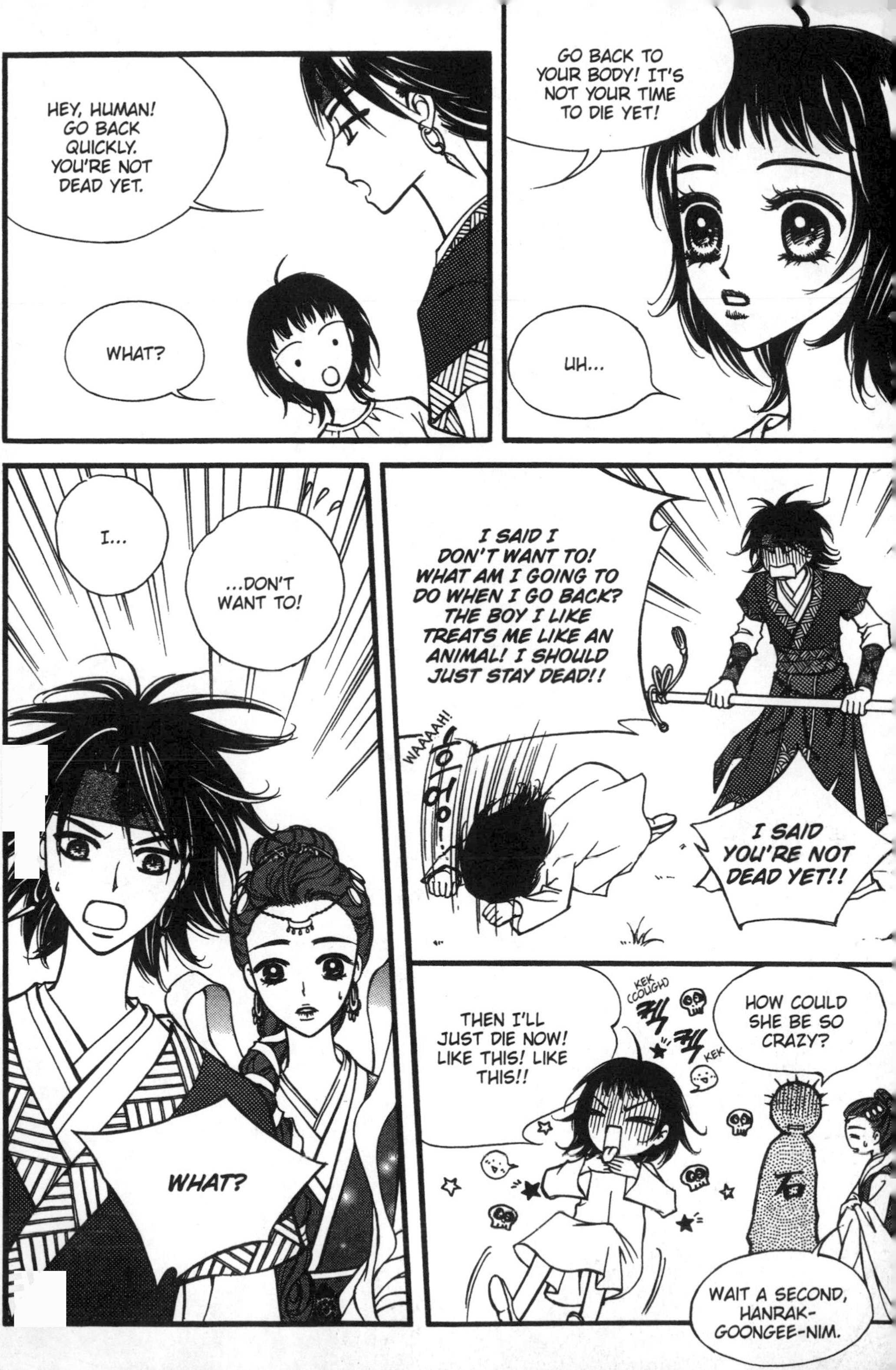
HEY, HUMAN! GO BACK QUICKLY. YOU'RE NOT DEAD YET.
WHAT?
GO BACK TO YOUR BODY! IT'S NOT YOUR TIME TO DIE YET!
UH...
I...
...DON'T WANT TO!
WHAT?
I SAID I DON'T WANT TO! WHAT AM I GOING TO DO WHEN I GO BACK? THE BOY I LIKE TREATS ME LIKE AN ANIMAL! I SHOULD JUST STAY DEAD!!
WAAAAH!
I SAID YOU'RE NOT DEAD YET!!
THEN I'LL JUST DIE NOW! LIKE THIS! LIKE THIS!!
KEK (COUGH)
KEK
HOW COULD SHE BE SO CRAZY?
WAIT A SECOND, HANRAK-GOONGEE-NIM.

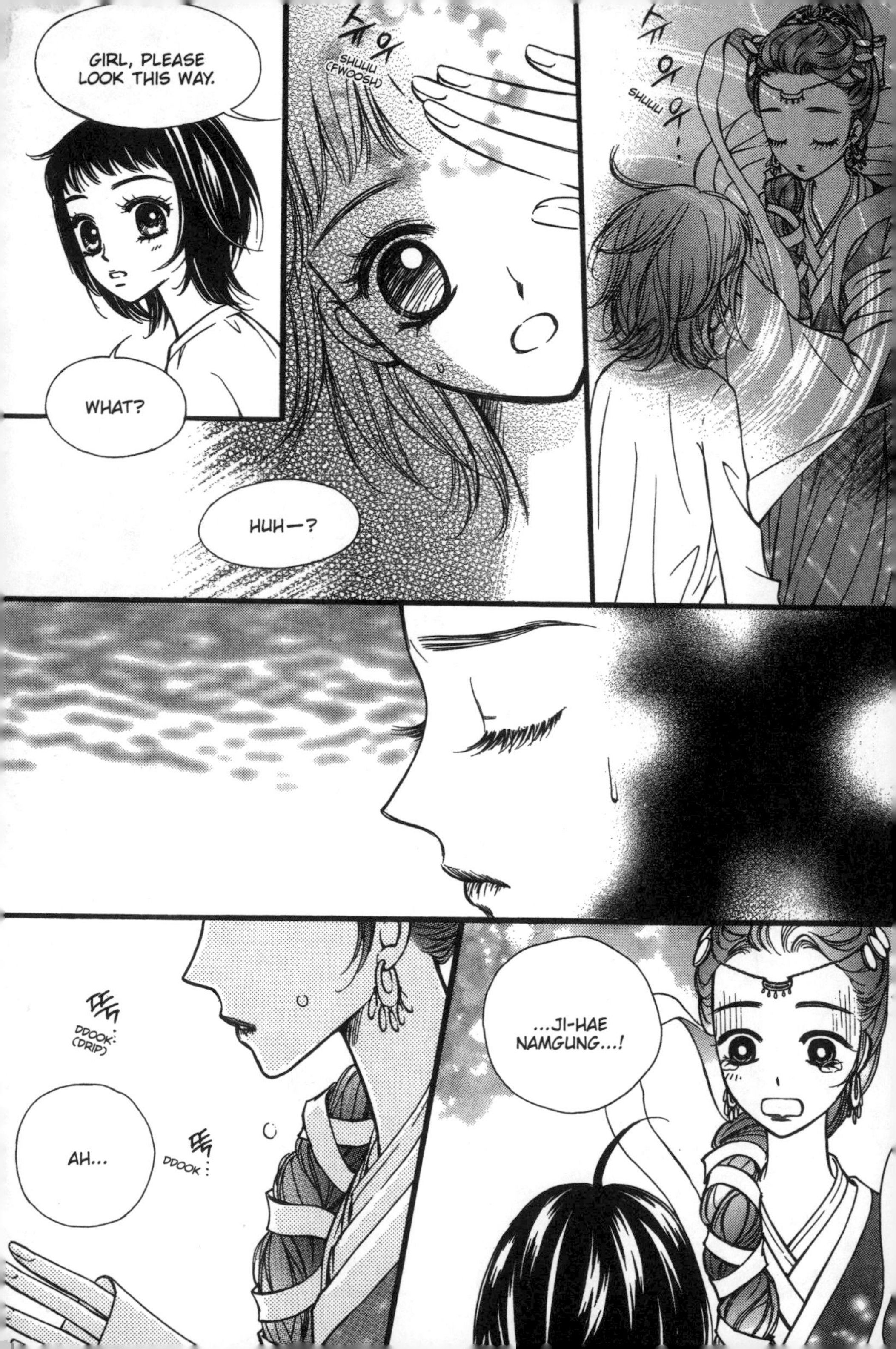
GIRL, PLEASE LOOK THIS WAY.
WHAT?
SHUUU (FWOOSH)
HUH—?
SHUUU
DDOOK (DRIP)
AH...
DDOOK
...JI-HAE NAMGUNG...!

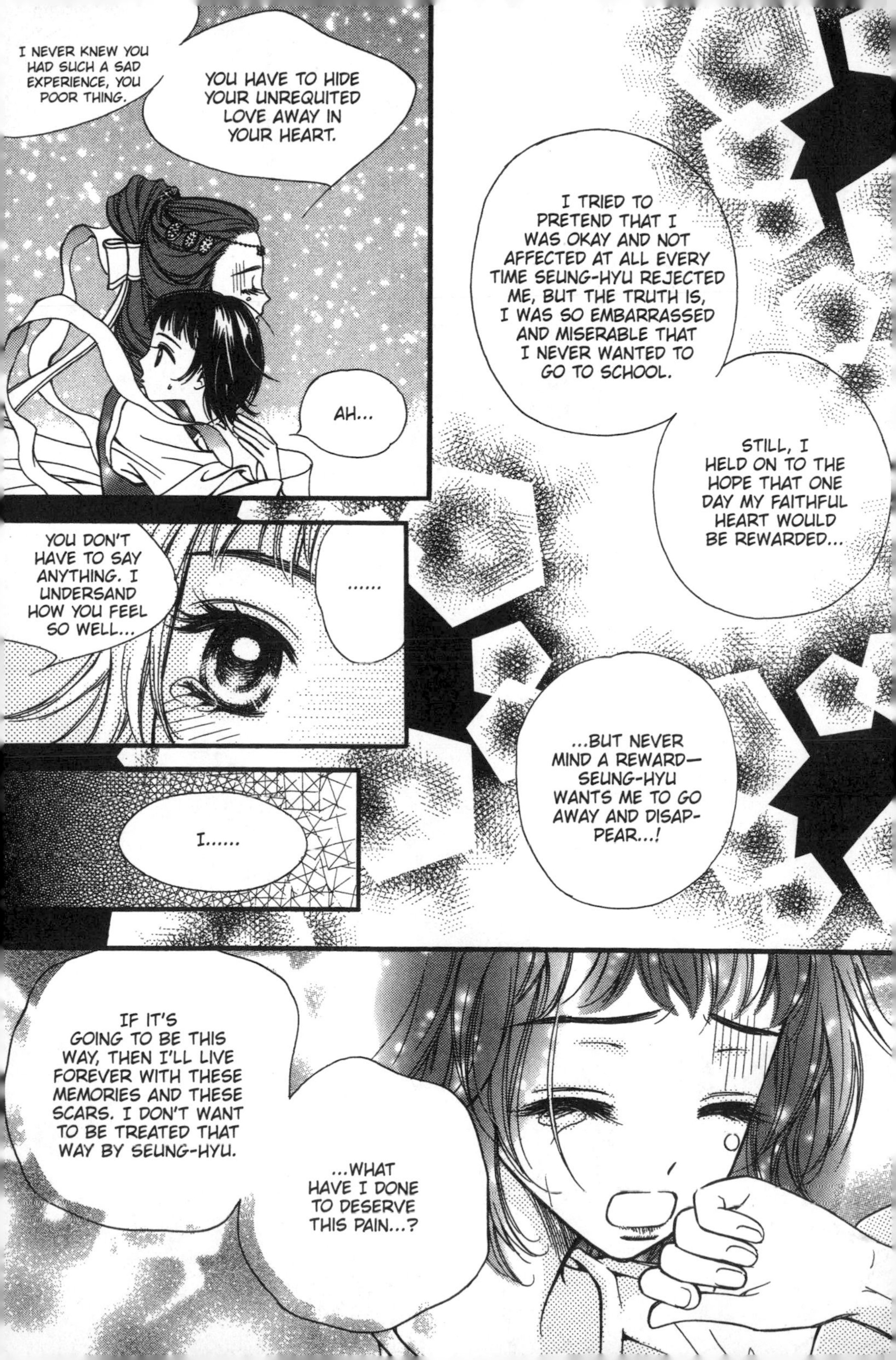
I NEVER KNEW YOU HAD SUCH A SAD EXPERIENCE, YOU POOR THING.
YOU HAVE TO HIDE YOUR UNREQUITED LOVE AWAY IN YOUR HEART.
AH...
YOU DON'T HAVE TO SAY ANYTHING. I UNDERSAND HOW YOU FEEL SO WELL...
......
I......
I TRIED TO PRETEND THAT I WAS OKAY AND NOT AFFECTED AT ALL EVERY TIME SEUNG-HYU REJECTED ME, BUT THE TRUTH IS, I WAS SO EMBARRASSED AND MISERABLE THAT I NEVER WANTED TO GO TO SCHOOL.
STILL, I HELD ON TO THE HOPE THAT ONE DAY MY FAITHFUL HEART WOULD BE REWARDED...
...BUT NEVER MIND A REWARD— SEUNG-HYU WANTS ME TO GO AWAY AND DISAP- PEAR...!
IF IT'S GOING TO BE THIS WAY, THEN I'LL LIVE FOREVER WITH THESE MEMORIES AND THESE SCARS. I DON'T WANT TO BE TREATED THAT WAY BY SEUNG-HYU.
...WHAT HAVE I DONE TO DESERVE THIS PAIN...?

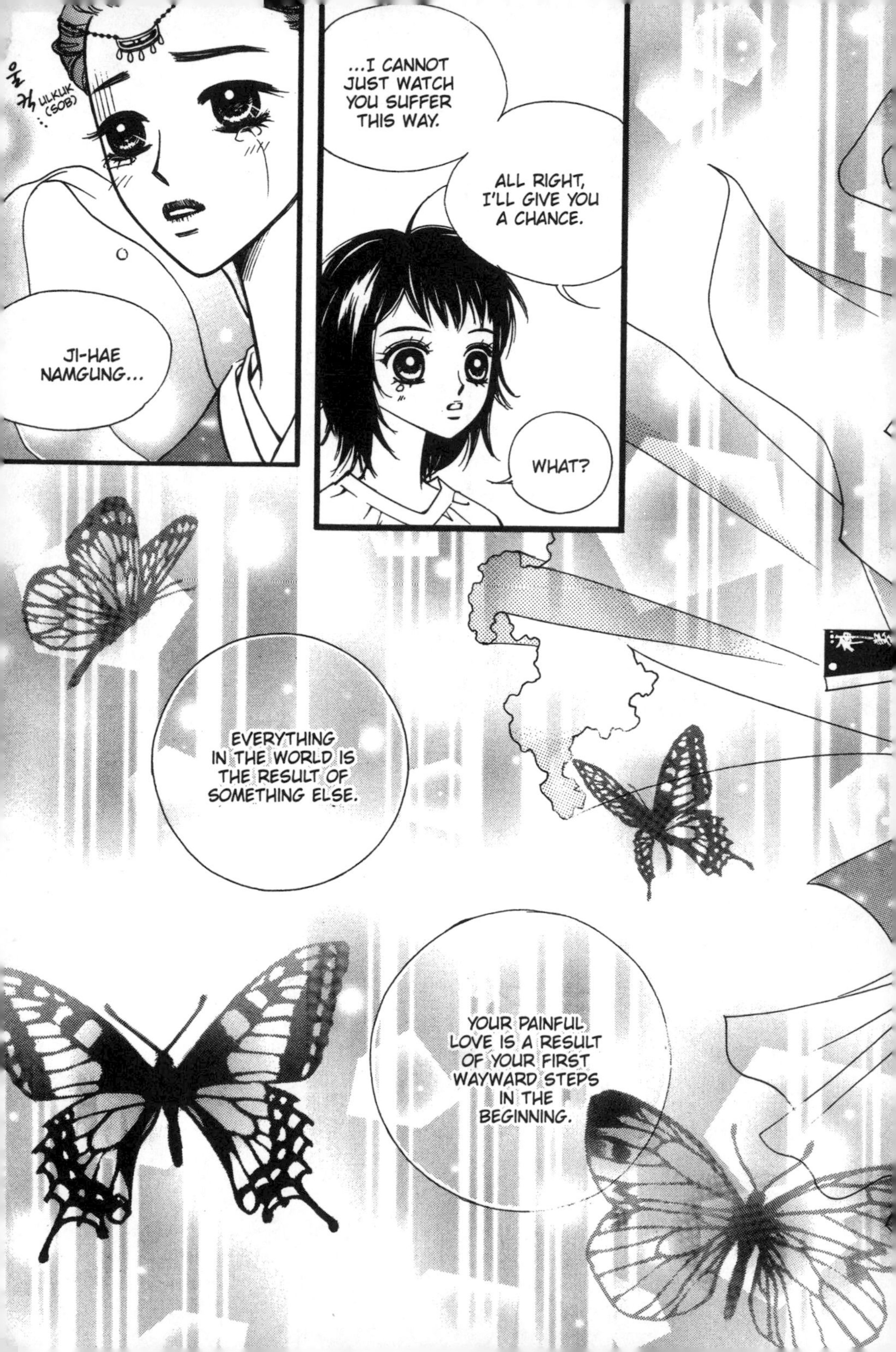
울컥
ULKUK (SOB)
JI-HAE NAMGUNG...
...I CANNOT JUST WATCH YOU SUFFER THIS WAY.
ALL RIGHT, I'LL GIVE YOU A CHANCE.
WHAT?
EVERYTHING IN THE WORLD IS THE RESULT OF SOMETHING ELSE.
YOUR PAINFUL LOVE IS A RESULT OF YOUR FIRST WAYWARD STEPS IN THE BEGINNING.

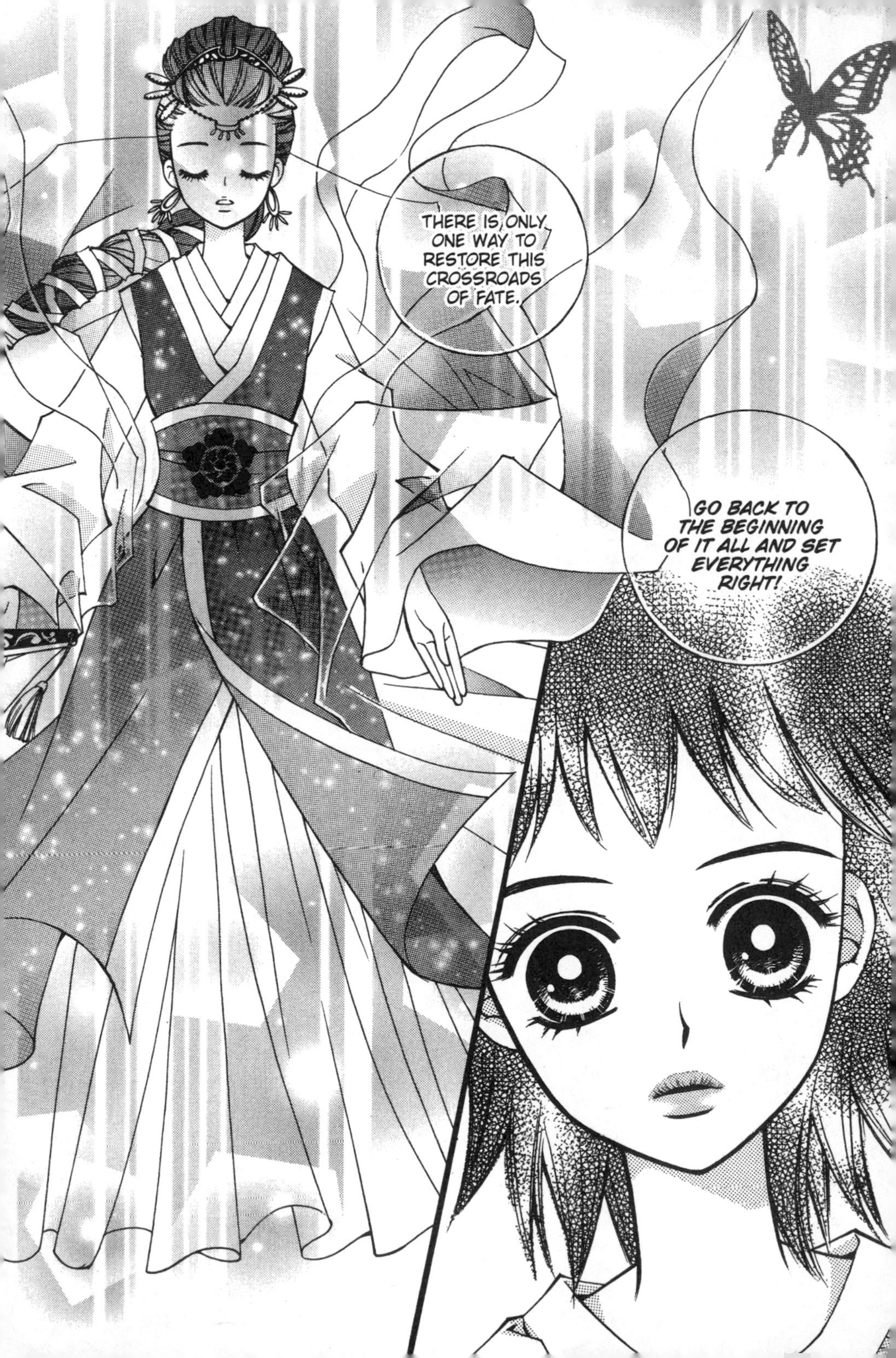
THERE IS ONLY ONE WAY TO RESTORE THIS CROSSROADS OF FATE.
GO BACK TO THE BEGINNING OF IT ALL AND SET EVERYTHING RIGHT!

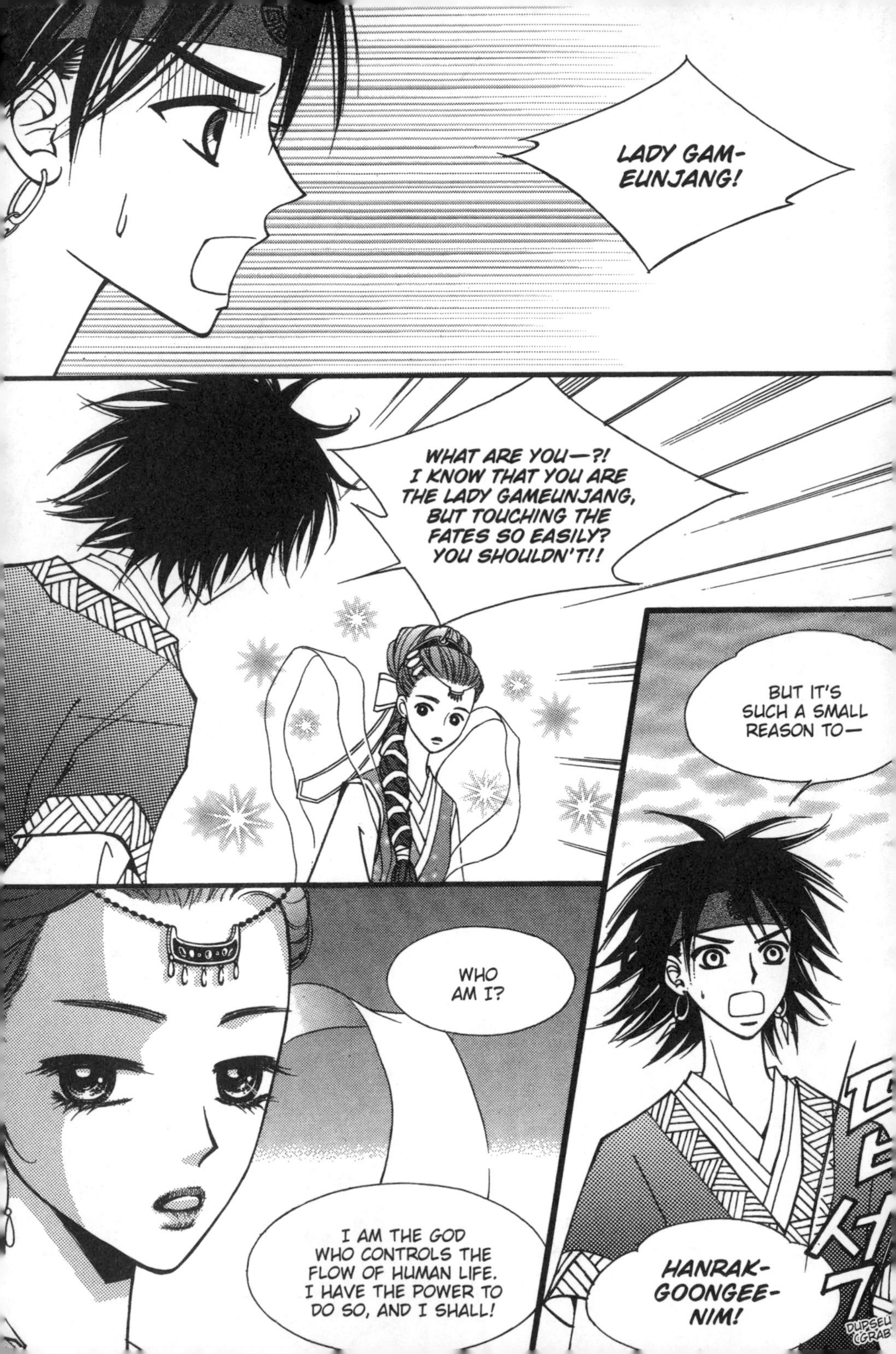
LADY GAM-EUNJANG!
WHAT ARE YOU—?! I KNOW THAT YOU ARE THE LADY GAMEUNJANG, BUT TOUCHING THE FATES SO EASILY? YOU SHOULDN'T!!
BUT IT'S SUCH A SMALL REASON TO—
WHO AM I?
I AM THE GOD WHO CONTROLS THE FLOW OF HUMAN LIFE. I HAVE THE POWER TO DO SO, AND I SHALL!
HANRAK-GOONGEE-NIM!
DUPSEU (GRAB

PLEASE HELP.

DON'T YOU KNOW THAT FEELING? THE FEELING YOU GET WHEN YOU DON'T WANT ANYTHING BUT HIM...

IT MIGHT BE NOTHING TO YOU, BUT IT'S A LOVE THAT'S WORTH MY LIFE.

EVERY TIME HE TELLS ME HE HATES ME, I FEEL LIKE MY WORLD IS COLLAPSING.

...HANRAK-GOONGEE-NIM.

HOW DID YOU FEEL WHEN YOU FACED YOUR MOTHER'S DEATH?

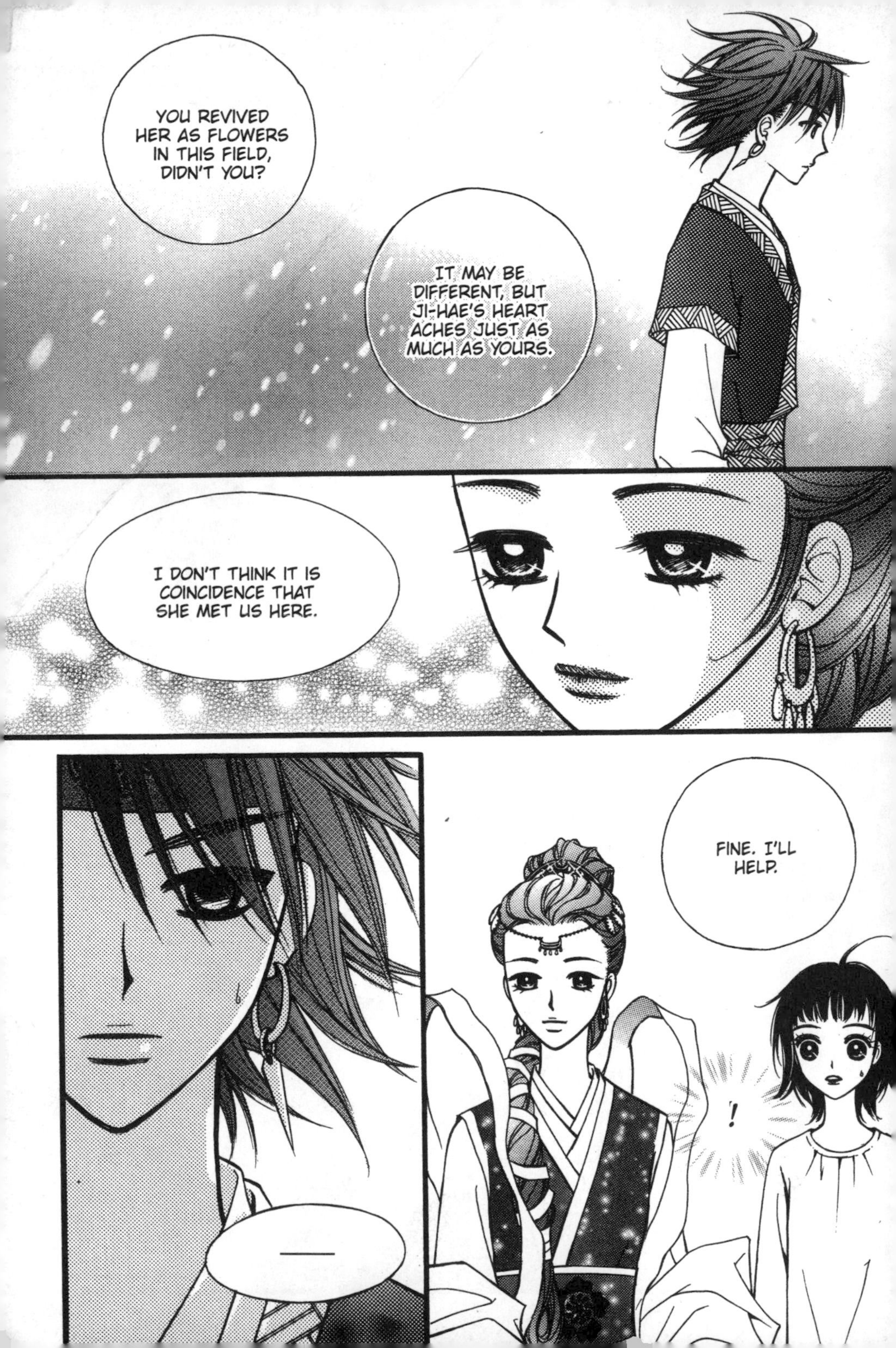
YOU REVIVED HER AS FLOWERS IN THIS FIELD, DIDN'T YOU?
IT MAY BE DIFFERENT, BUT JI-HAE'S HEART ACHES JUST AS MUCH AS YOURS.
I DON'T THINK IT IS COINCIDENCE THAT SHE MET US HERE.
——
FINE. I'LL HELP.
!

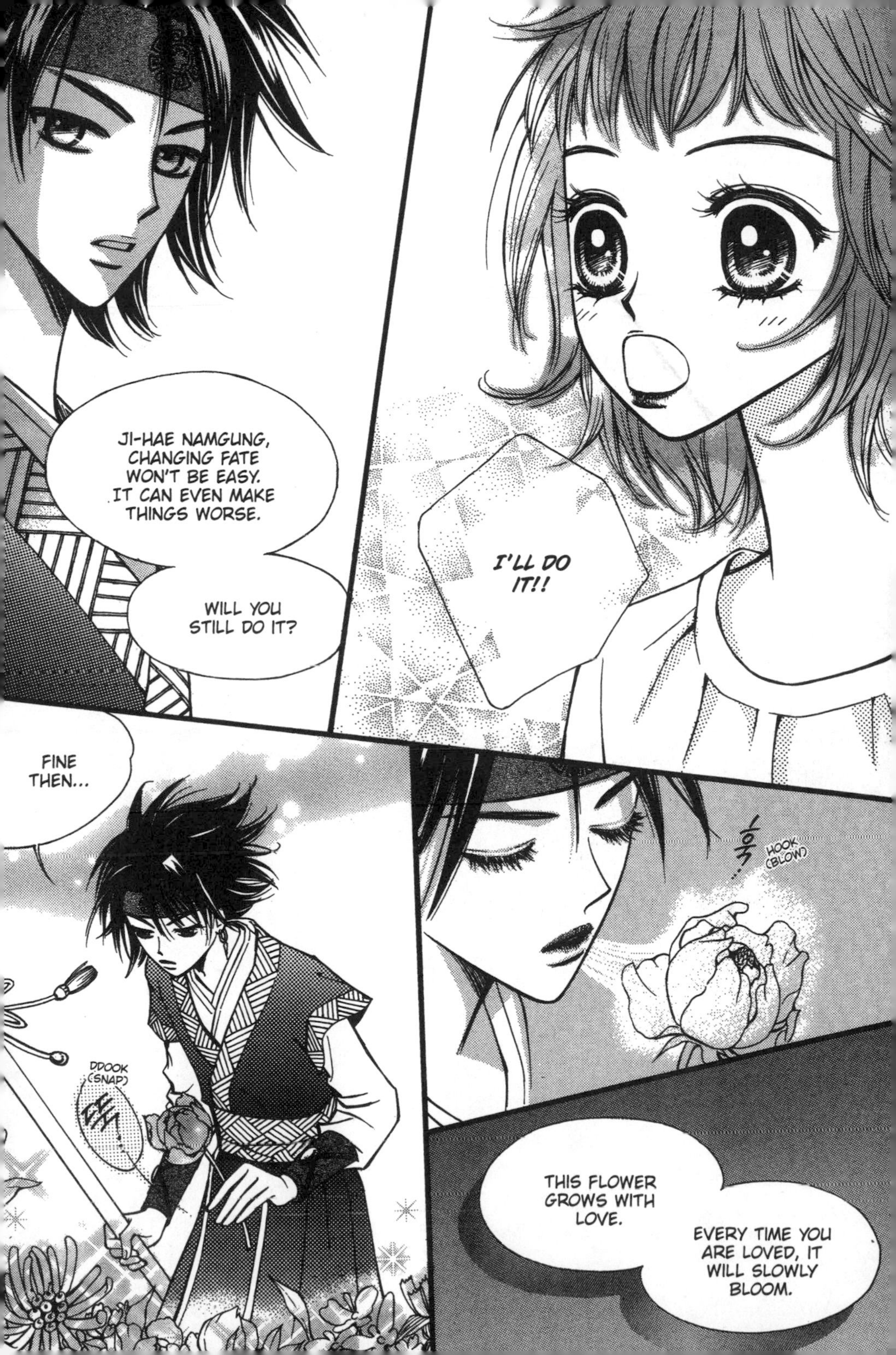
JI-HAE NAMGUNG, CHANGING FATE WON'T BE EASY. IT CAN EVEN MAKE THINGS WORSE.
WILL YOU STILL DO IT?
I'LL DO IT!!
FINE THEN...
DDOOK (SNAP)
HOOK (BLOW)
THIS FLOWER GROWS WITH LOVE.
EVERY TIME YOU ARE LOVED, IT WILL SLOWLY BLOOM.

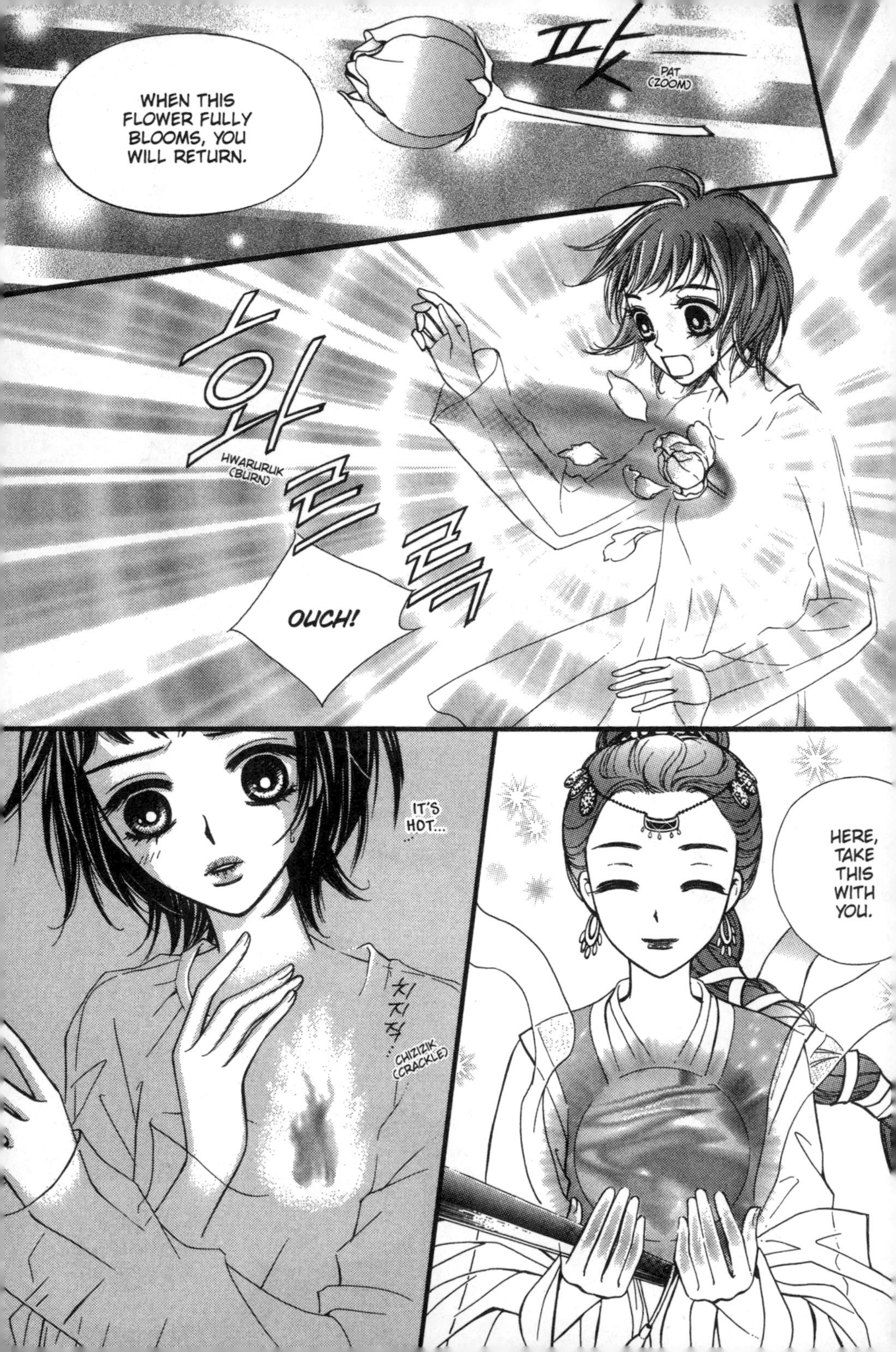
WHEN THIS FLOWER FULLY BLOOMS, YOU WILL RETURN.
팍—
PAT (ZOOM)
화르륵
HWARURUK (BURN)
OUCH!
IT'S HOT...
치지직
CHIZIZIK (CRACKLE)
HERE, TAKE THIS WITH YOU.

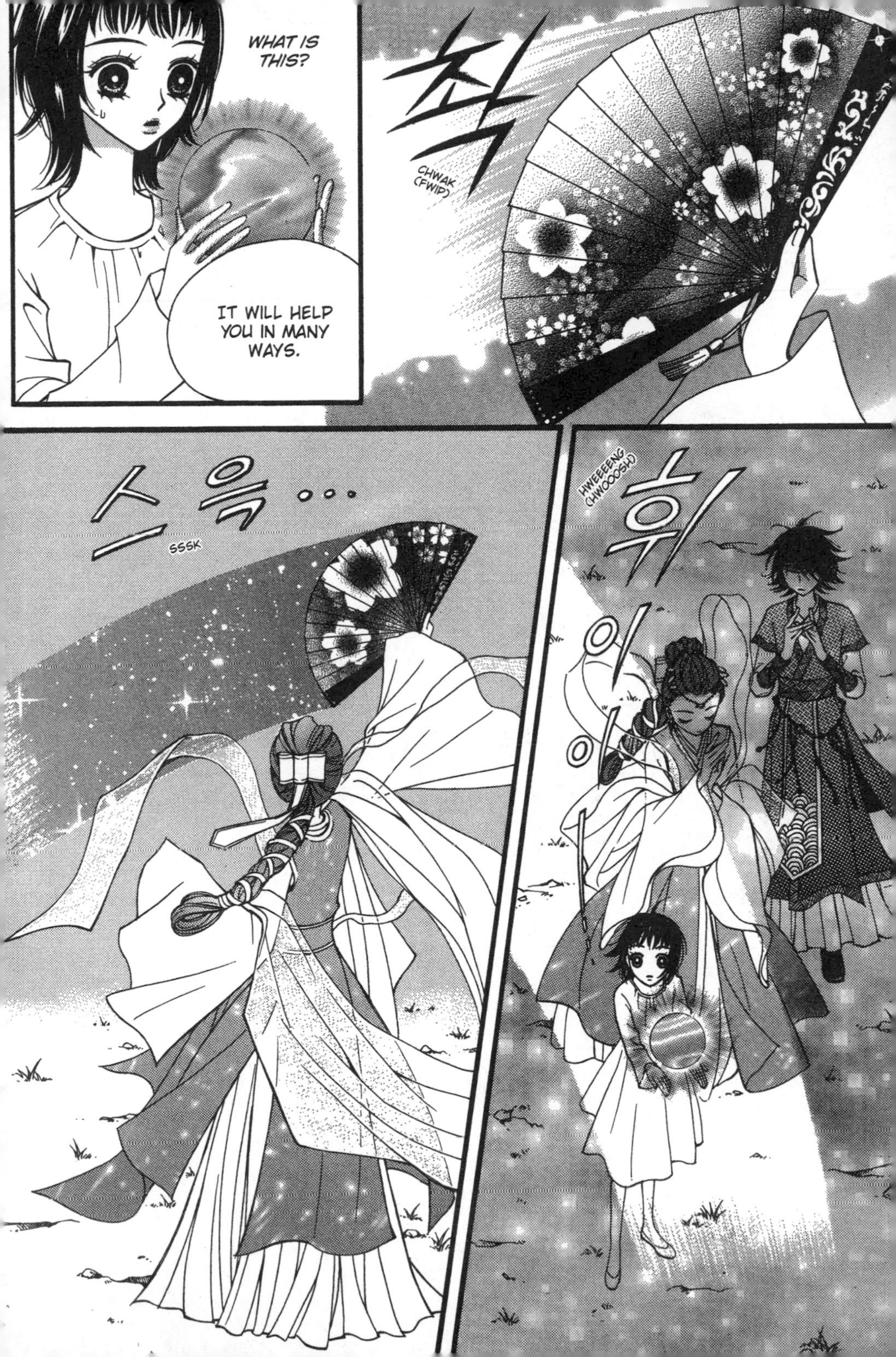
WHAT IS THIS?
IT WILL HELP YOU IN MANY WAYS.
CHWAK (FWIP)
스윽...
SSSK
HWEEEENG (HWOOOSH)

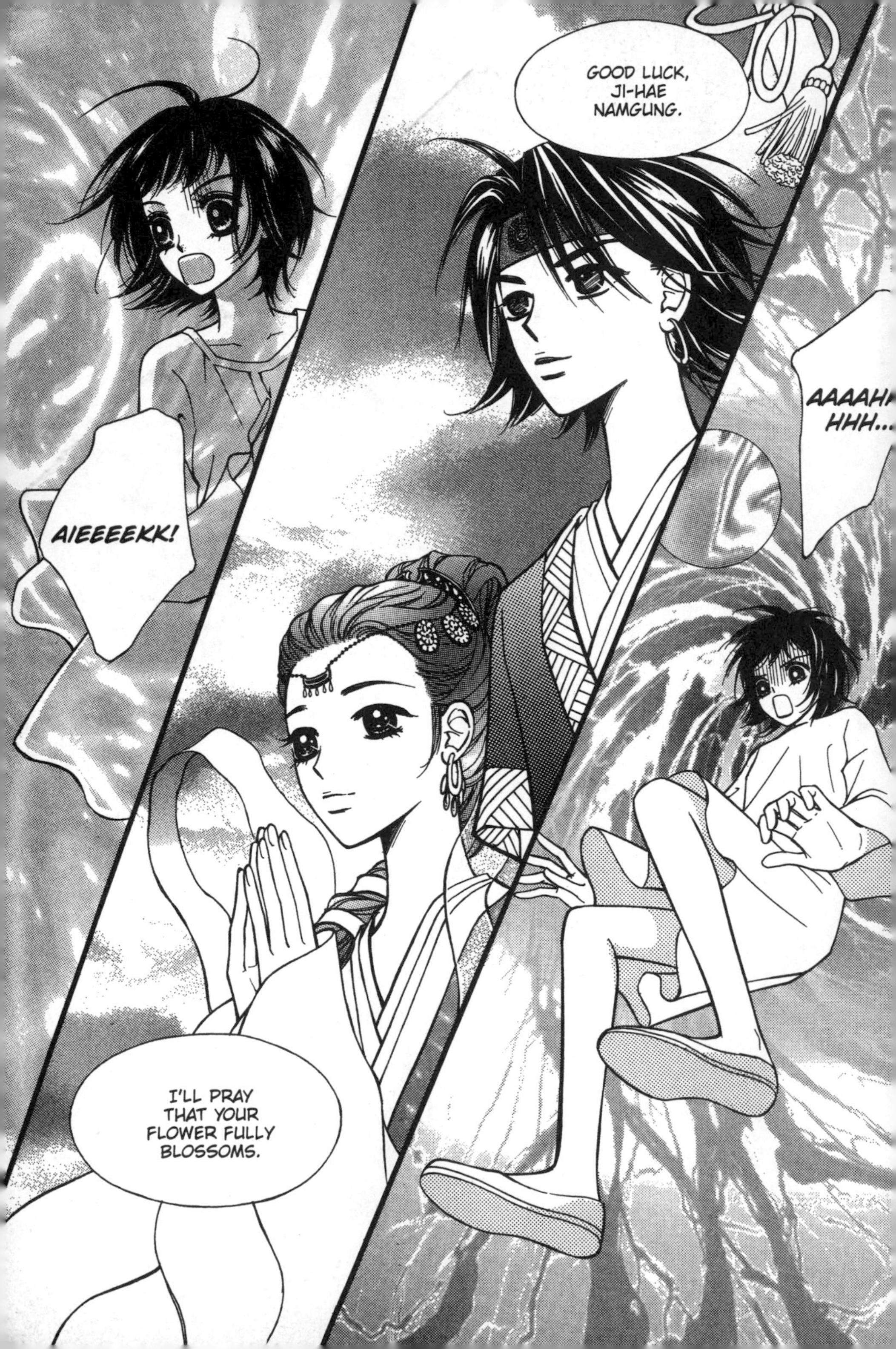
AIEEEEKK!
GOOD LUCK, JI-HAE NAMGUNG.
I'LL PRAY THAT YOUR FLOWER FULLY BLOSSOMS.
AAAAHHHH...

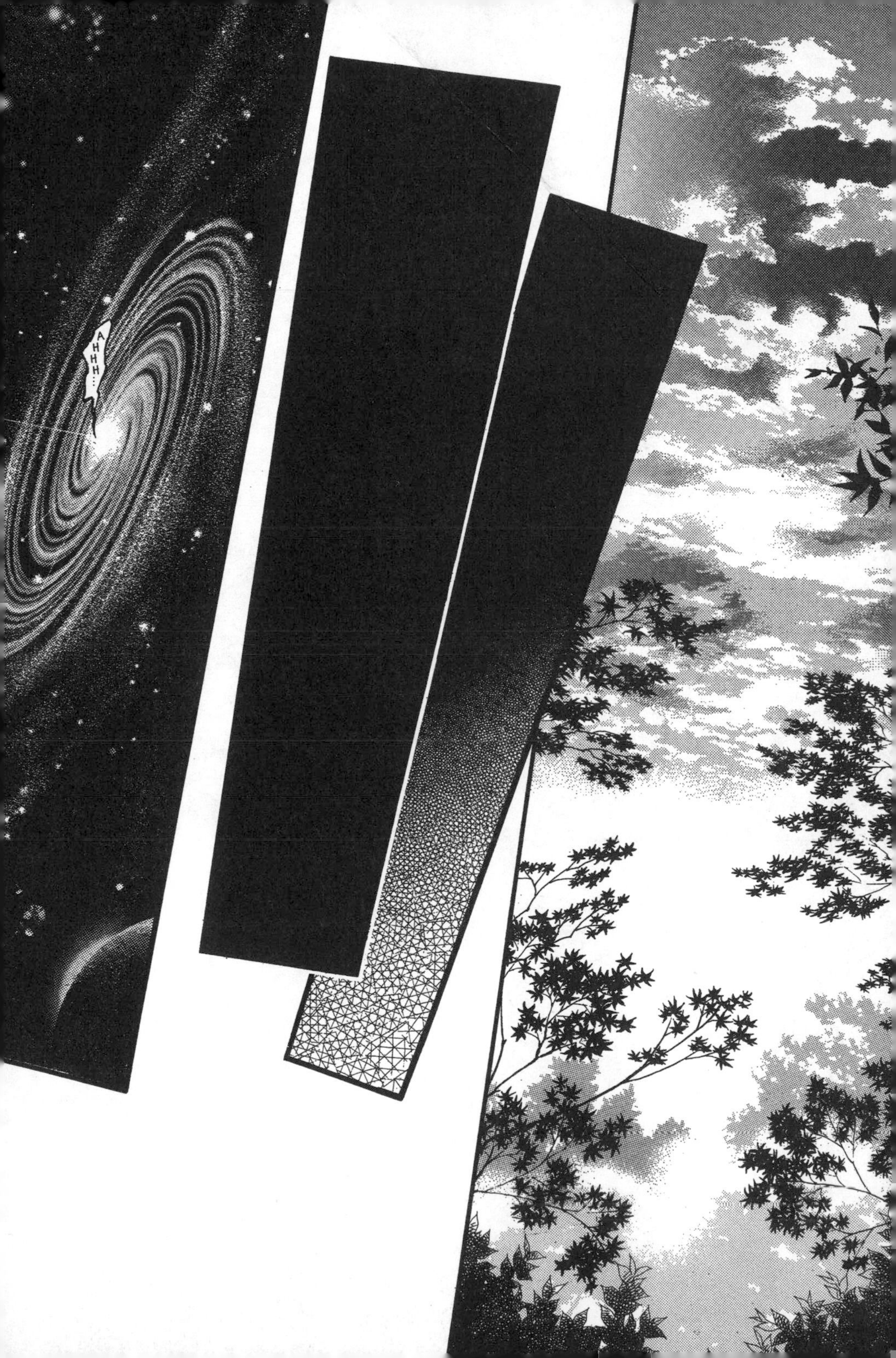
AHHH…

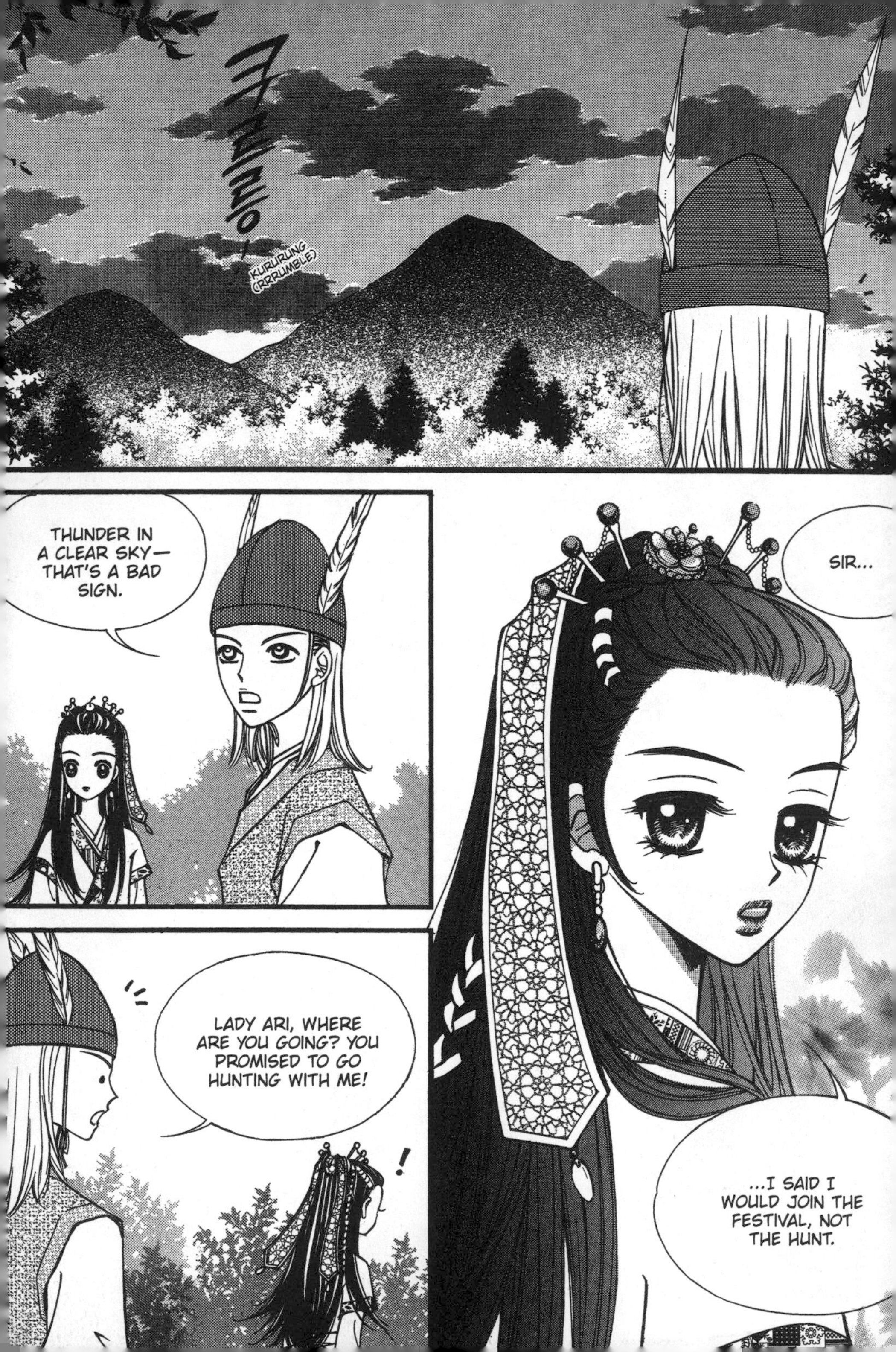
KURURUNG (RRRUMBLE)
THUNDER IN A CLEAR SKY— THAT'S A BAD SIGN.
LADY ARI, WHERE ARE YOU GOING? YOU PROMISED TO GO HUNTING WITH ME!
!
SIR...
...I SAID I WOULD JOIN THE FESTIVAL, NOT THE HUNT.

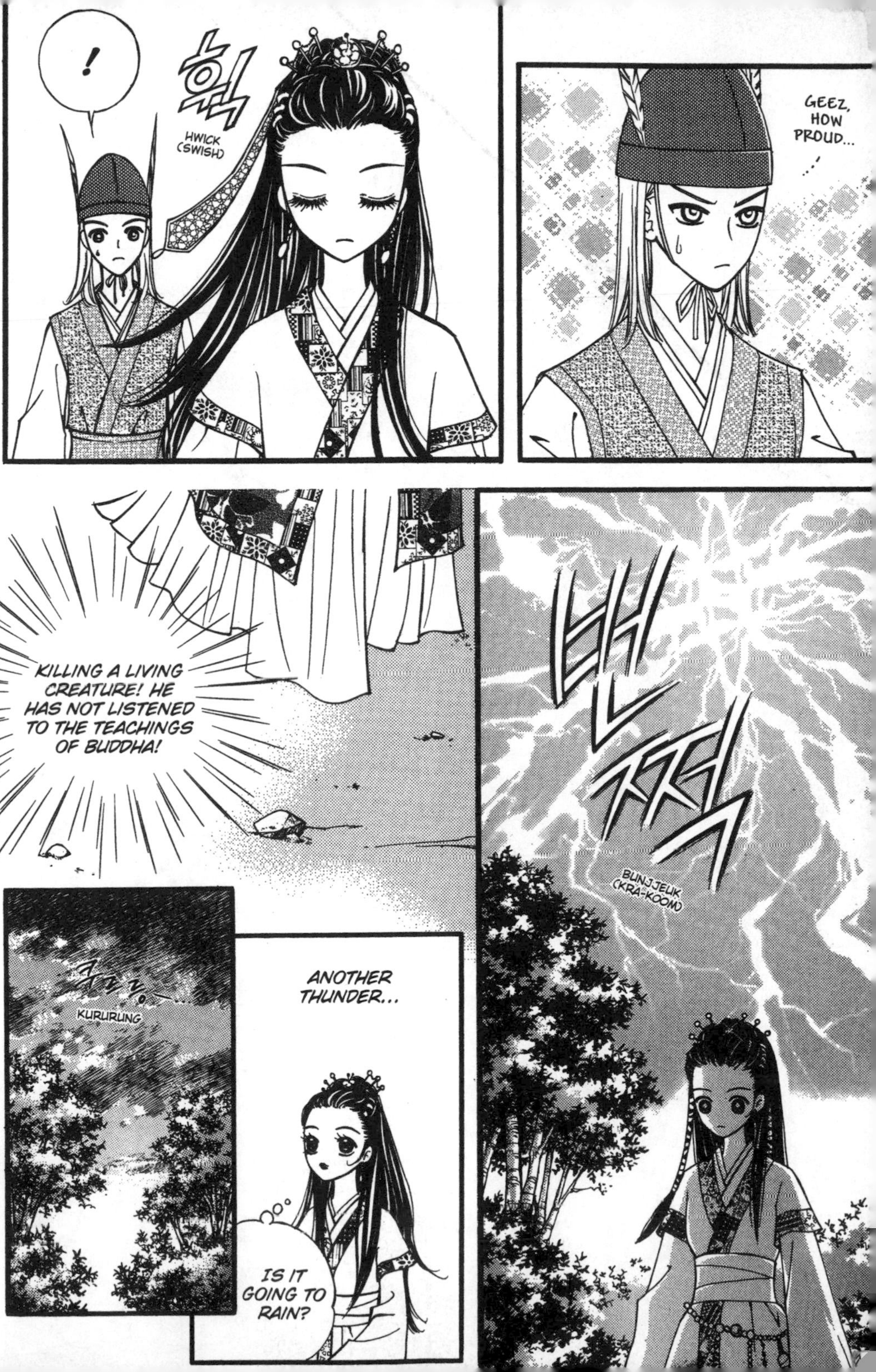
!
휙
HWICK (SWISH)
GEEZ, HOW PROUD...
KILLING A LIVING CREATURE! HE HAS NOT LISTENED TO THE TEACHINGS OF BUDDHA!
쿠르릉
KURURUNG
ANOTHER THUNDER...
IS IT GOING TO RAIN?
번쩍
BUNJJEUK (KRA-KOOM)

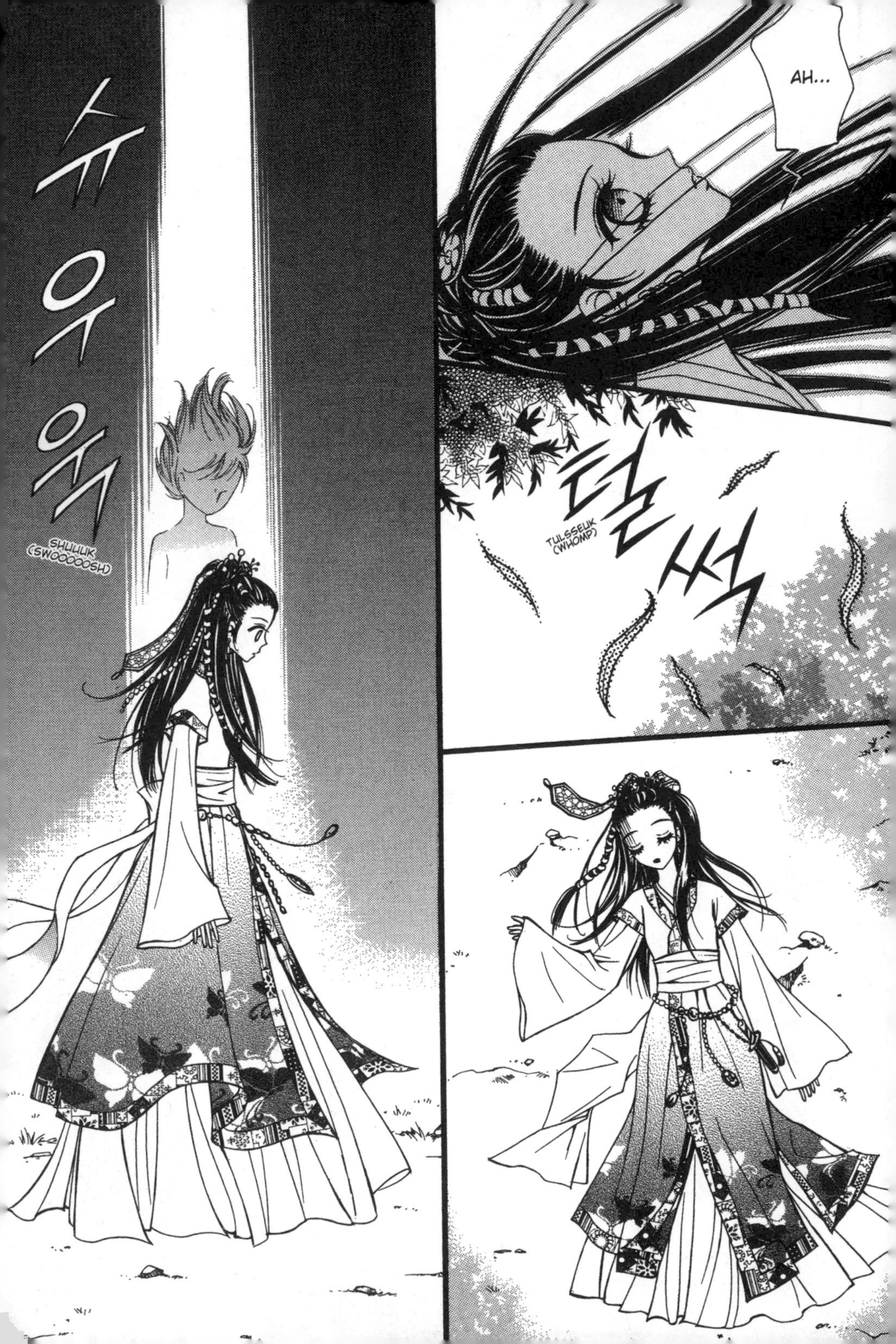
SHUUUK (SWOOOOOSH)
AH...
TULSSEUK (WHOMP)

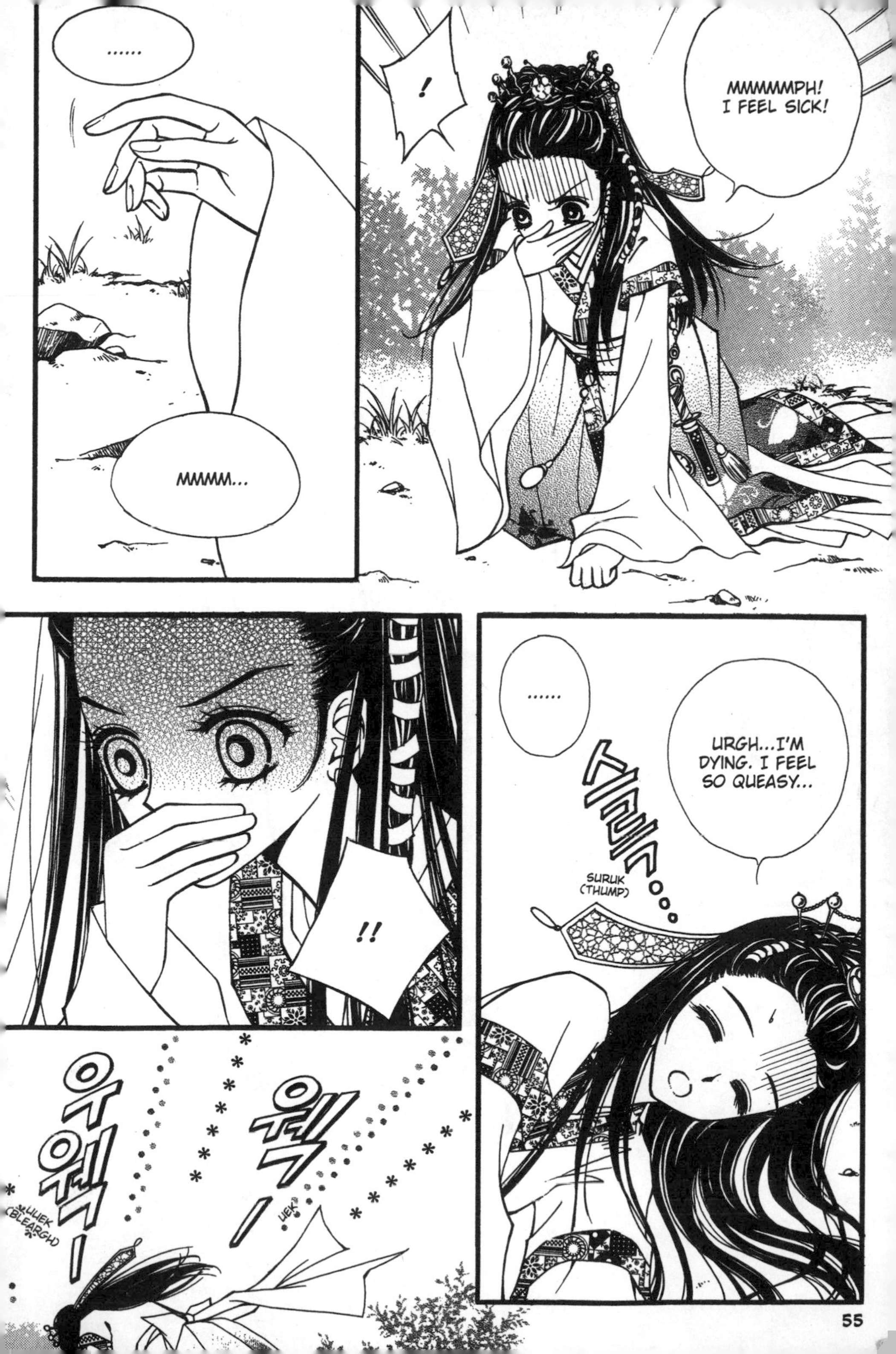
......
MMMM...
!
MMMMMMPH! I FEEL SICK!
!!
우웩—
UWEK (BLEARGH)
웩—
UEK
......
URGH...I'M DYING. I FEEL SO QUEASY...
SURUK (THUMP)

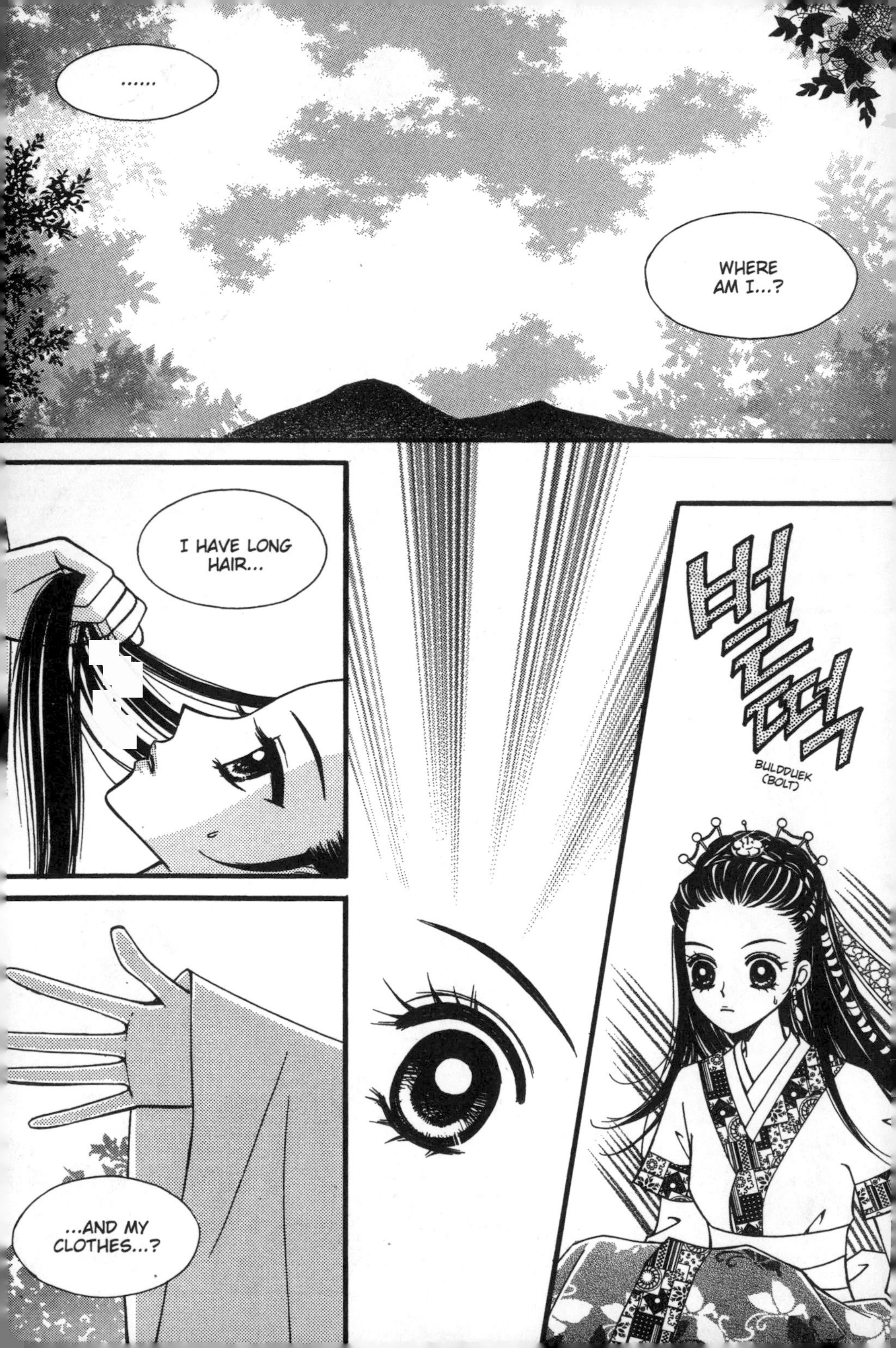
......
WHERE AM I...?
I HAVE LONG HAIR...
...AND MY CLOTHES...?
벌떡
BULDDUEK (BOLT)

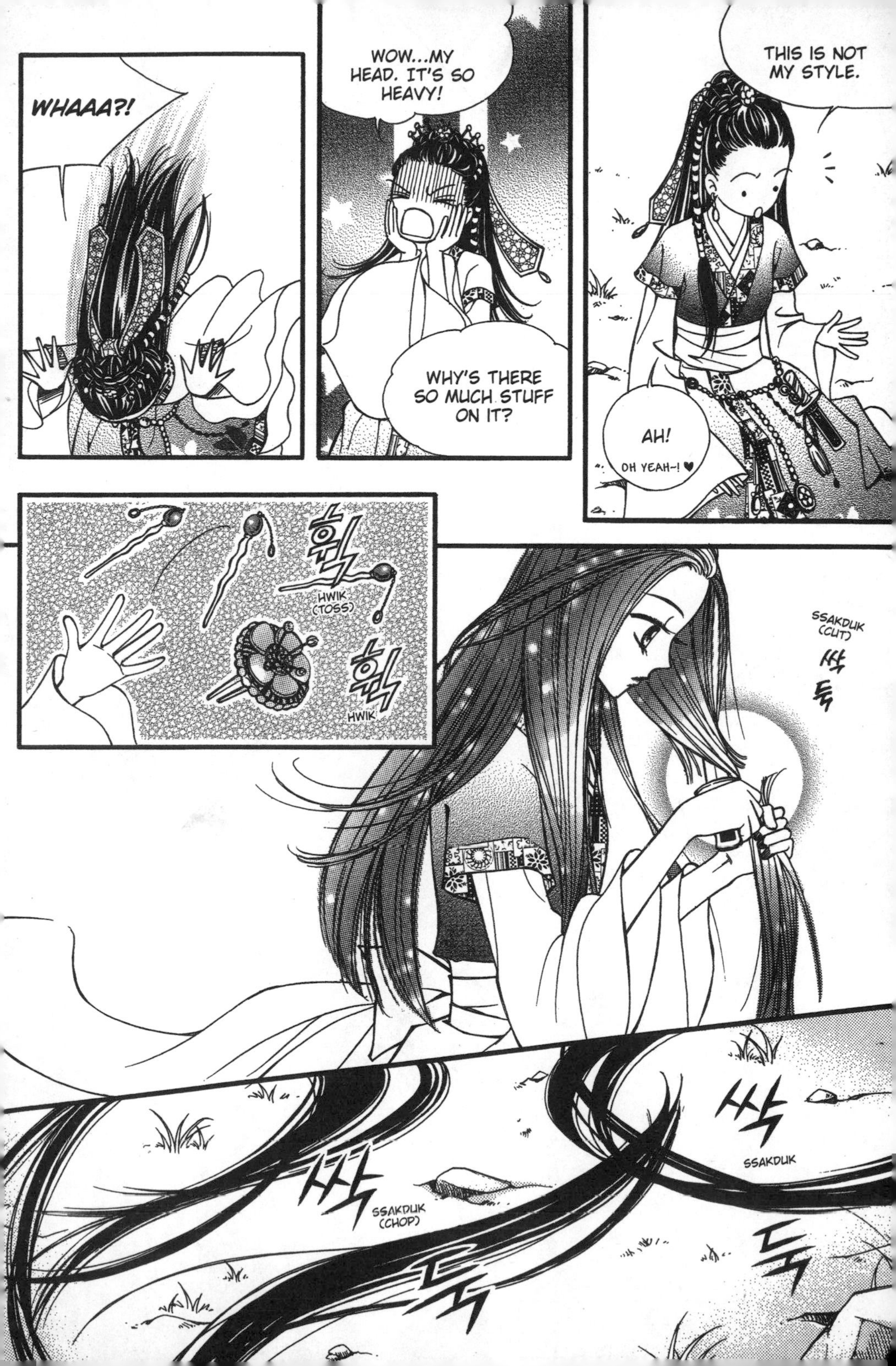
WHAAA?!
WOW...MY HEAD. IT'S SO HEAVY!
WHY'S THERE SO MUCH STUFF ON IT?
THIS IS NOT MY STYLE.
AH!
OH YEAH~! ♥
휙
HWIK (TOSS)
휙
HWIK
SSAKDUK (CUT)
싹둑
싹둑
SSAKDUK (CHOP)
싹둑
SSAKDUK

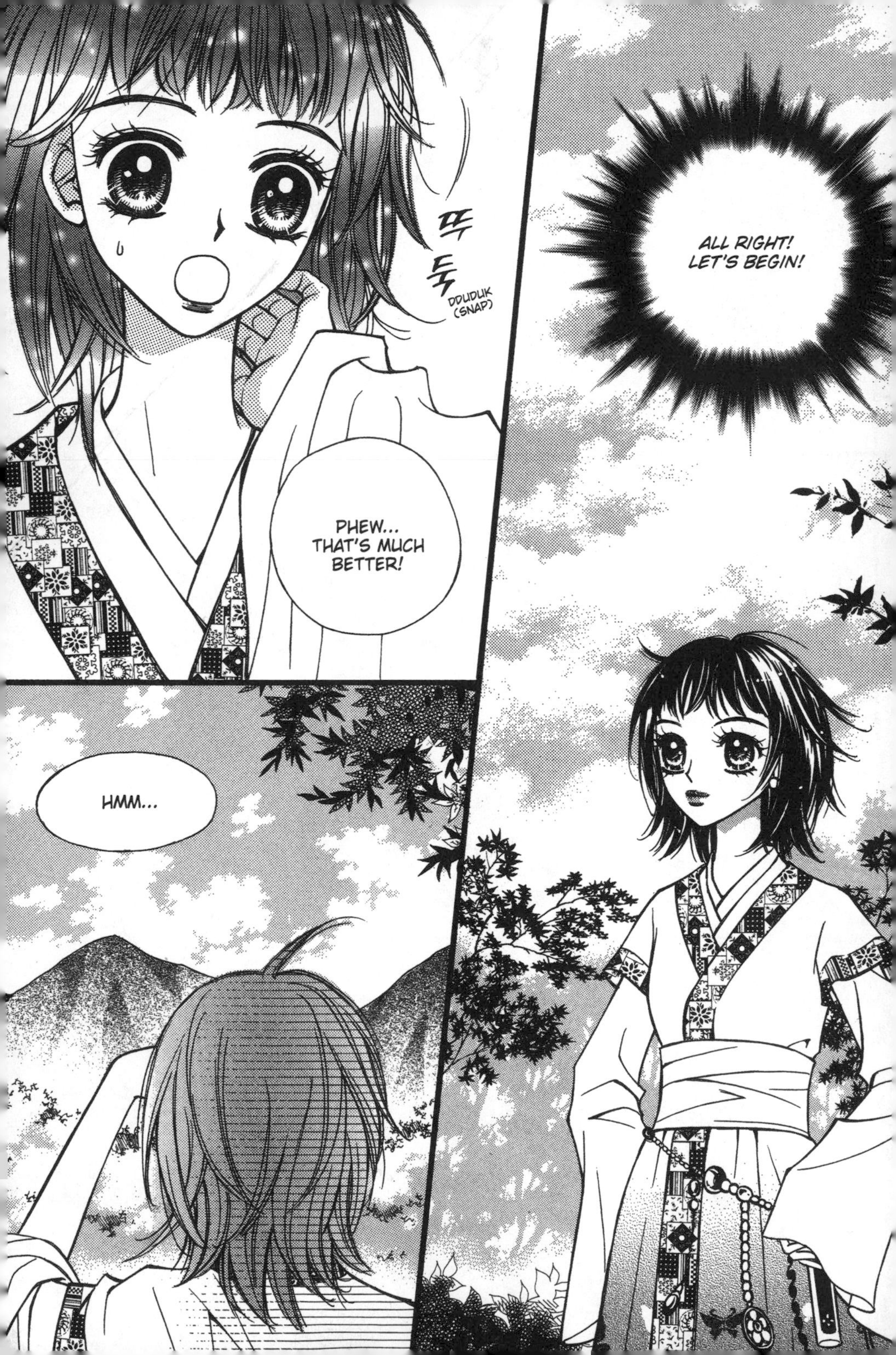

뚜둑
DDUDUK (SNAP)
PHEW... THAT'S MUCH BETTER!
HMM...
ALL RIGHT! LET'S BEGIN!

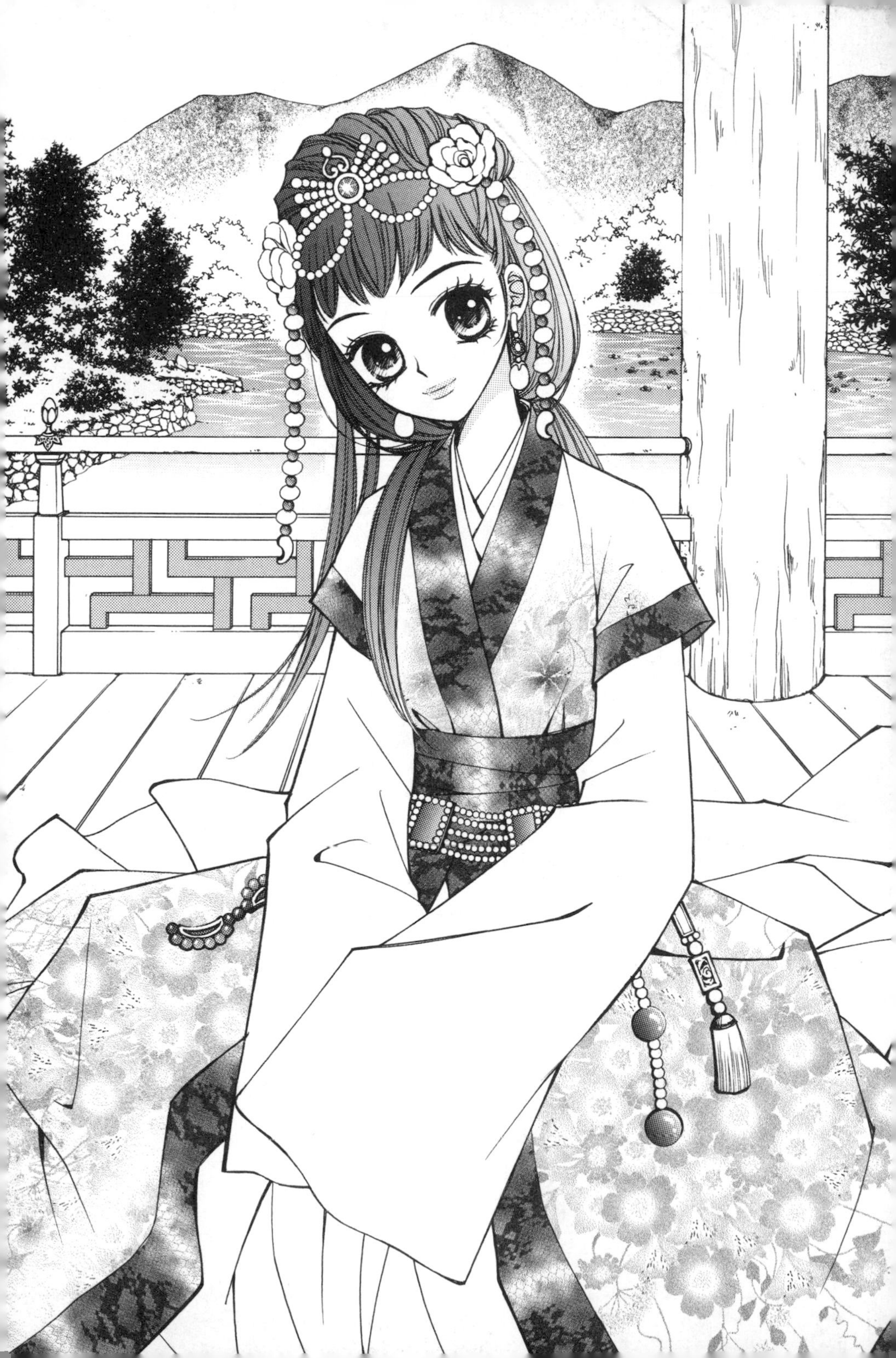

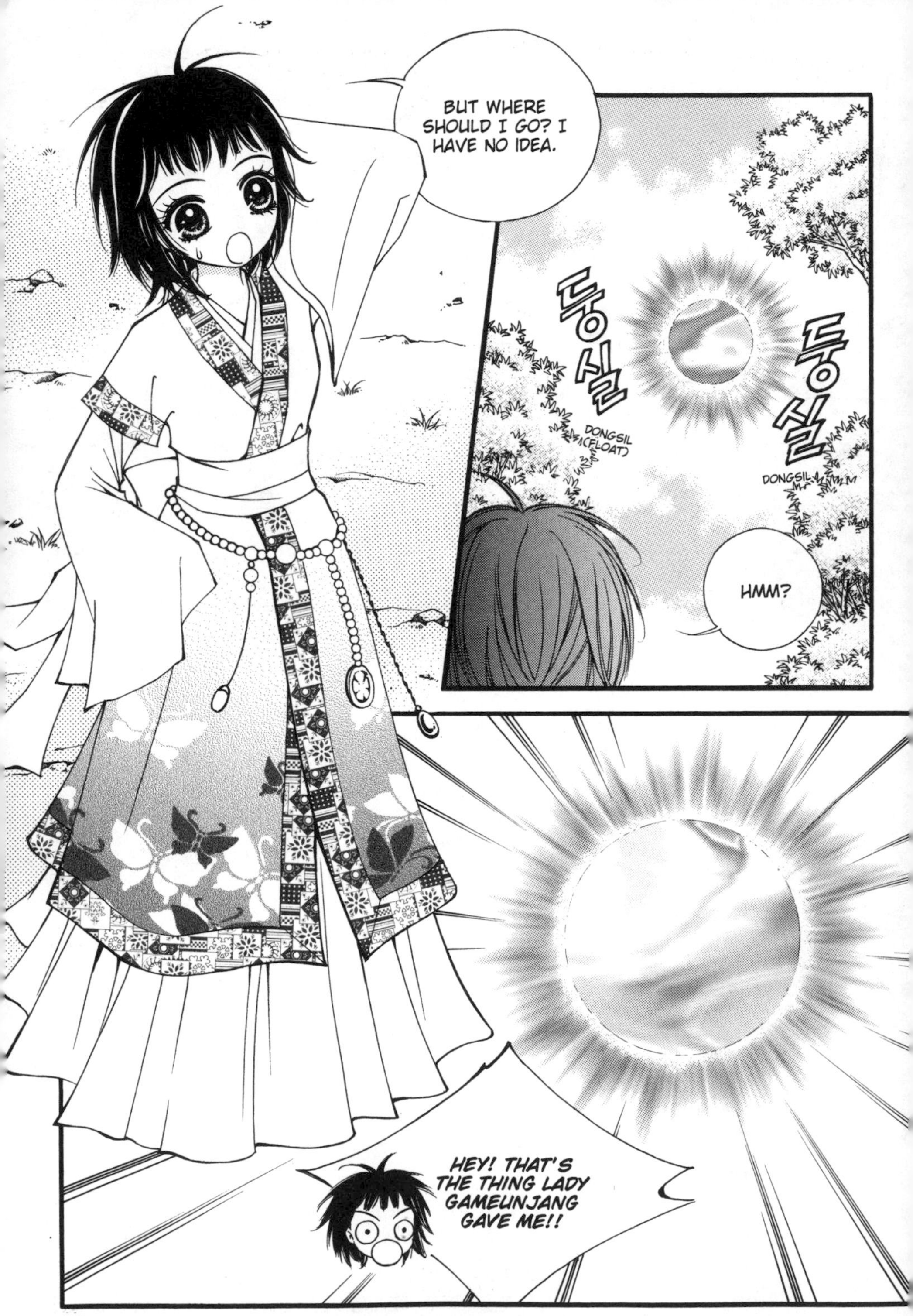

BUT WHERE SHOULD I GO? I HAVE NO IDEA.
둥실
DONGSIL (FLOAT)
둥실
DONGSIL
HMM?
HEY! THAT'S THE THING LADY GAMEUNJANG GAVE ME!!

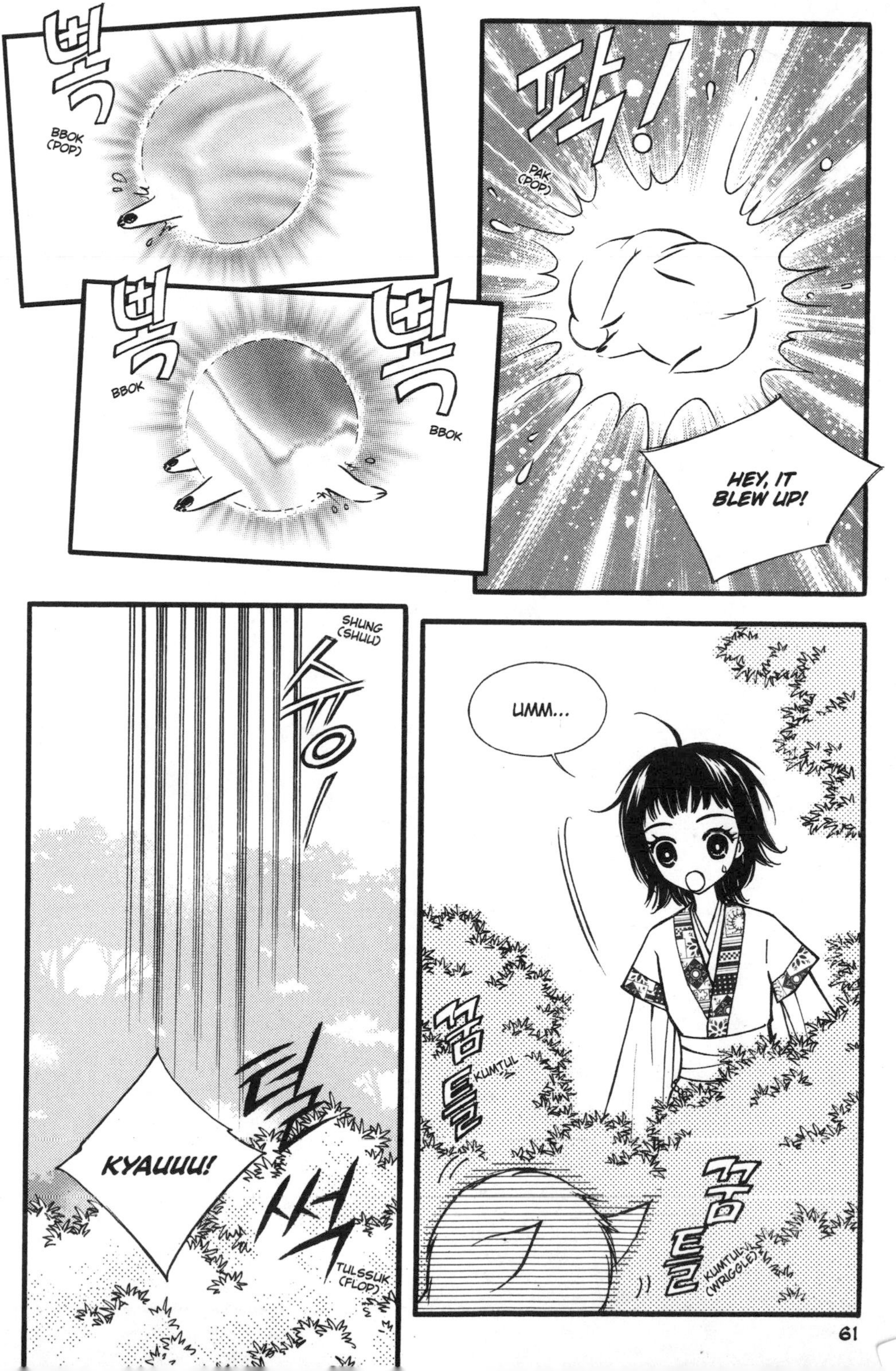

뽁
BBOK (POP)
뽁
BBOK
뽁
BBOK
팍!
PAK (POP)
HEY, IT BLEW UP!
SHUNG (SHUU)
KYAUUU!
TULSSUK (FLOP)
UMM...
꿈틀
KUMTUL
꿈틀
KUMTUL (WRIGGLE)

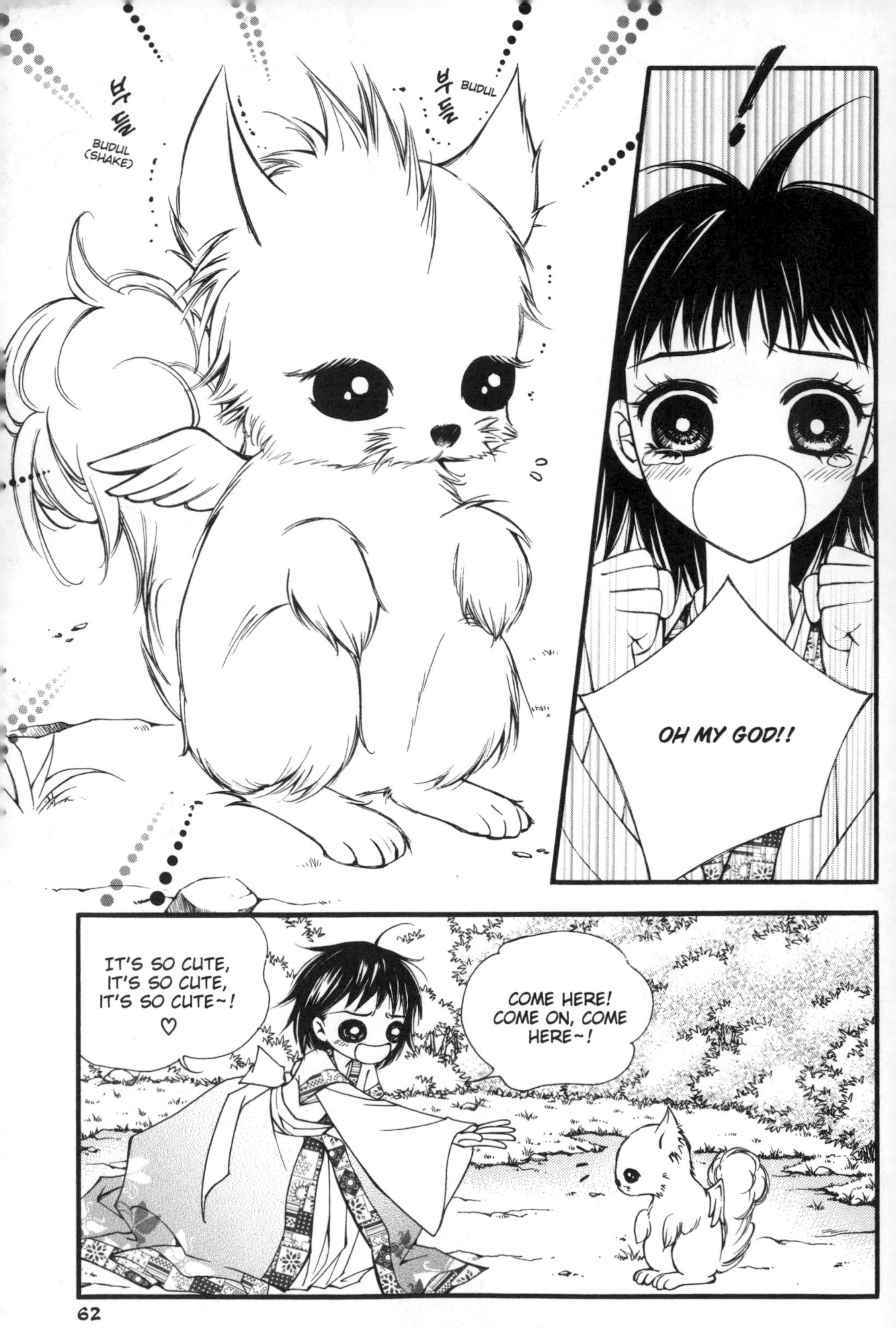
부들
BUDUL (SHAKE)
부들
BUDUL
!
OH MY GOD!!
IT'S SO CUTE, IT'S SO CUTE, IT'S SO CUTE~! ♡
COME HERE! COME ON, COME HERE~!

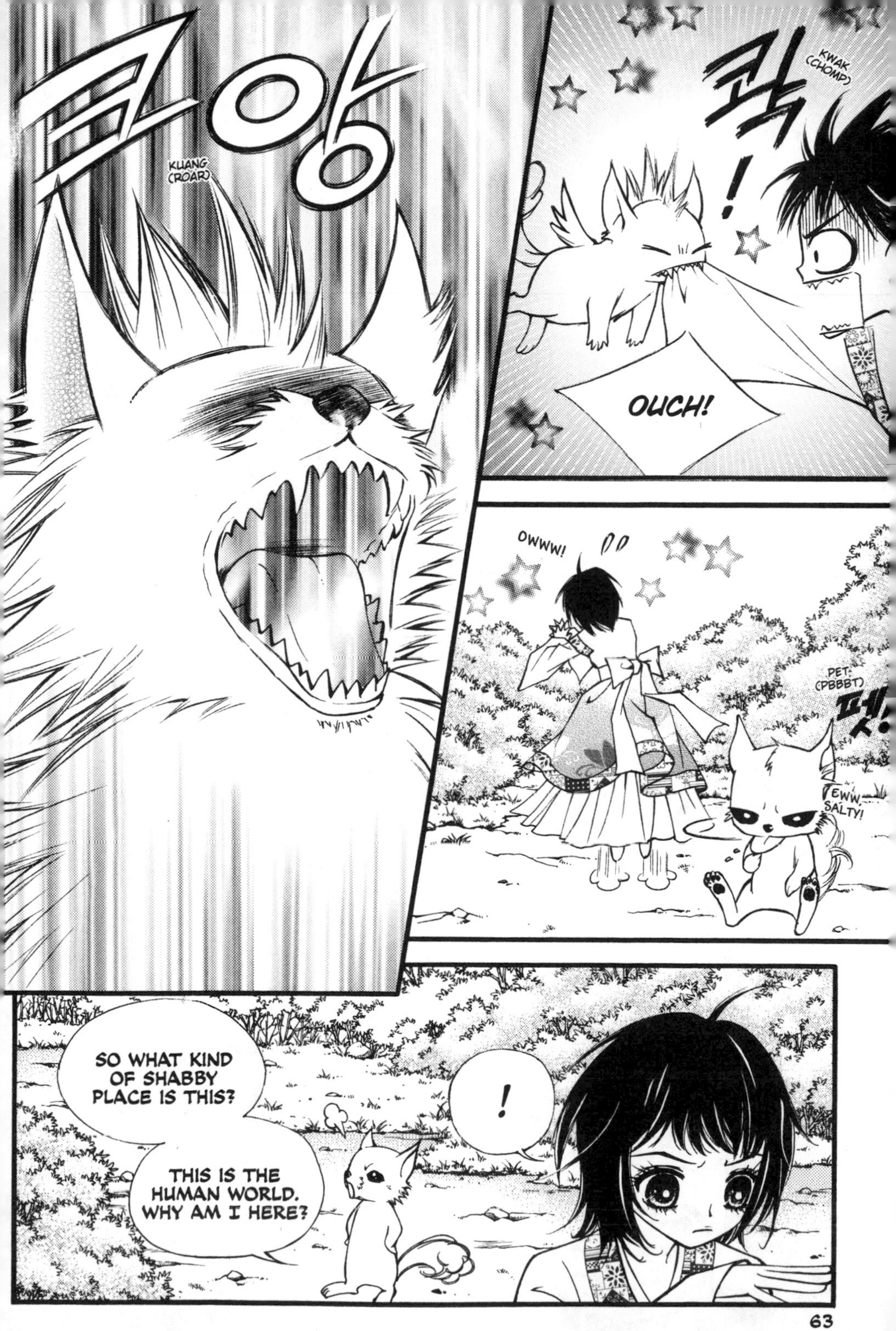
KUANG
(ROAR)
콱
KWAK
(CHOMP)
OUCH!
OWWW!
PET
(PBBBT)
EWW, SALTY!
SO WHAT KIND OF SHABBY PLACE IS THIS?
THIS IS THE HUMAN WORLD. WHY AM I HERE?
!

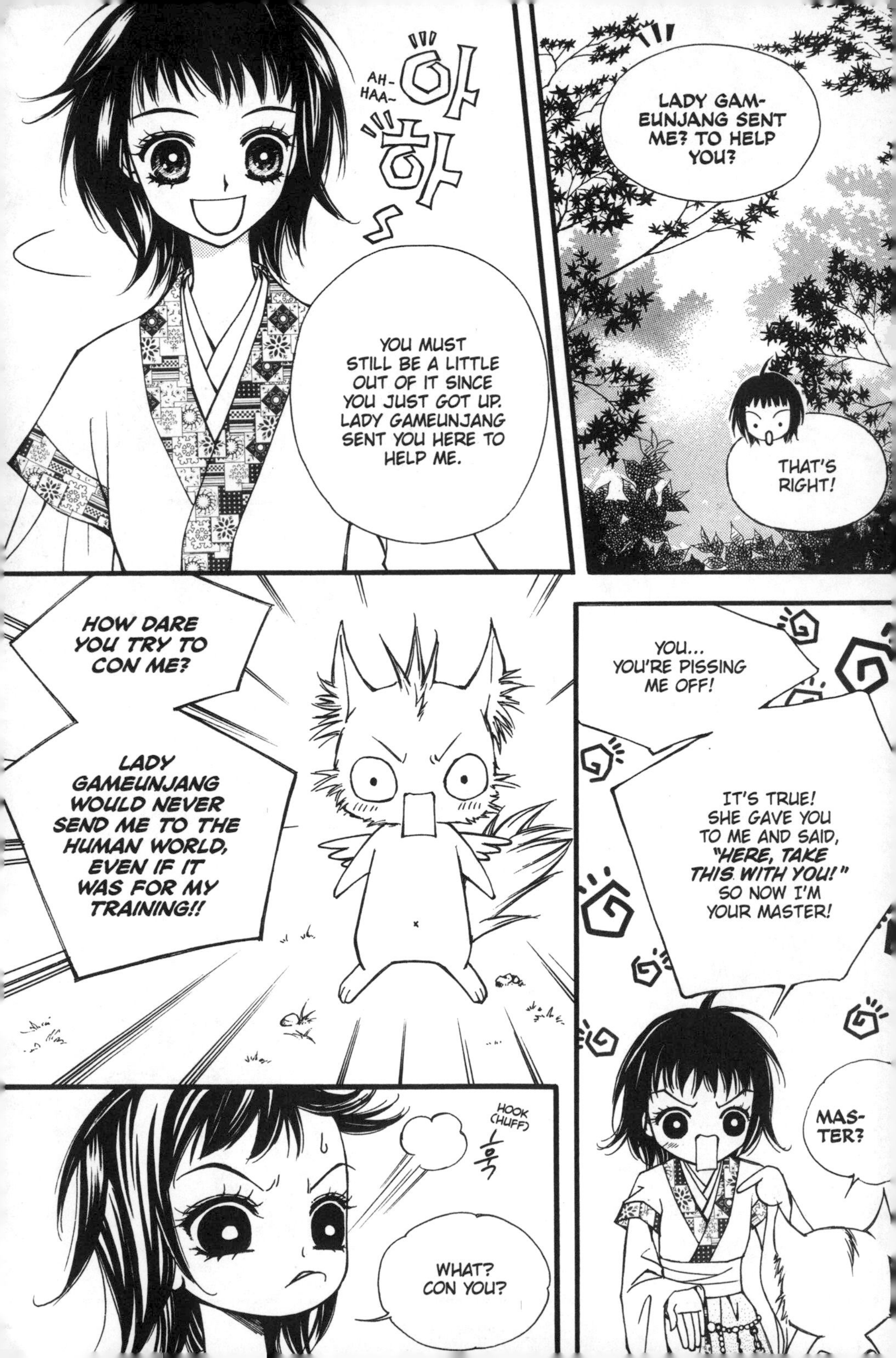

AH-HAA~
아하~
YOU MUST STILL BE A LITTLE OUT OF IT SINCE YOU JUST GOT UP. LADY GAMEUNJANG SENT YOU HERE TO HELP ME.
LADY GAM-EUNJANG SENT ME? TO HELP YOU?
THAT'S RIGHT!
HOW DARE YOU TRY TO CON ME?
LADY GAMEUNJANG WOULD NEVER SEND ME TO THE HUMAN WORLD, EVEN IF IT WAS FOR MY TRAINING!!
HOOK (HUFF)
훅
WHAT? CON YOU?
YOU... YOU'RE PISSING ME OFF!
IT'S TRUE! SHE GAVE YOU TO ME AND SAID, "HERE, TAKE THIS WITH YOU!" SO NOW I'M YOUR MASTER!
MAS-TER?

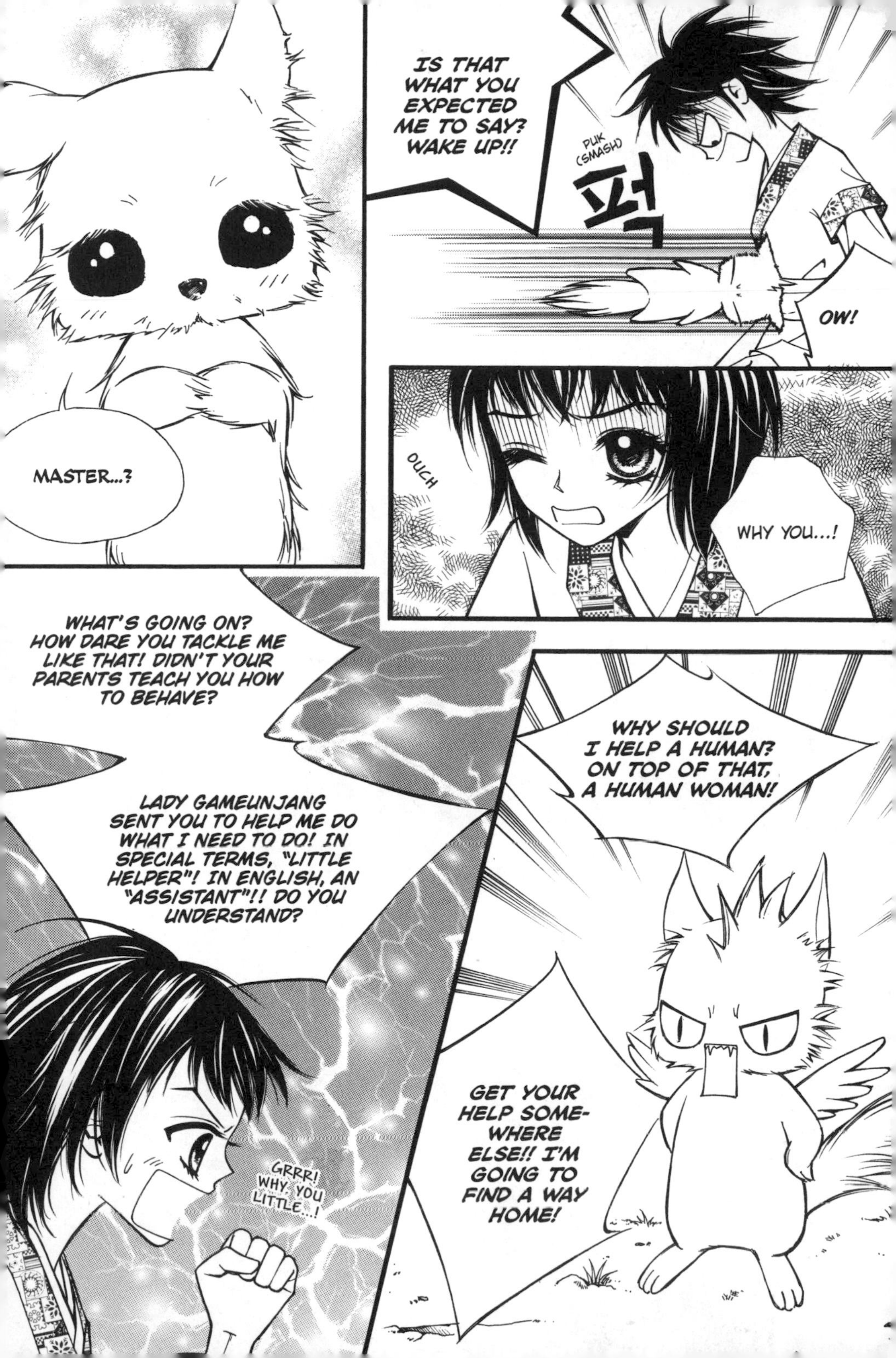
MASTER...?
IS THAT WHAT YOU EXPECTED ME TO SAY? WAKE UP!!
PUK (SMASH)
퍽
OW!
OUCH
WHY YOU...!
WHAT'S GOING ON? HOW DARE YOU TACKLE ME LIKE THAT! DIDN'T YOUR PARENTS TEACH YOU HOW TO BEHAVE?
LADY GAMEUNJANG SENT YOU TO HELP ME DO WHAT I NEED TO DO! IN SPECIAL TERMS, "LITTLE HELPER"! IN ENGLISH, AN "ASSISTANT"!! DO YOU UNDERSTAND?
GRRR! WHY, YOU LITTLE...!
WHY SHOULD I HELP A HUMAN? ON TOP OF THAT, A HUMAN WOMAN!
GET YOUR HELP SOME-WHERE ELSE!! I'M GOING TO FIND A WAY HOME!

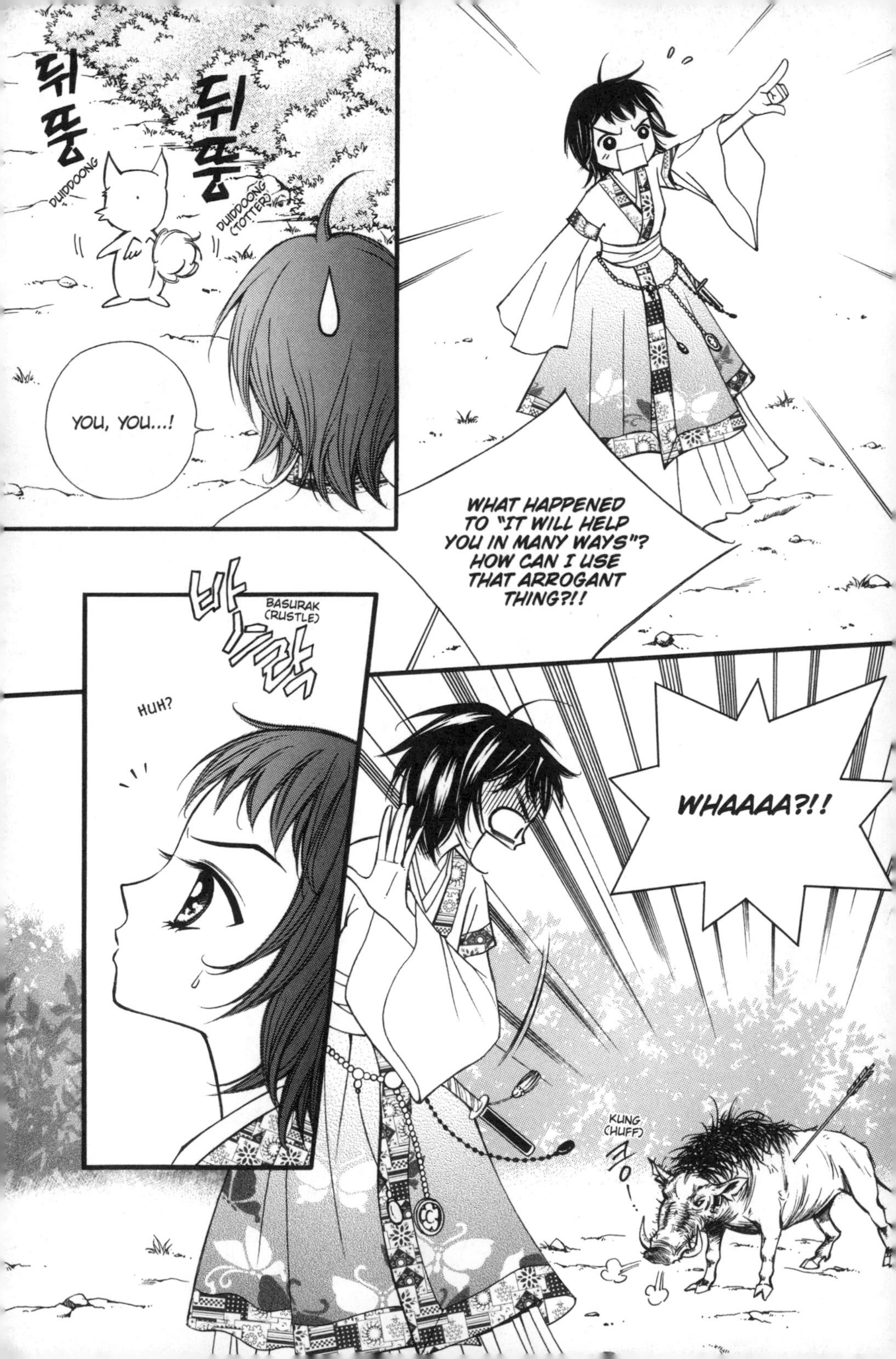

뒤뚱
DUIDDOONG
뒤뚱
DUIDDOONG (TOTTER)
YOU, YOU...!
WHAT HAPPENED TO "IT WILL HELP YOU IN MANY WAYS"? HOW CAN I USE THAT ARROGANT THING?!!
바스락
BASURAK (RUSTLE)
HUH?
WHAAAA?!!
KUNG (CHUFF)
쿵

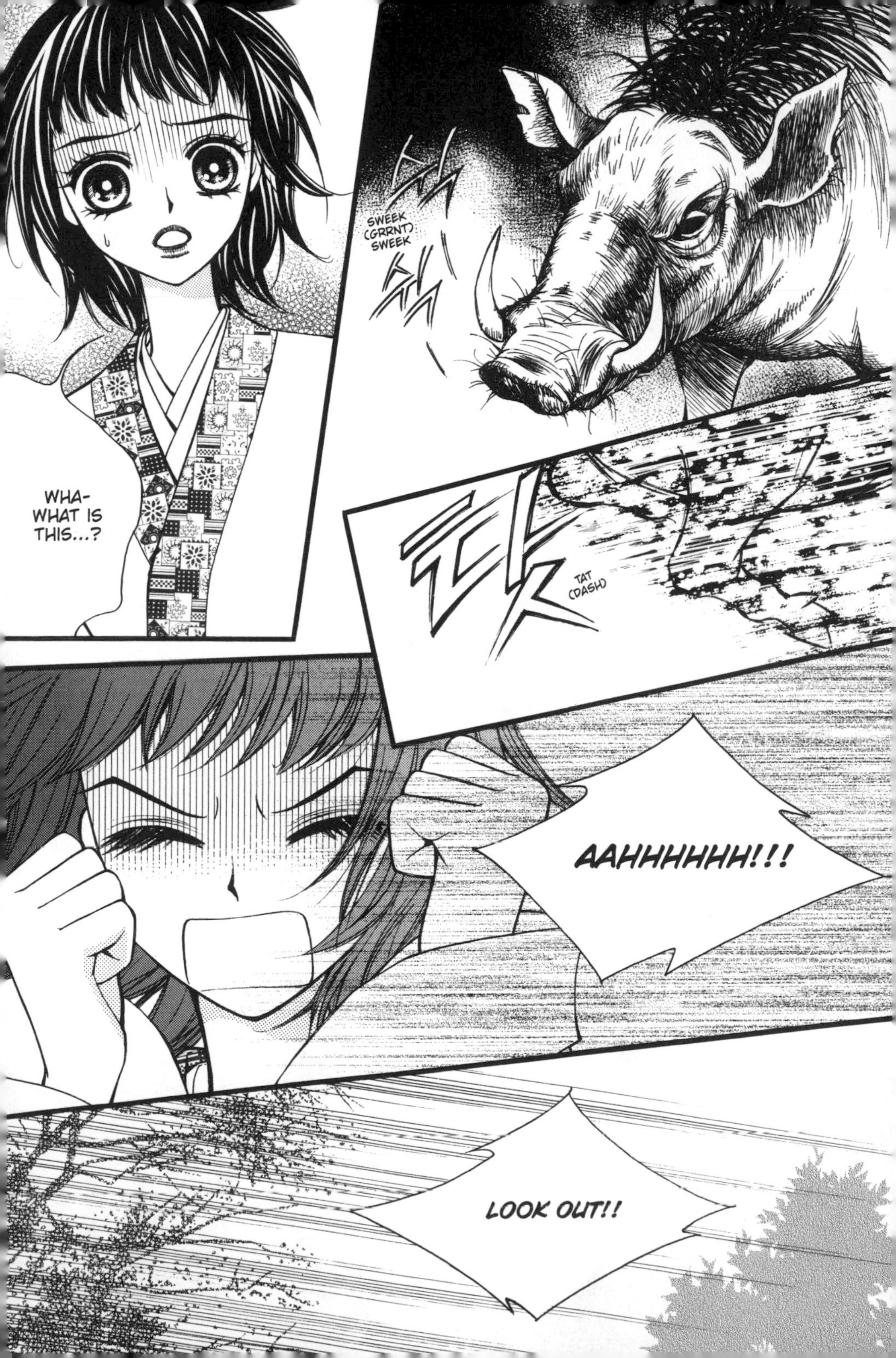
WHA-
WHAT IS
THIS...?
SWEEK
(GRRNT)
SWEEK
TAT
(DASH)
AAHHHHHH!!!
LOOK OUT!!

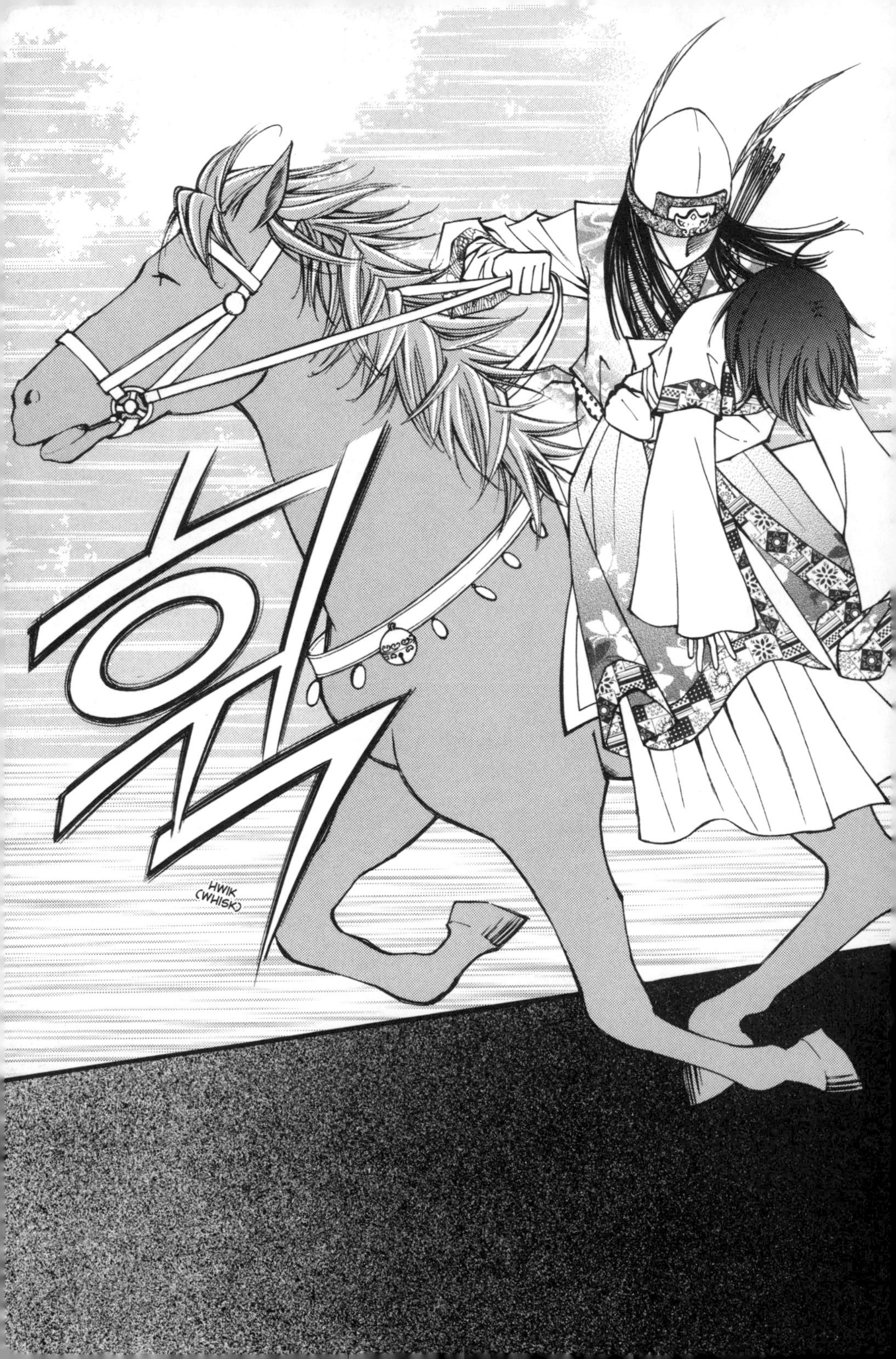
HWIK
(WHISK)

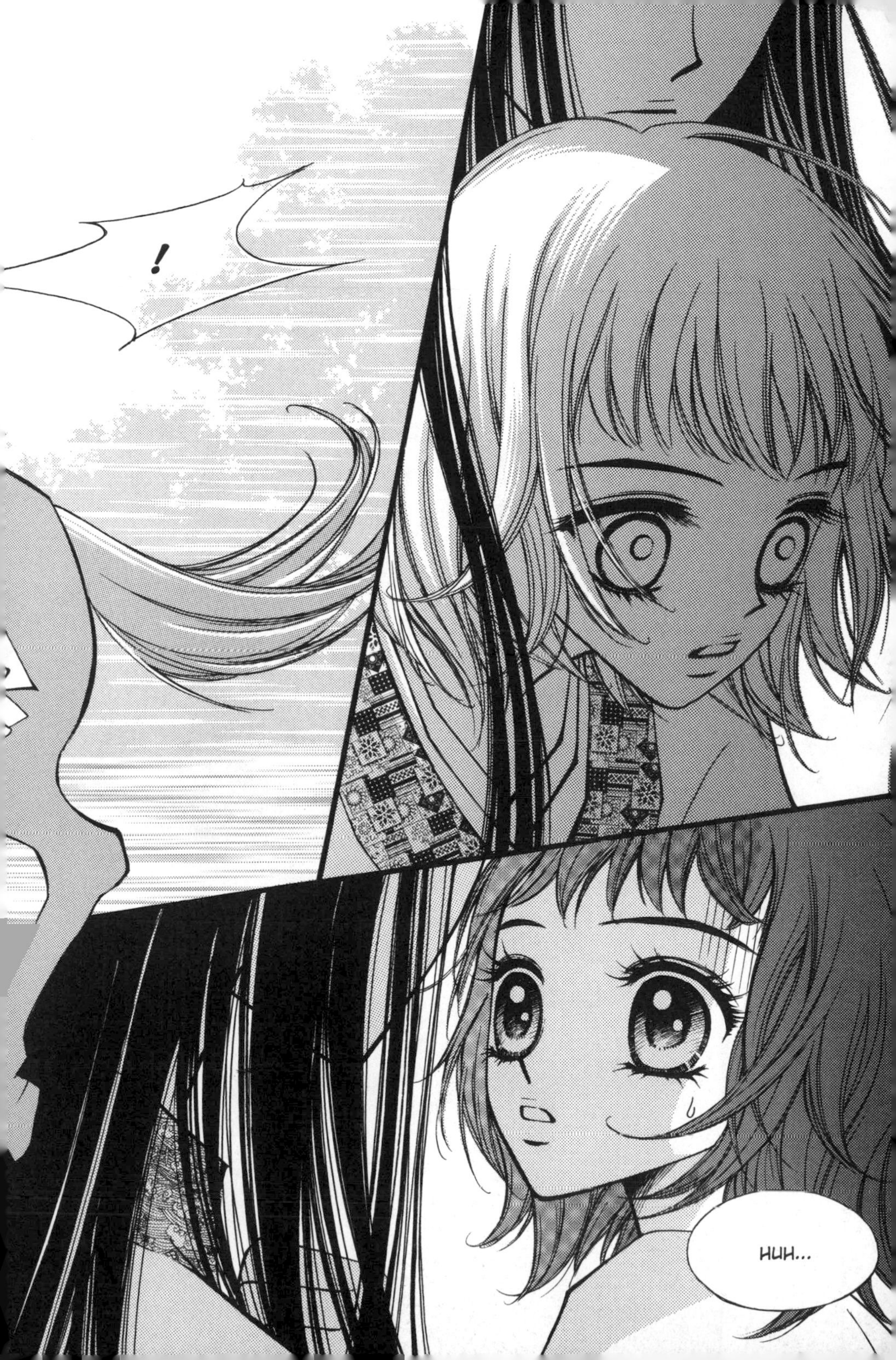
!
HUH...

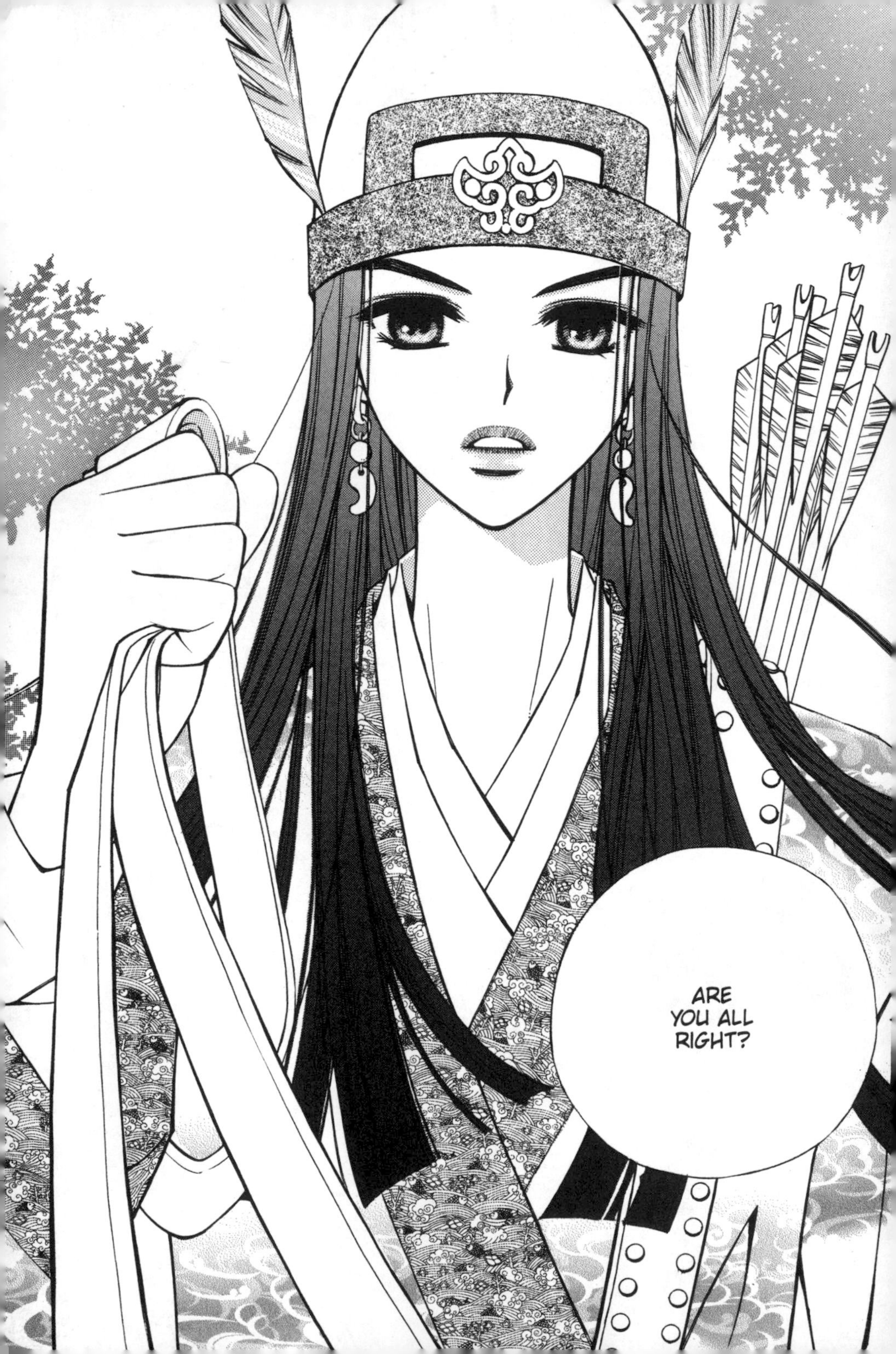
ARE YOU ALL RIGHT?

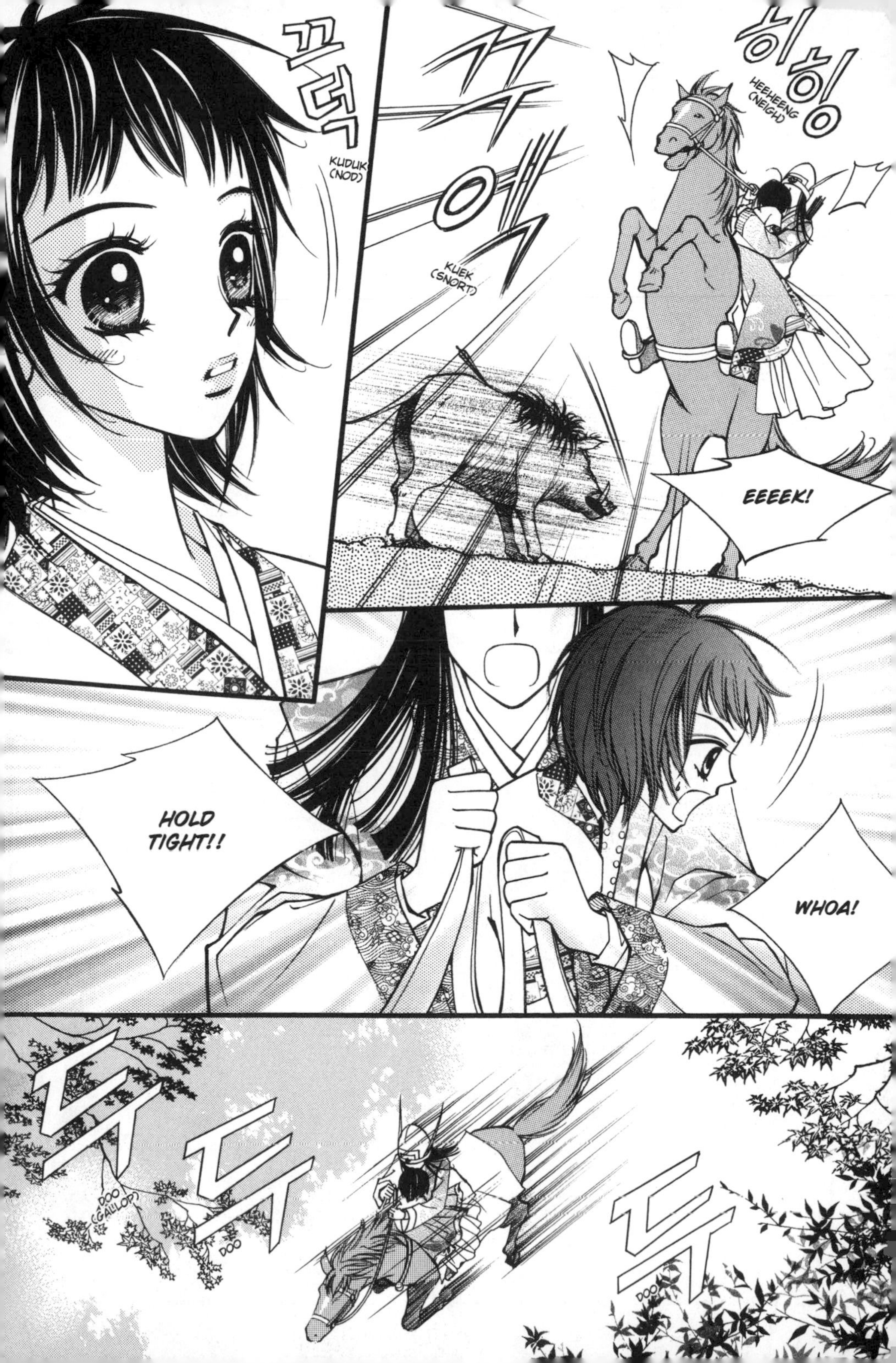
끄덕
KUDUK (NOD)
KUEK (SNORT)
히힝
HEEHEENG (NEIGH)
EEEEK!
HOLD TIGHT!!
WHOA!
두
DOO (GALLOP)
두
DOO
두
DOO

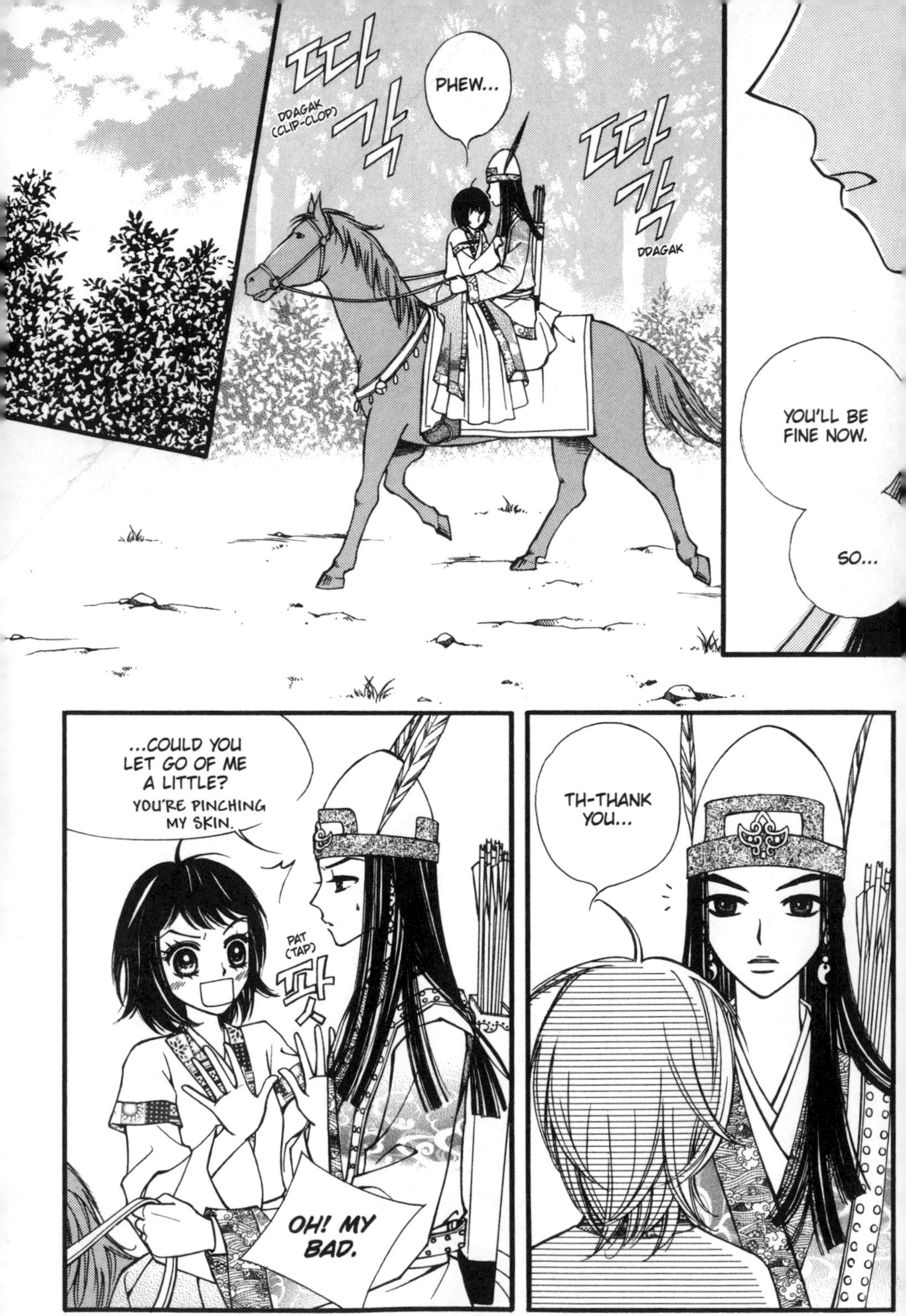
따각
DDAGAK (CLIP-CLOP)
PHEW...
따각
DDAGAK
YOU'LL BE FINE NOW.
SO...
...COULD YOU LET GO OF ME A LITTLE?
YOU'RE PINCHING MY SKIN.
PAT (TAP)
팟
OH! MY BAD.
TH-THANK YOU...

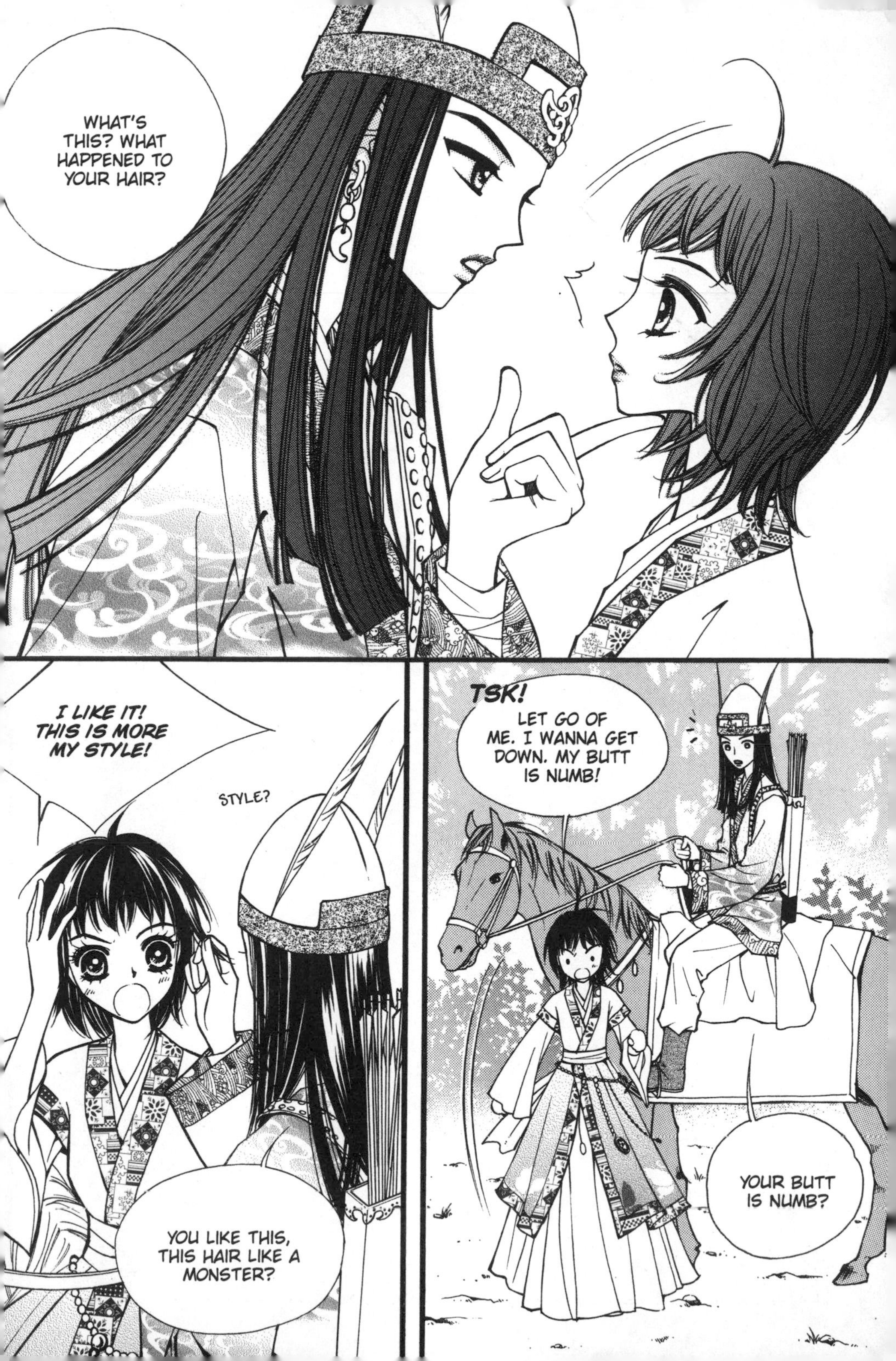
WHAT'S THIS? WHAT HAPPENED TO YOUR HAIR?
I LIKE IT! THIS IS MORE MY STYLE!
STYLE?
YOU LIKE THIS, THIS HAIR LIKE A MONSTER?
TSK!
LET GO OF ME. I WANNA GET DOWN. MY BUTT IS NUMB!
YOUR BUTT IS NUMB?

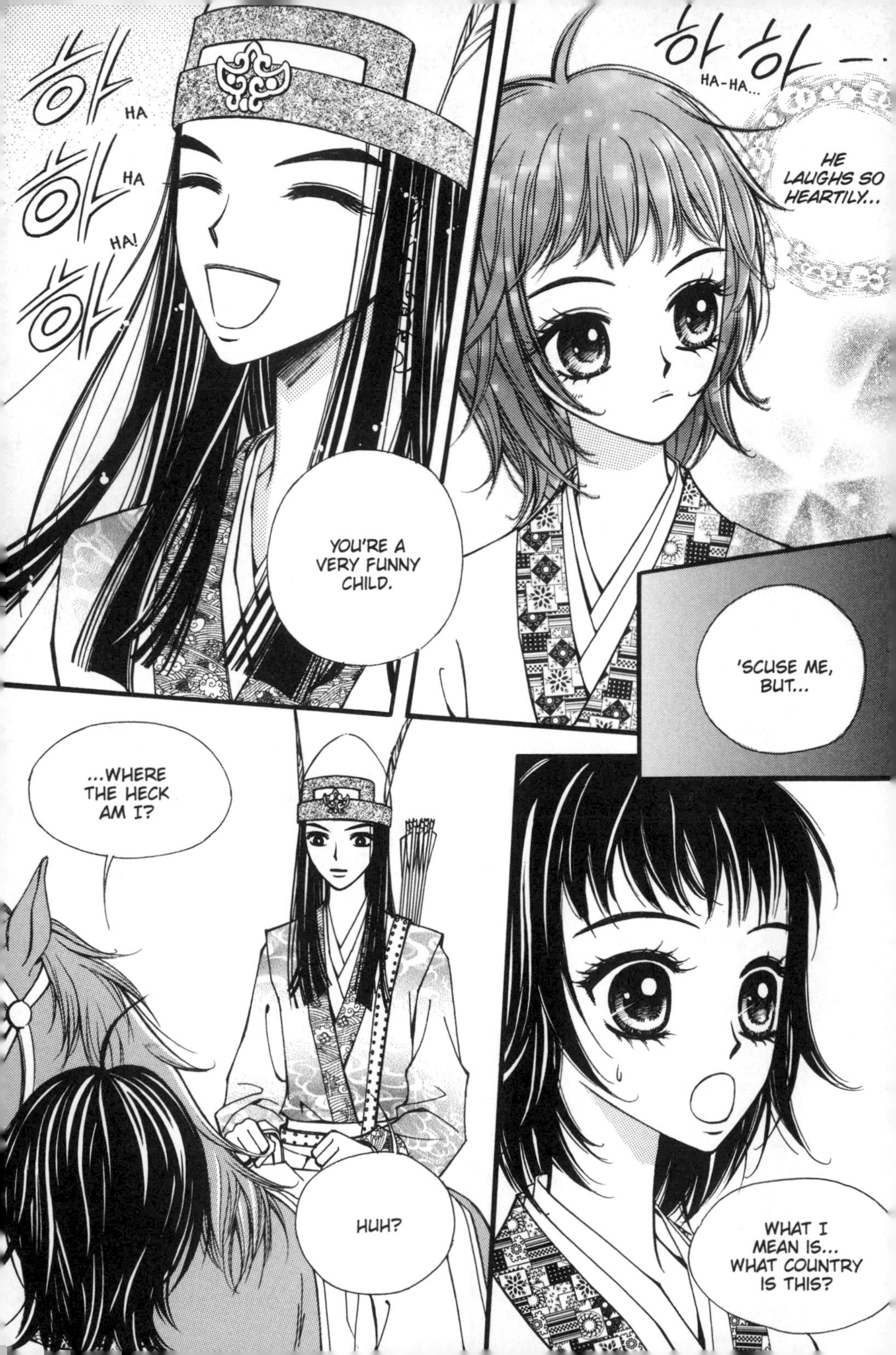

하
HA
하
HA
하
HA!
YOU'RE A VERY FUNNY CHILD.
하하-.
HA-HA...
HE LAUGHS SO HEARTILY...
'SCUSE ME, BUT...
...WHERE THE HECK AM I?
HUH?
WHAT I MEAN IS... WHAT COUNTRY IS THIS?

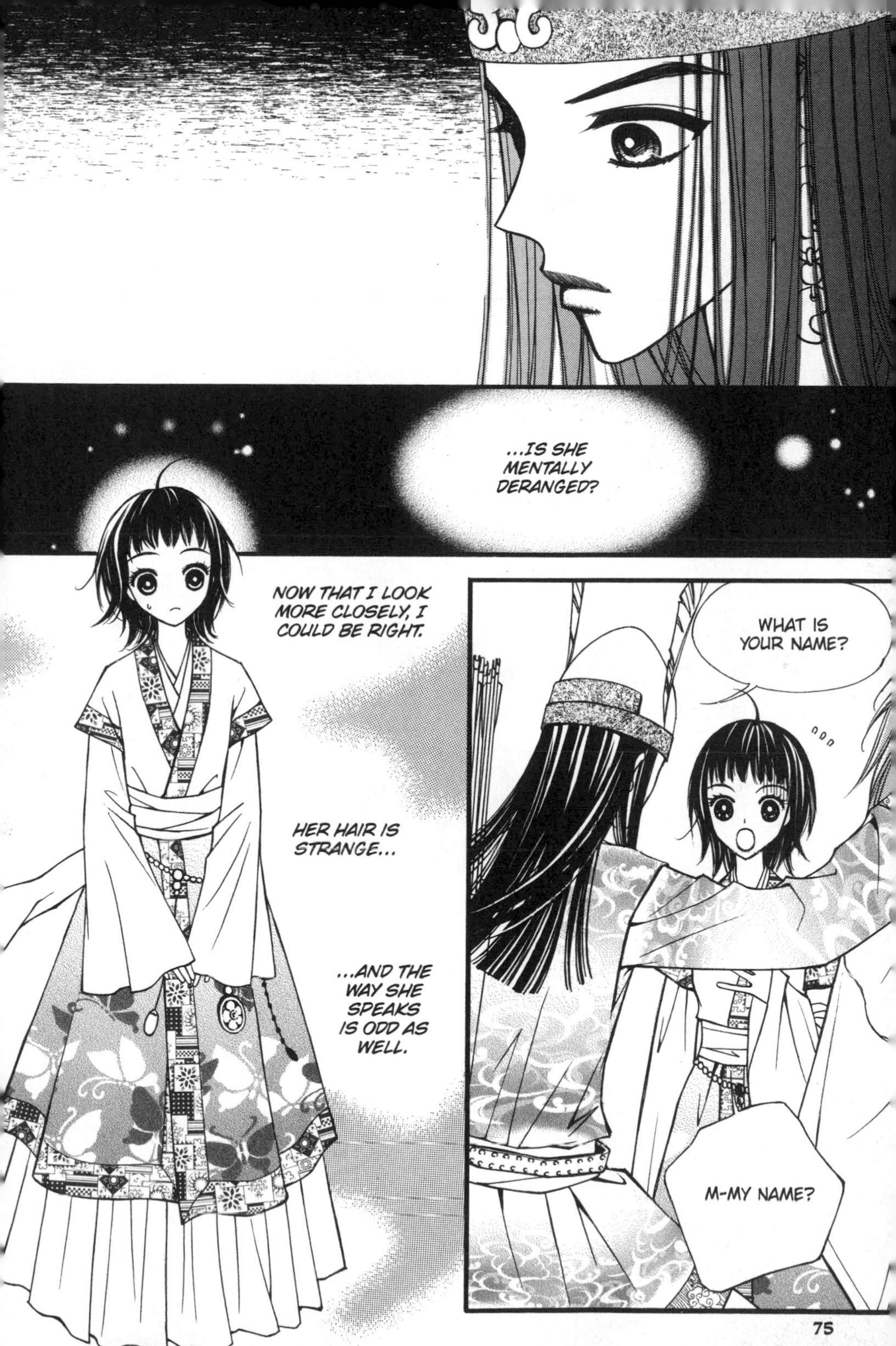
...IS SHE MENTALLY DERANGED?
NOW THAT I LOOK MORE CLOSELY, I COULD BE RIGHT.
HER HAIR IS STRANGE...
...AND THE WAY SHE SPEAKS IS ODD AS WELL.
WHAT IS YOUR NAME?
M-MY NAME?

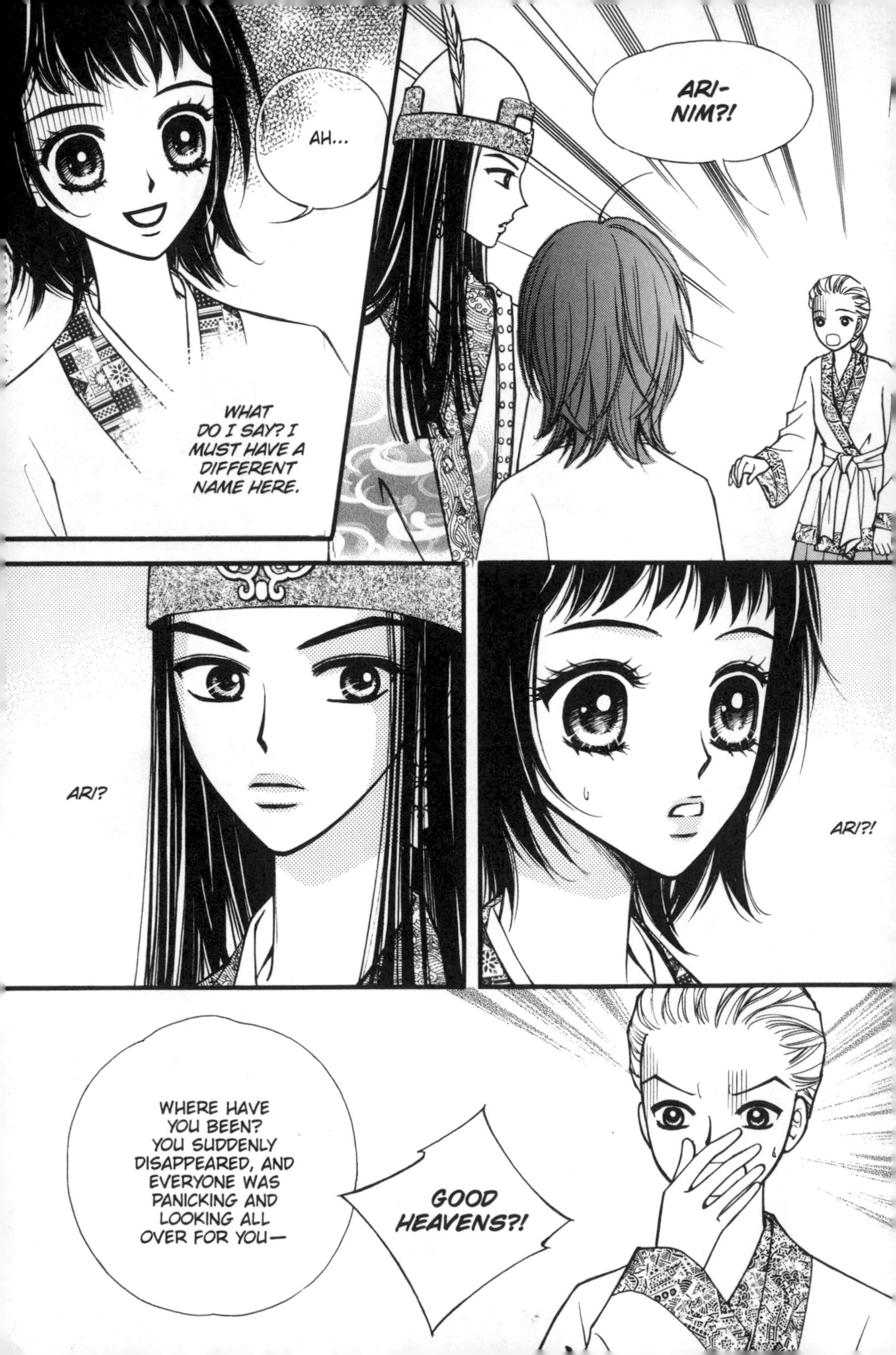
AH...
WHAT DO I SAY? I MUST HAVE A DIFFERENT NAME HERE.
ARI-NIM?!
ARI?
ARI?!
WHERE HAVE YOU BEEN? YOU SUDDENLY DISAPPEARED, AND EVERYONE WAS PANICKING AND LOOKING ALL OVER FOR YOU—
GOOD HEAVENS?!

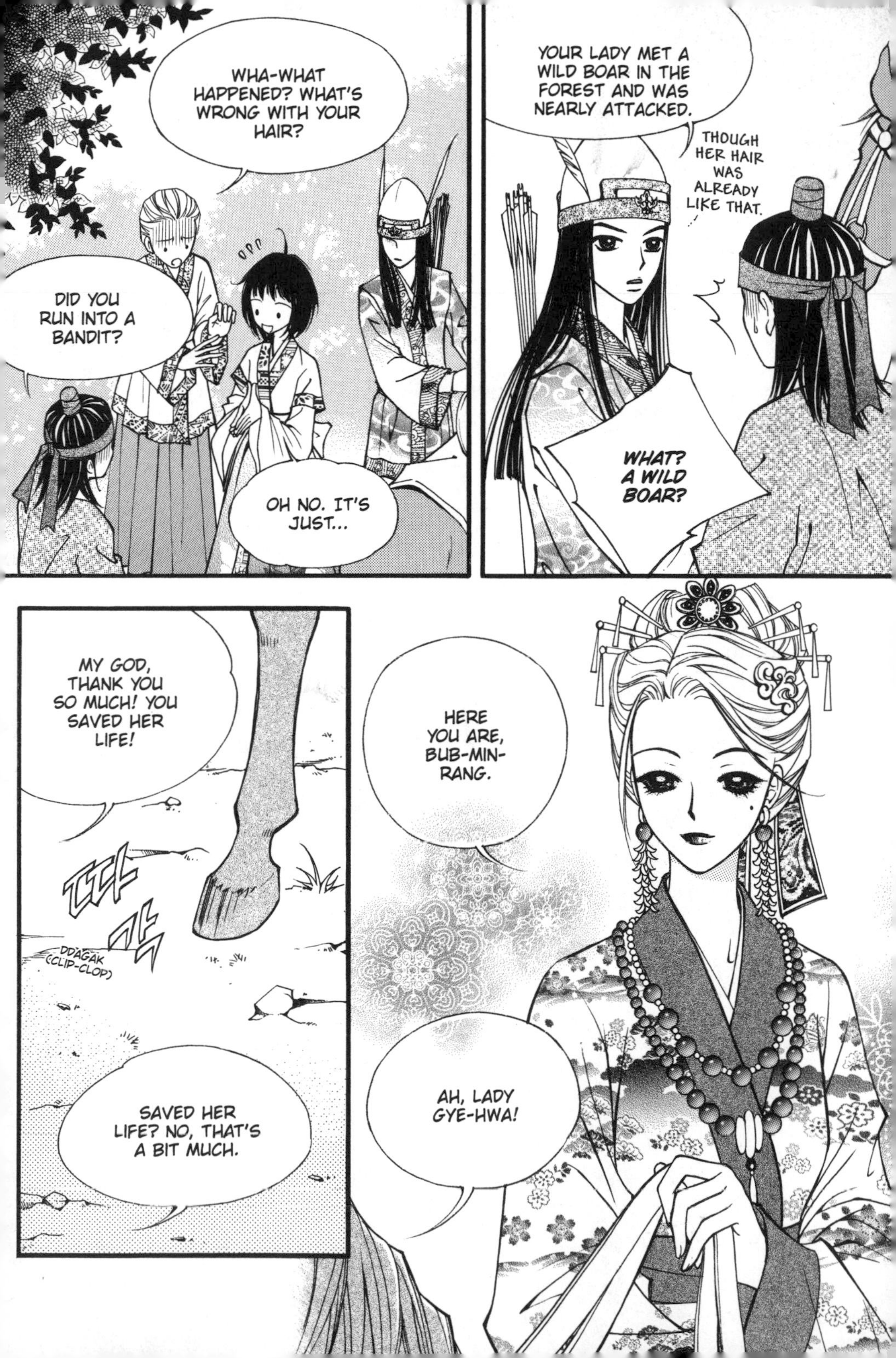
WHA-WHAT HAPPENED? WHAT'S WRONG WITH YOUR HAIR?
DID YOU RUN INTO A BANDIT?
OH NO. IT'S JUST...
YOUR LADY MET A WILD BOAR IN THE FOREST AND WAS NEARLY ATTACKED.
THOUGH HER HAIR WAS ALREADY LIKE THAT.
WHAT? A WILD BOAR?
MY GOD, THANK YOU SO MUCH! YOU SAVED HER LIFE!
DDAGAK (CLIP-CLOP)
SAVED HER LIFE? NO, THAT'S A BIT MUCH.
HERE YOU ARE, BUB-MIN-RANG.
AH, LADY GYE-HWA!

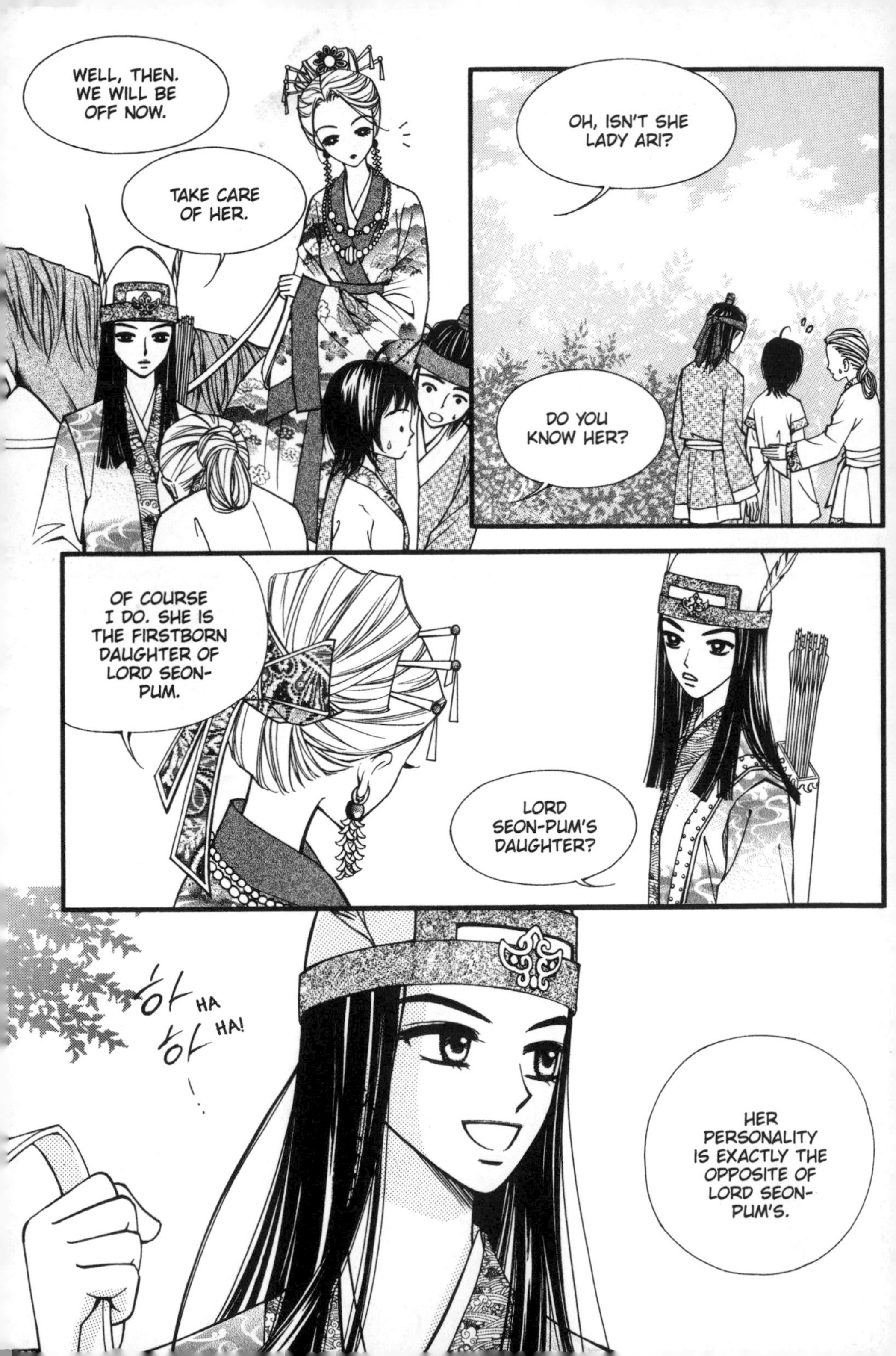
WELL, THEN. WE WILL BE OFF NOW.
TAKE CARE OF HER.
OH, ISN'T SHE LADY ARI?
DO YOU KNOW HER?
OF COURSE I DO. SHE IS THE FIRSTBORN DAUGHTER OF LORD SEON-PUM.
LORD SEON-PUM'S DAUGHTER?
하 HA
하 HA!
HER PERSONALITY IS EXACTLY THE OPPOSITE OF LORD SEON-PUM'S.

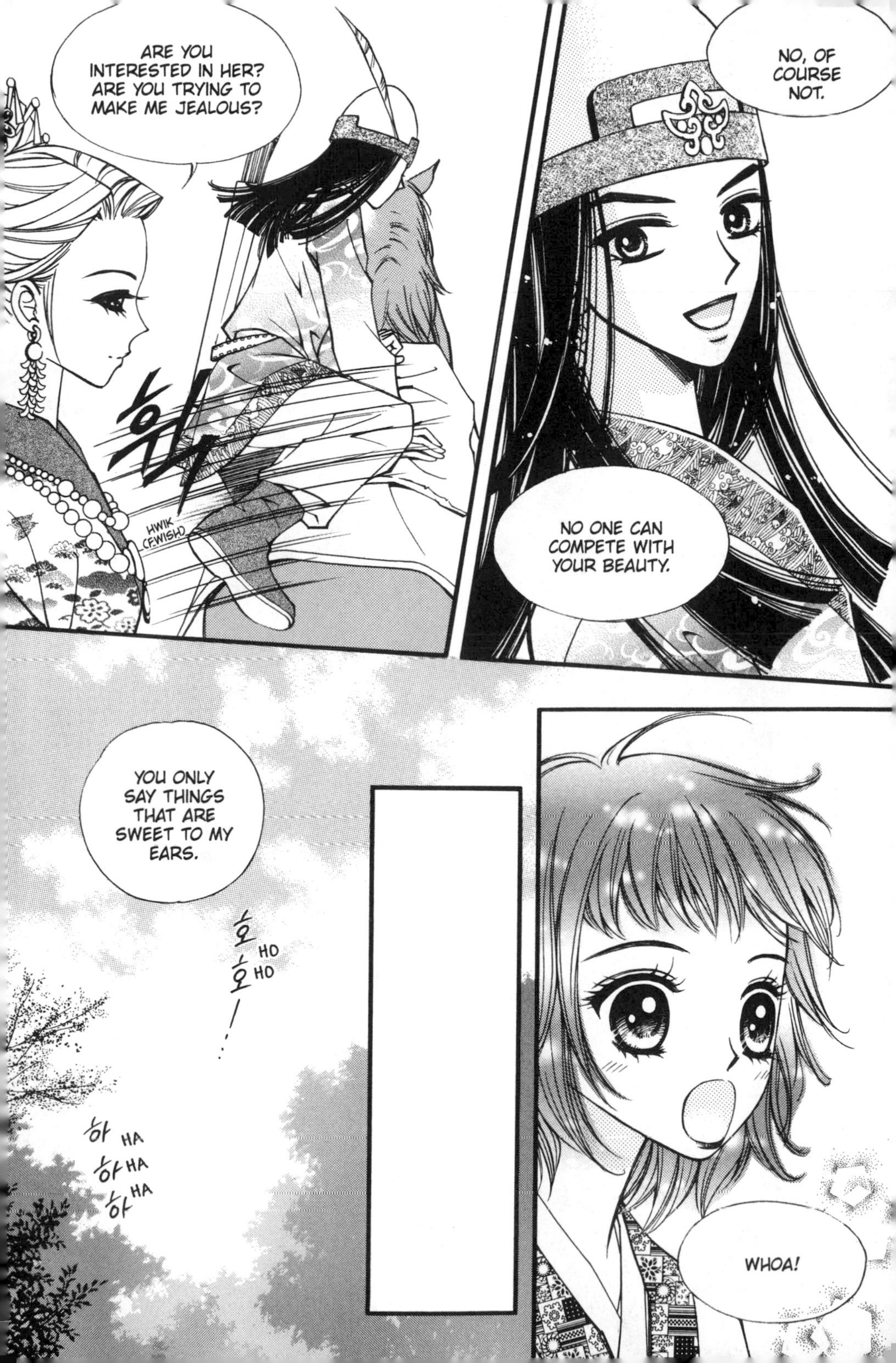
ARE YOU INTERESTED IN HER? ARE YOU TRYING TO MAKE ME JEALOUS?
HWIK (FWISH)
NO, OF COURSE NOT.
NO ONE CAN COMPETE WITH YOUR BEAUTY.
YOU ONLY SAY THINGS THAT ARE SWEET TO MY EARS.
호 HO 호 HO
하 HA 하 HA 하 HA
WHOA!

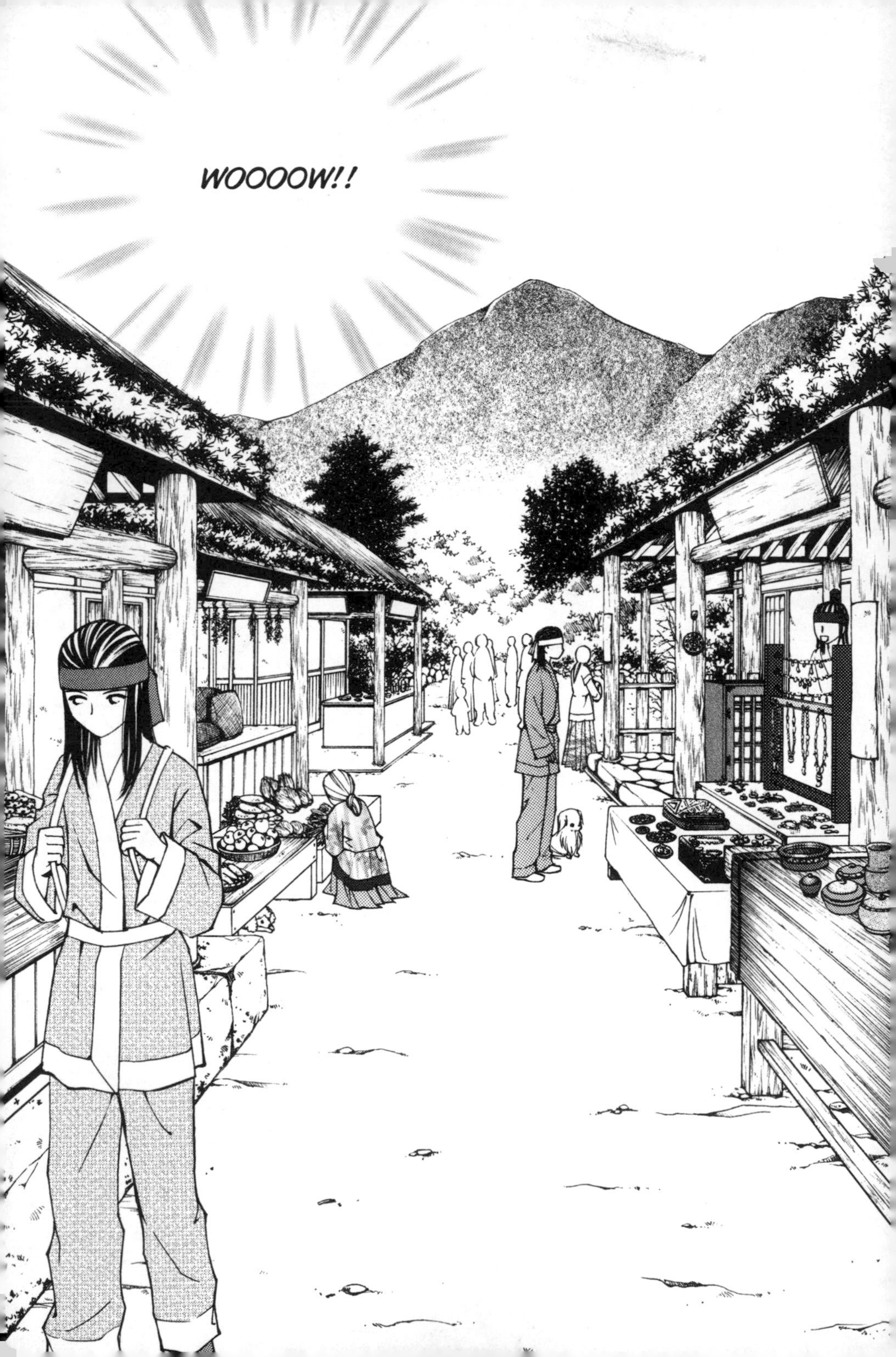
WOOOOW!!

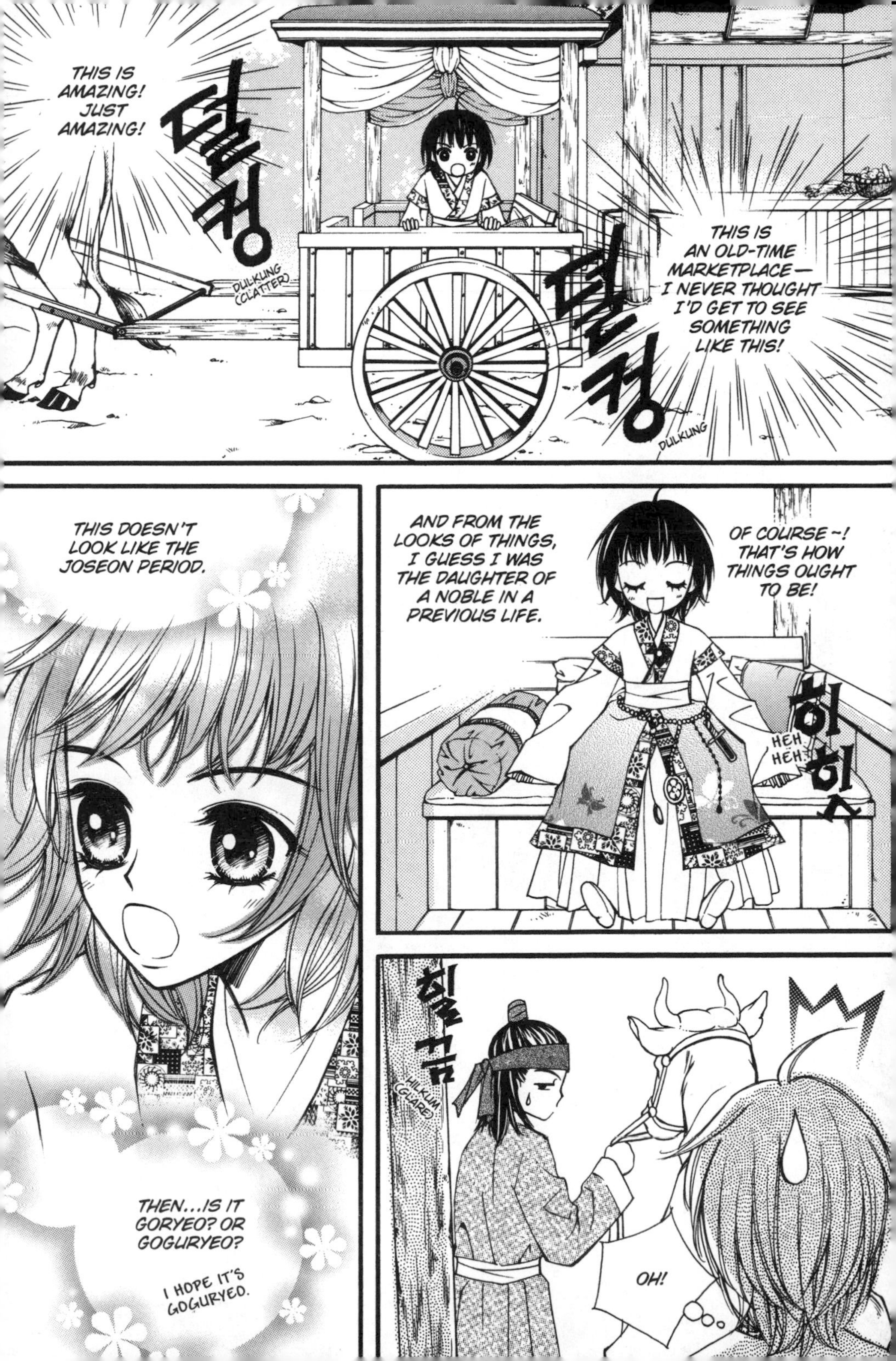
THIS IS AMAZING! JUST AMAZING!
덜컹
DUL-KUNG (CLATTER)
THIS IS AN OLD-TIME MARKETPLACE— I NEVER THOUGHT I'D GET TO SEE SOMETHING LIKE THIS!
덜컹
DULKUNG
THIS DOESN'T LOOK LIKE THE JOSEON PERIOD.
THEN...IS IT GORYEO? OR GOGURYEO?
I HOPE IT'S GOGURYEO.
AND FROM THE LOOKS OF THINGS, I GUESS I WAS THE DAUGHTER OF A NOBLE IN A PREVIOUS LIFE.
OF COURSE~! THAT'S HOW THINGS OUGHT TO BE!
히히
HEH HEH
힐끔
HILKUM (GLARE)
OH!

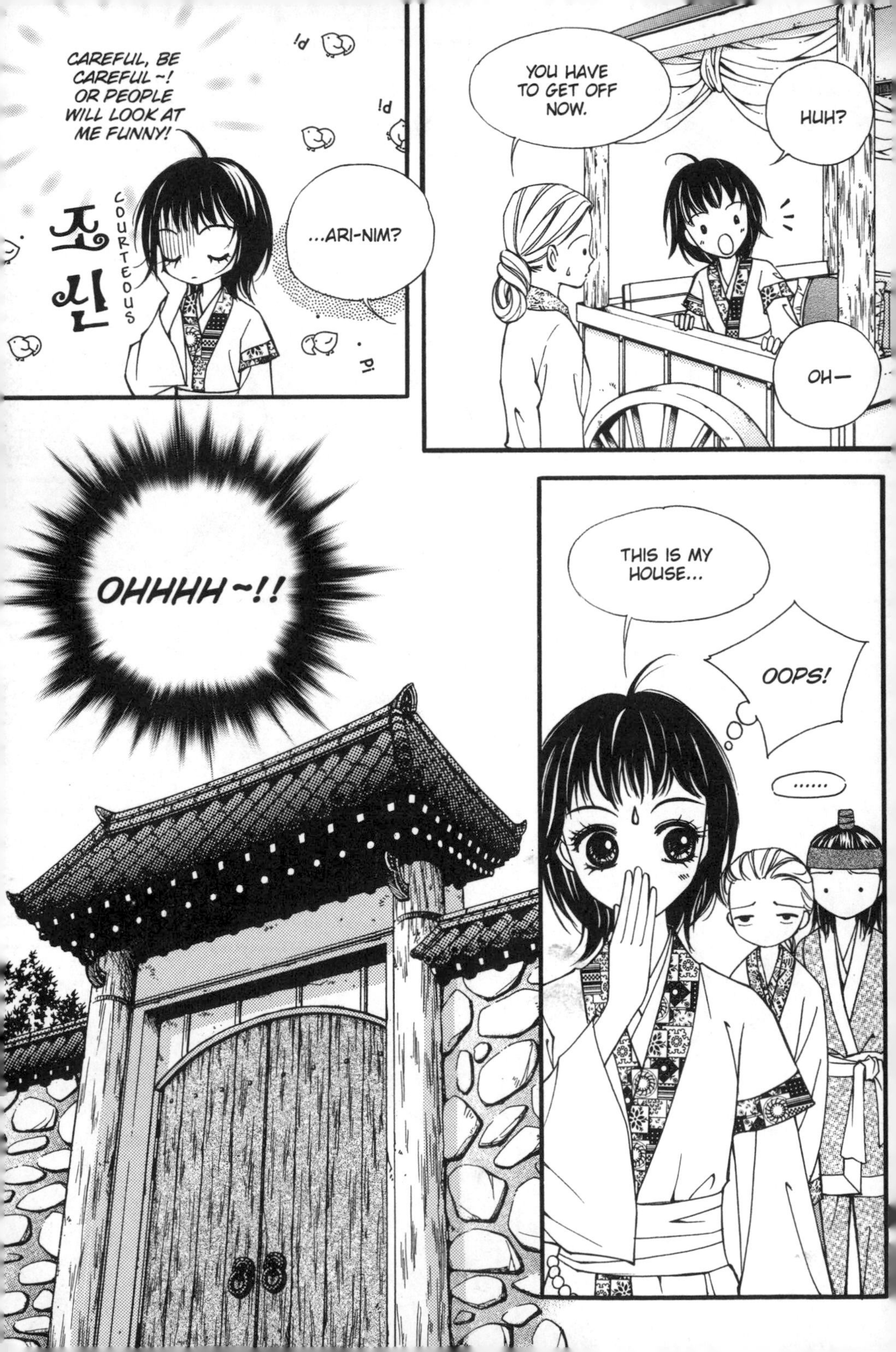
CAREFUL, BE CAREFUL~! OR PEOPLE WILL LOOK AT ME FUNNY!
Pi!
Pi!
조신
COURTEOUS
...ARI-NIM?
Pi
YOU HAVE TO GET OFF NOW.
HUH?
OH—
OHHHH~!!
THIS IS MY HOUSE...
OOPS!
......

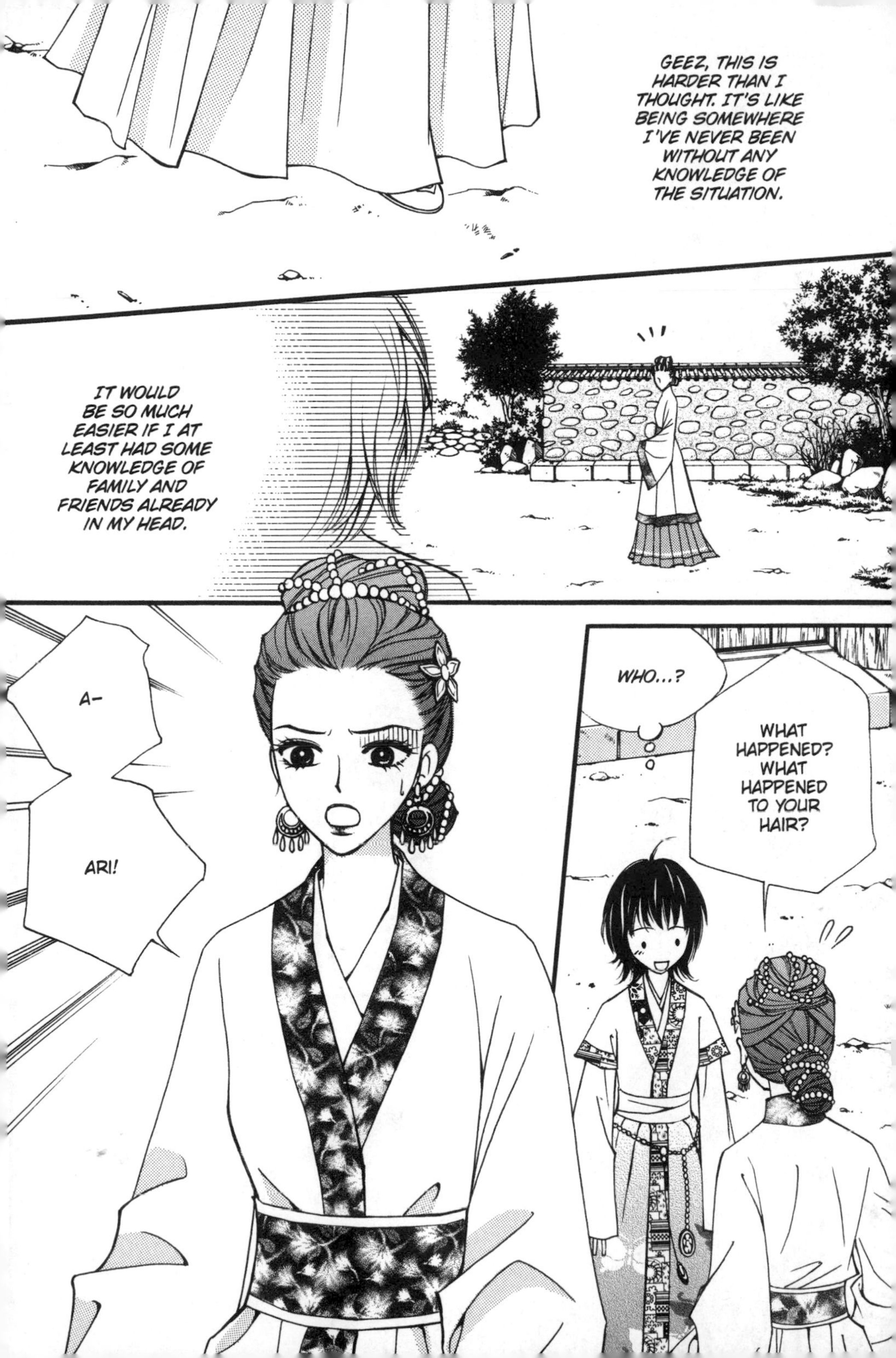
GEEZ, THIS IS HARDER THAN I THOUGHT. IT'S LIKE BEING SOMEWHERE I'VE NEVER BEEN WITHOUT ANY KNOWLEDGE OF THE SITUATION.
IT WOULD BE SO MUCH EASIER IF I AT LEAST HAD SOME KNOWLEDGE OF FAMILY AND FRIENDS ALREADY IN MY HEAD.
A-
ARI!
WHO...?
WHAT HAPPENED? WHAT HAPPENED TO YOUR HAIR?

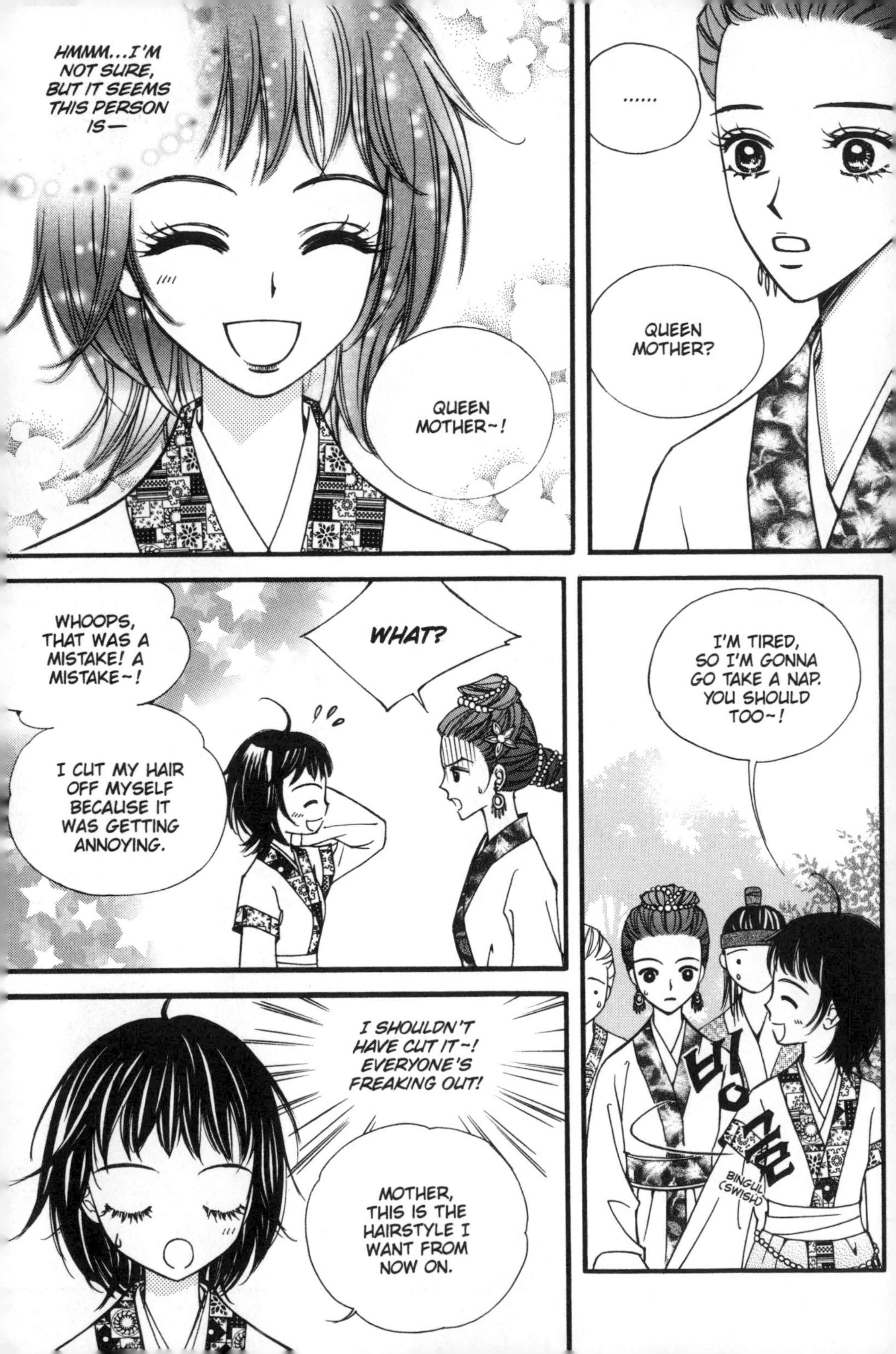
HMMM...I'M NOT SURE, BUT IT SEEMS THIS PERSON IS—
QUEEN MOTHER~!
......
QUEEN MOTHER?
WHOOPS, THAT WAS A MISTAKE! A MISTAKE~!
WHAT?
I CUT MY HAIR OFF MYSELF BECAUSE IT WAS GETTING ANNOYING.
I SHOULDN'T HAVE CUT IT~! EVERYONE'S FREAKING OUT!
MOTHER, THIS IS THE HAIRSTYLE I WANT FROM NOW ON.
I'M TIRED, SO I'M GONNA GO TAKE A NAP. YOU SHOULD TOO~!
BINGUL (SWISH)

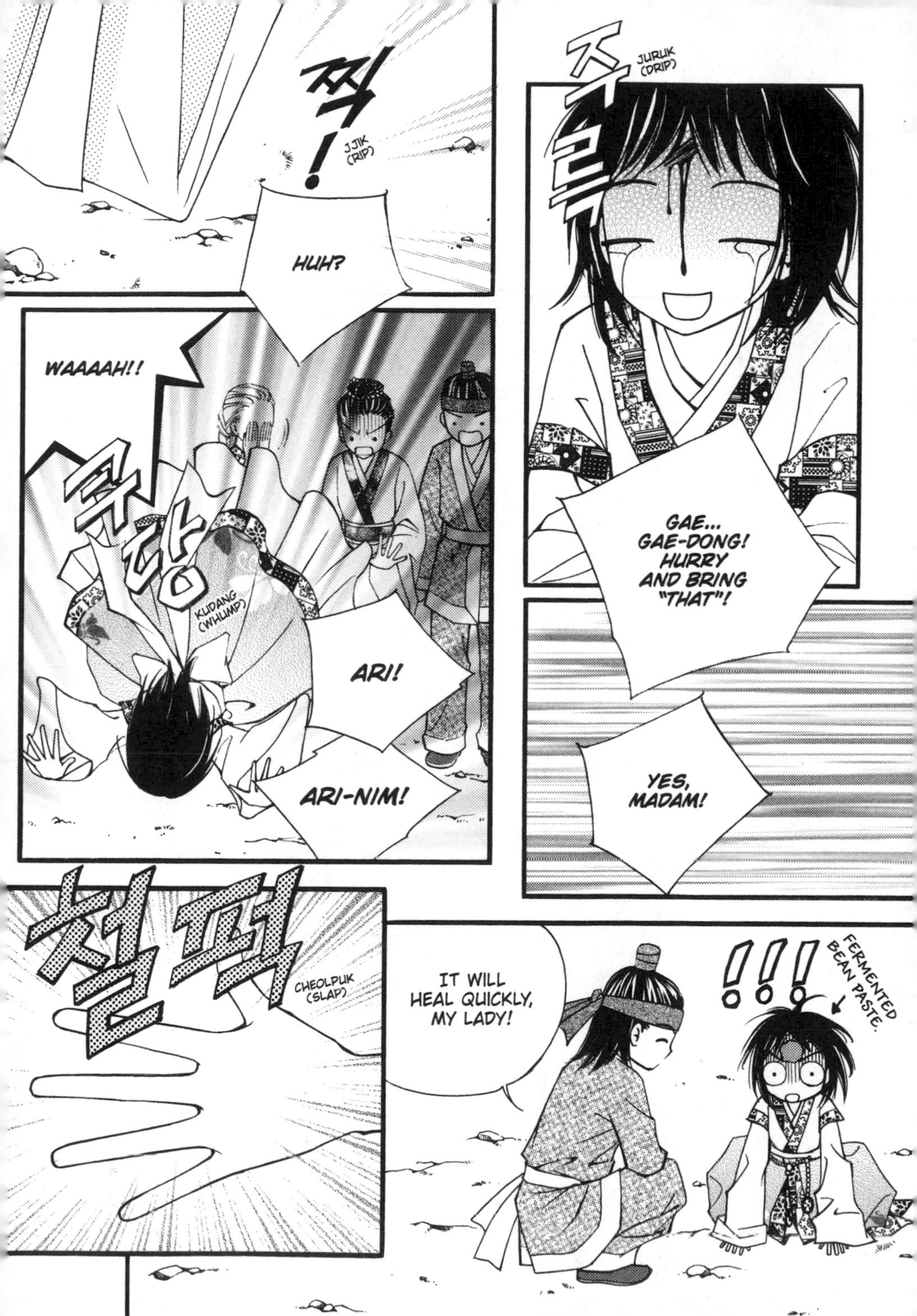
찍!
JJIK (RIP)
HUH?
WAAAAH!!
쿠당
KUDANG (WHUMP)
ARI!
ARI-NIM!
주륵
JURUK (DRIP)
GAE... GAE-DONG! HURRY AND BRING "THAT"!
YES, MADAM!
철퍽
CHEOLPUK (SLAP)
IT WILL HEAL QUICKLY, MY LADY!
!!!
FERMENTED BEAN PASTE.

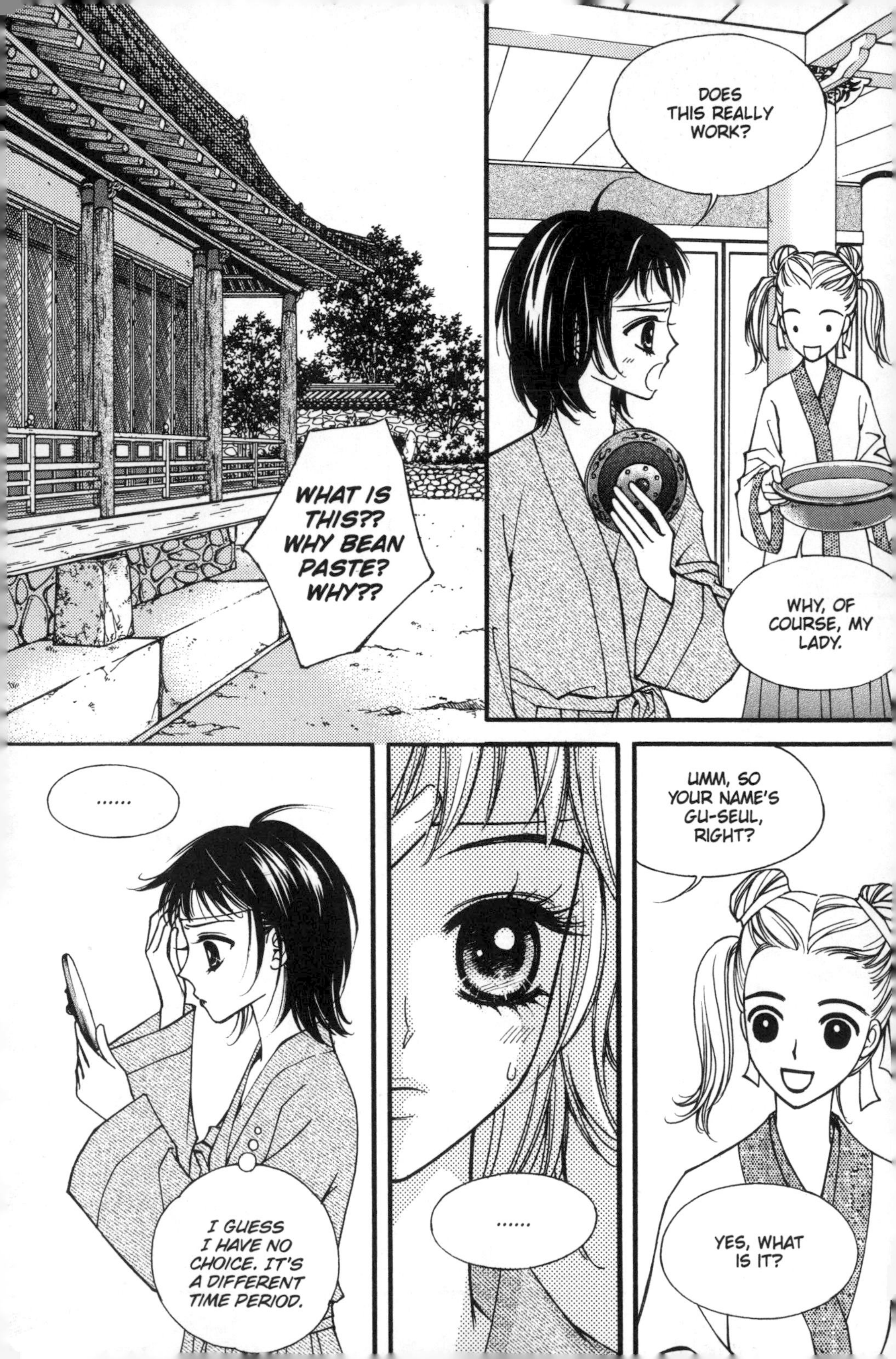
WHAT IS THIS?? WHY BEAN PASTE? WHY??
DOES THIS REALLY WORK?
WHY, OF COURSE, MY LADY.
......
I GUESS I HAVE NO CHOICE. IT'S A DIFFERENT TIME PERIOD.
......
UMM, SO YOUR NAME'S GU-SEUL, RIGHT?
YES, WHAT IS IT?

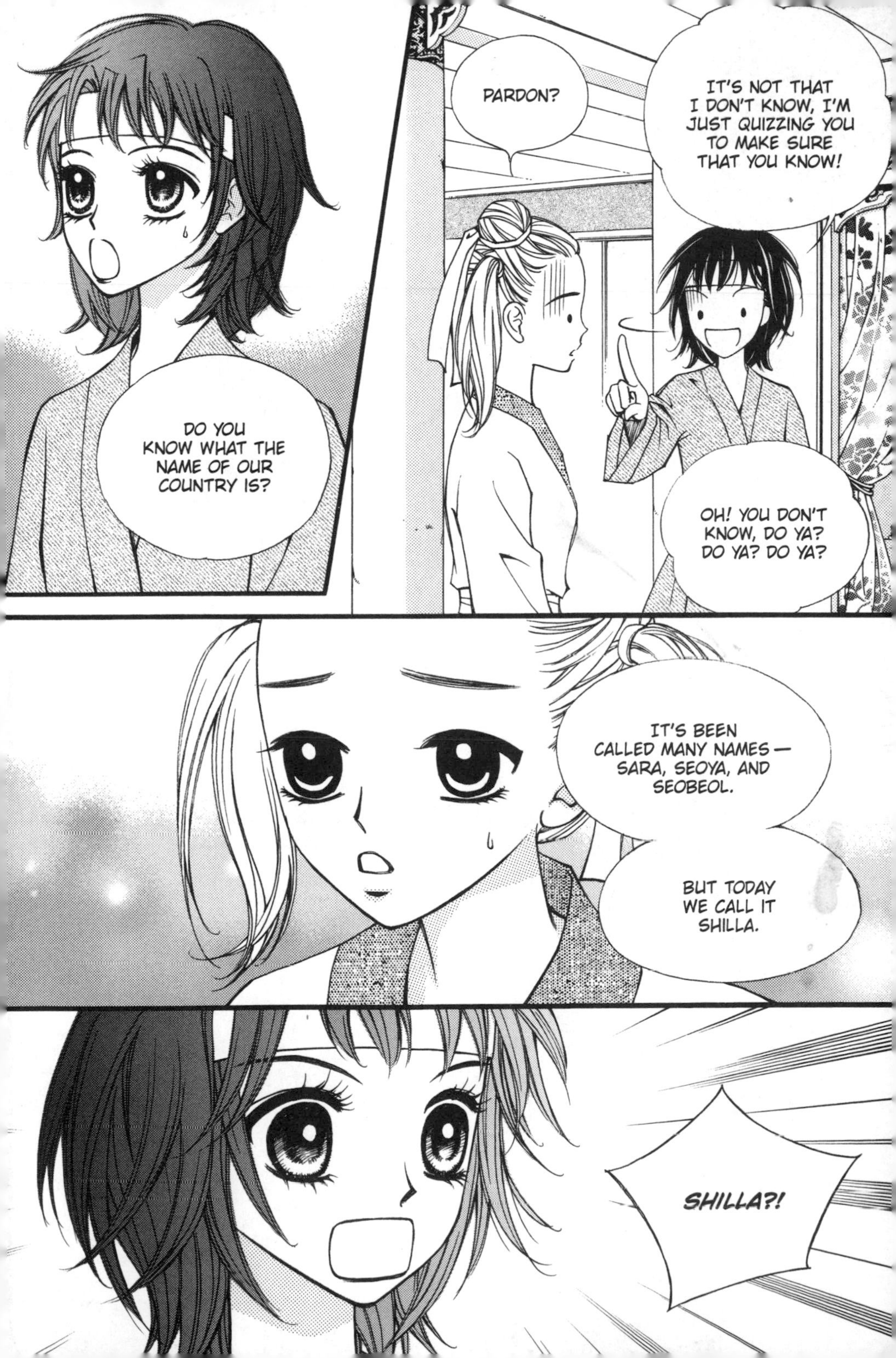
DO YOU KNOW WHAT THE NAME OF OUR COUNTRY IS?
PARDON?
IT'S NOT THAT I DON'T KNOW, I'M JUST QUIZZING YOU TO MAKE SURE THAT YOU KNOW!
OH! YOU DON'T KNOW, DO YA? DO YA? DO YA?
IT'S BEEN CALLED MANY NAMES— SARA, SEOYA, AND SEOBEOL.
BUT TODAY WE CALL IT SHILLA.
SHILLA?!

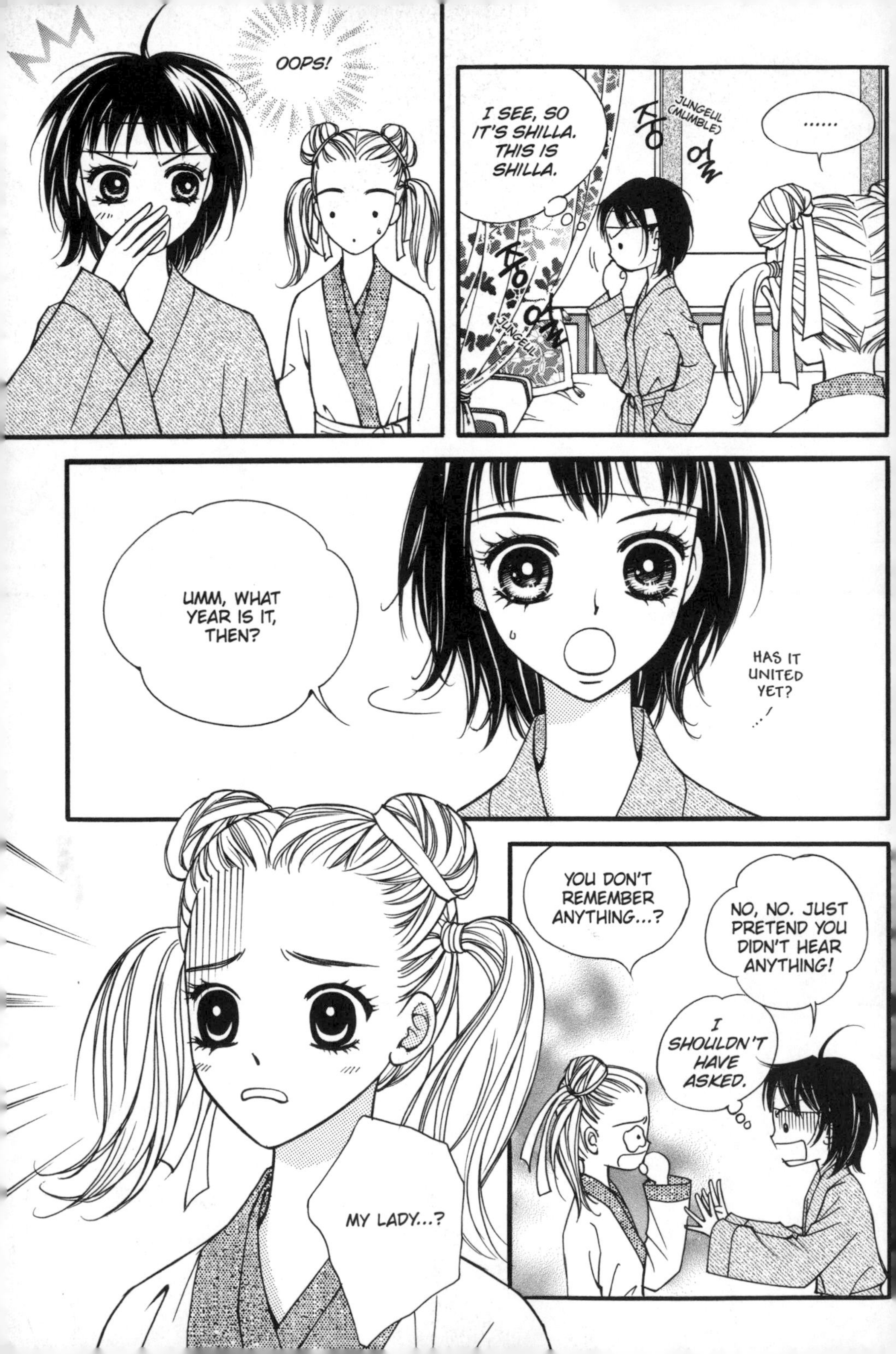

OOPS!
I SEE, SO IT'S SHILLA. THIS IS SHILLA.
중얼
JUNGEUL (MUMBLE)
......
중얼
JUNGEUL
UMM, WHAT YEAR IS IT, THEN?
HAS IT UNITED YET?
MY LADY...?
YOU DON'T REMEMBER ANYTHING...?
NO, NO. JUST PRETEND YOU DIDN'T HEAR ANYTHING!
I SHOULDN'T HAVE ASKED.

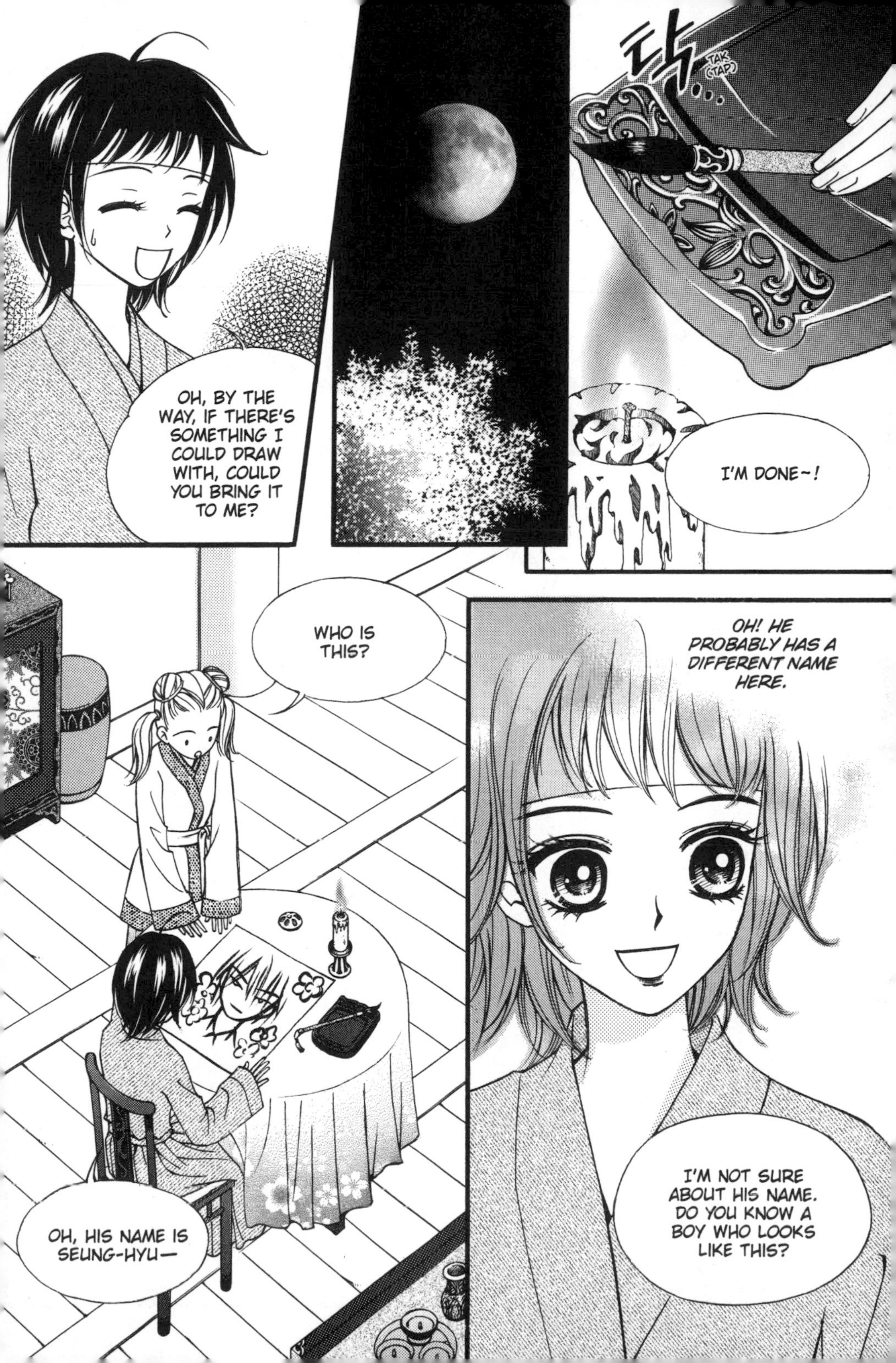

OH, BY THE WAY, IF THERE'S SOMETHING I COULD DRAW WITH, COULD YOU BRING IT TO ME?
탁
TAK (TAP)
I'M DONE~!
WHO IS THIS?
OH, HIS NAME IS SEUNG-HYU—
OH! HE PROBABLY HAS A DIFFERENT NAME HERE.
I'M NOT SURE ABOUT HIS NAME. DO YOU KNOW A BOY WHO LOOKS LIKE THIS?

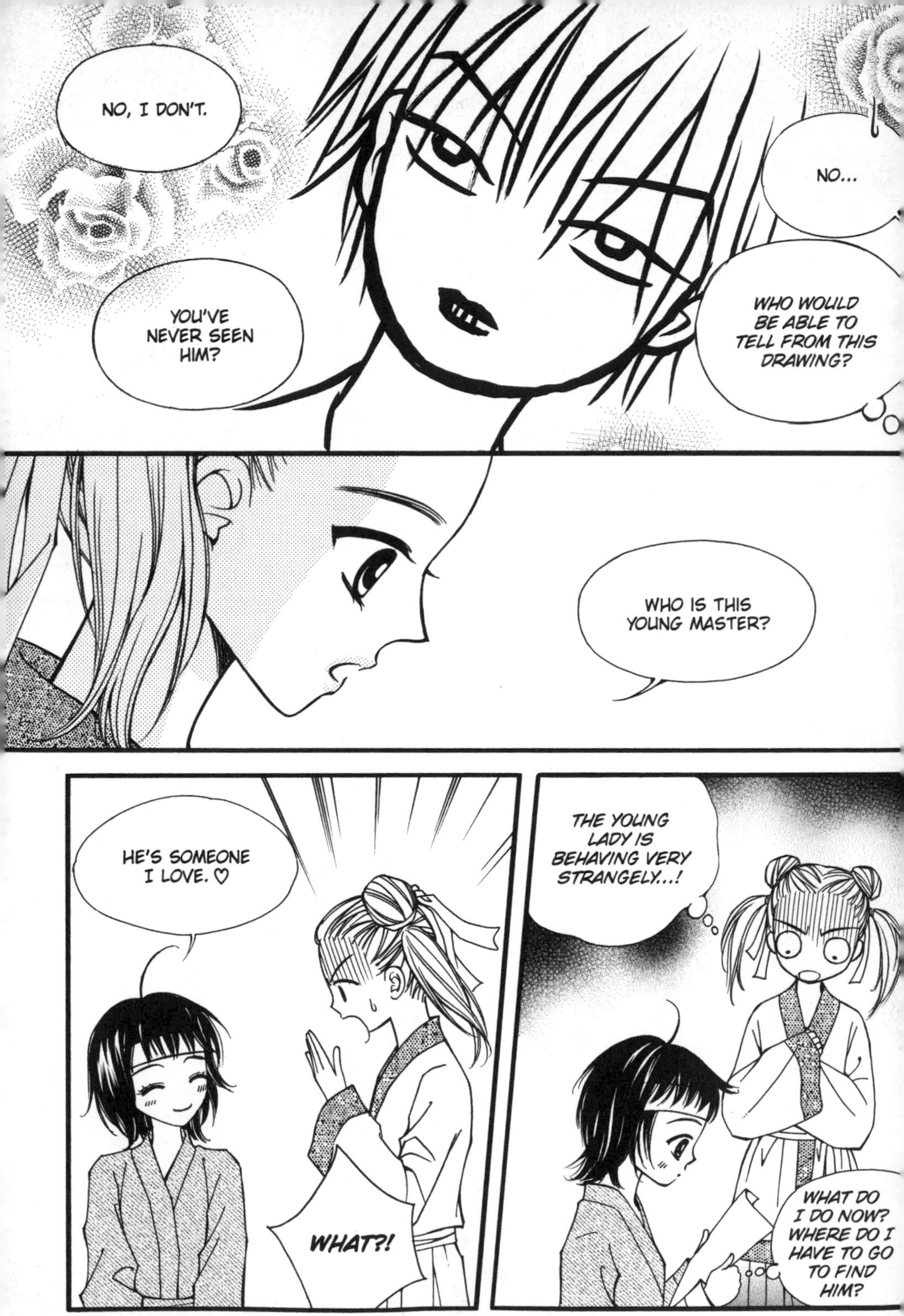
NO, I DON'T.
YOU'VE NEVER SEEN HIM?
NO...
WHO WOULD BE ABLE TO TELL FROM THIS DRAWING?
WHO IS THIS YOUNG MASTER?
HE'S SOMEONE I LOVE. ♡
WHAT?!
THE YOUNG LADY IS BEHAVING VERY STRANGELY...!
WHAT DO I DO NOW? WHERE DO I HAVE TO GO TO FIND HIM?

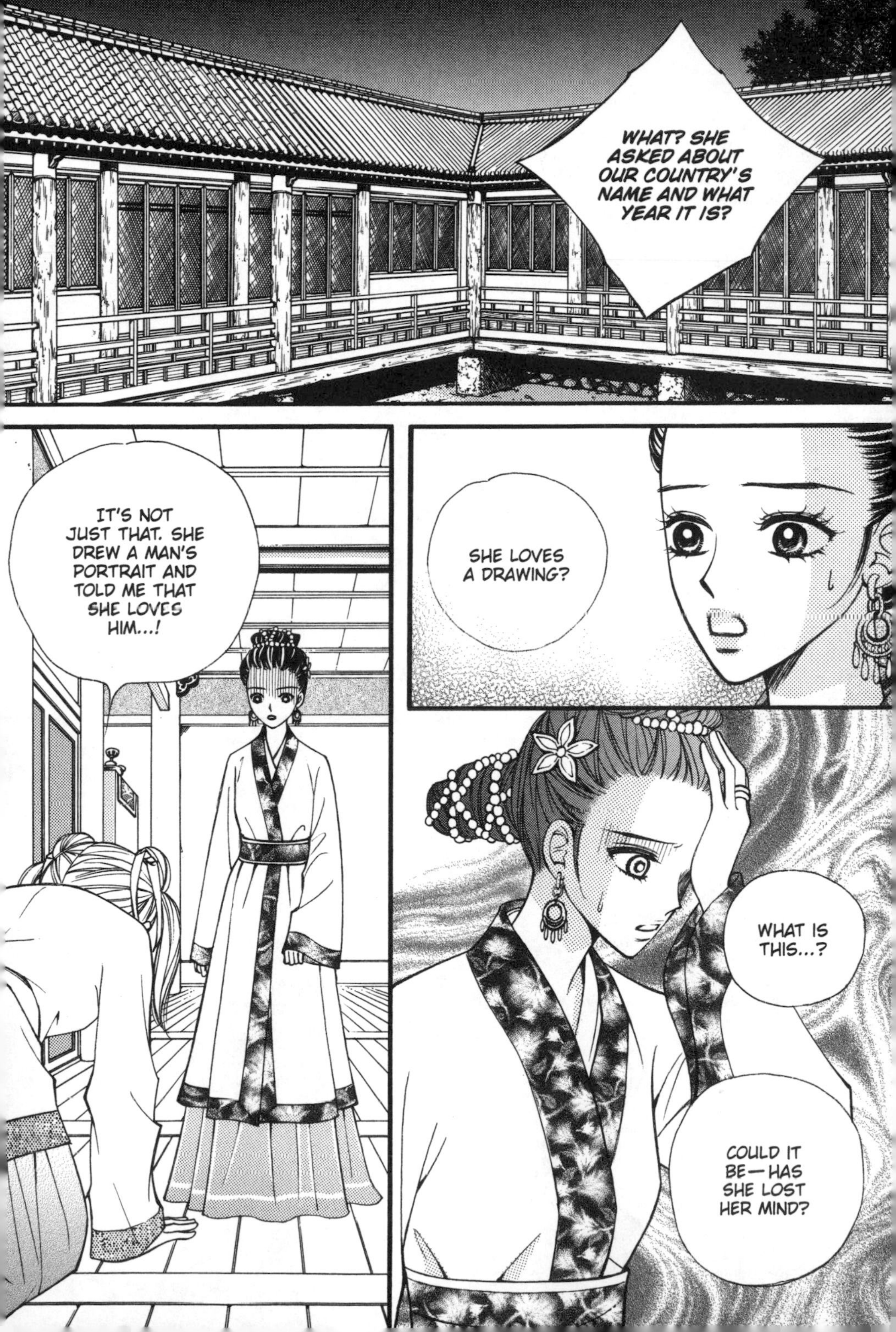
WHAT? SHE ASKED ABOUT OUR COUNTRY'S NAME AND WHAT YEAR IT IS?
IT'S NOT JUST THAT. SHE DREW A MAN'S PORTRAIT AND TOLD ME THAT SHE LOVES HIM...!
SHE LOVES A DRAWING?
WHAT IS THIS...?
COULD IT BE—HAS SHE LOST HER MIND?

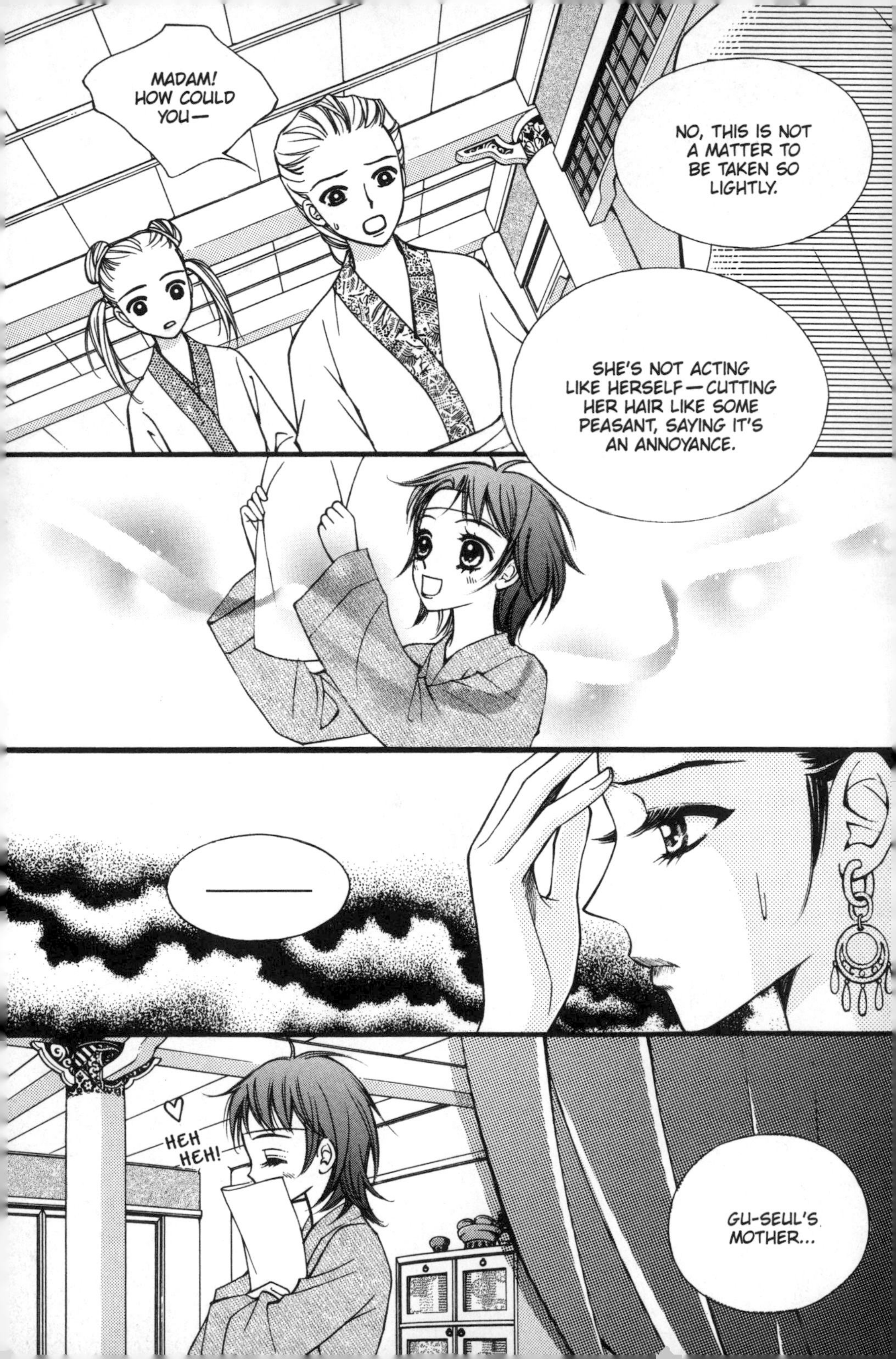
MADAM! HOW COULD YOU—
NO, THIS IS NOT A MATTER TO BE TAKEN SO LIGHTLY.
SHE'S NOT ACTING LIKE HERSELF—CUTTING HER HAIR LIKE SOME PEASANT, SAYING IT'S AN ANNOYANCE.
——
HEH HEH!
GU-SEUL'S MOTHER...

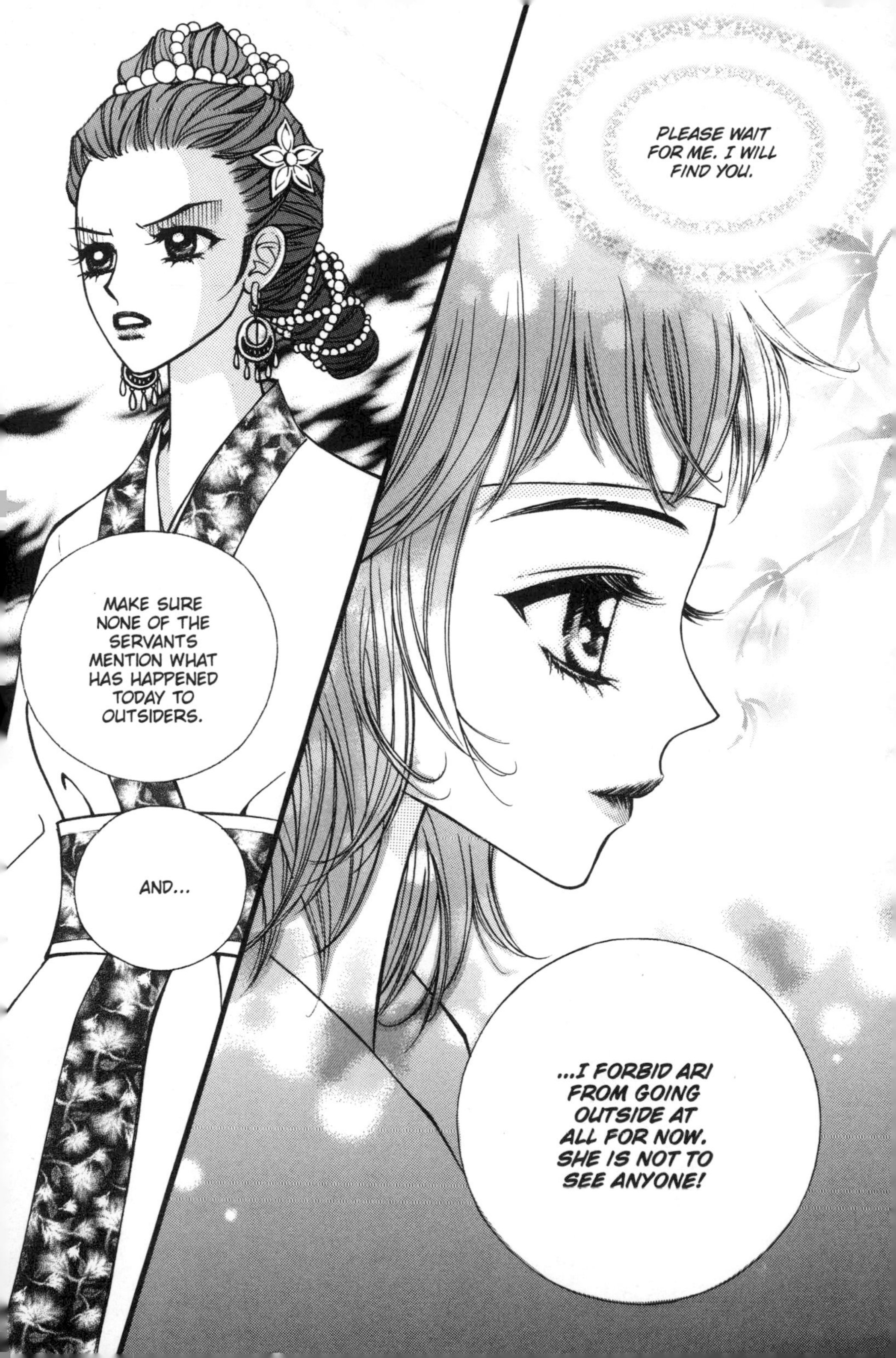
MAKE SURE NONE OF THE SERVANTS MENTION WHAT HAS HAPPENED TODAY TO OUTSIDERS.
AND...
PLEASE WAIT FOR ME. I WILL FIND YOU.
...I FORBID ARI FROM GOING OUTSIDE AT ALL FOR NOW. SHE IS NOT TO SEE ANYONE!

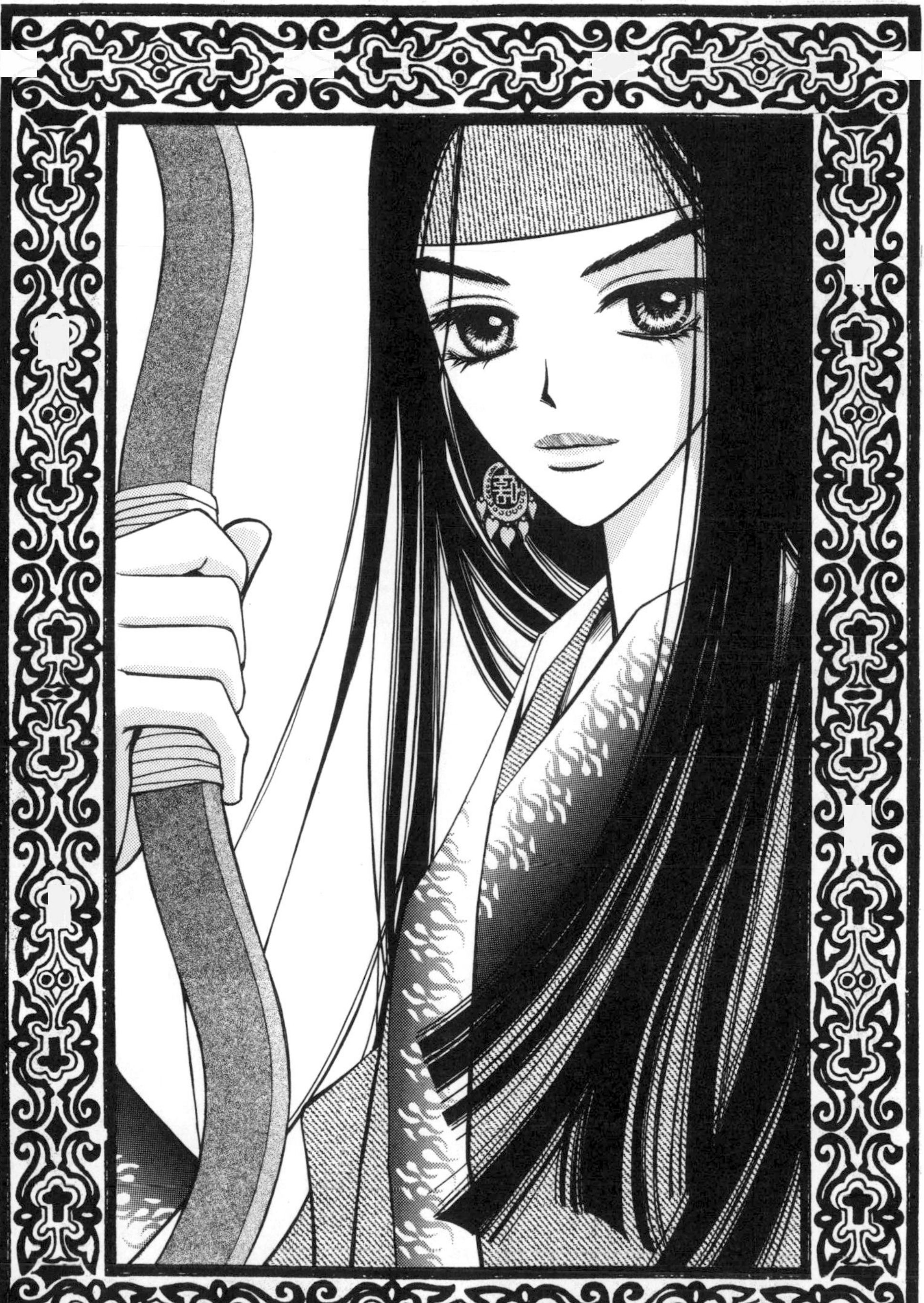

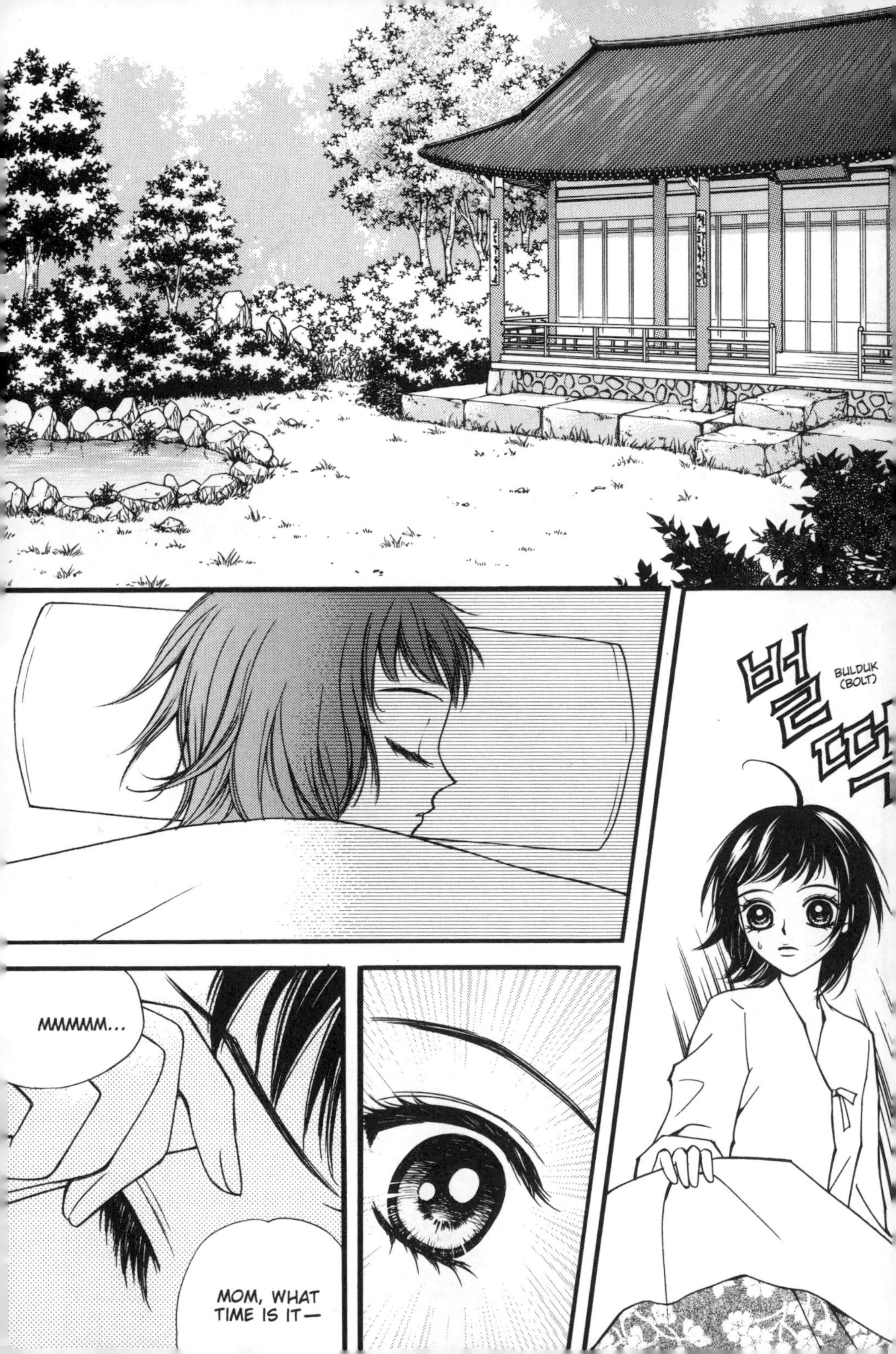
MMMMM...
MOM, WHAT TIME IS IT—
벌떡
BULDUK (BOLT)

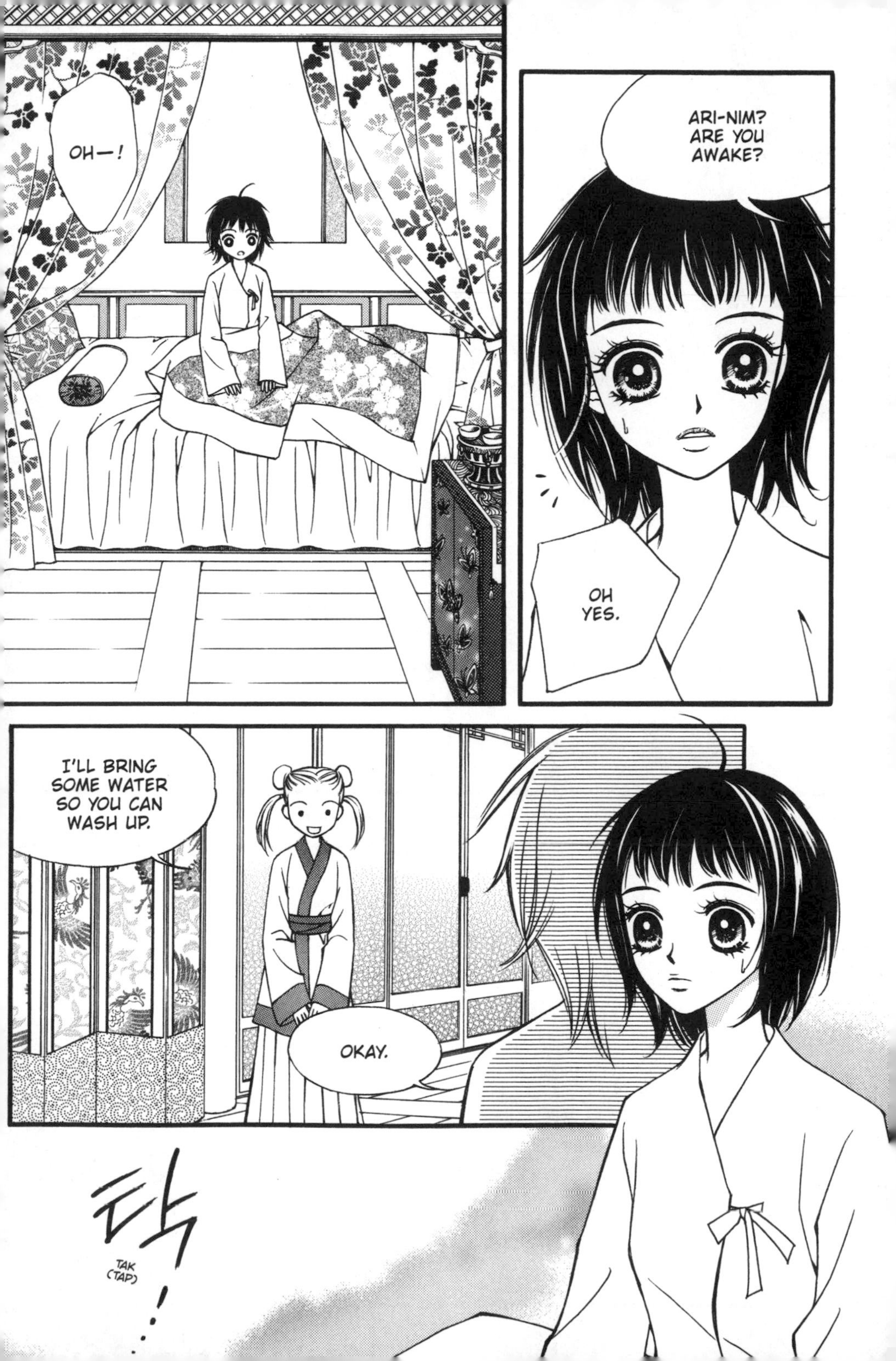
OH—!
ARI-NIM? ARE YOU AWAKE?
OH YES.
I'LL BRING SOME WATER SO YOU CAN WASH UP.
OKAY.
TAK (TAP)

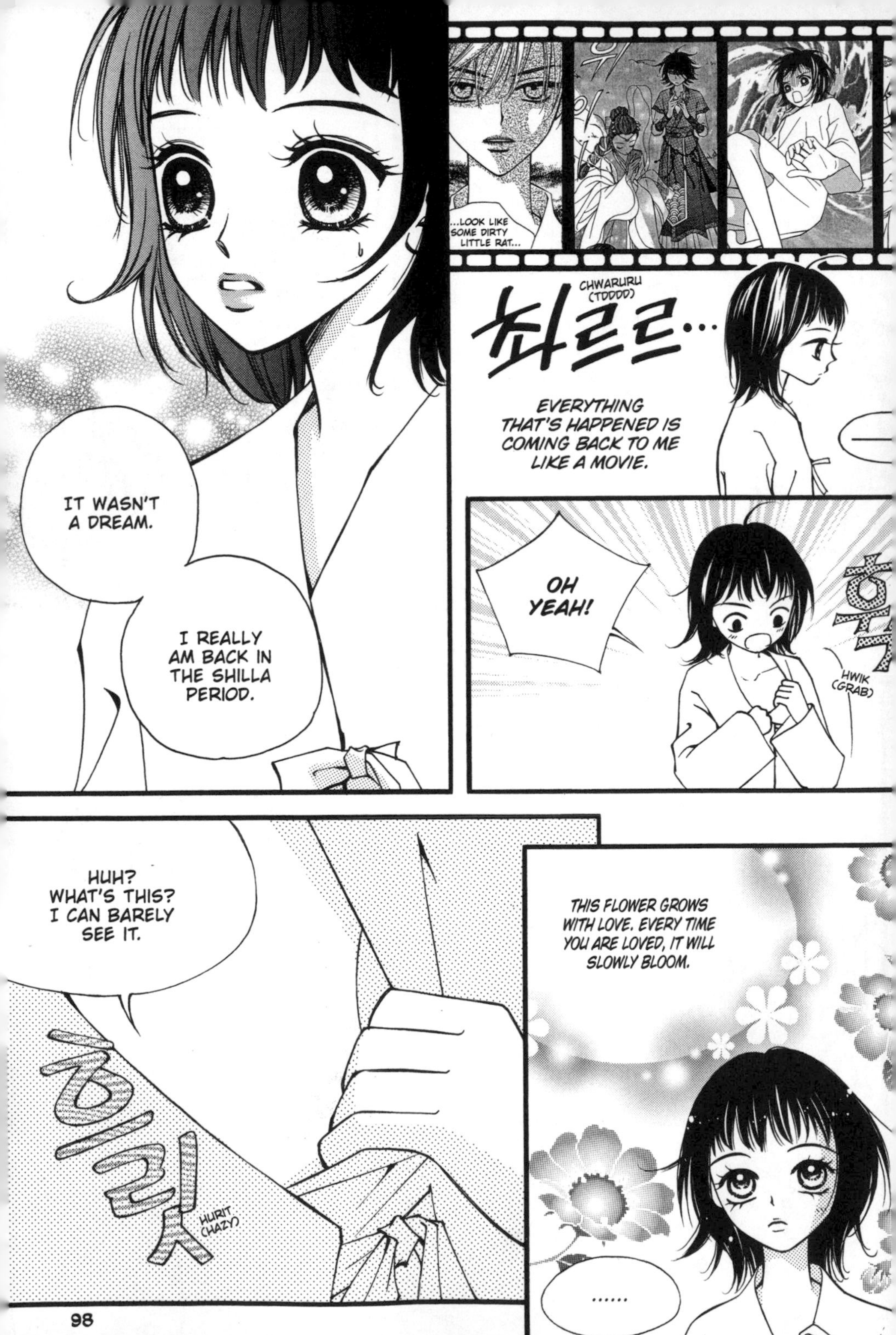
IT WASN'T A DREAM.
I REALLY AM BACK IN THE SHILLA PERIOD.
...LOOK LIKE SOME DIRTY LITTLE RAT...
촤르르…
CHWARURU (TDDDD)
EVERYTHING THAT'S HAPPENED IS COMING BACK TO ME LIKE A MOVIE.
OH YEAH!
HWIK (GRAB)
HUH? WHAT'S THIS? I CAN BARELY SEE IT.
HURIT (HAZY)
THIS FLOWER GROWS WITH LOVE. EVERY TIME YOU ARE LOVED, IT WILL SLOWLY BLOOM.
......

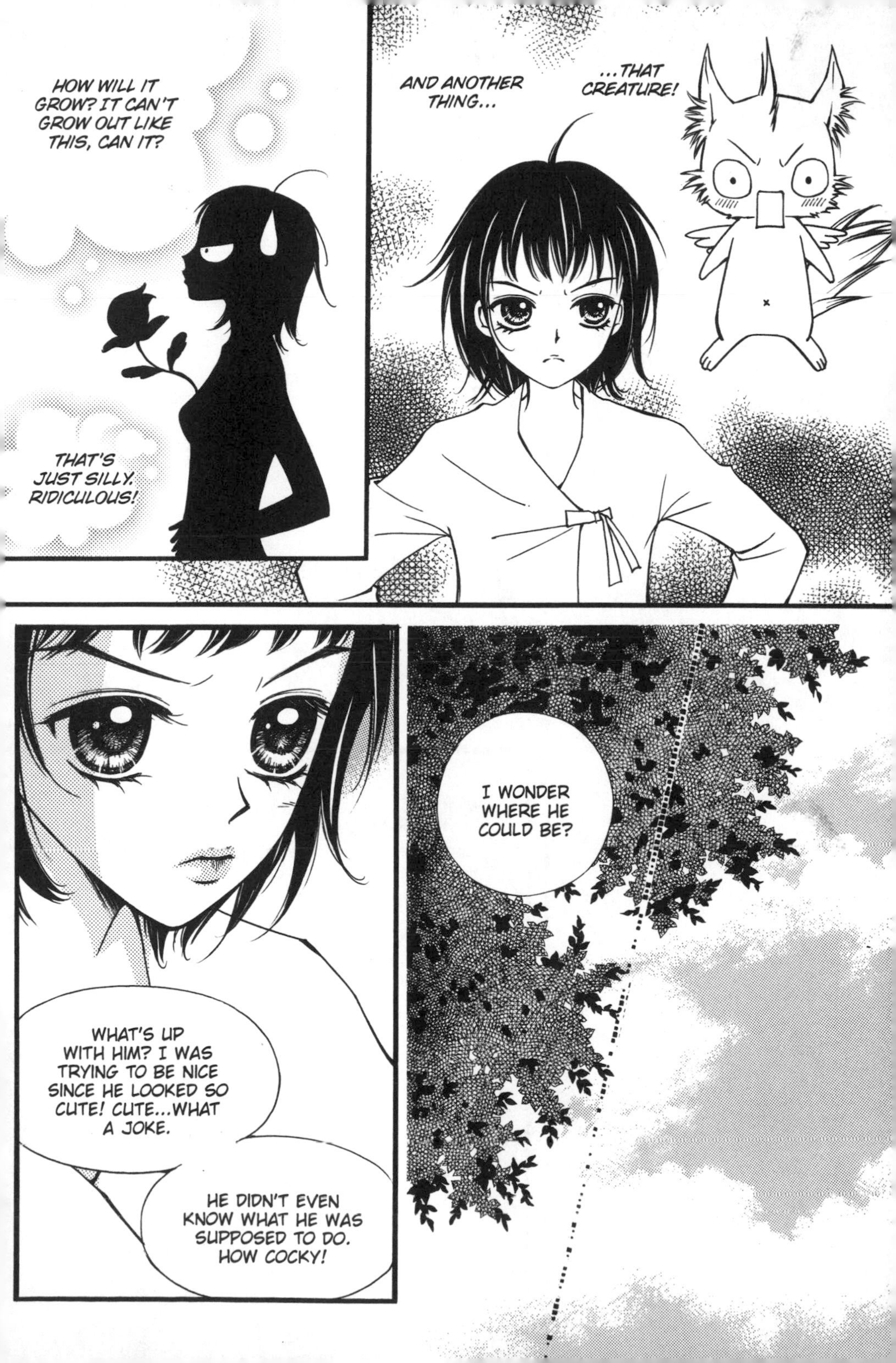
HOW WILL IT GROW? IT CAN'T GROW OUT LIKE THIS, CAN IT?
THAT'S JUST SILLY. RIDICULOUS!
AND ANOTHER THING...
...THAT CREATURE!
WHAT'S UP WITH HIM? I WAS TRYING TO BE NICE SINCE HE LOOKED SO CUTE! CUTE...WHAT A JOKE.
HE DIDN'T EVEN KNOW WHAT HE WAS SUPPOSED TO DO. HOW COCKY!
I WONDER WHERE HE COULD BE?

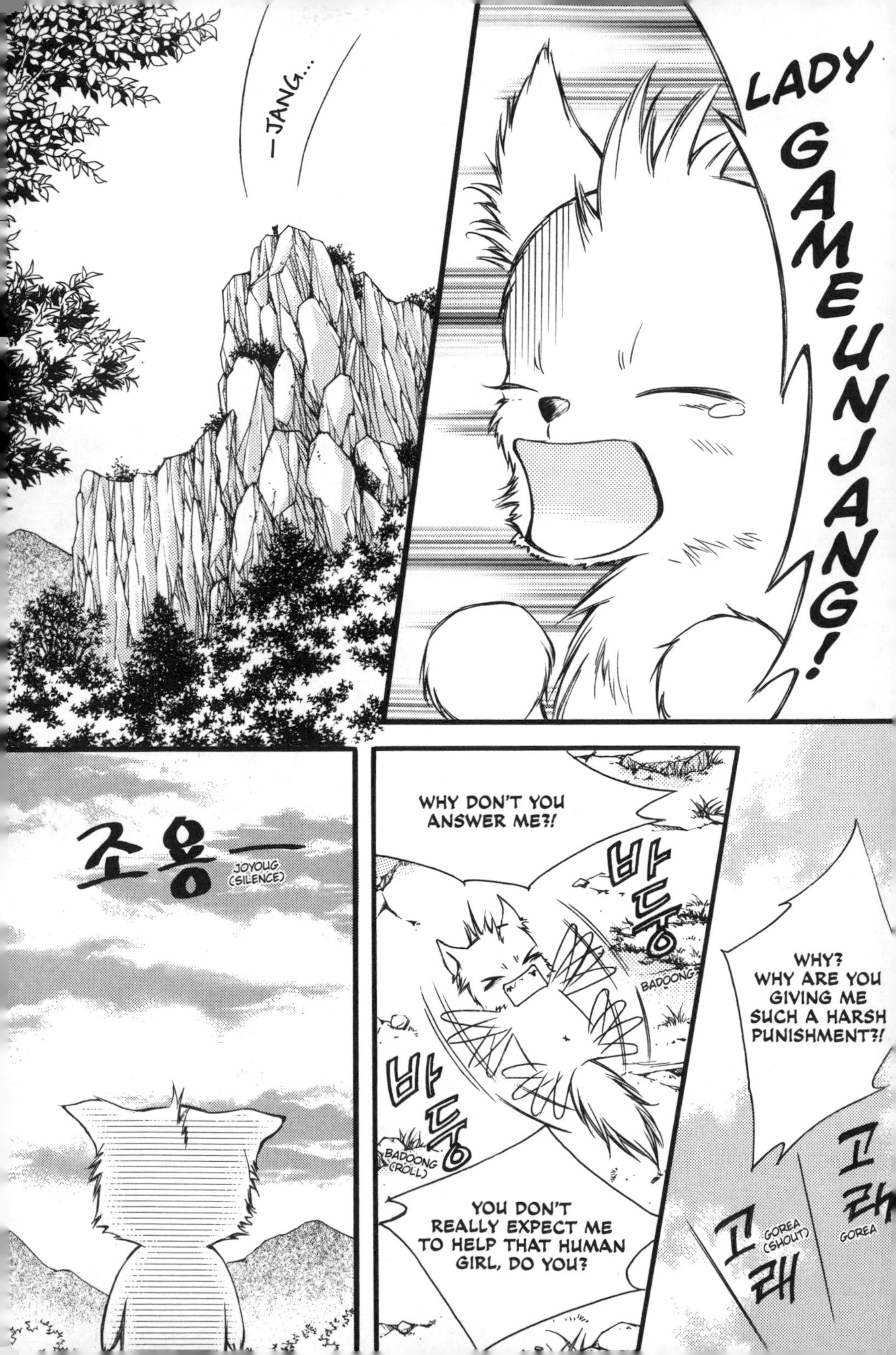

—JANG...
LADY GAMEUNJANG!
조용—
JOYOUG (SILENCE)
WHY DON'T YOU ANSWER ME?!
바둥
BADOONG
바둥
BADOONG (ROLL)
YOU DON'T REALLY EXPECT ME TO HELP THAT HUMAN GIRL, DO YOU?
WHY? WHY ARE YOU GIVING ME SUCH A HARSH PUNISHMENT?!
고래
GOREA (SHOUT)
고래
GOREA

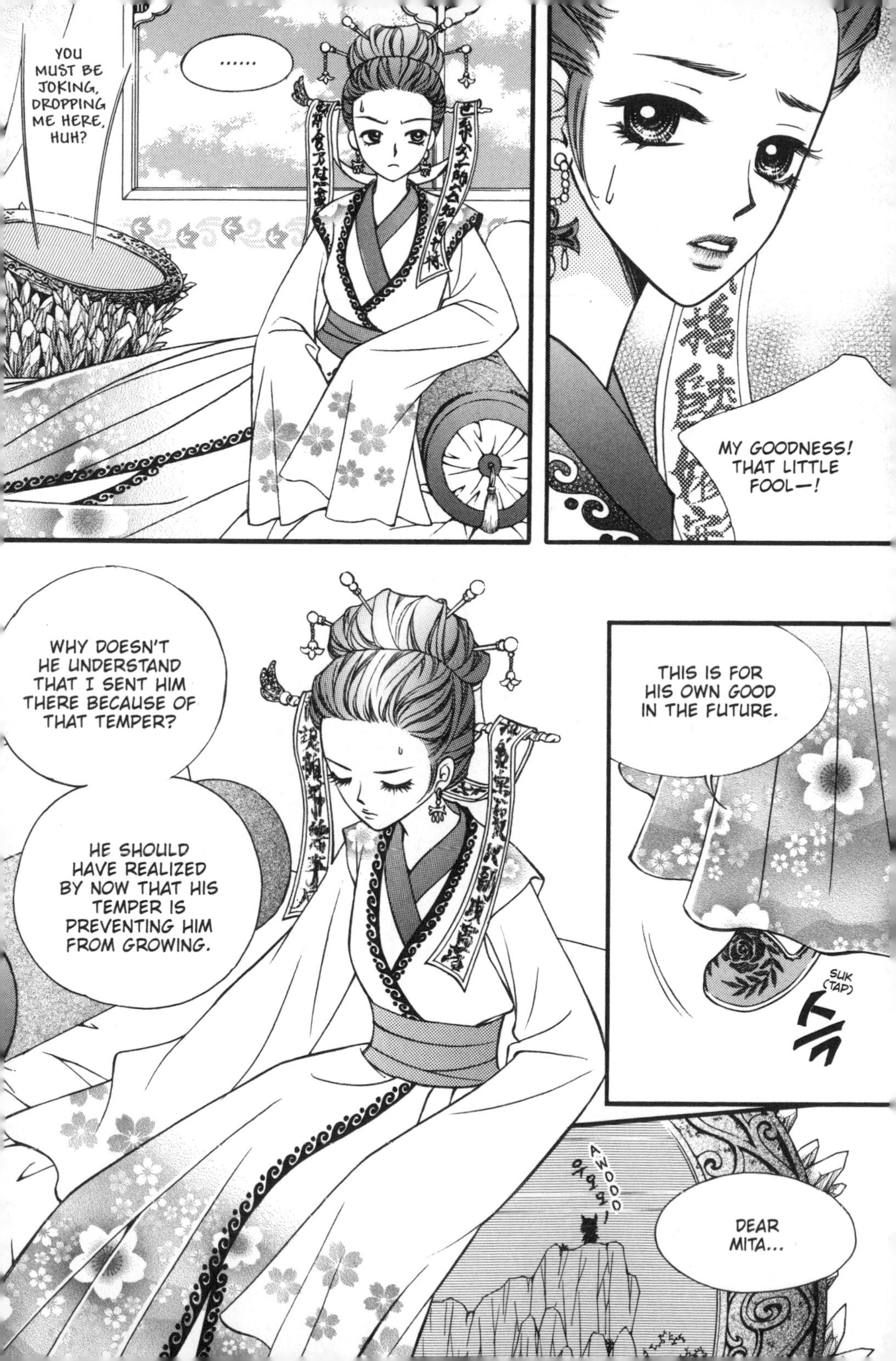
YOU MUST BE JOKING, DROPPING ME HERE, HUH?
......
MY GOODNESS! THAT LITTLE FOOL—!
WHY DOESN'T HE UNDERSTAND THAT I SENT HIM THERE BECAUSE OF THAT TEMPER?
HE SHOULD HAVE REALIZED BY NOW THAT HIS TEMPER IS PREVENTING HIM FROM GROWING.
THIS IS FOR HIS OWN GOOD IN THE FUTURE.
SUK (TAP)
A-WOOO
DEAR MITA...

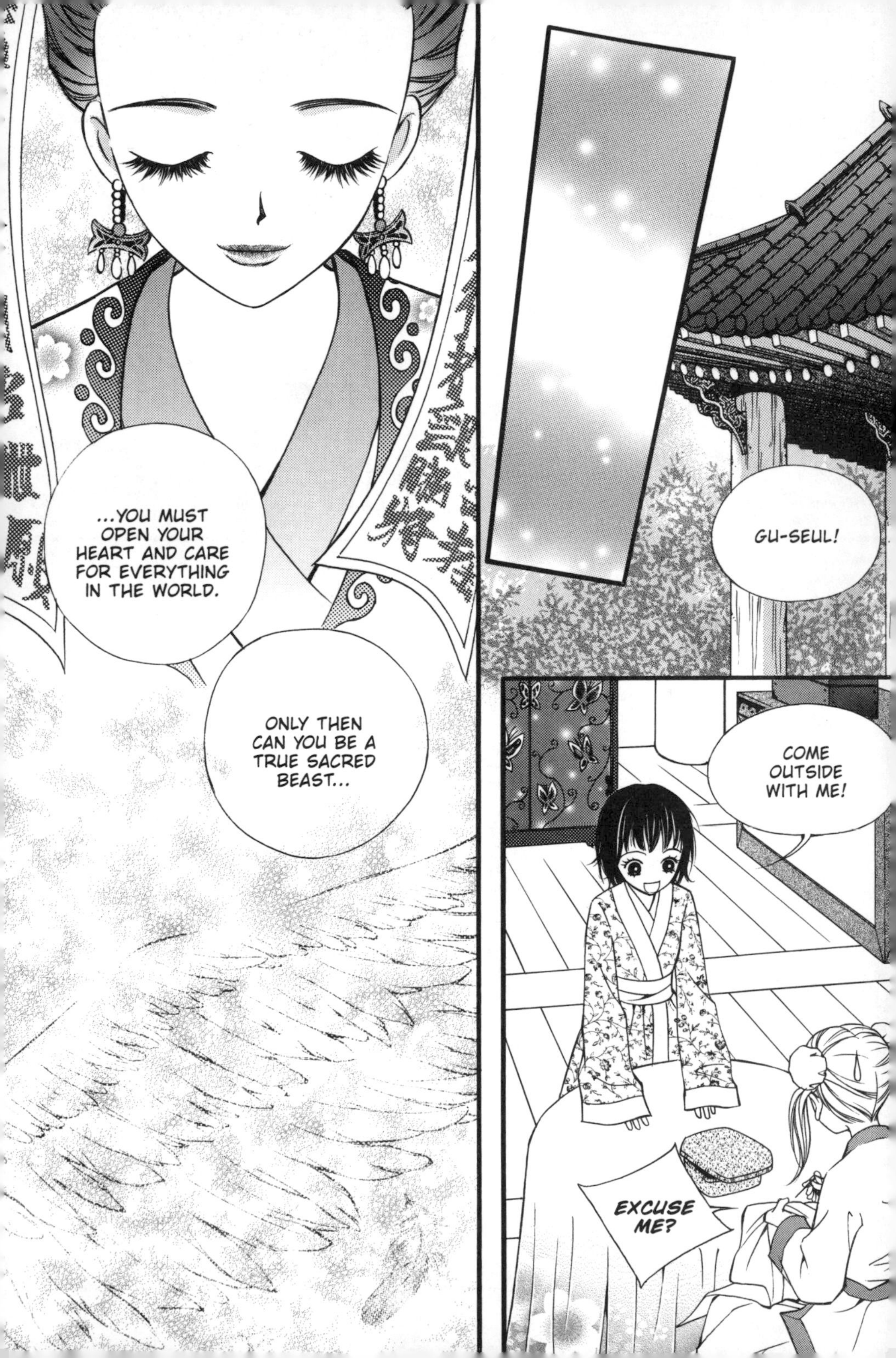
...YOU MUST OPEN YOUR HEART AND CARE FOR EVERYTHING IN THE WORLD.
ONLY THEN CAN YOU BE A TRUE SACRED BEAST...
GU-SEUL!
COME OUTSIDE WITH ME!
EXCUSE ME?

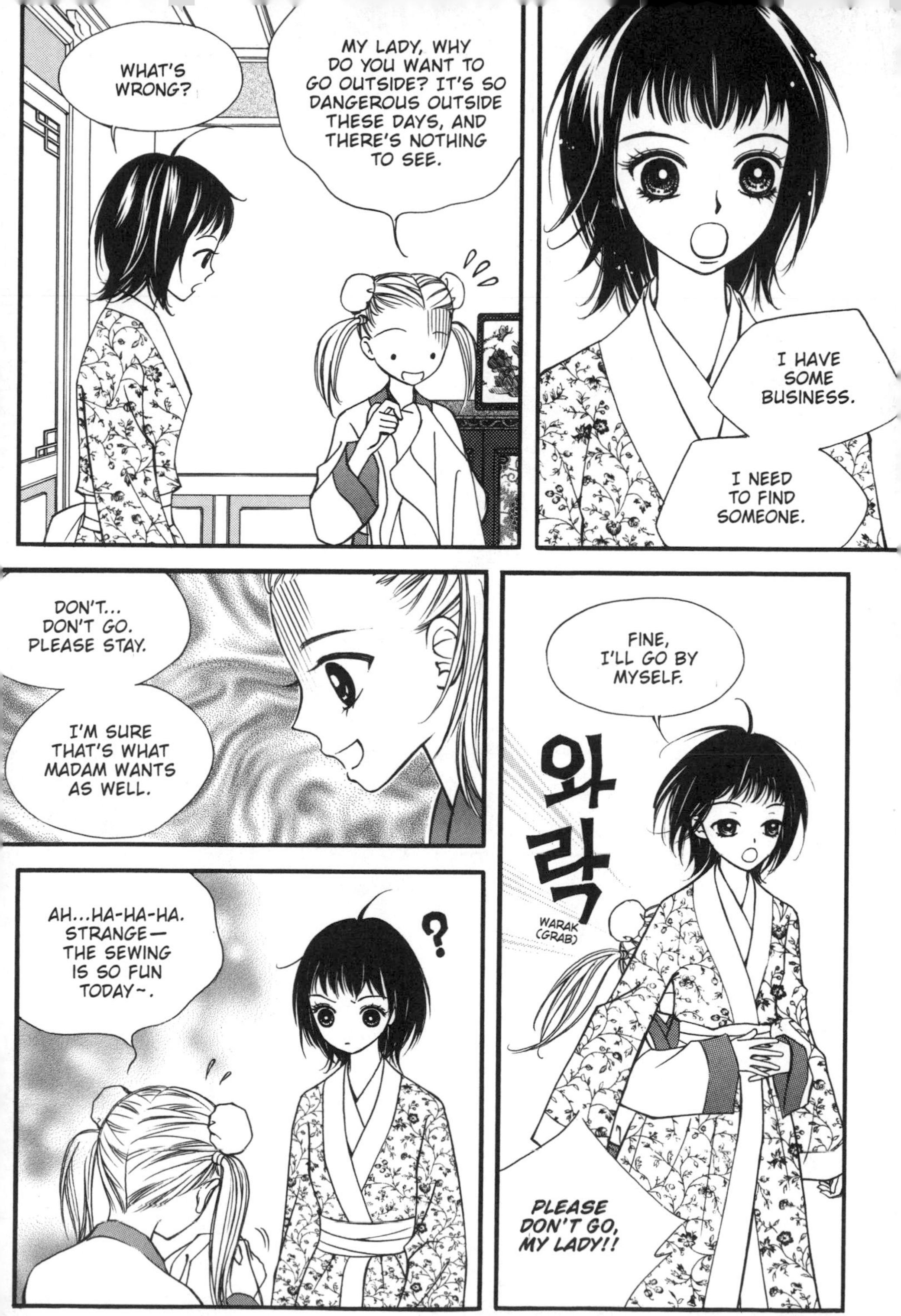

WHAT'S WRONG?
MY LADY, WHY DO YOU WANT TO GO OUTSIDE? IT'S SO DANGEROUS OUTSIDE THESE DAYS, AND THERE'S NOTHING TO SEE.
I HAVE SOME BUSINESS.
I NEED TO FIND SOMEONE.
DON'T... DON'T GO. PLEASE STAY.
I'M SURE THAT'S WHAT MADAM WANTS AS WELL.
AH...HA-HA-HA. STRANGE— THE SEWING IS SO FUN TODAY~.
?
FINE, I'LL GO BY MYSELF.
와락
WARAK (GRAB)
PLEASE DON'T GO, MY LADY!!

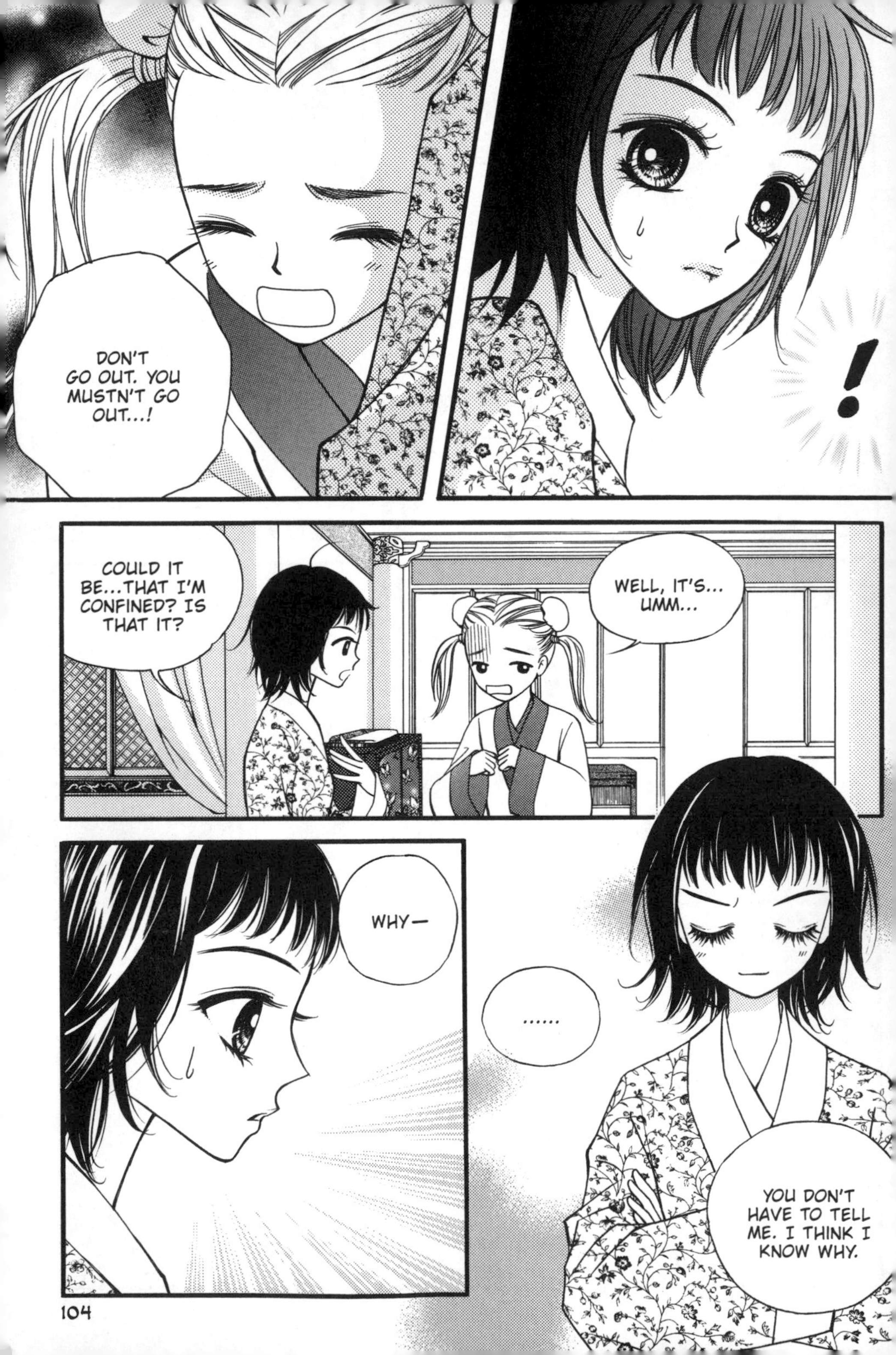
DON'T GO OUT. YOU MUSTN'T GO OUT...!
!
COULD IT BE...THAT I'M CONFINED? IS THAT IT?
WELL, IT'S... UMM...
WHY—
......
YOU DON'T HAVE TO TELL ME. I THINK I KNOW WHY.

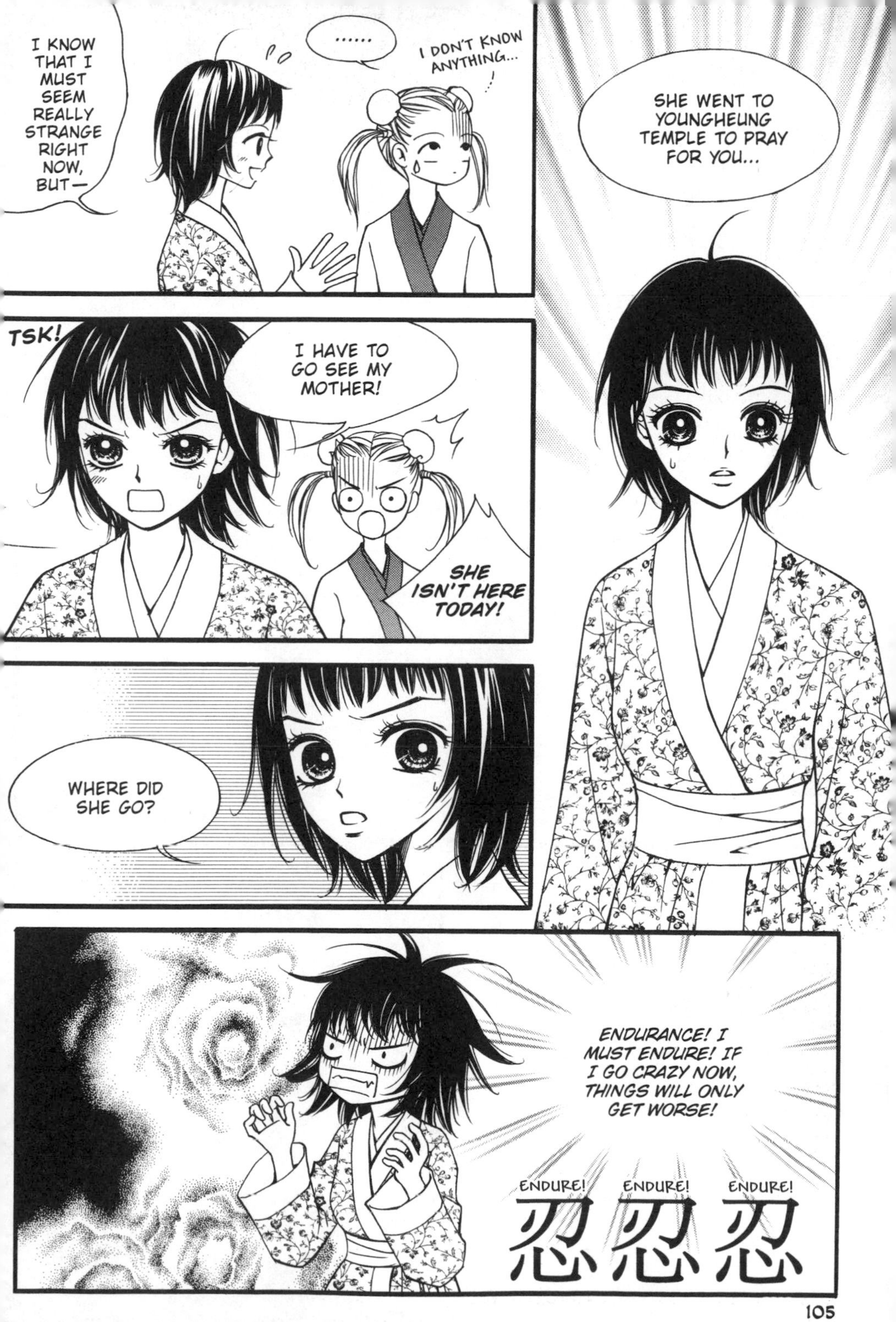
I KNOW THAT I MUST SEEM REALLY STRANGE RIGHT NOW, BUT—
......
I DON'T KNOW ANYTHING...
TSK!
I HAVE TO GO SEE MY MOTHER!
SHE ISN'T HERE TODAY!
WHERE DID SHE GO?
SHE WENT TO YOUNGHEUNG TEMPLE TO PRAY FOR YOU...
ENDURANCE! I MUST ENDURE! IF I GO CRAZY NOW, THINGS WILL ONLY GET WORSE!
ENDURE! ENDURE! ENDURE!
忍忍忍

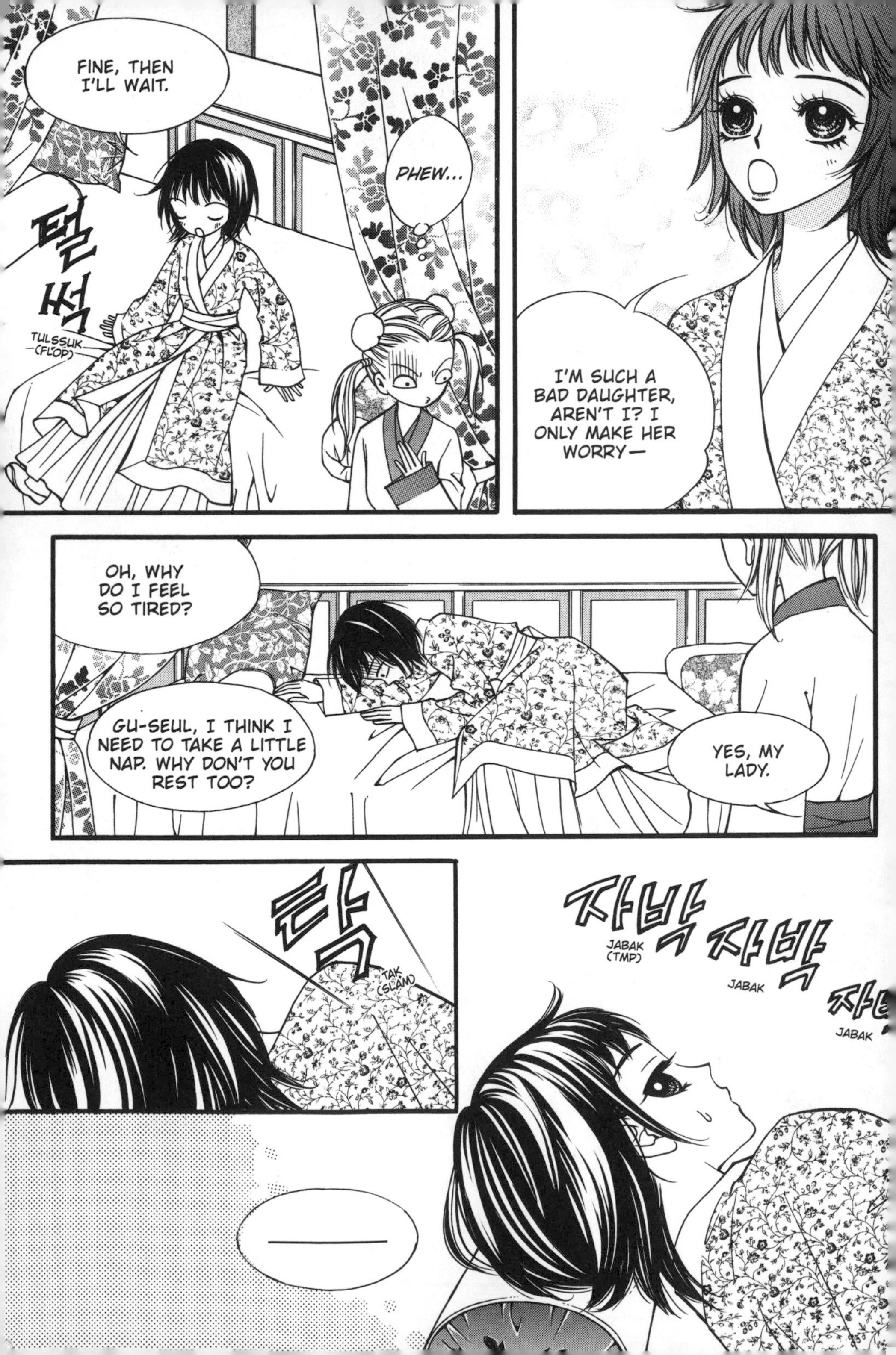
FINE, THEN I'LL WAIT.
털썩
TULSSUK (FLOP)
PHEW...
I'M SUCH A BAD DAUGHTER, AREN'T I? I ONLY MAKE HER WORRY—
OH, WHY DO I FEEL SO TIRED?
GU-SEUL, I THINK I NEED TO TAKE A LITTLE NAP. WHY DON'T YOU REST TOO?
YES, MY LADY.
탁
TAK (SLAM)
자박
JABAK (TMP)
자박
JABAK
JABAK
—

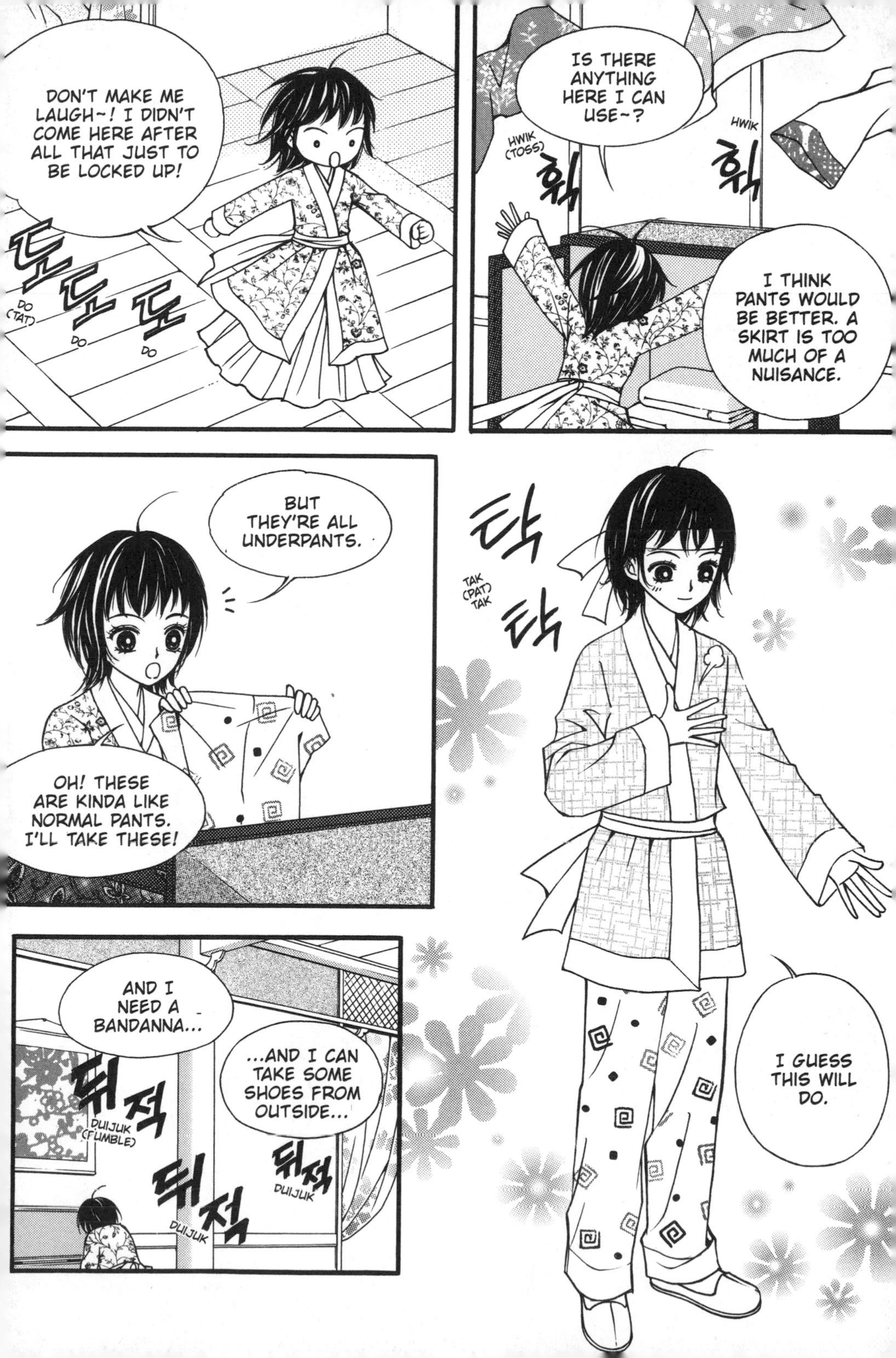
DON'T MAKE ME LAUGH~! I DIDN'T COME HERE AFTER ALL THAT JUST TO BE LOCKED UP!
도
DO (TAT)
도
DO
도
DO
IS THERE ANYTHING HERE I CAN USE~?
홱
HWIK (TOSS)
홱
HWIK
I THINK PANTS WOULD BE BETTER. A SKIRT IS TOO MUCH OF A NUISANCE.
BUT THEY'RE ALL UNDERPANTS.
OH! THESE ARE KINDA LIKE NORMAL PANTS. I'LL TAKE THESE!
AND I NEED A BANDANNA...
...AND I CAN TAKE SOME SHOES FROM OUTSIDE...
뒤적
DUIJUK (FUMBLE)
뒤적
DUIJUK
뒤적
DUIJUK
탁
TAK (PAT) TAK
탁
I GUESS THIS WILL DO.

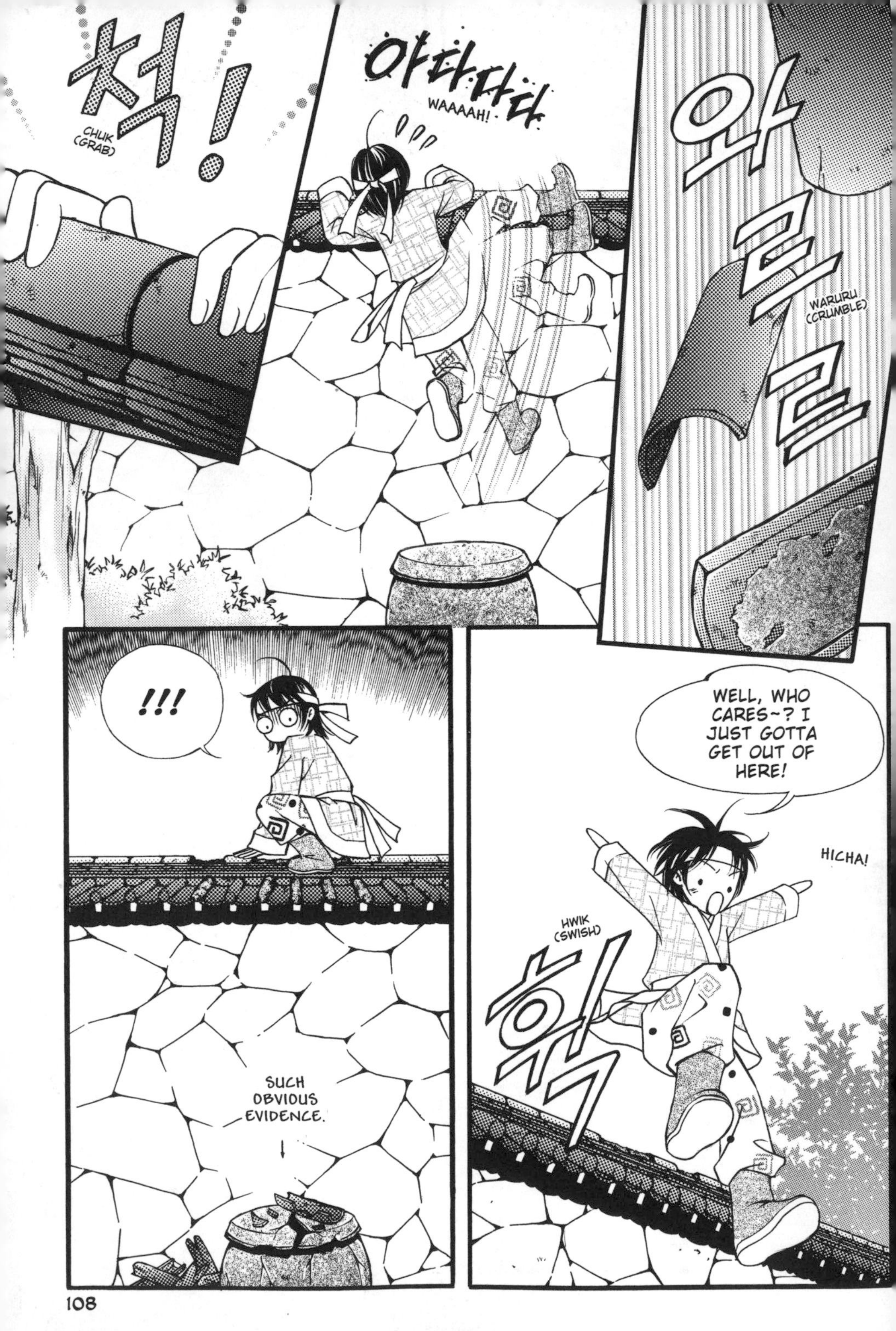
척!
CHUK (GRAB)
WAAAAH!
와르르
WARURU (CRUMBLE)
!!!
SUCH OBVIOUS EVIDENCE.
WELL, WHO CARES~? I JUST GOTTA GET OUT OF HERE!
HICHA!
HWIK (SWISH)
휙

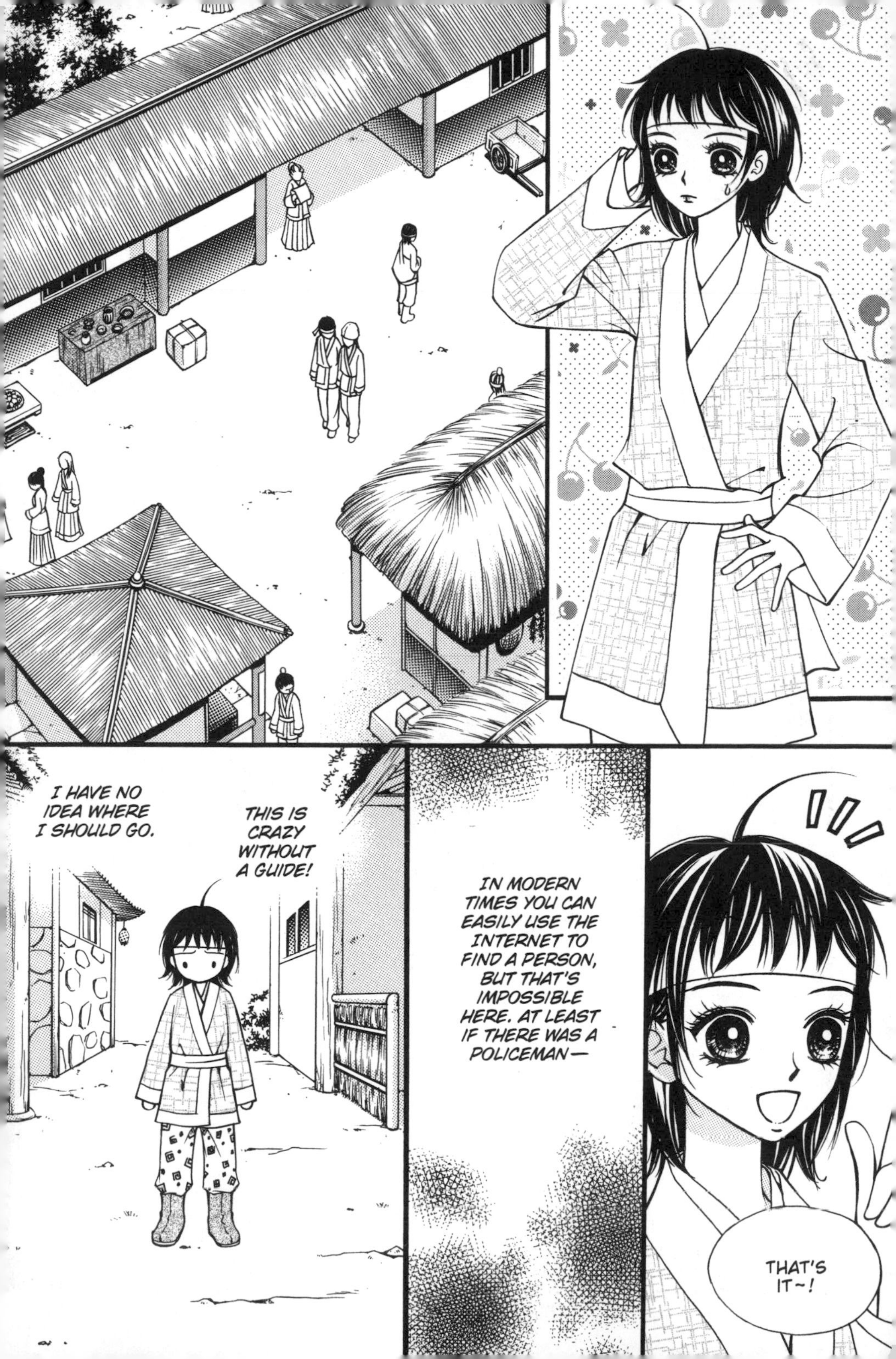
I HAVE NO IDEA WHERE I SHOULD GO.
THIS IS CRAZY WITHOUT A GUIDE!
IN MODERN TIMES YOU CAN EASILY USE THE INTERNET TO FIND A PERSON, BUT THAT'S IMPOSSIBLE HERE. AT LEAST IF THERE WAS A POLICEMAN—
THAT'S IT~!

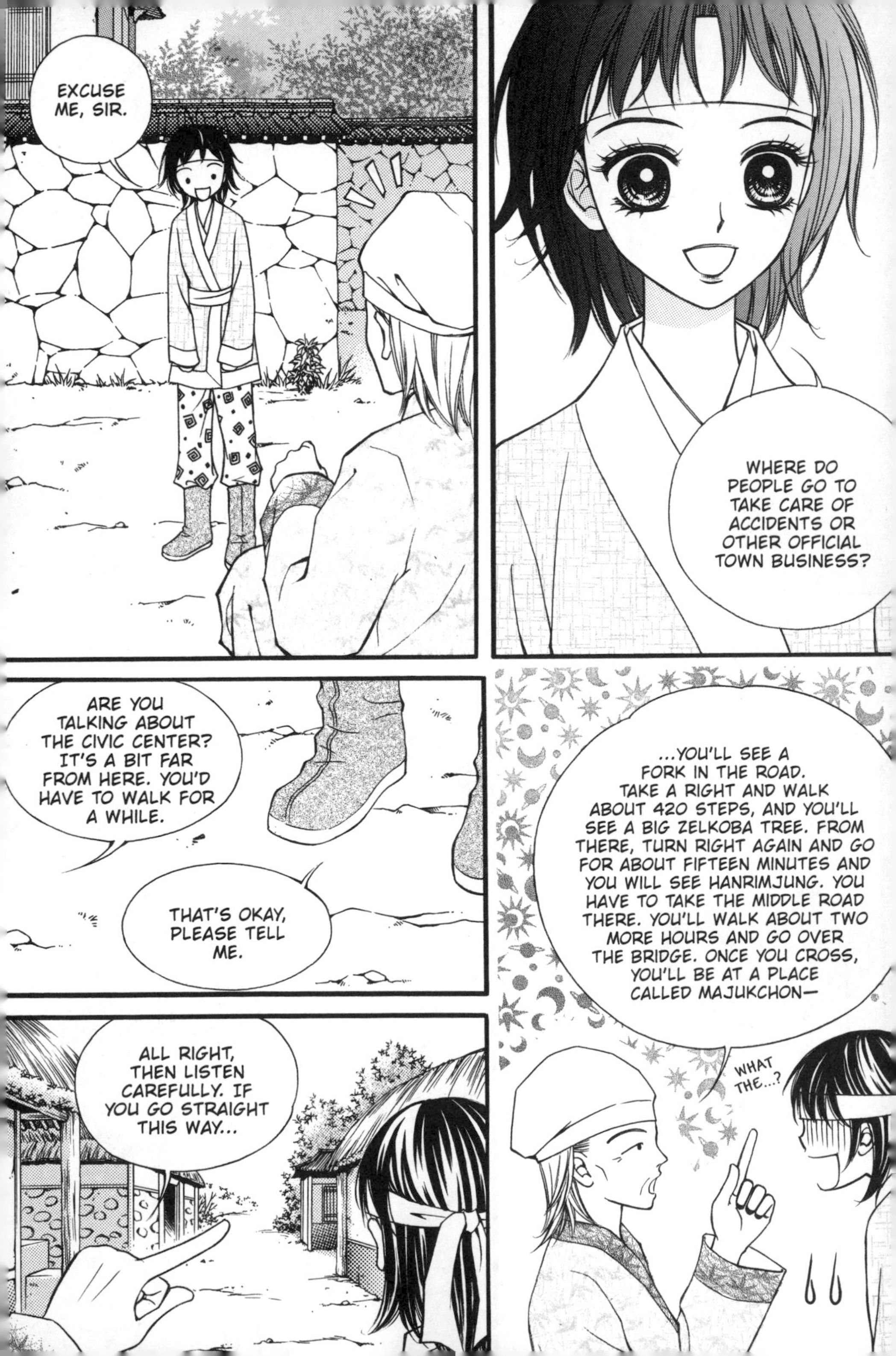
EXCUSE ME, SIR.
WHERE DO PEOPLE GO TO TAKE CARE OF ACCIDENTS OR OTHER OFFICIAL TOWN BUSINESS?
ARE YOU TALKING ABOUT THE CIVIC CENTER? IT'S A BIT FAR FROM HERE. YOU'D HAVE TO WALK FOR A WHILE.
THAT'S OKAY, PLEASE TELL ME.
...YOU'LL SEE A FORK IN THE ROAD. TAKE A RIGHT AND WALK ABOUT 420 STEPS, AND YOU'LL SEE A BIG ZELKOBA TREE. FROM THERE, TURN RIGHT AGAIN AND GO FOR ABOUT FIFTEEN MINUTES AND YOU WILL SEE HANRIMJUNG. YOU HAVE TO TAKE THE MIDDLE ROAD THERE. YOU'LL WALK ABOUT TWO MORE HOURS AND GO OVER THE BRIDGE. ONCE YOU CROSS, YOU'LL BE AT A PLACE CALLED MAJUKCHON—
ALL RIGHT, THEN LISTEN CAREFULLY. IF YOU GO STRAIGHT THIS WAY...
WHAT THE...?

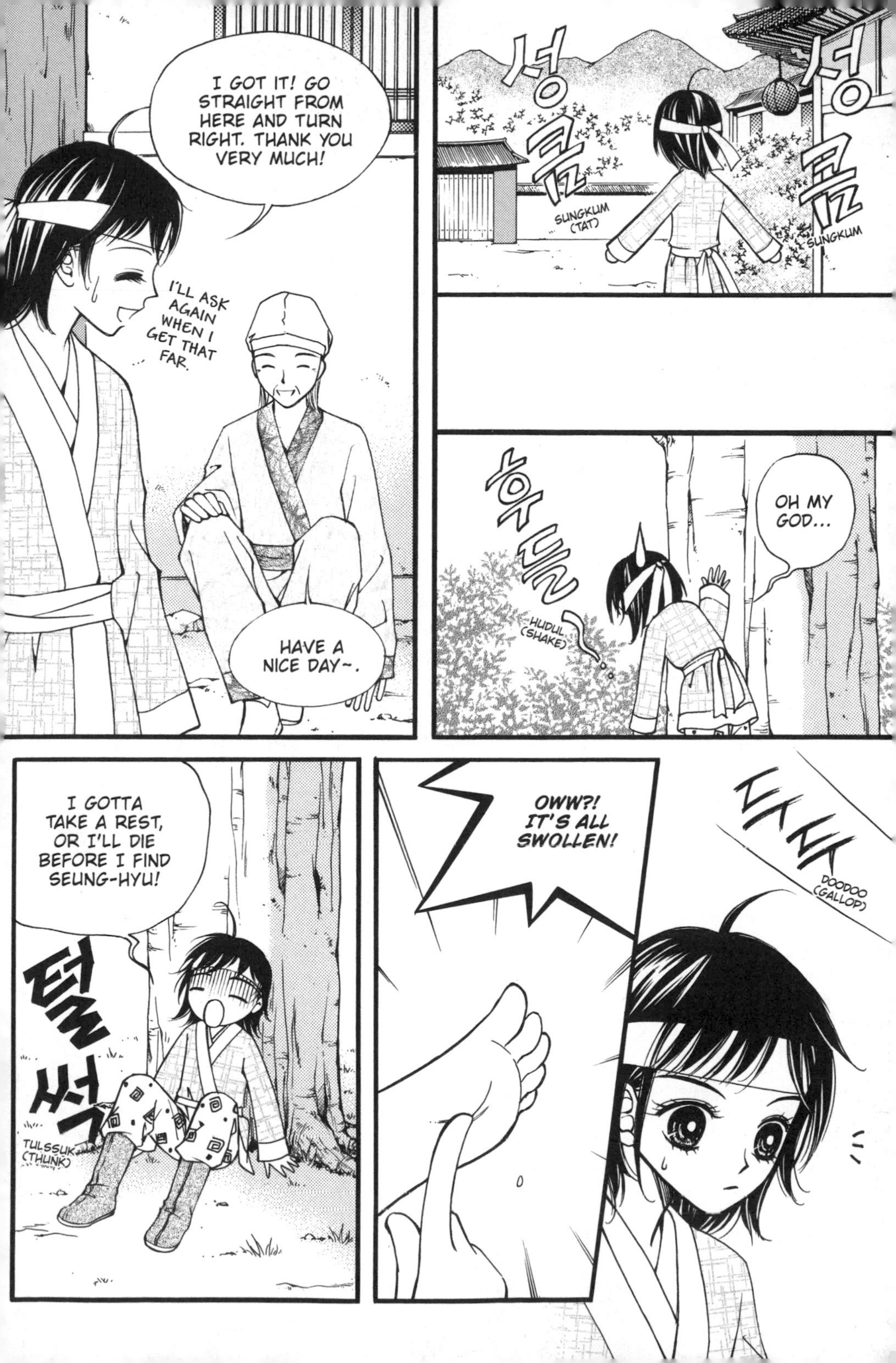
I GOT IT! GO STRAIGHT FROM HERE AND TURN RIGHT. THANK YOU VERY MUCH!
I'LL ASK AGAIN WHEN I GET THAT FAR.
HAVE A NICE DAY~.
성큼
SUNGKUM (TAT)
성큼
SUNGKUM
후들
HUDUL (SHAKE)
OH MY GOD...
I GOTTA TAKE A REST, OR I'LL DIE BEFORE I FIND SEUNG-HYU!
털썩
TULSSUK (THUNK)
OWW?! IT'S ALL SWOLLEN!
DOODOO (GALLOP)

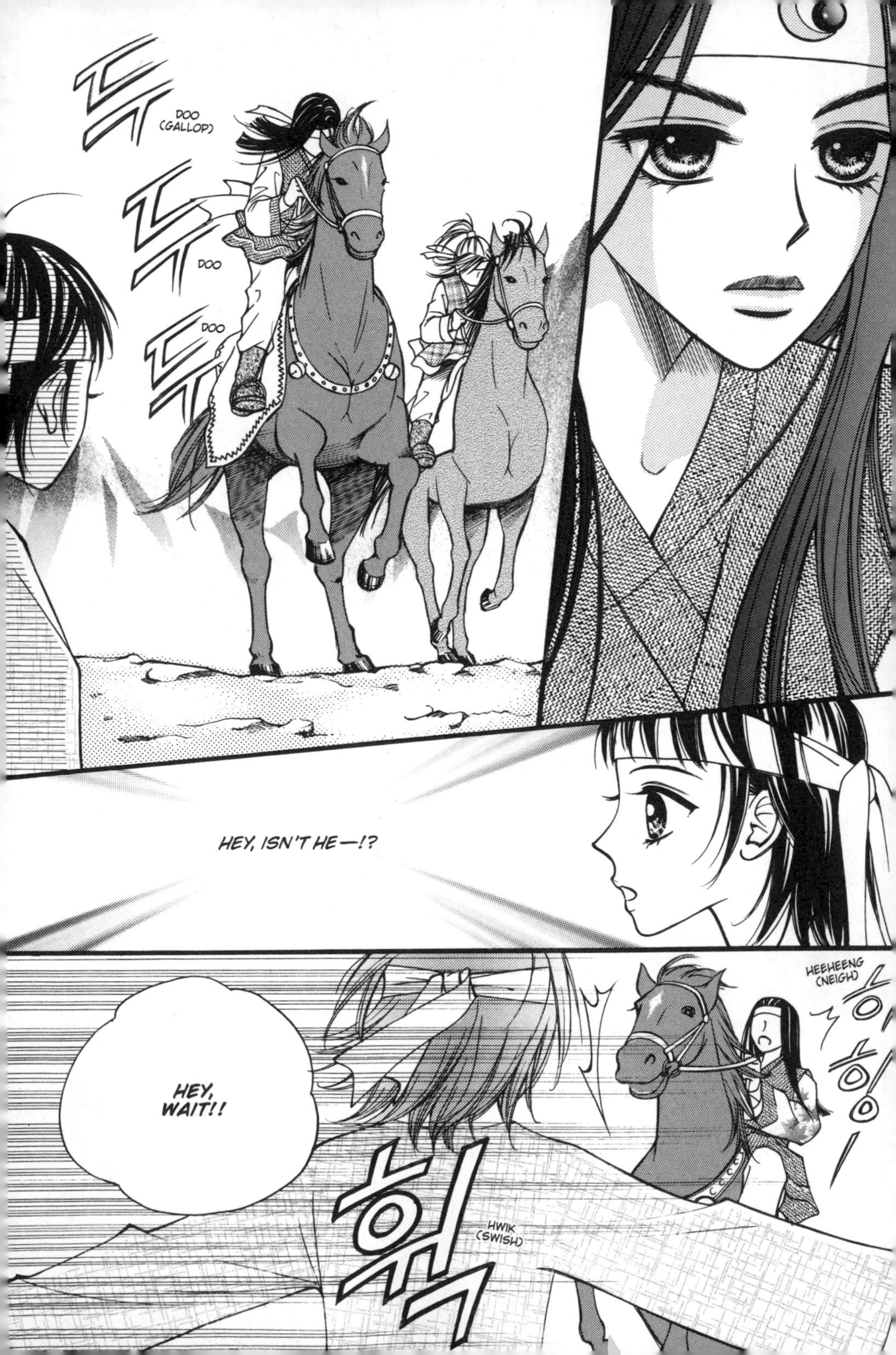
DOO (GALLOP)
DOO
DOO
HEY, ISN'T HE—!?
HEY, WAIT!!
HWIK (SWISH)
HEEHEENG (NEIGH)

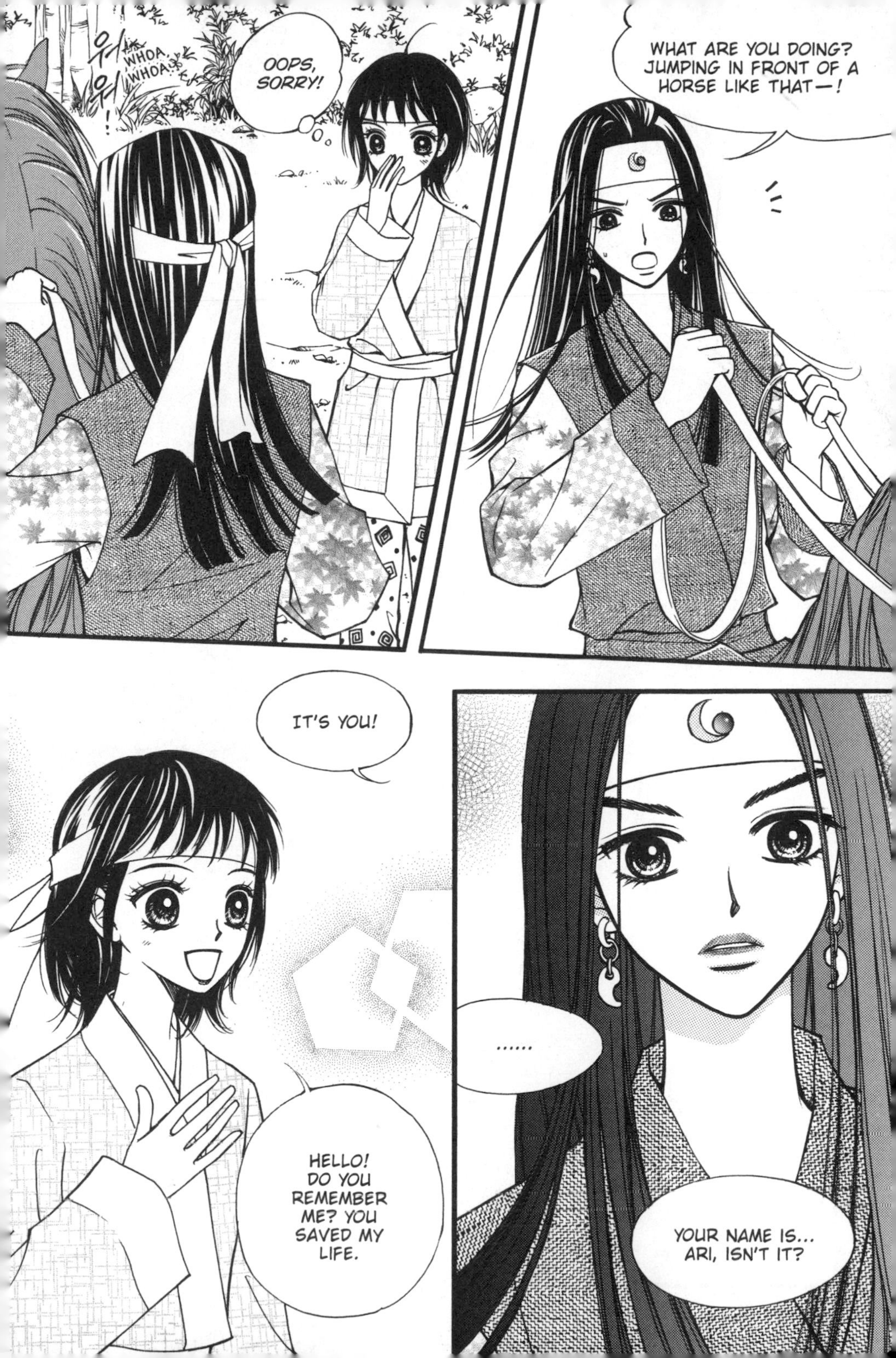

워 워!
WHOA, WHOA!
OOPS, SORRY!
WHAT ARE YOU DOING? JUMPING IN FRONT OF A HORSE LIKE THAT—!
IT'S YOU!
HELLO! DO YOU REMEMBER ME? YOU SAVED MY LIFE.
......
YOUR NAME IS... ARI, ISN'T IT?

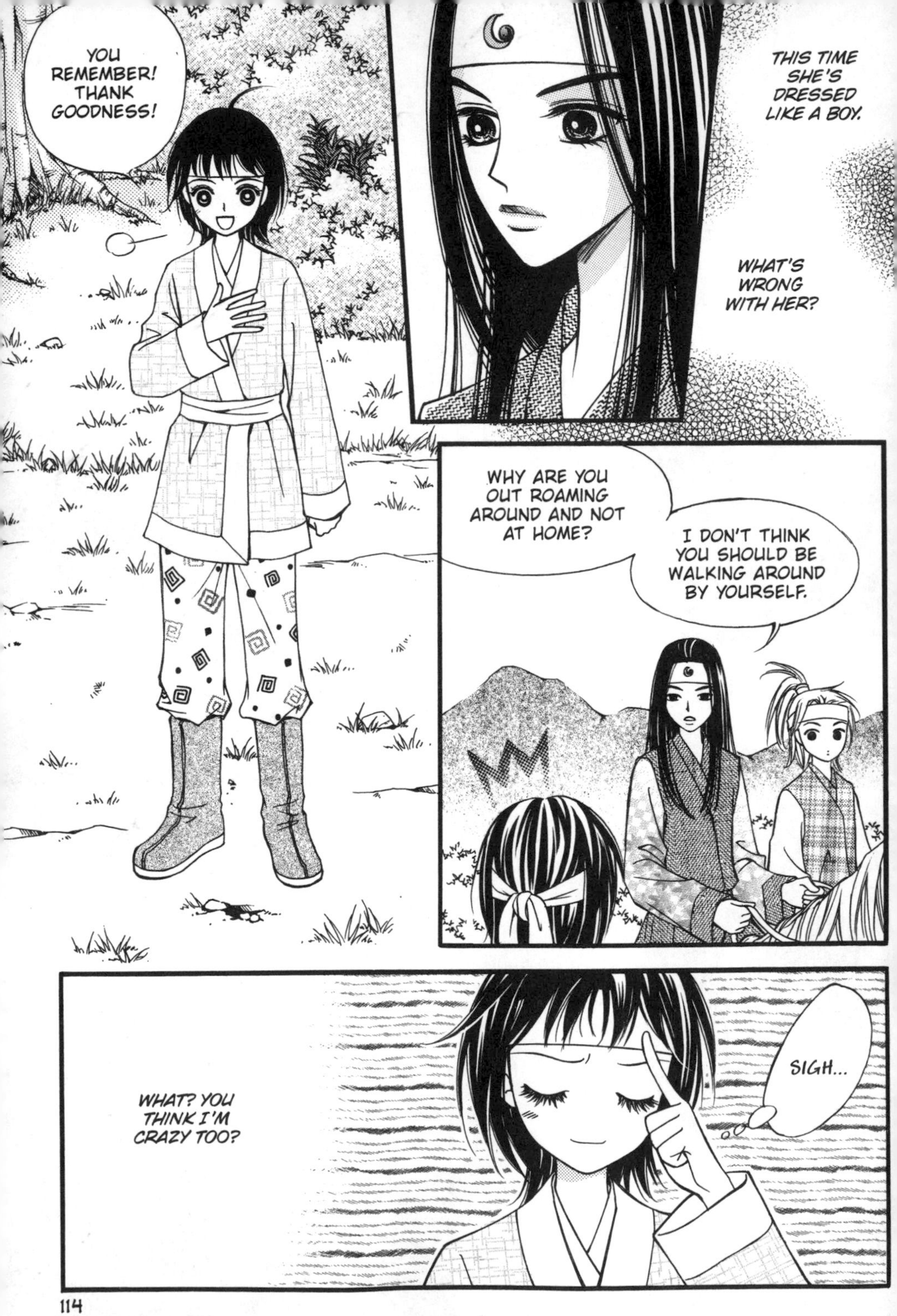
YOU REMEMBER! THANK GOODNESS!
THIS TIME SHE'S DRESSED LIKE A BOY.
WHAT'S WRONG WITH HER?
WHY ARE YOU OUT ROAMING AROUND AND NOT AT HOME?
I DON'T THINK YOU SHOULD BE WALKING AROUND BY YOURSELF.
WHAT? YOU THINK I'M CRAZY TOO?
SIGH...

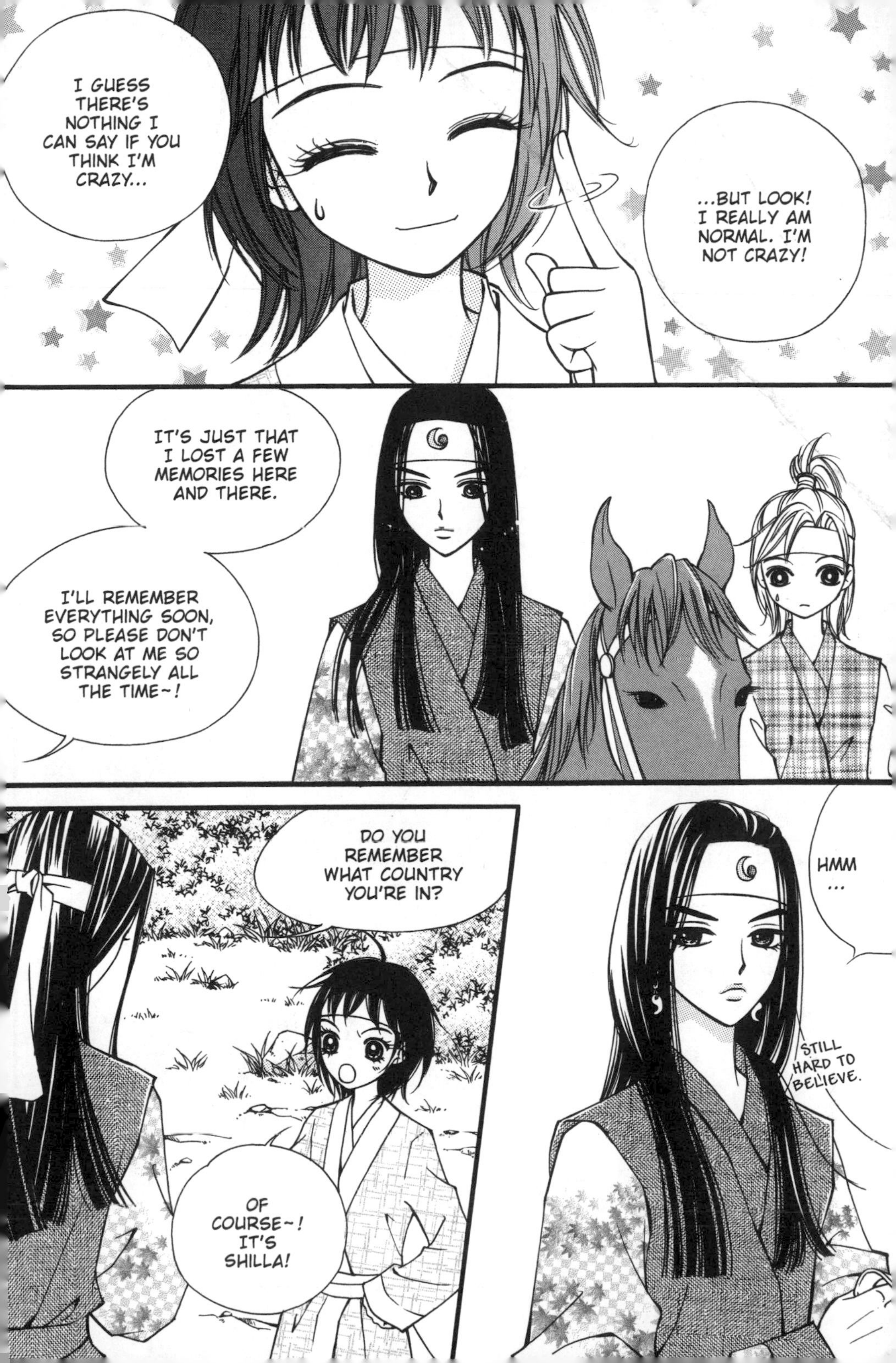
I GUESS THERE'S NOTHING I CAN SAY IF YOU THINK I'M CRAZY...
...BUT LOOK! I REALLY AM NORMAL. I'M NOT CRAZY!
IT'S JUST THAT I LOST A FEW MEMORIES HERE AND THERE.
I'LL REMEMBER EVERYTHING SOON, SO PLEASE DON'T LOOK AT ME SO STRANGELY ALL THE TIME~!
DO YOU REMEMBER WHAT COUNTRY YOU'RE IN?
OF COURSE~! IT'S SHILLA!
HMM ...
STILL HARD TO BELIEVE.

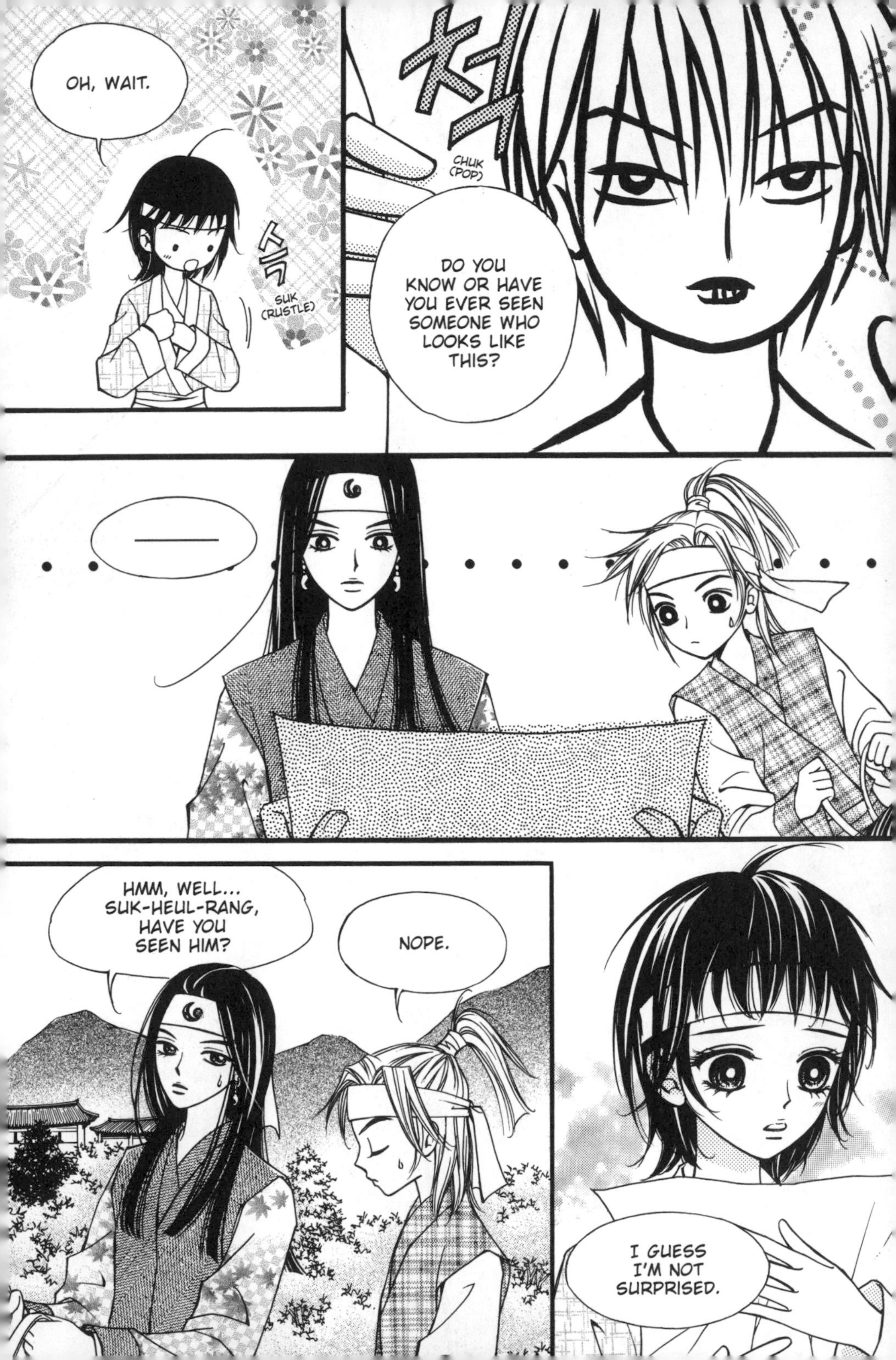
OH, WAIT.
SUK (RUSTLE)
CHUK (POP)
DO YOU KNOW OR HAVE YOU EVER SEEN SOMEONE WHO LOOKS LIKE THIS?
———
HMM, WELL... SUK-HEUL-RANG, HAVE YOU SEEN HIM?
NOPE.
I GUESS I'M NOT SURPRISED.

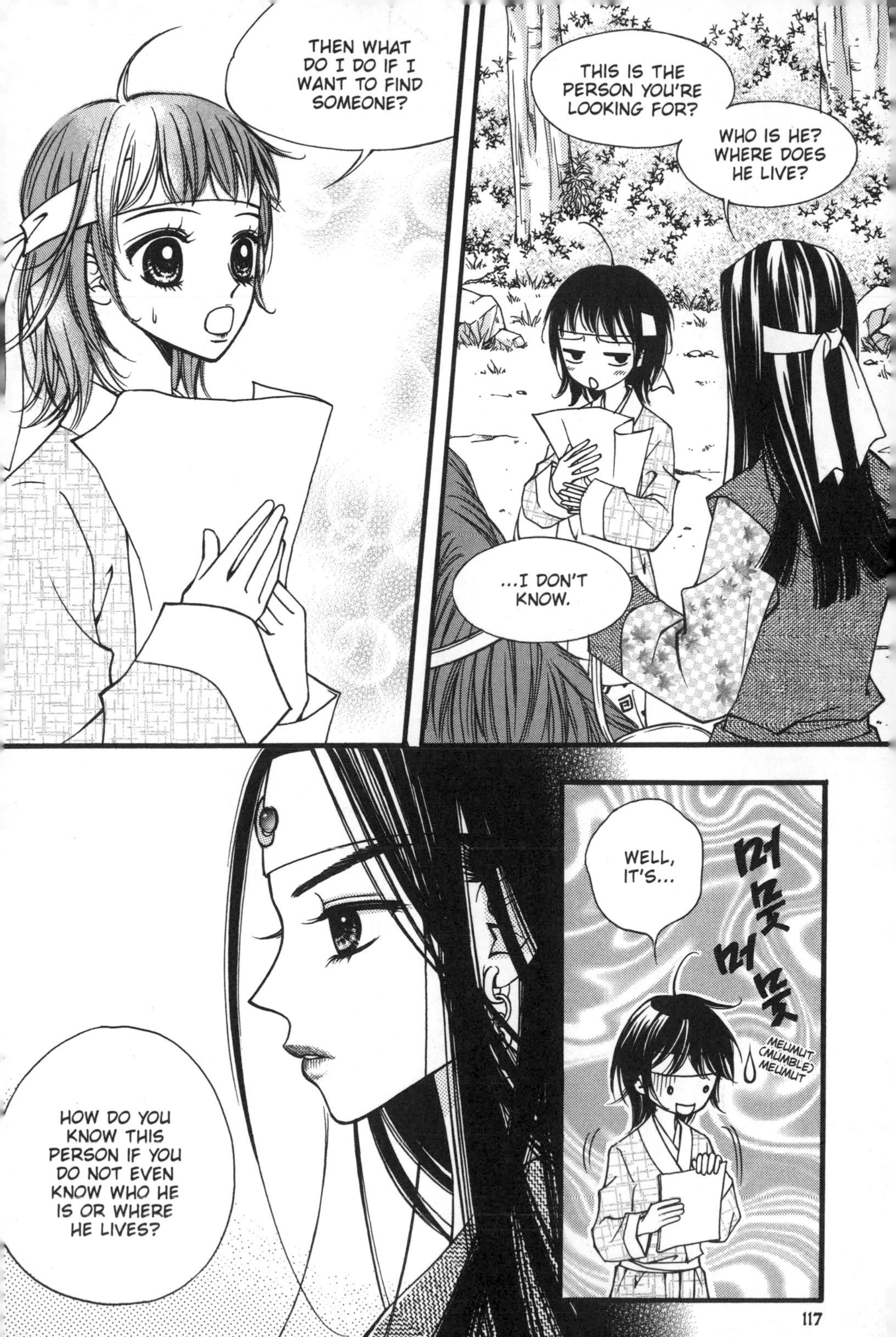
THEN WHAT DO I DO IF I WANT TO FIND SOMEONE?
THIS IS THE PERSON YOU'RE LOOKING FOR?
WHO IS HE? WHERE DOES HE LIVE?
...I DON'T KNOW.
HOW DO YOU KNOW THIS PERSON IF YOU DO NOT EVEN KNOW WHO HE IS OR WHERE HE LIVES?
WELL, IT'S...
머뭇 머뭇
MEUMUT (MUMBLE) MEUMUT

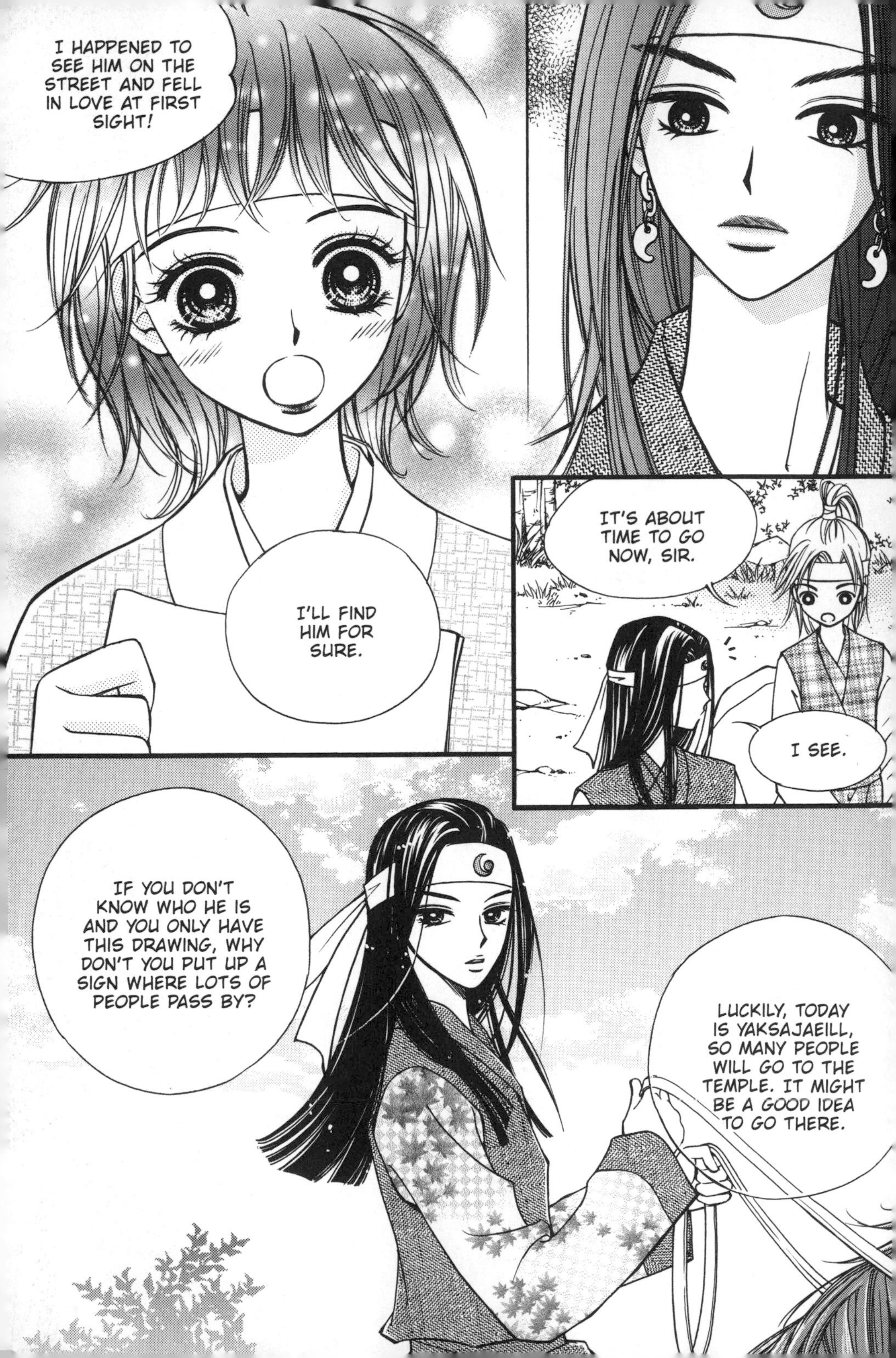
I HAPPENED TO SEE HIM ON THE STREET AND FELL IN LOVE AT FIRST SIGHT!
I'LL FIND HIM FOR SURE.
IT'S ABOUT TIME TO GO NOW, SIR.
I SEE.
IF YOU DON'T KNOW WHO HE IS AND YOU ONLY HAVE THIS DRAWING, WHY DON'T YOU PUT UP A SIGN WHERE LOTS OF PEOPLE PASS BY?
LUCKILY, TODAY IS YAKSAJAEILL, SO MANY PEOPLE WILL GO TO THE TEMPLE. IT MIGHT BE A GOOD IDEA TO GO THERE.

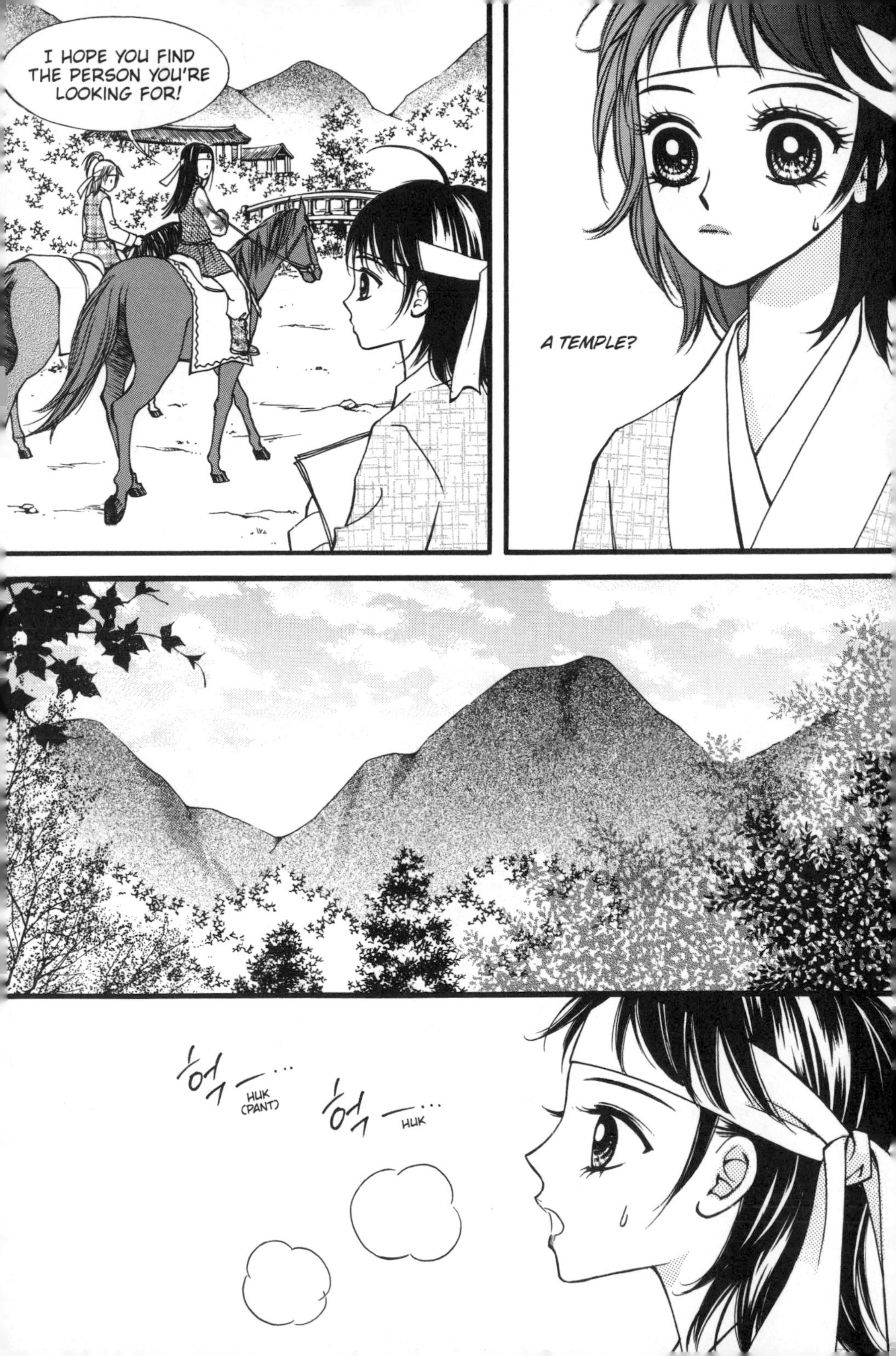
I HOPE YOU FIND THE PERSON YOU'RE LOOKING FOR!
A TEMPLE?
헉—...
HUK (PANT)
헉—...
HUK

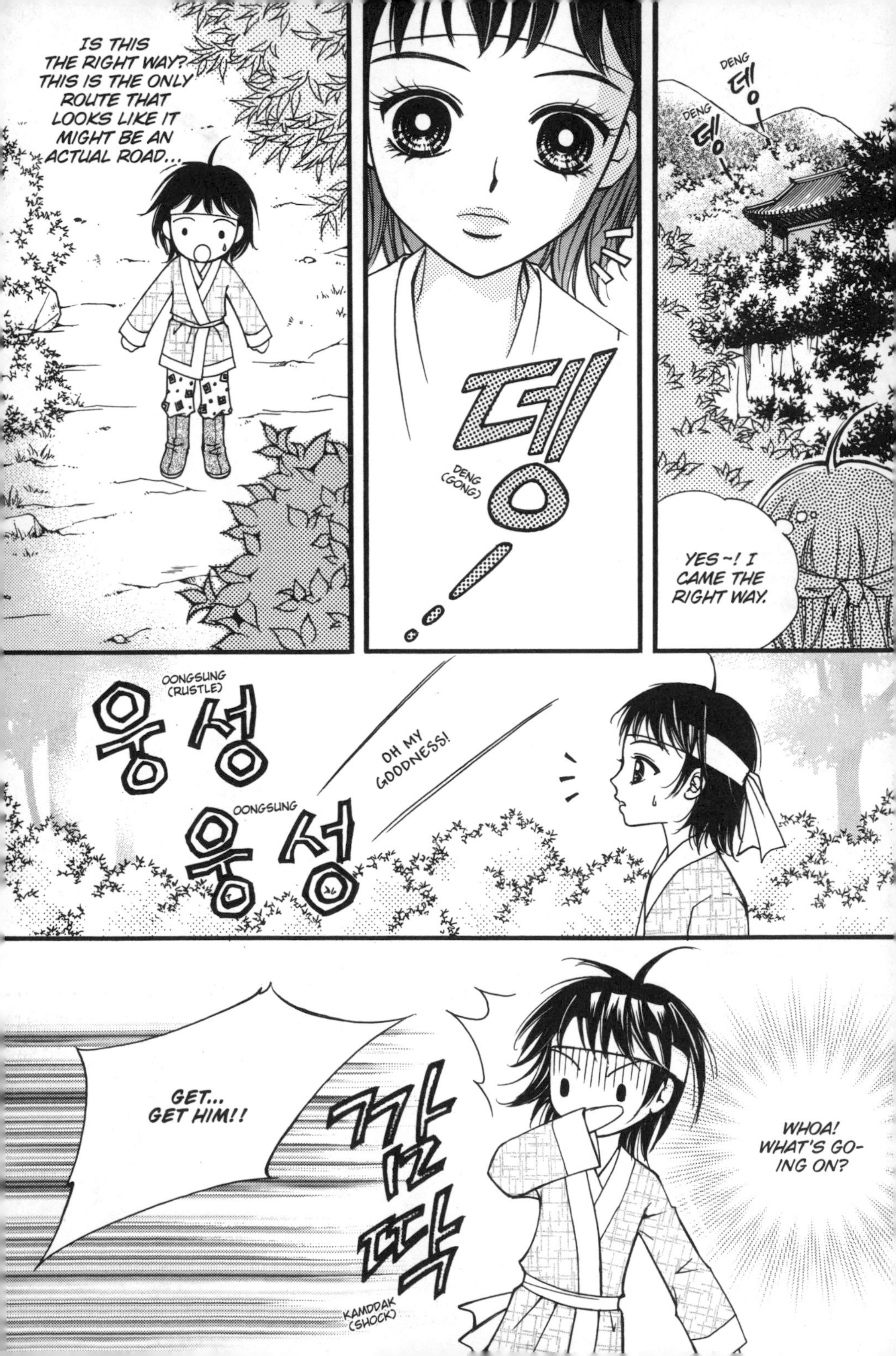
IS THIS THE RIGHT WAY? THIS IS THE ONLY ROUTE THAT LOOKS LIKE IT MIGHT BE AN ACTUAL ROAD...
뎅
DENG (GONG)
DENG 뎅
DENG 뎅
YES~! I CAME THE RIGHT WAY.
OONGSUNG (RUSTLE) 웅성
OONGSUNG 웅성
OH MY GOODNESS!
GET... GET HIM!!
깜딱
KAMDDAK (SHOCK)
WHOA! WHAT'S GO-ING ON?

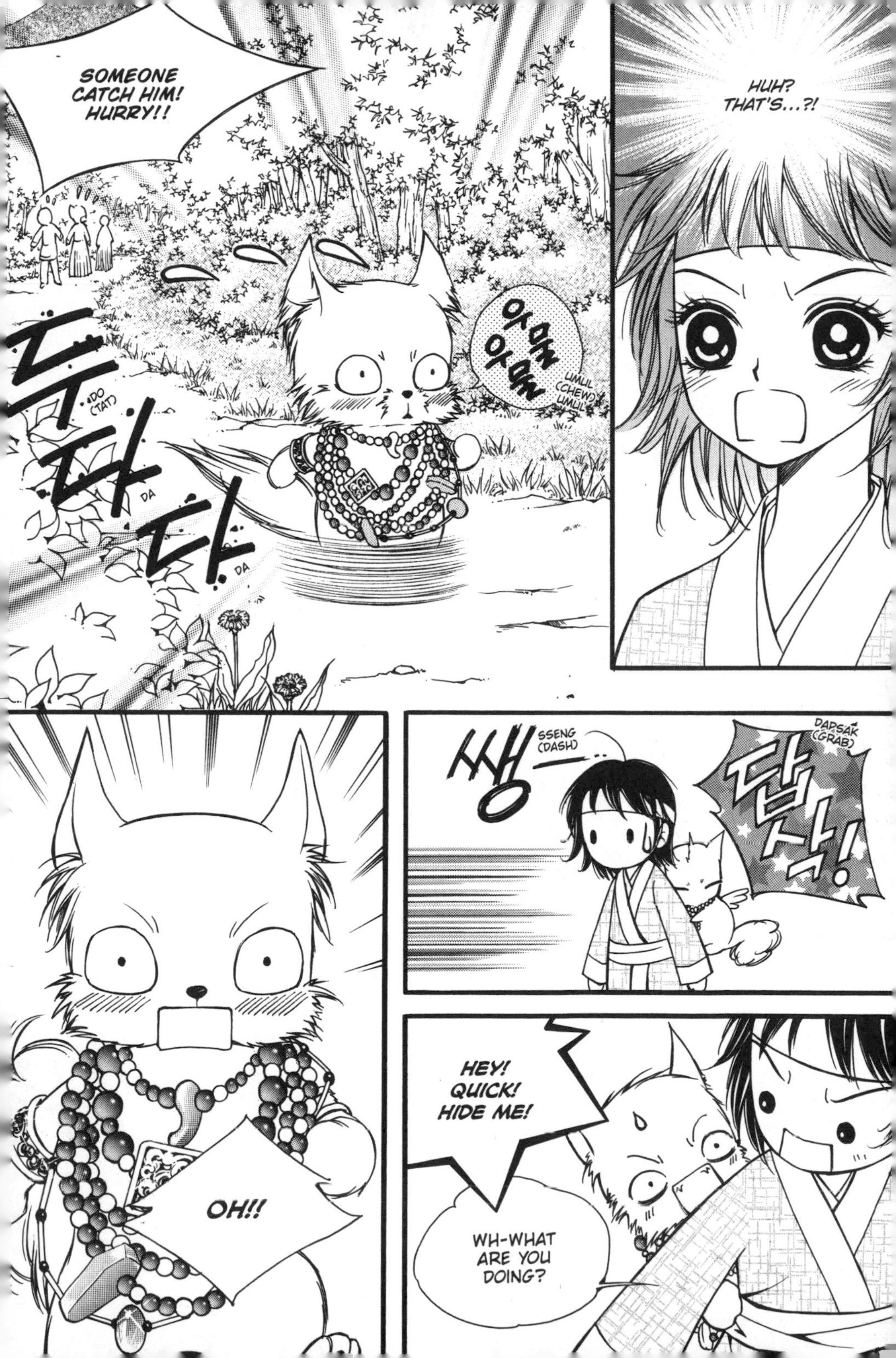
SOMEONE CATCH HIM! HURRY!!
두다다
DO (TAT) DA DA
우물우물
UMUL (CHEW) UMUL
HUH? THAT'S...?!
OH!!
쌩—
SSENG (DASH)
답삭!
DAPSAK (GRAB)
HEY! QUICK! HIDE ME!
WH-WHAT ARE YOU DOING?

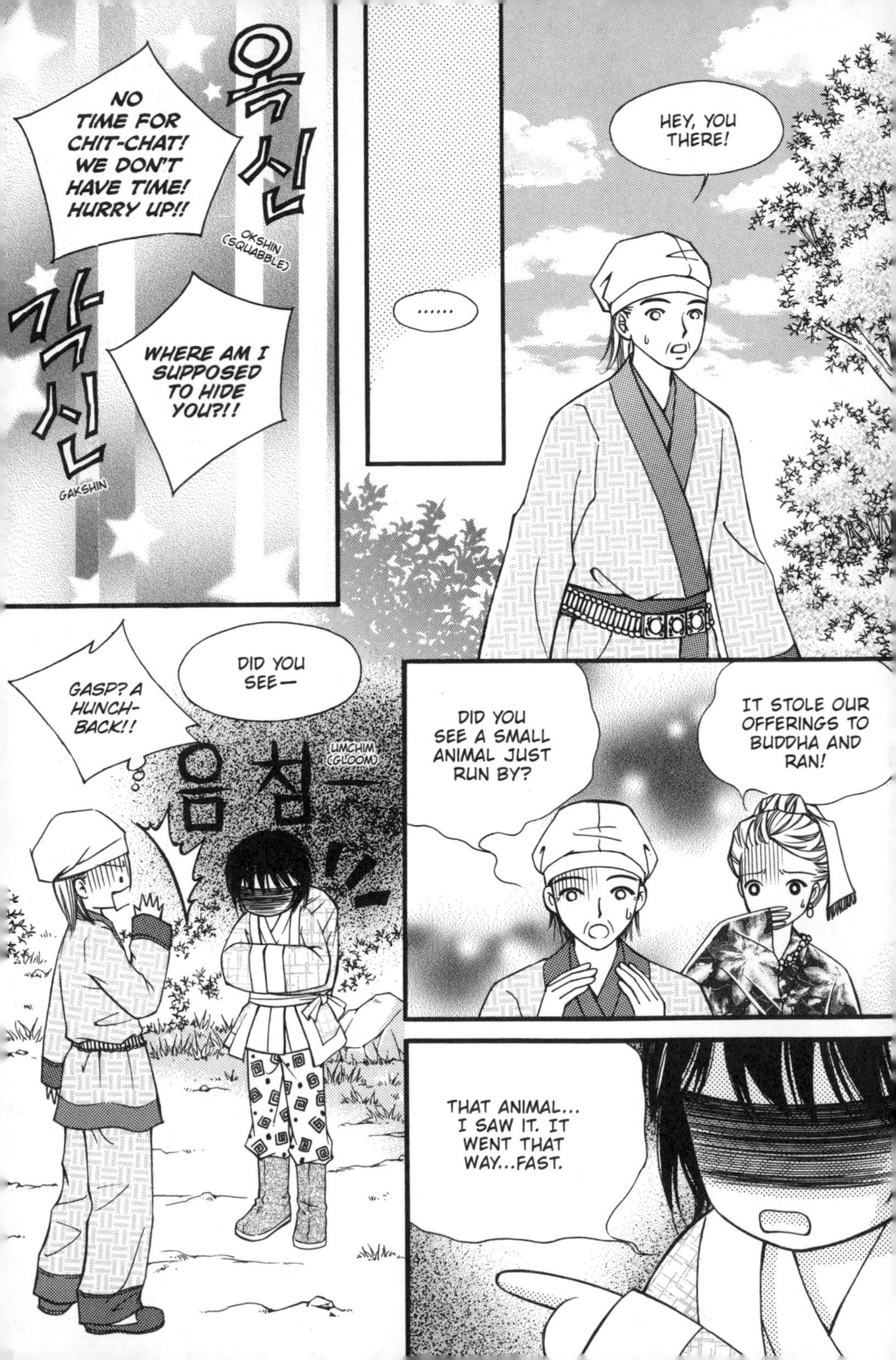

NO TIME FOR CHIT-CHAT! WE DON'T HAVE TIME! HURRY UP!!
옥신
OKSHIN (SQUABBLE)
WHERE AM I SUPPOSED TO HIDE YOU?!!
각신
GAKSHIN
......
HEY, YOU THERE!
GASP? A HUNCH-BACK!!
DID YOU SEE—
음침
UMCHIM (GLOOM)
DID YOU SEE A SMALL ANIMAL JUST RUN BY?
IT STOLE OUR OFFERINGS TO BUDDHA AND RAN!
THAT ANIMAL... I SAW IT. IT WENT THAT WAY...FAST.

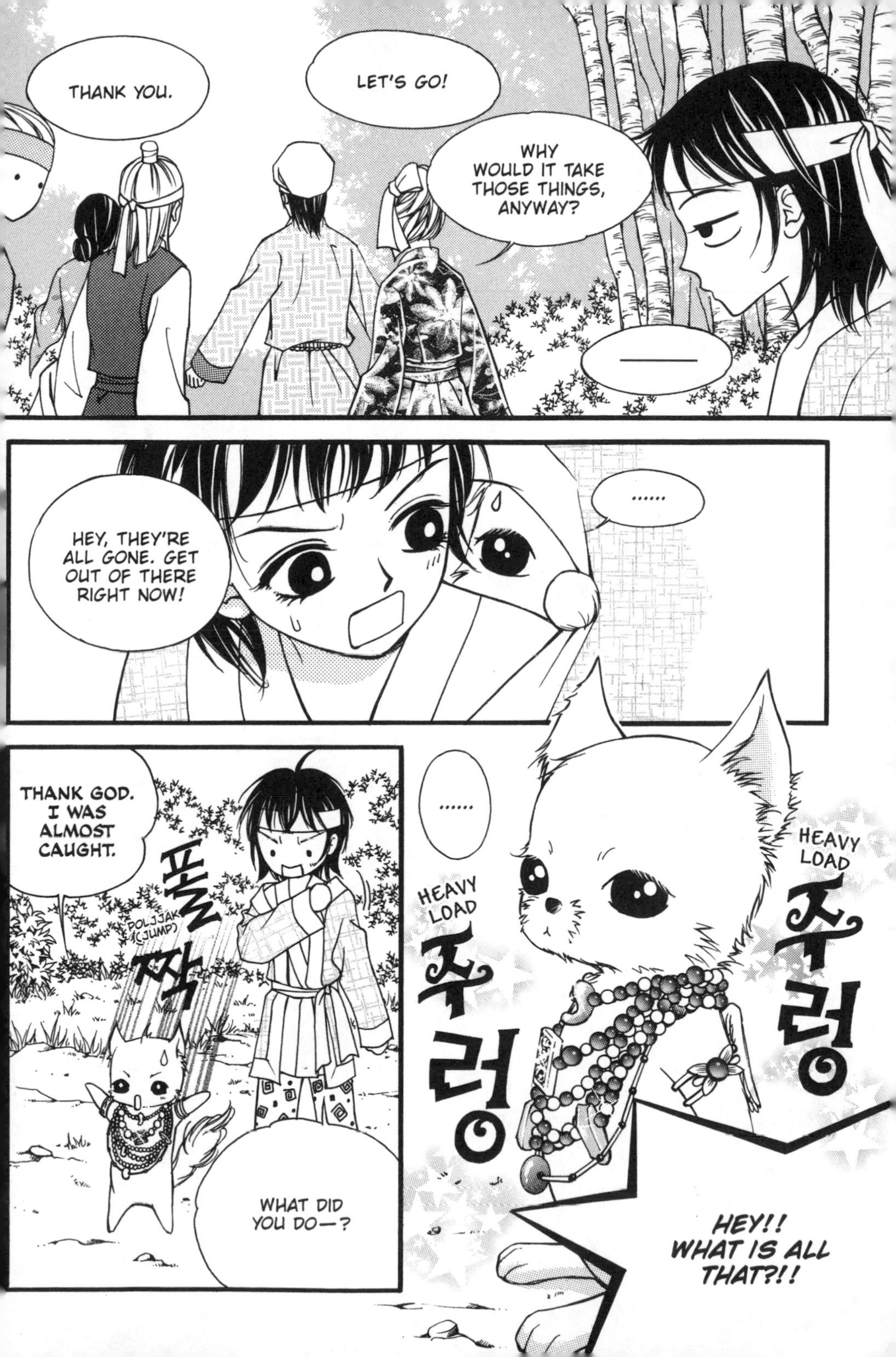
THANK YOU.
LET'S GO!
WHY WOULD IT TAKE THOSE THINGS, ANYWAY?
———
HEY, THEY'RE ALL GONE. GET OUT OF THERE RIGHT NOW!
......
THANK GOD. I WAS ALMOST CAUGHT.
폴짝
POLJJAK (JUMP)
WHAT DID YOU DO—?
......
HEAVY LOAD
주렁
HEAVY LOAD
주렁
HEY!! WHAT IS ALL THAT?!!

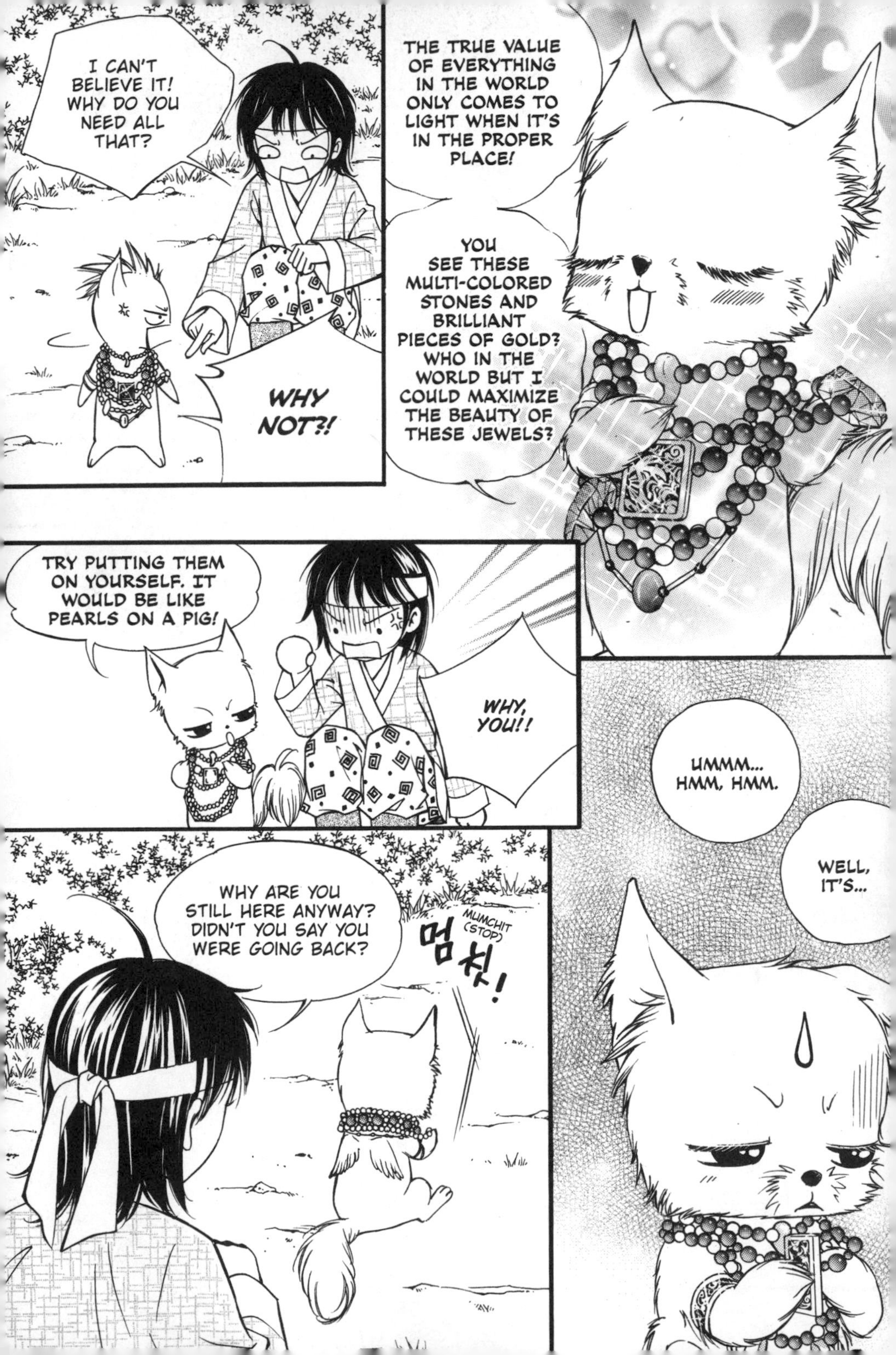

I CAN'T BELIEVE IT! WHY DO YOU NEED ALL THAT?
WHY NOT?!
THE TRUE VALUE OF EVERYTHING IN THE WORLD ONLY COMES TO LIGHT WHEN IT'S IN THE PROPER PLACE!
YOU SEE THESE MULTI-COLORED STONES AND BRILLIANT PIECES OF GOLD? WHO IN THE WORLD BUT I COULD MAXIMIZE THE BEAUTY OF THESE JEWELS?
TRY PUTTING THEM ON YOURSELF. IT WOULD BE LIKE PEARLS ON A PIG!
WHY, YOU!!
WHY ARE YOU STILL HERE ANYWAY? DIDN'T YOU SAY YOU WERE GOING BACK?
멈칫!
MUMCHIT (STOP)
UMMM... HMM, HMM.
WELL, IT'S...

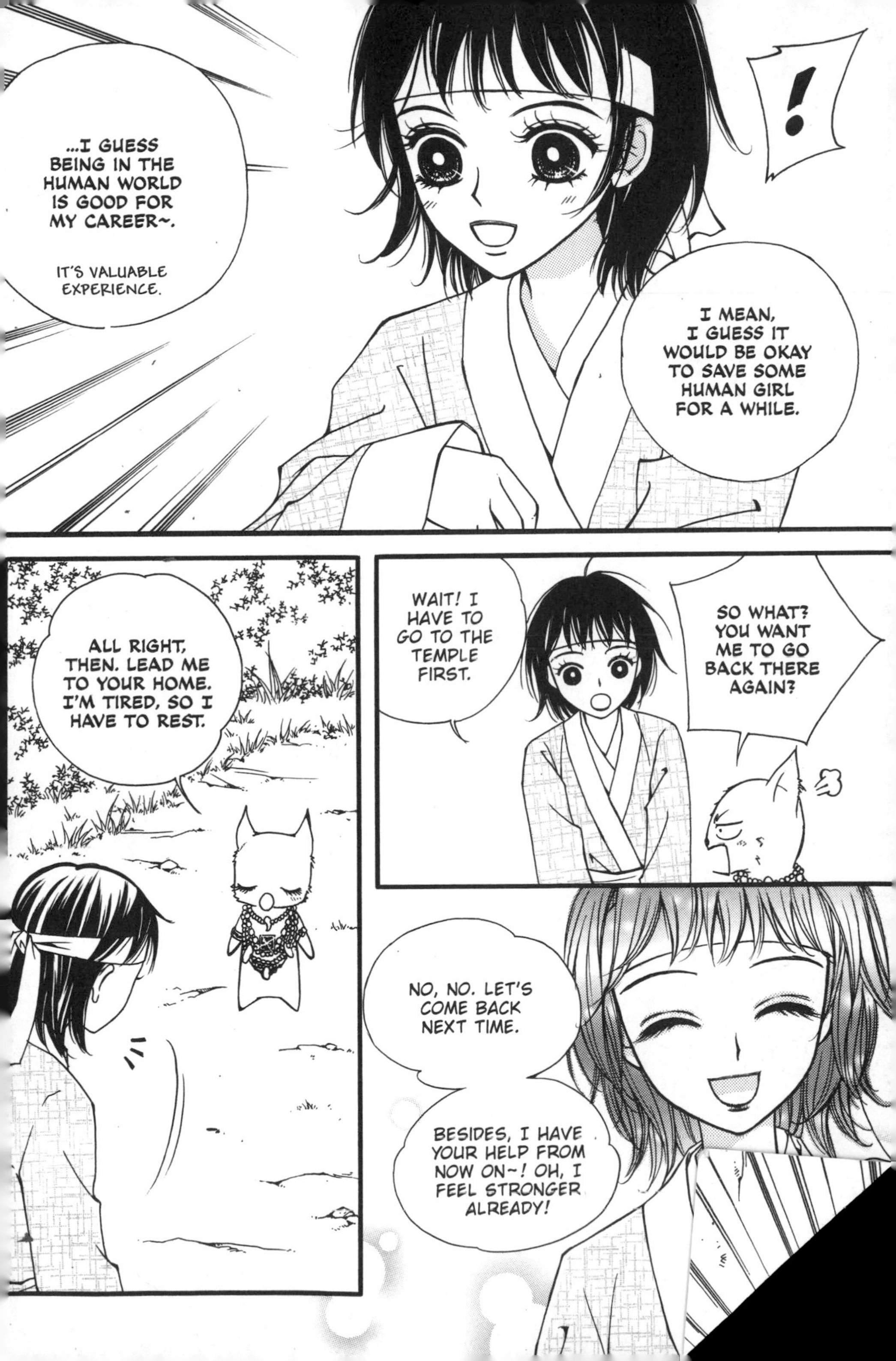
...I GUESS BEING IN THE HUMAN WORLD IS GOOD FOR MY CAREER~.
IT'S VALUABLE EXPERIENCE.
!
I MEAN, I GUESS IT WOULD BE OKAY TO SAVE SOME HUMAN GIRL FOR A WHILE.
ALL RIGHT, THEN. LEAD ME TO YOUR HOME. I'M TIRED, SO I HAVE TO REST.
WAIT! I HAVE TO GO TO THE TEMPLE FIRST.
SO WHAT? YOU WANT ME TO GO BACK THERE AGAIN?
NO, NO. LET'S COME BACK NEXT TIME.
BESIDES, I HAVE YOUR HELP FROM NOW ON~! OH, I FEEL STRONGER ALREADY!

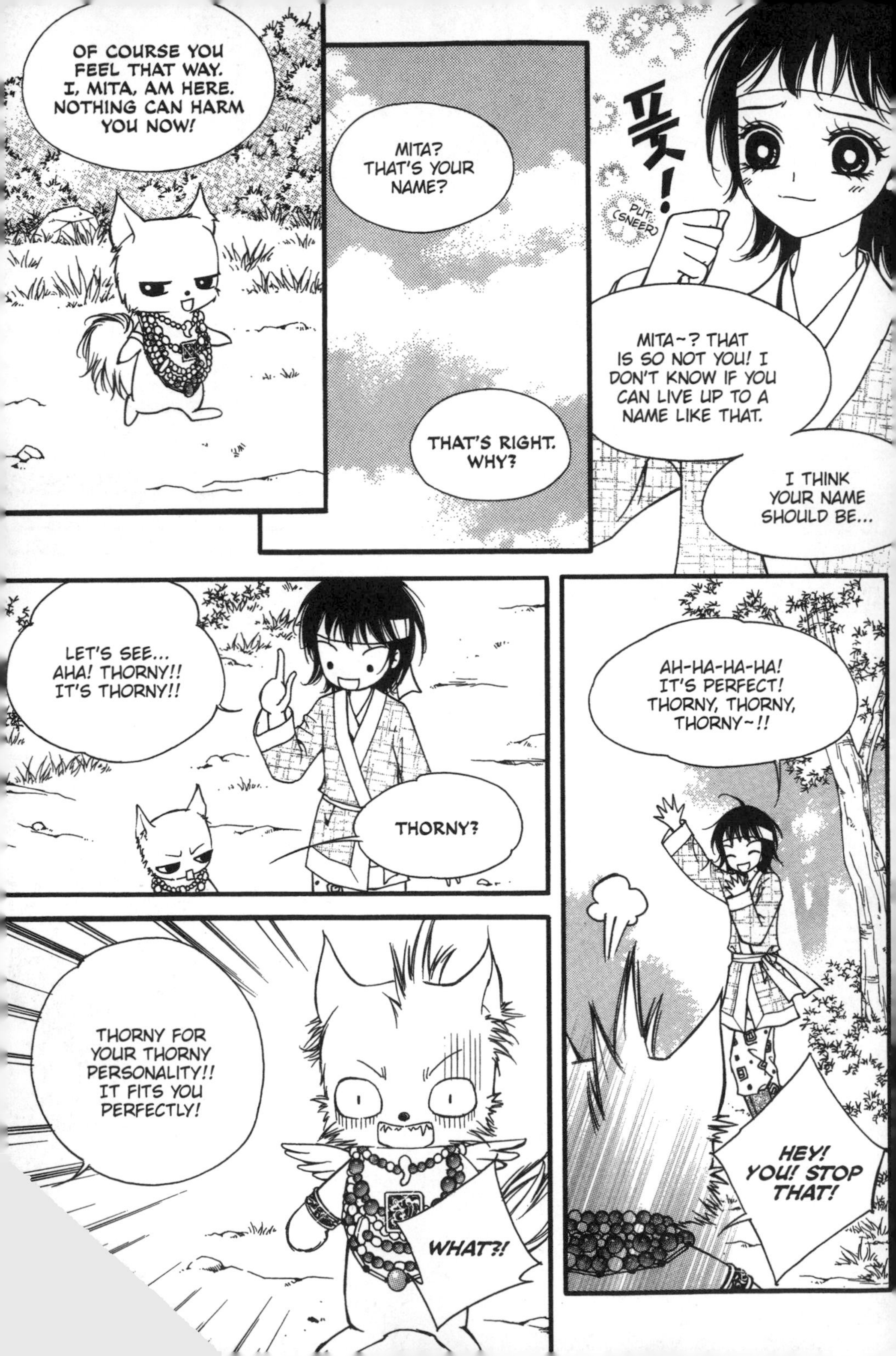

OF COURSE YOU FEEL THAT WAY. I, MITA, AM HERE. NOTHING CAN HARM YOU NOW!
MITA? THAT'S YOUR NAME?
THAT'S RIGHT. WHY?
풋!
PUT (SNEER)
MITA~? THAT IS SO NOT YOU! I DON'T KNOW IF YOU CAN LIVE UP TO A NAME LIKE THAT.
I THINK YOUR NAME SHOULD BE...
LET'S SEE... AHA! THORNY!! IT'S THORNY!!
THORNY?
THORNY FOR YOUR THORNY PERSONALITY!! IT FITS YOU PERFECTLY!
WHAT?!
AH-HA-HA-HA! IT'S PERFECT! THORNY, THORNY, THORNY~!!
HEY! YOU! STOP THAT!

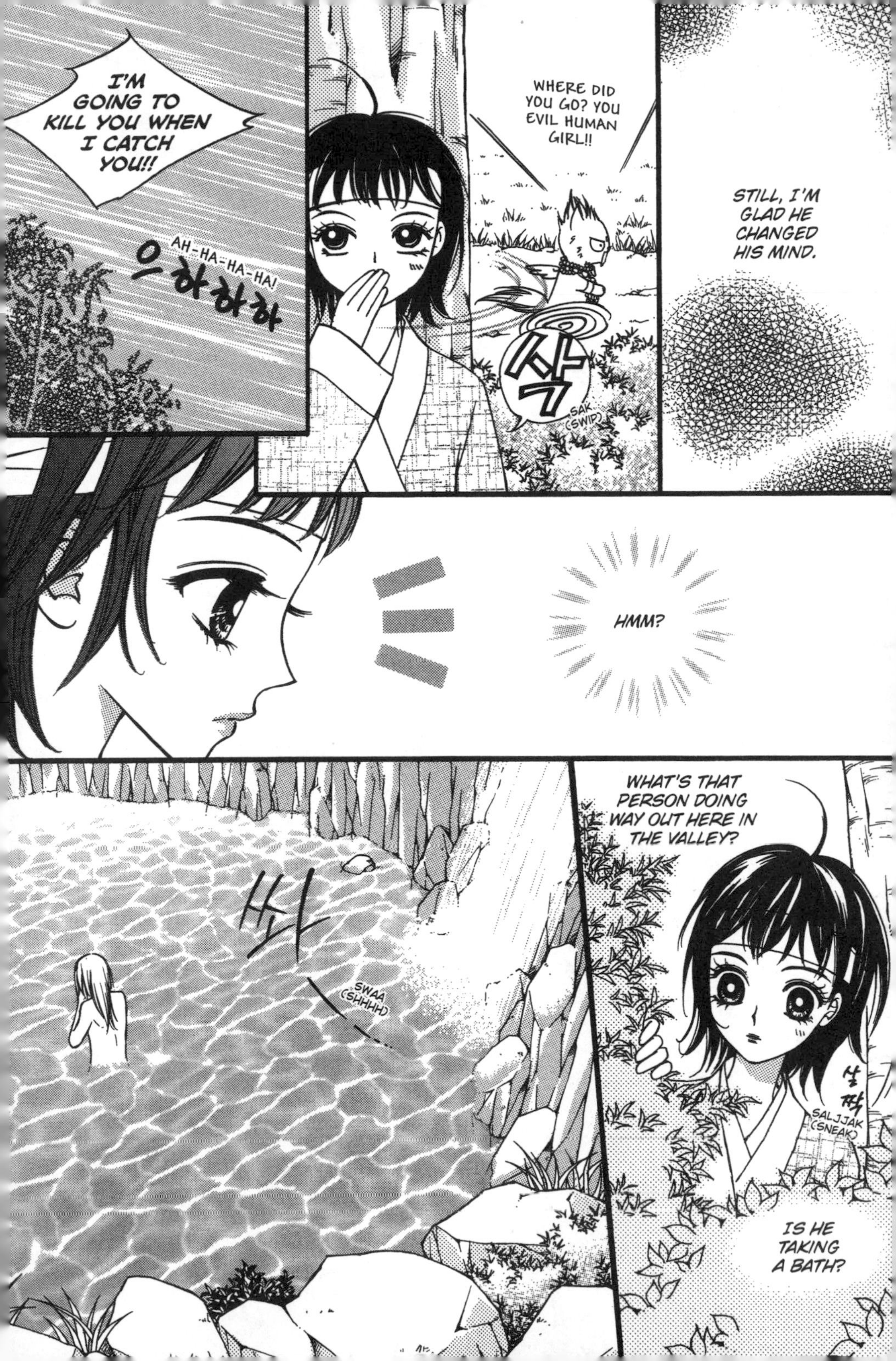
I'M GOING TO KILL YOU WHEN I CATCH YOU!!
으하하하
AH-HA-HA-HA!
WHERE DID YOU GO? YOU EVIL HUMAN GIRL!!
삭
SAK (SWIP)
STILL, I'M GLAD HE CHANGED HIS MIND.
HMM?
쏴
SWAA (SHHHH)
WHAT'S THAT PERSON DOING WAY OUT HERE IN THE VALLEY?
살짝
SALJJAK (SNEAK)
IS HE TAKING A BATH?

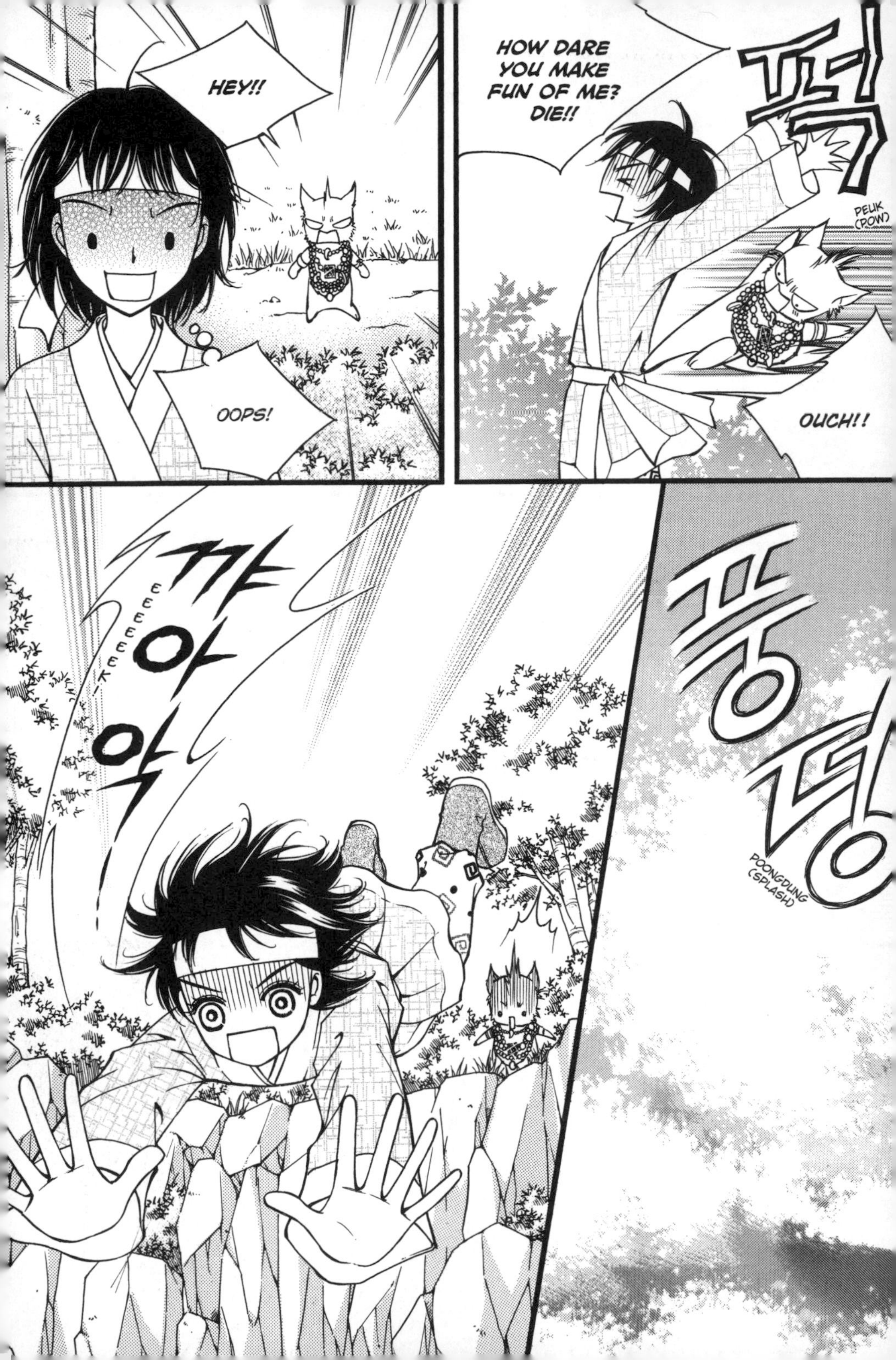
HEY!!
OOPS!
HOW DARE YOU MAKE FUN OF ME? DIE!!
퍽
PEUK (POW)
OUCH!!
까아악
EEEEEEK!
풍덩
POONGDUNG (SPLASH)

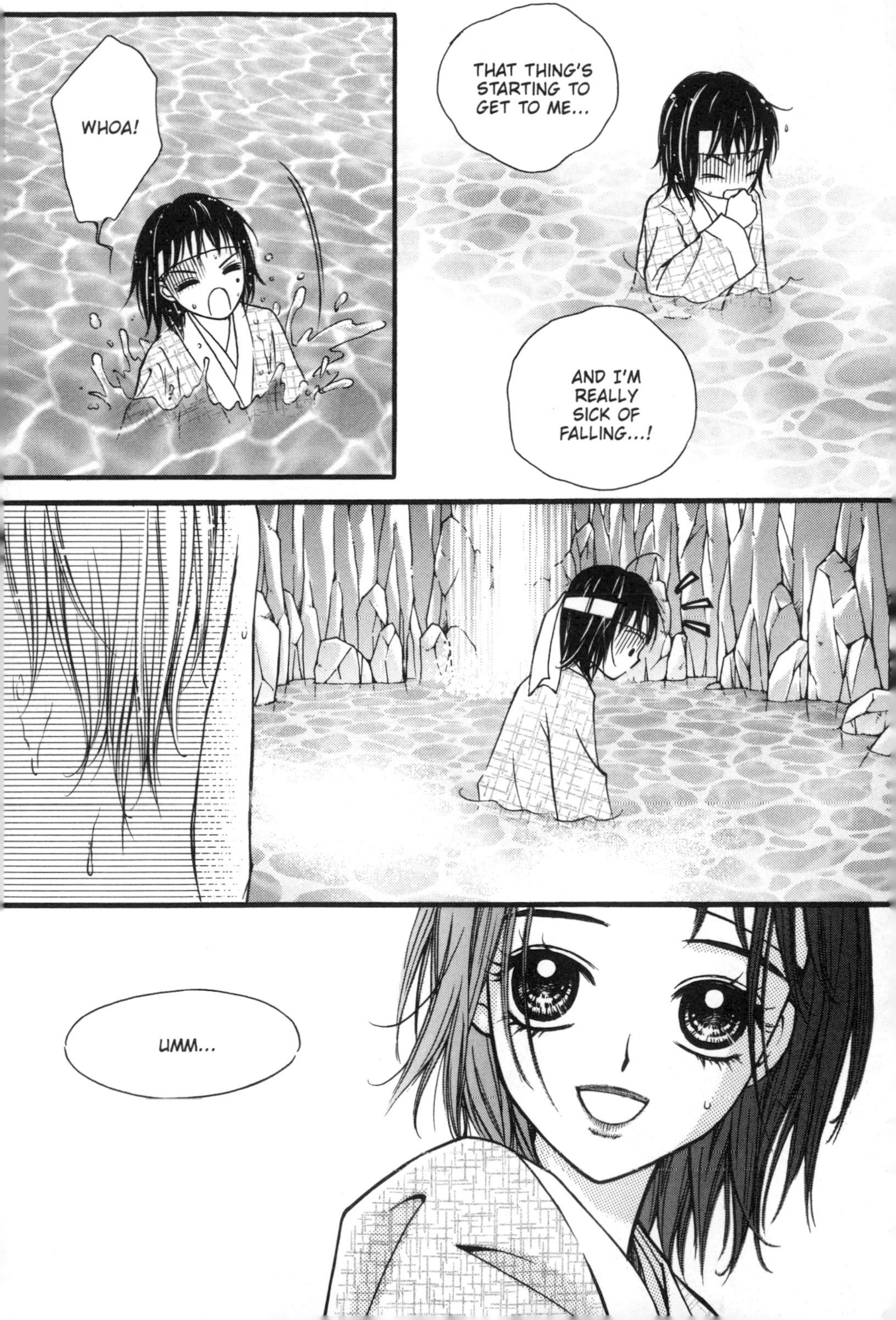
WHOA!
THAT THING'S STARTING TO GET TO ME...
AND I'M REALLY SICK OF FALLING...!
UMM...

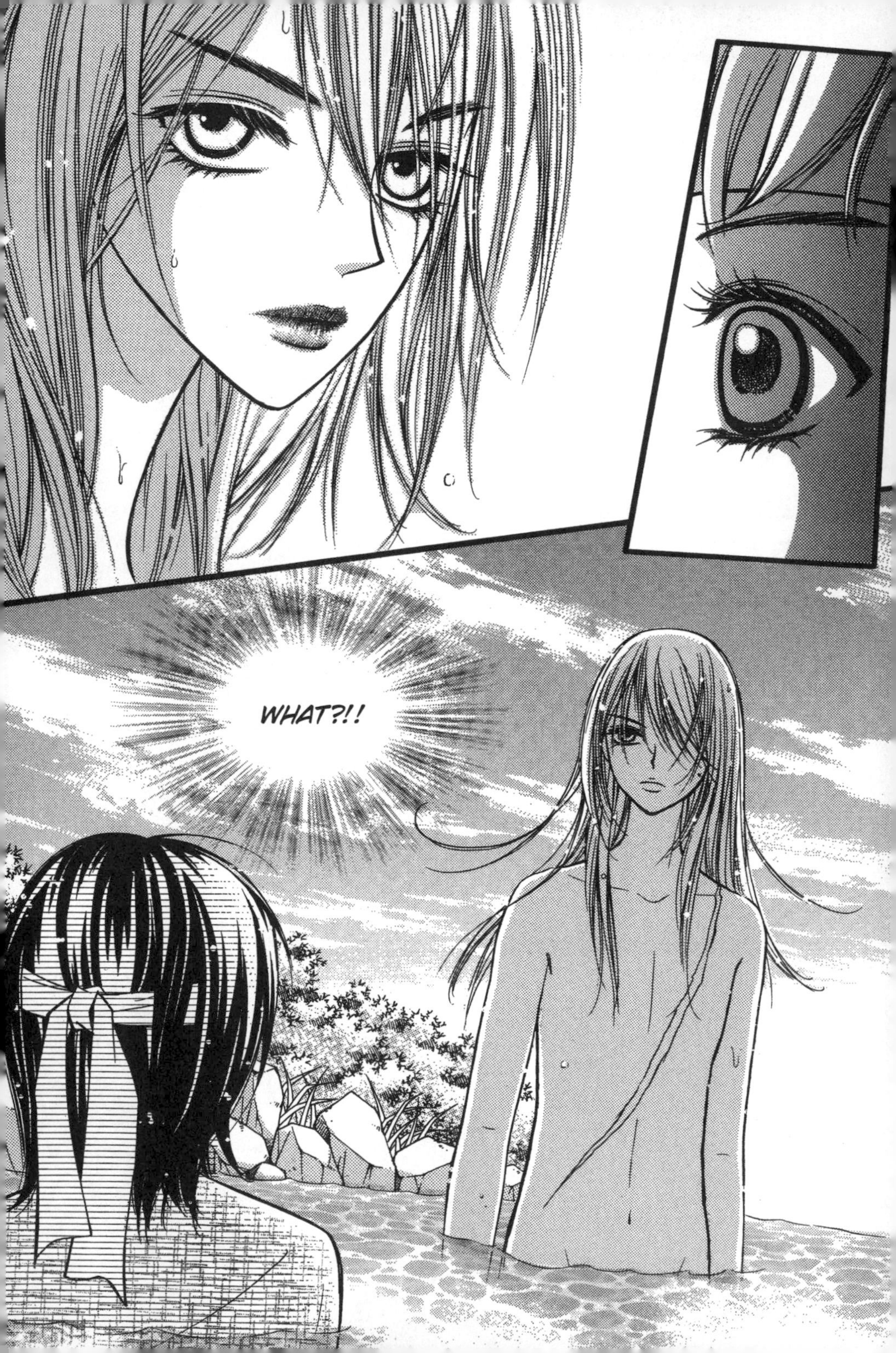
WHAT?!!

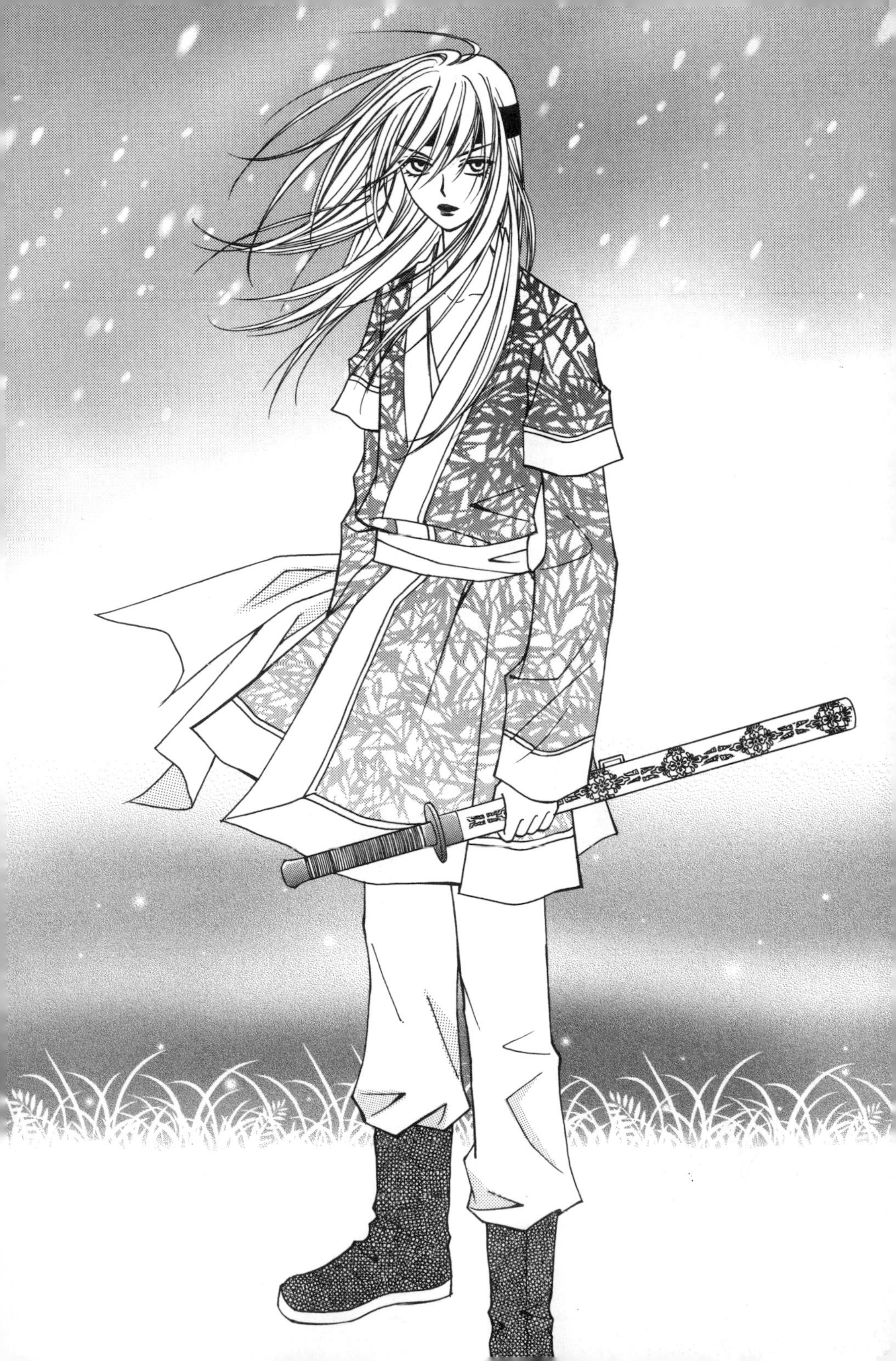

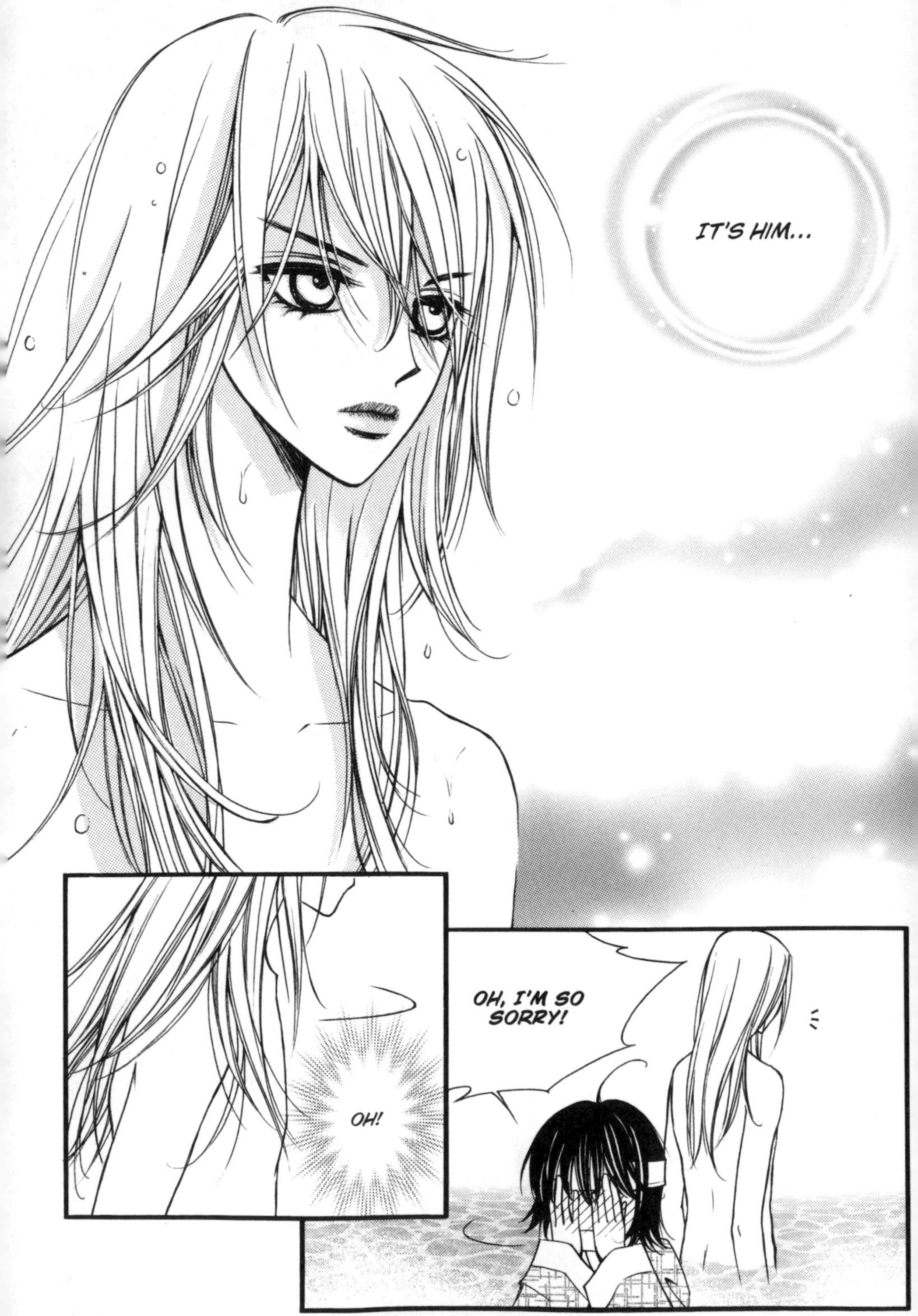
IT'S HIM...
OH!
OH, I'M SO SORRY!

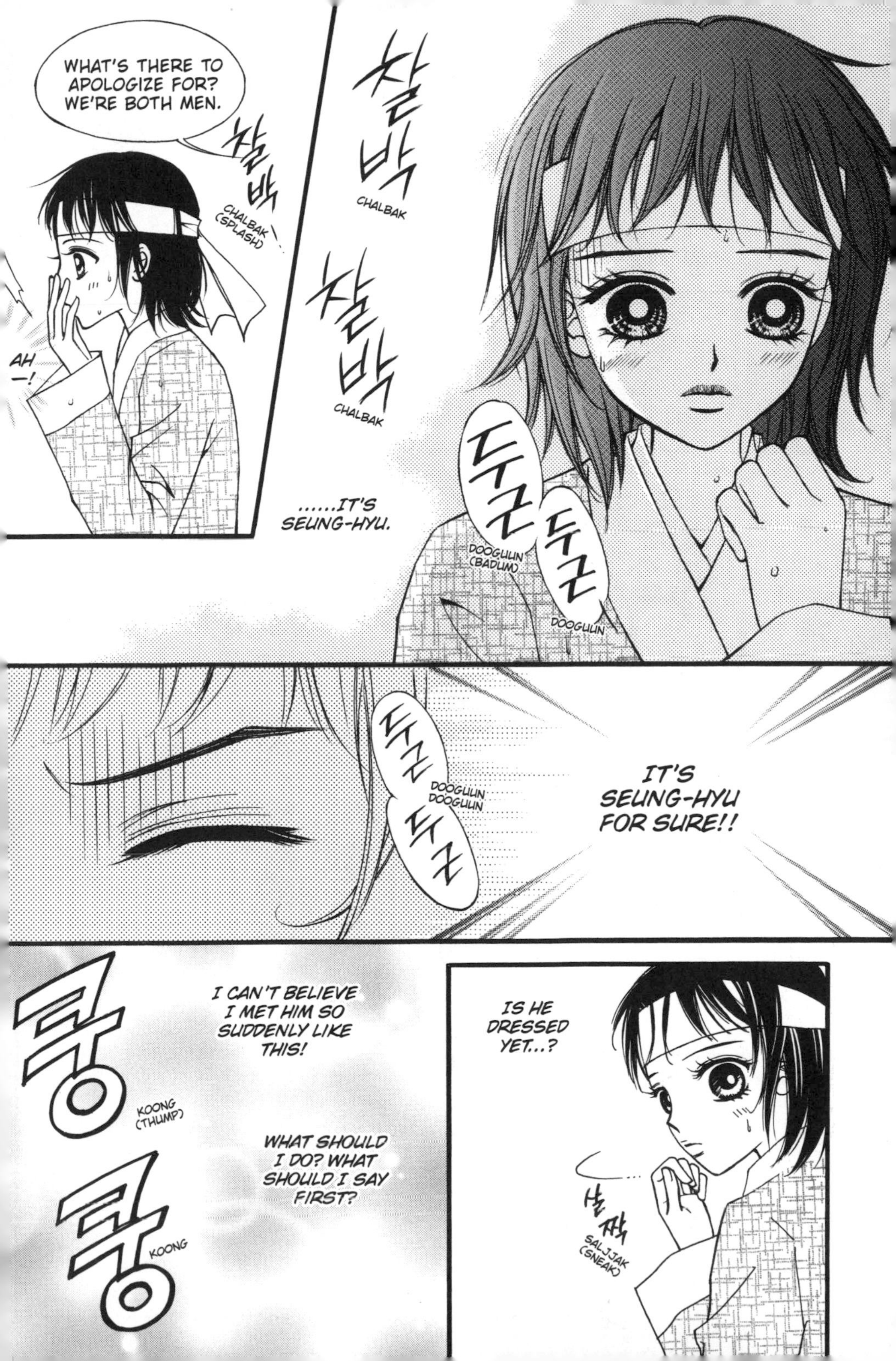
WHAT'S THERE TO APOLOGIZE FOR? WE'RE BOTH MEN.
찰박
CHALBAK (SPLASH)
AH—!
찰박
CHALBAK
찰박
CHALBAK
......IT'S SEUNG-HYU.
두근
DOOGUUN (BADUM)
두근
DOOGUUN
두근 두근
DOOGUUN DOOGUUN
IT'S SEUNG-HYU FOR SURE!!
쿵
KOONG (THUMP)
I CAN'T BELIEVE I MET HIM SO SUDDENLY LIKE THIS!
WHAT SHOULD I DO? WHAT SHOULD I SAY FIRST?
쿵
KOONG
IS HE DRESSED YET...?
살짝
SALJJAK (SNEAK)

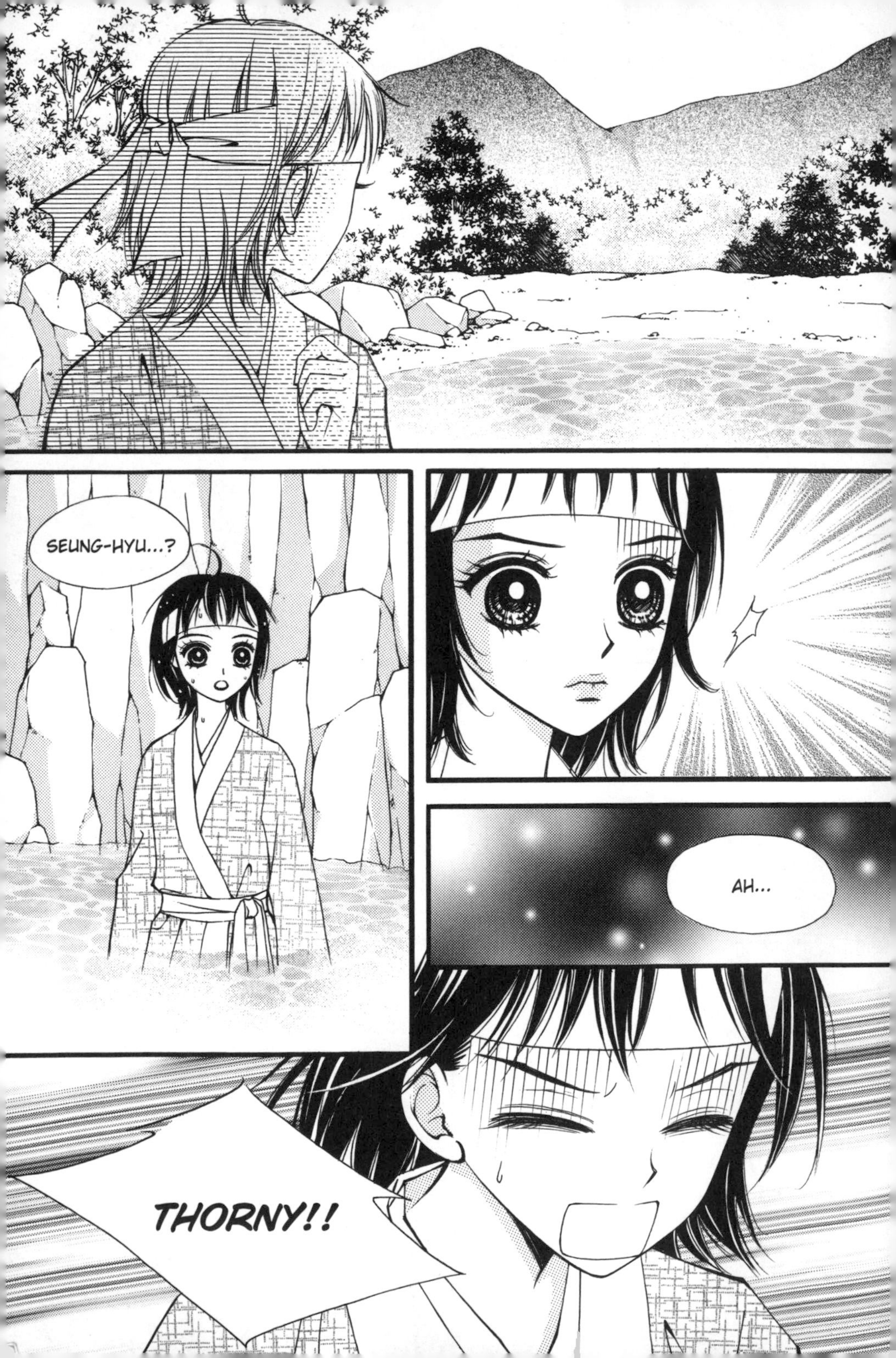
SEUNG-HYU...?
AH...
THORNY!!

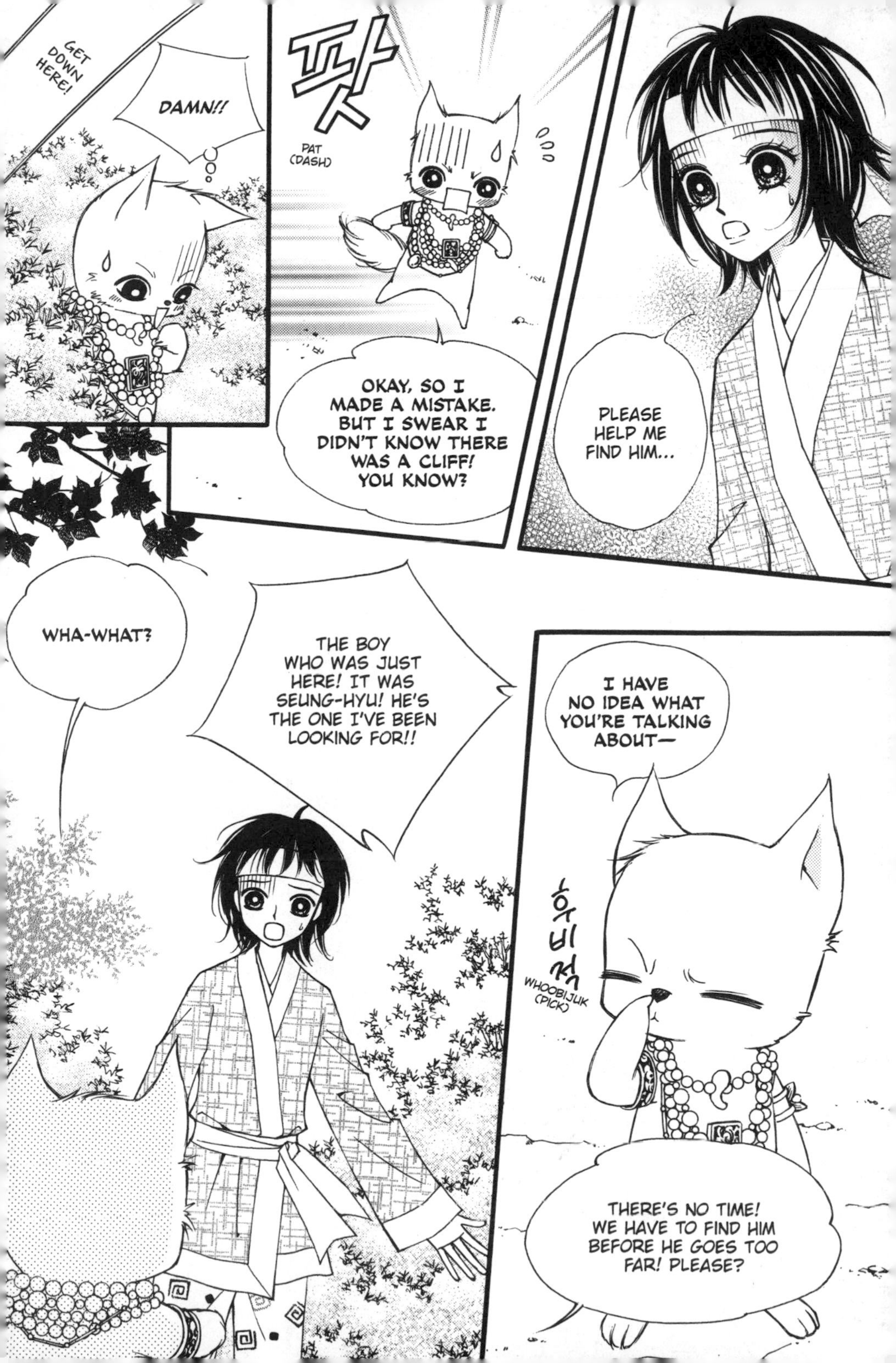
GET DOWN HERE!
DAMN!!
PAT (DASH)
OKAY, SO I MADE A MISTAKE. BUT I SWEAR I DIDN'T KNOW THERE WAS A CLIFF! YOU KNOW?
PLEASE HELP ME FIND HIM...
WHA-WHAT?
THE BOY WHO WAS JUST HERE! IT WAS SEUNG-HYU! HE'S THE ONE I'VE BEEN LOOKING FOR!!
I HAVE NO IDEA WHAT YOU'RE TALKING ABOUT—
후비적
WHOOBIJUK (PICK)
THERE'S NO TIME! WE HAVE TO FIND HIM BEFORE HE GOES TOO FAR! PLEASE?

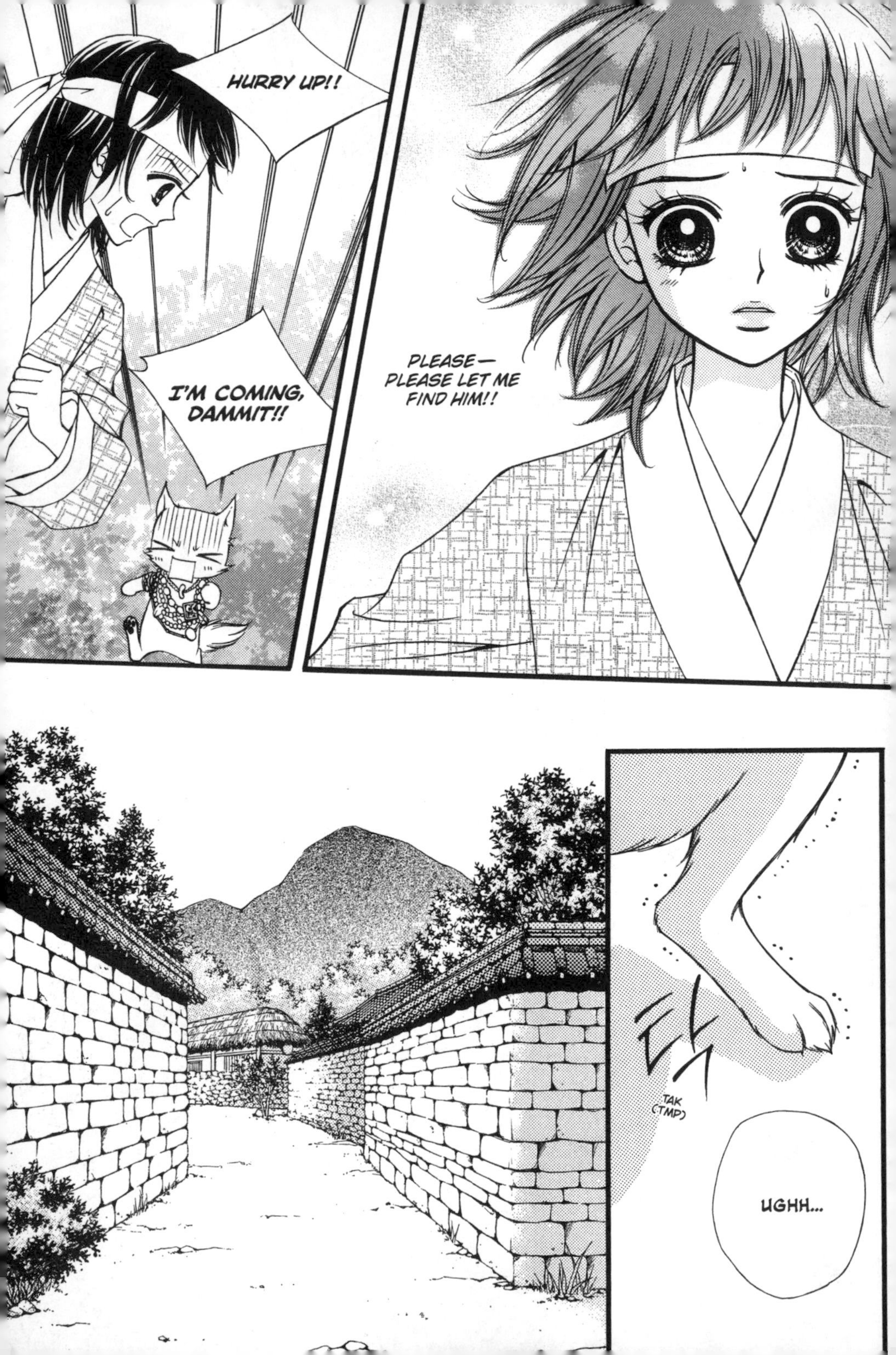
HURRY UP!!
I'M COMING, DAMMIT!!
PLEASE— PLEASE LET ME FIND HIM!!
TAK (TMP)
UGHH...

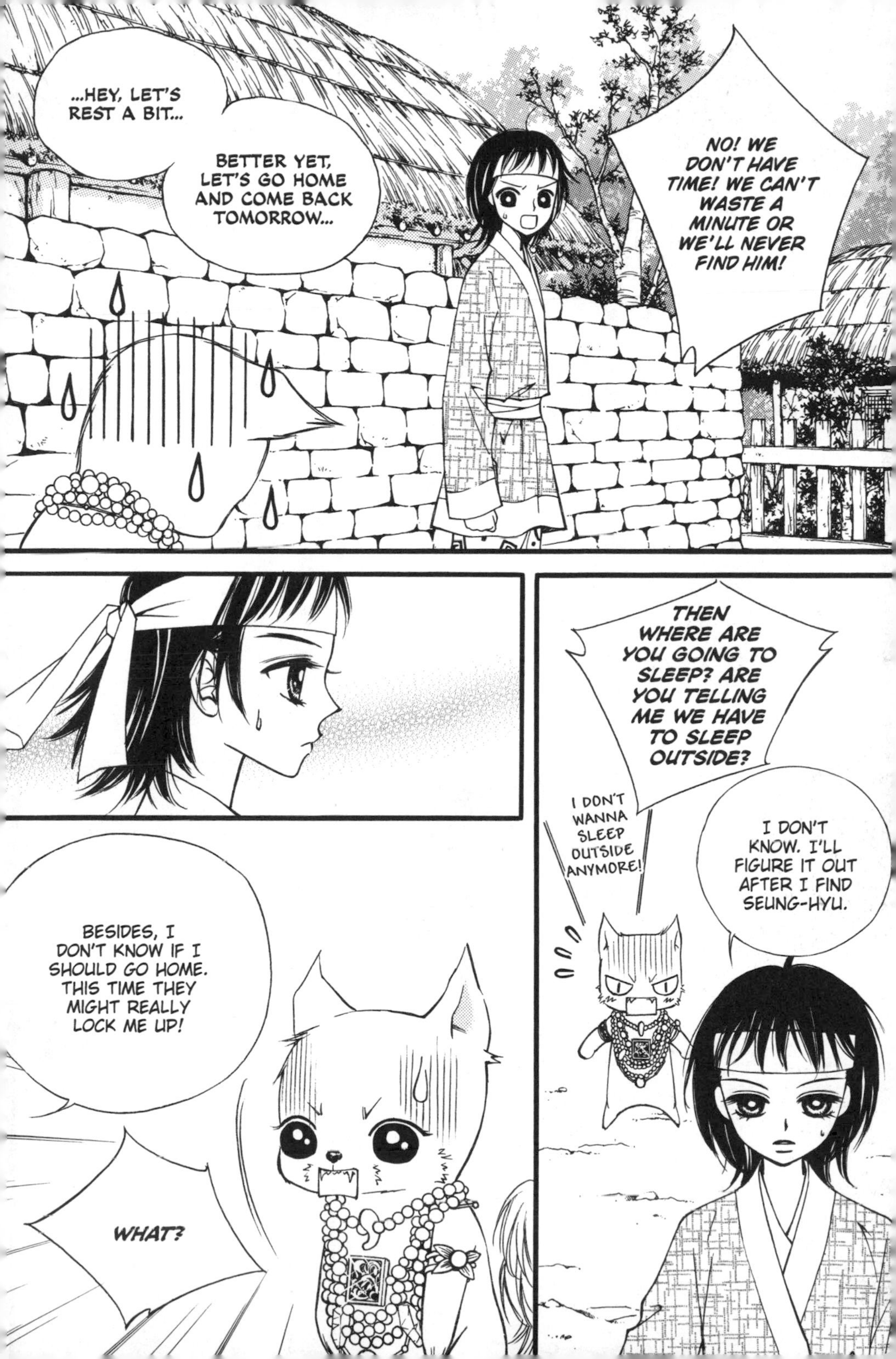
...HEY, LET'S REST A BIT...
BETTER YET, LET'S GO HOME AND COME BACK TOMORROW...
NO! WE DON'T HAVE TIME! WE CAN'T WASTE A MINUTE OR WE'LL NEVER FIND HIM!
BESIDES, I DON'T KNOW IF I SHOULD GO HOME. THIS TIME THEY MIGHT REALLY LOCK ME UP!
WHAT?
THEN WHERE ARE YOU GOING TO SLEEP? ARE YOU TELLING ME WE HAVE TO SLEEP OUTSIDE?
I DON'T WANNA SLEEP OUTSIDE ANYMORE!
I DON'T KNOW. I'LL FIGURE IT OUT AFTER I FIND SEUNG-HYU.

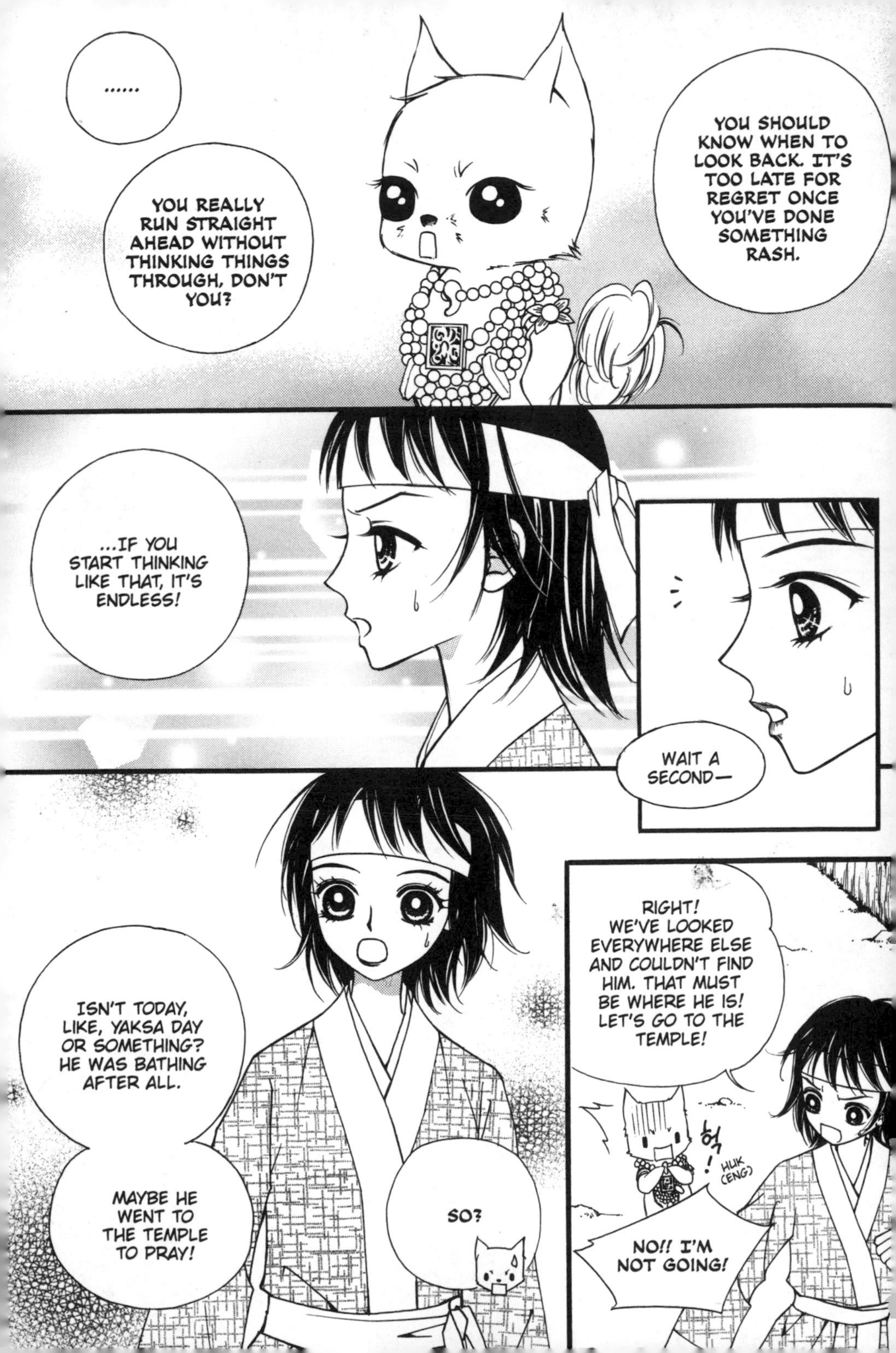
......
YOU REALLY RUN STRAIGHT AHEAD WITHOUT THINKING THINGS THROUGH, DON'T YOU?
YOU SHOULD KNOW WHEN TO LOOK BACK. IT'S TOO LATE FOR REGRET ONCE YOU'VE DONE SOMETHING RASH.
...IF YOU START THINKING LIKE THAT, IT'S ENDLESS!
WAIT A SECOND—
ISN'T TODAY, LIKE, YAKSA DAY OR SOMETHING? HE WAS BATHING AFTER ALL.
MAYBE HE WENT TO THE TEMPLE TO PRAY!
SO?
RIGHT! WE'VE LOOKED EVERYWHERE ELSE AND COULDN'T FIND HIM. THAT MUST BE WHERE HE IS! LET'S GO TO THE TEMPLE!
HUK (ENG)
NO!! I'M NOT GOING!

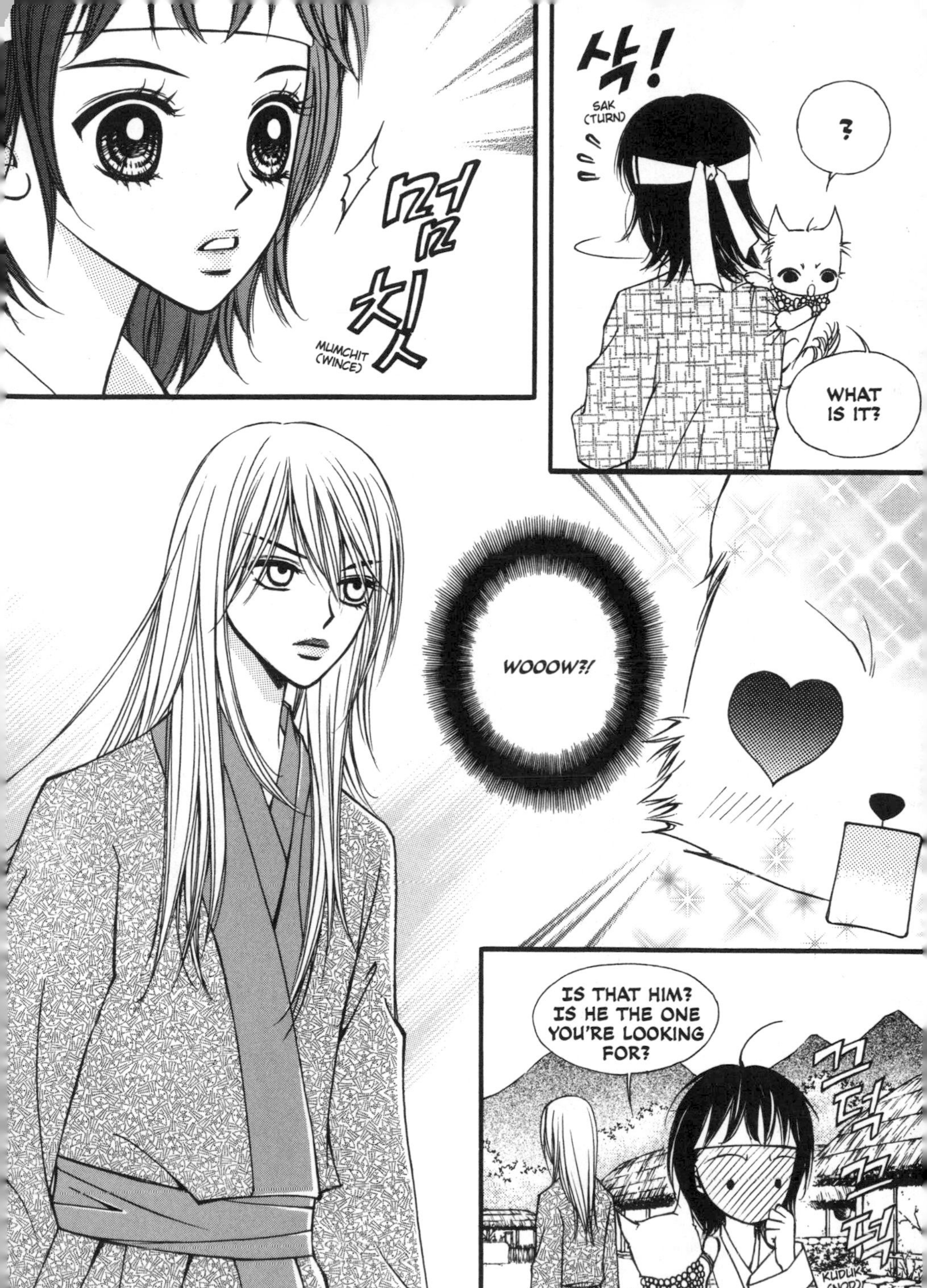

멈칫
MUMCHIT (WINCE)
삭!
SAK (TURN)
?
WHAT IS IT?
WOOOW?!
IS THAT HIM? IS HE THE ONE YOU'RE LOOKING FOR?
끄덕끄덕
KUDUK (NOD) KUDUK

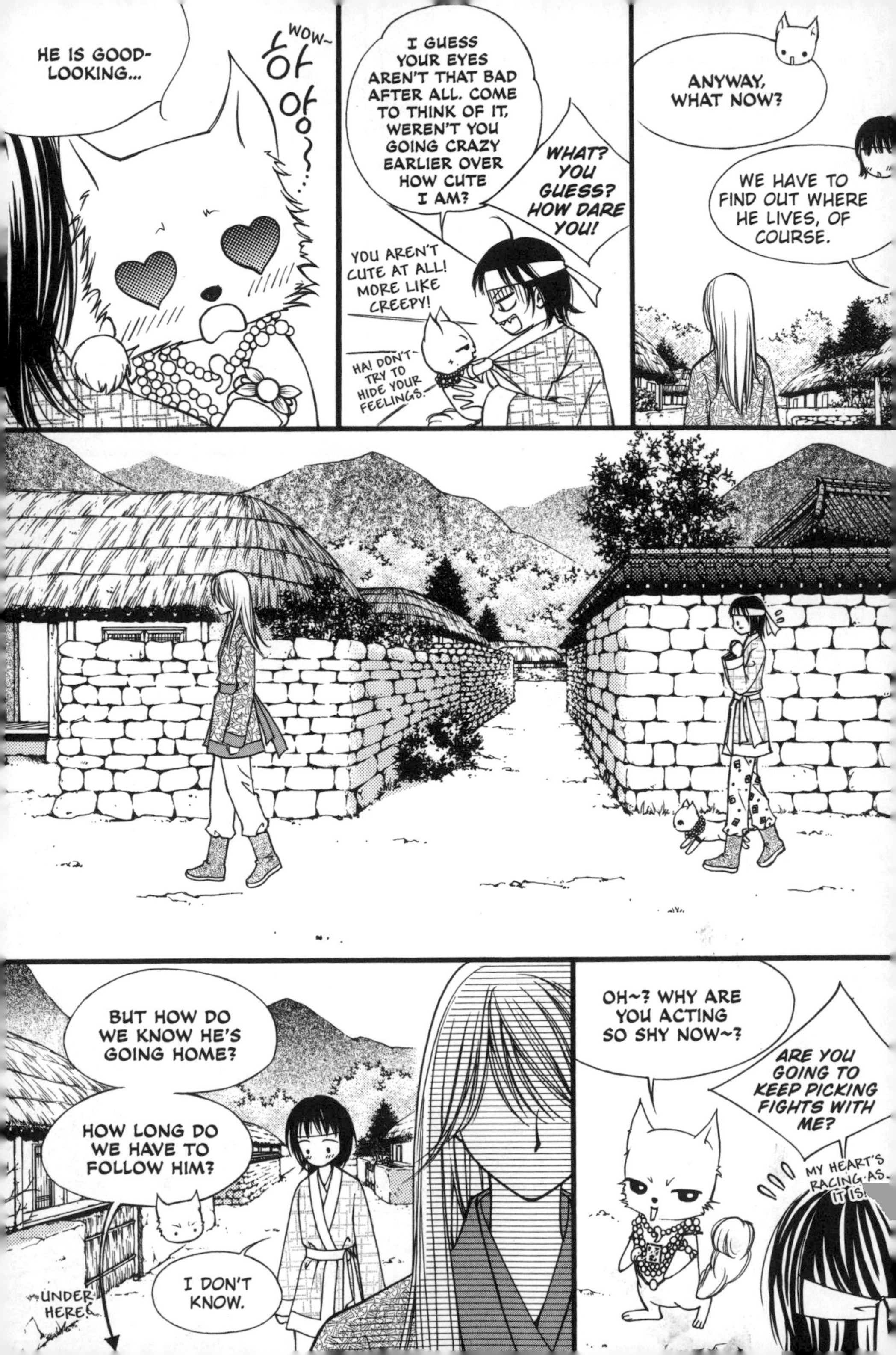
HE IS GOOD-LOOKING...
WOW~
하아아~
I GUESS YOUR EYES AREN'T THAT BAD AFTER ALL. COME TO THINK OF IT, WEREN'T YOU GOING CRAZY EARLIER OVER HOW CUTE I AM?
WHAT? YOU GUESS? HOW DARE YOU!
YOU AREN'T CUTE AT ALL! MORE LIKE CREEPY!
HA! DON'T TRY TO HIDE YOUR FEELINGS.
ANYWAY, WHAT NOW?
WE HAVE TO FIND OUT WHERE HE LIVES, OF COURSE.
BUT HOW DO WE KNOW HE'S GOING HOME?
HOW LONG DO WE HAVE TO FOLLOW HIM?
I DON'T KNOW.
UNDER HERE.
OH~? WHY ARE YOU ACTING SO SHY NOW~?
ARE YOU GOING TO KEEP PICKING FIGHTS WITH ME?
MY HEART'S RACING AS IT IS!

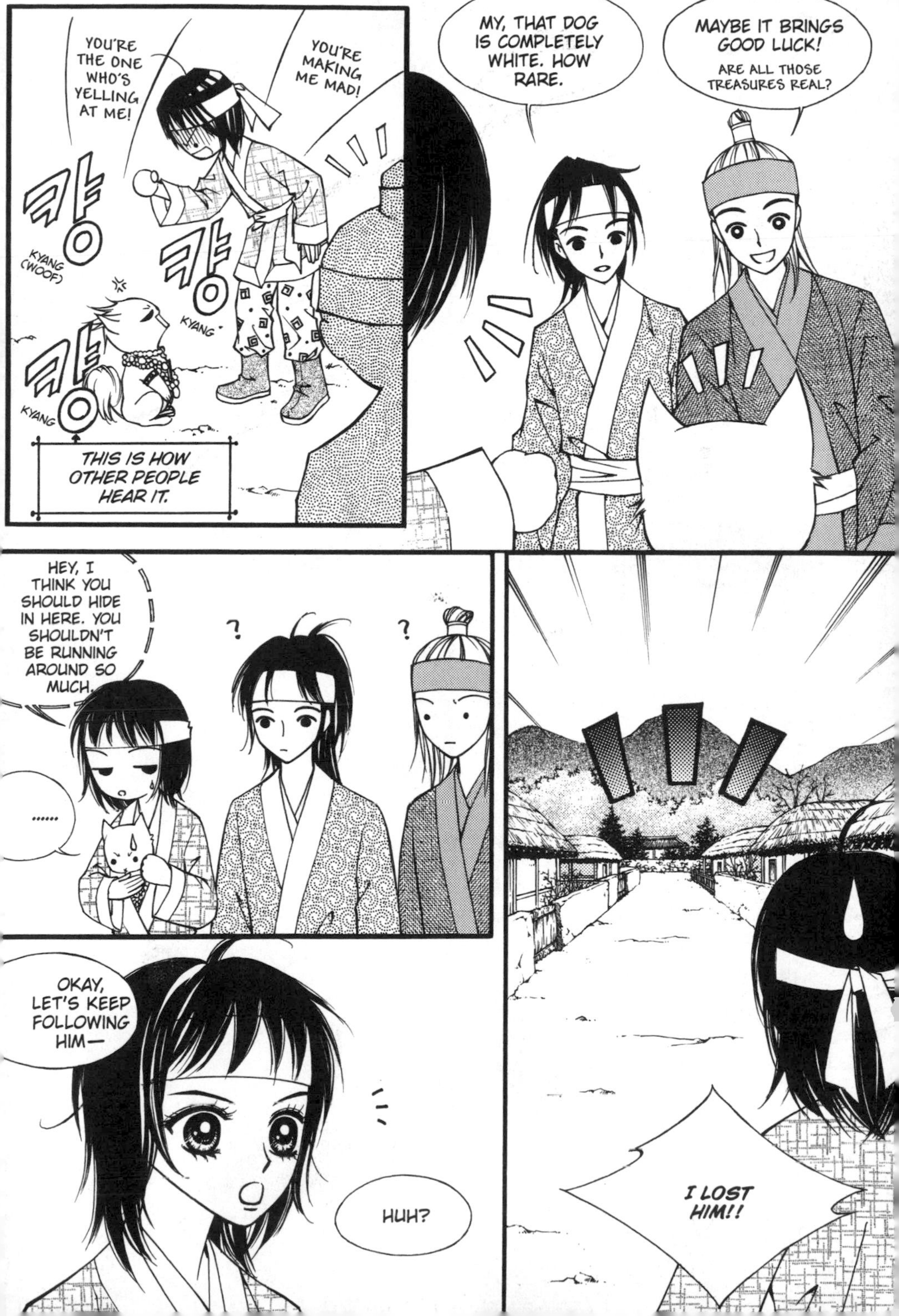
YOU'RE THE ONE WHO'S YELLING AT ME!
YOU'RE MAKING ME MAD!
컁
KYANG (WOOF)
컁
KYANG
컁
KYANG
THIS IS HOW OTHER PEOPLE HEAR IT.
MY, THAT DOG IS COMPLETELY WHITE. HOW RARE.
MAYBE IT BRINGS GOOD LUCK!
ARE ALL THOSE TREASURES REAL?
HEY, I THINK YOU SHOULD HIDE IN HERE. YOU SHOULDN'T BE RUNNING AROUND SO MUCH.
?
?
......
OKAY, LET'S KEEP FOLLOWING HIM—
HUH?
I LOST HIM!!

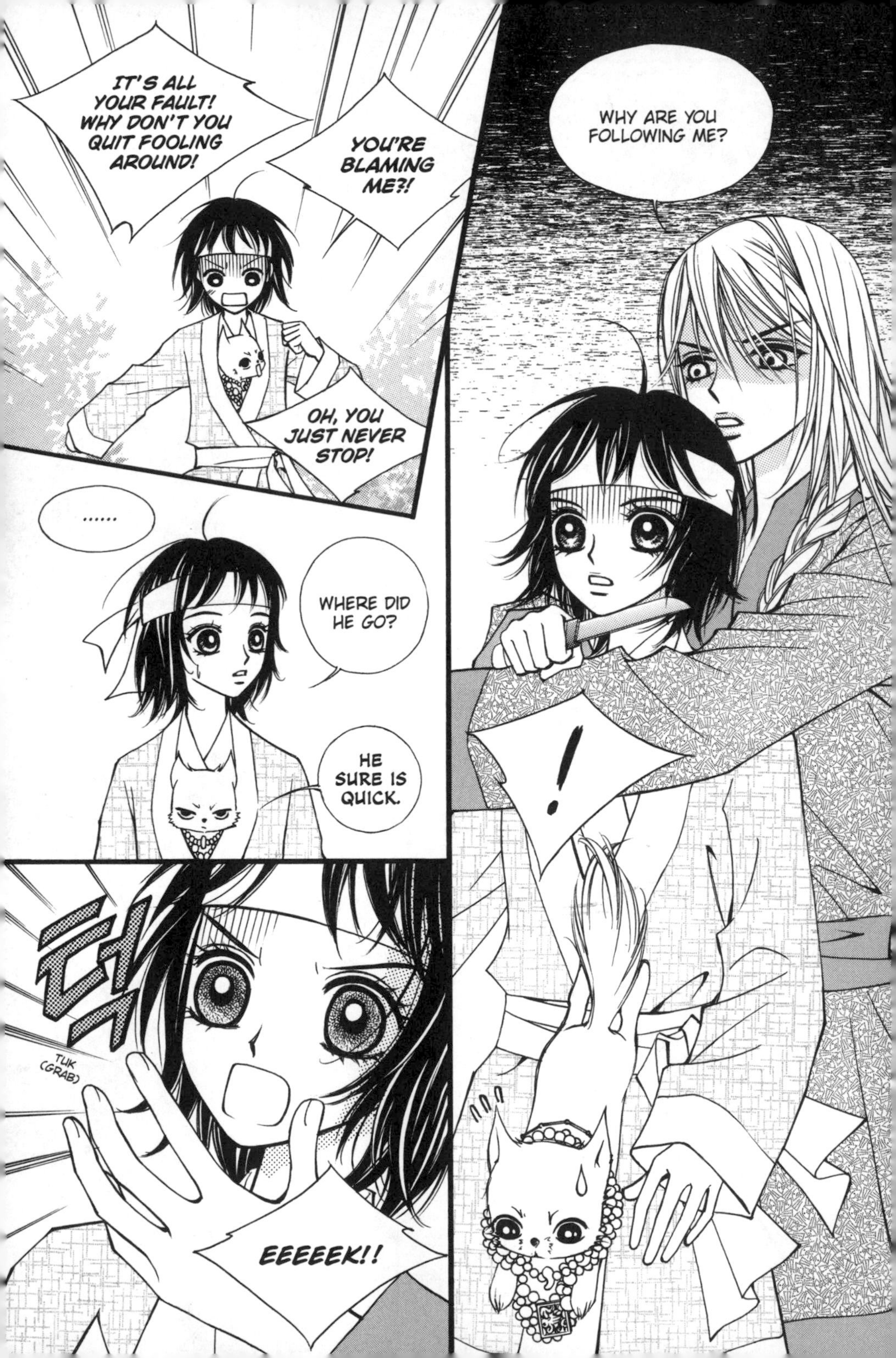
IT'S ALL YOUR FAULT! WHY DON'T YOU QUIT FOOLING AROUND!
YOU'RE BLAMING ME?!
OH, YOU JUST NEVER STOP!
......
WHERE DID HE GO?
HE SURE IS QUICK.
TUK (GRAB)
EEEEEK!!
WHY ARE YOU FOLLOWING ME?
!

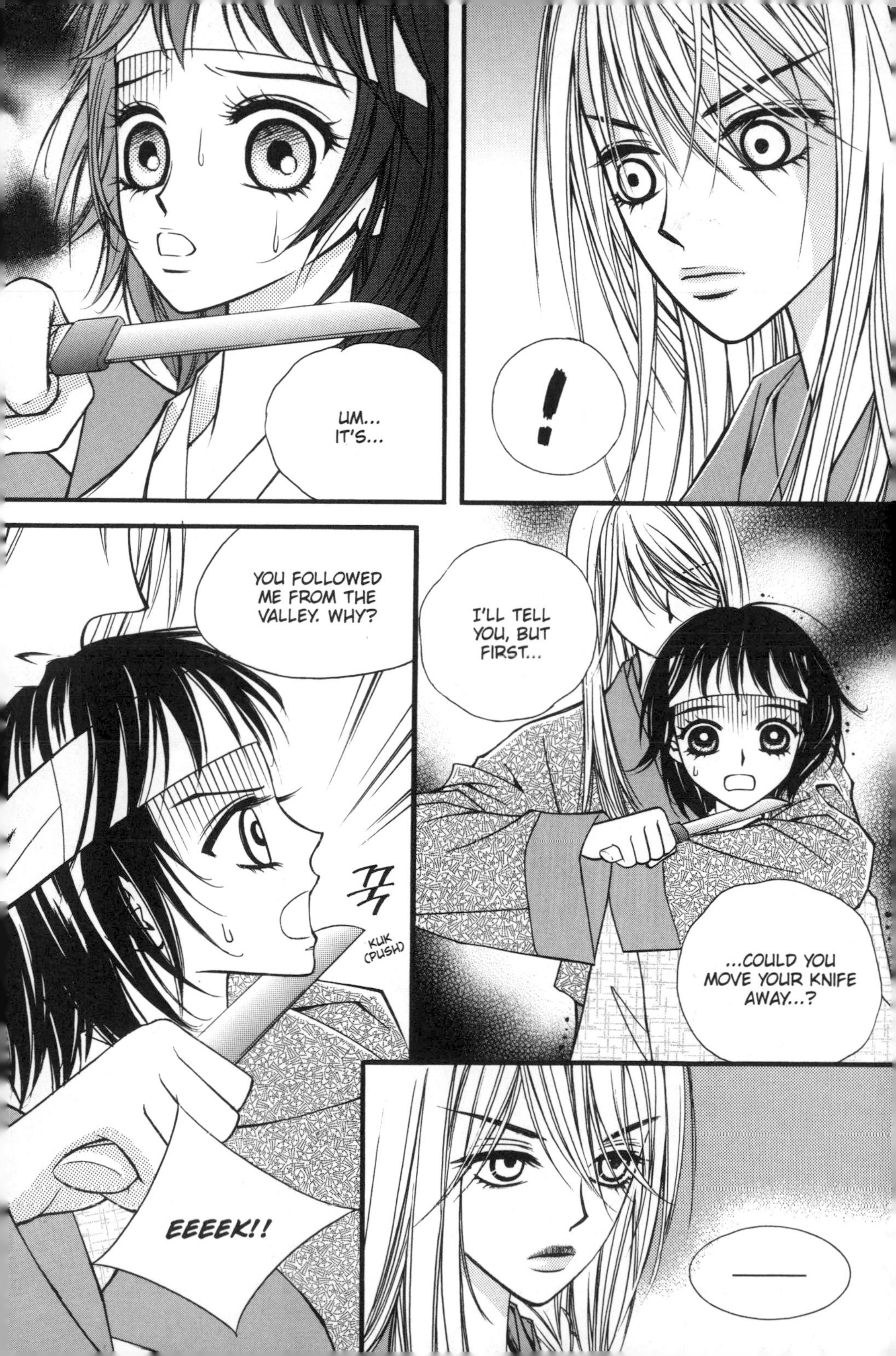
UM... IT'S...
!
YOU FOLLOWED ME FROM THE VALLEY. WHY?
KUK (PUSH)
EEEEK!!
I'LL TELL YOU, BUT FIRST...
...COULD YOU MOVE YOUR KNIFE AWAY...?
——

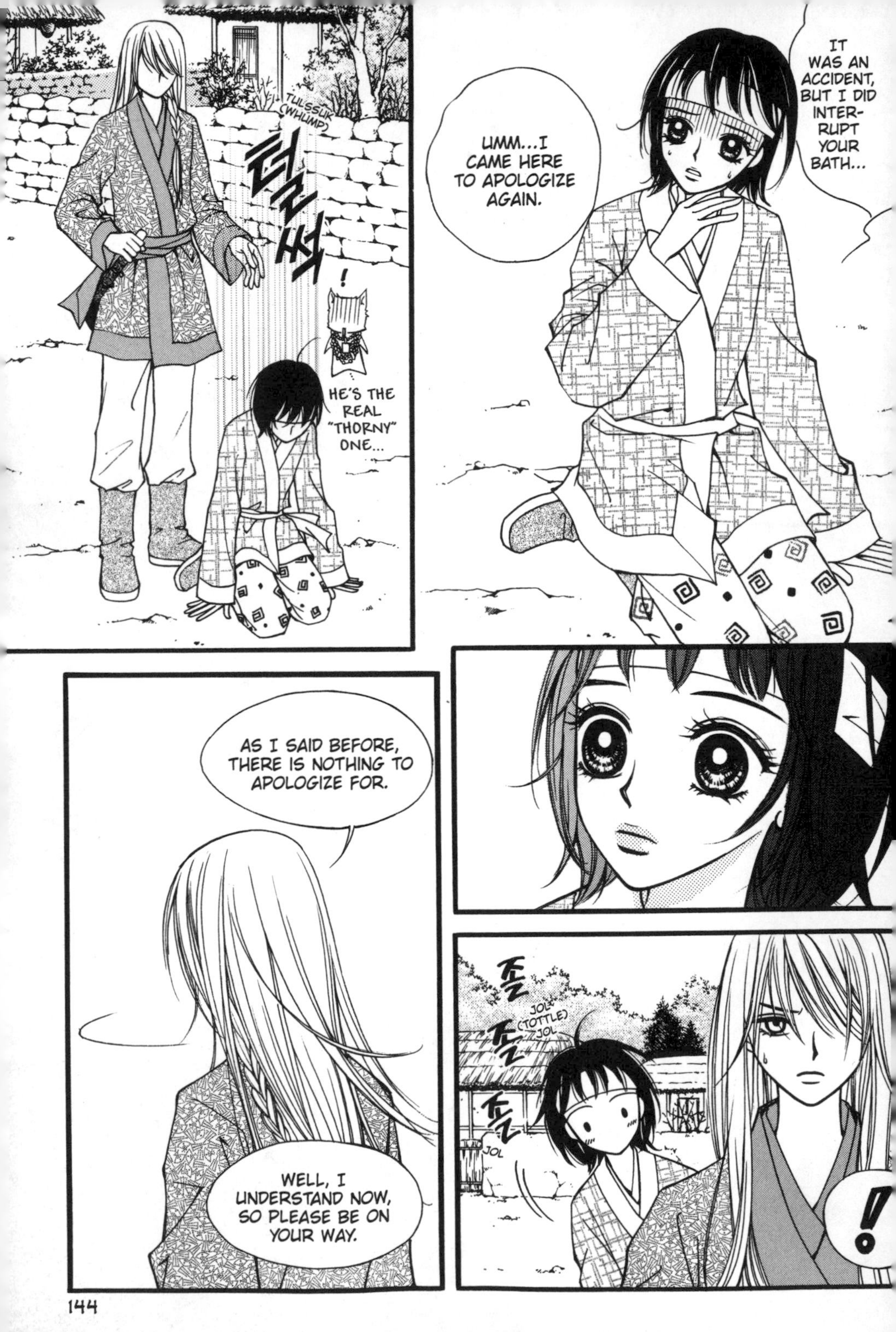
TULSSUK (WHUMP)
털썩
!
HE'S THE REAL "THORNY" ONE...
UMM...I CAME HERE TO APOLOGIZE AGAIN.
IT WAS AN ACCIDENT, BUT I DID INTER-RUPT YOUR BATH...
AS I SAID BEFORE, THERE IS NOTHING TO APOLOGIZE FOR.
WELL, I UNDERSTAND NOW, SO PLEASE BE ON YOUR WAY.
졸
JOL (TOTTLE) JOL
졸
졸
JOL
!

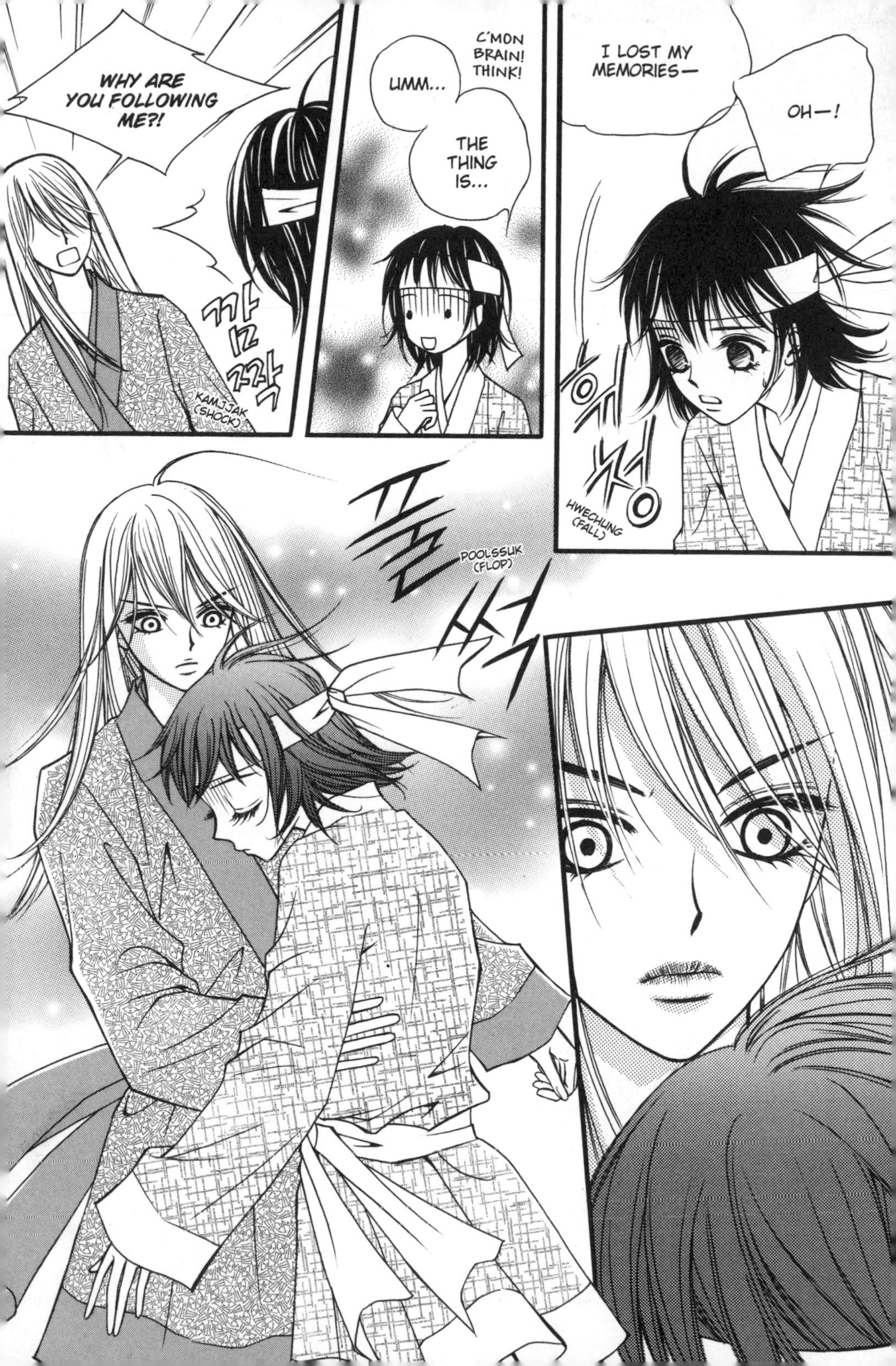
WHY ARE YOU FOLLOWING ME?!
KAMJJAK (SHOCK)
UMM...
C'MON BRAIN! THINK!
THE THING IS...
I LOST MY MEMORIES—
OH—!
HWECHUNG (FALL)
POOLSSUK (FLOP)

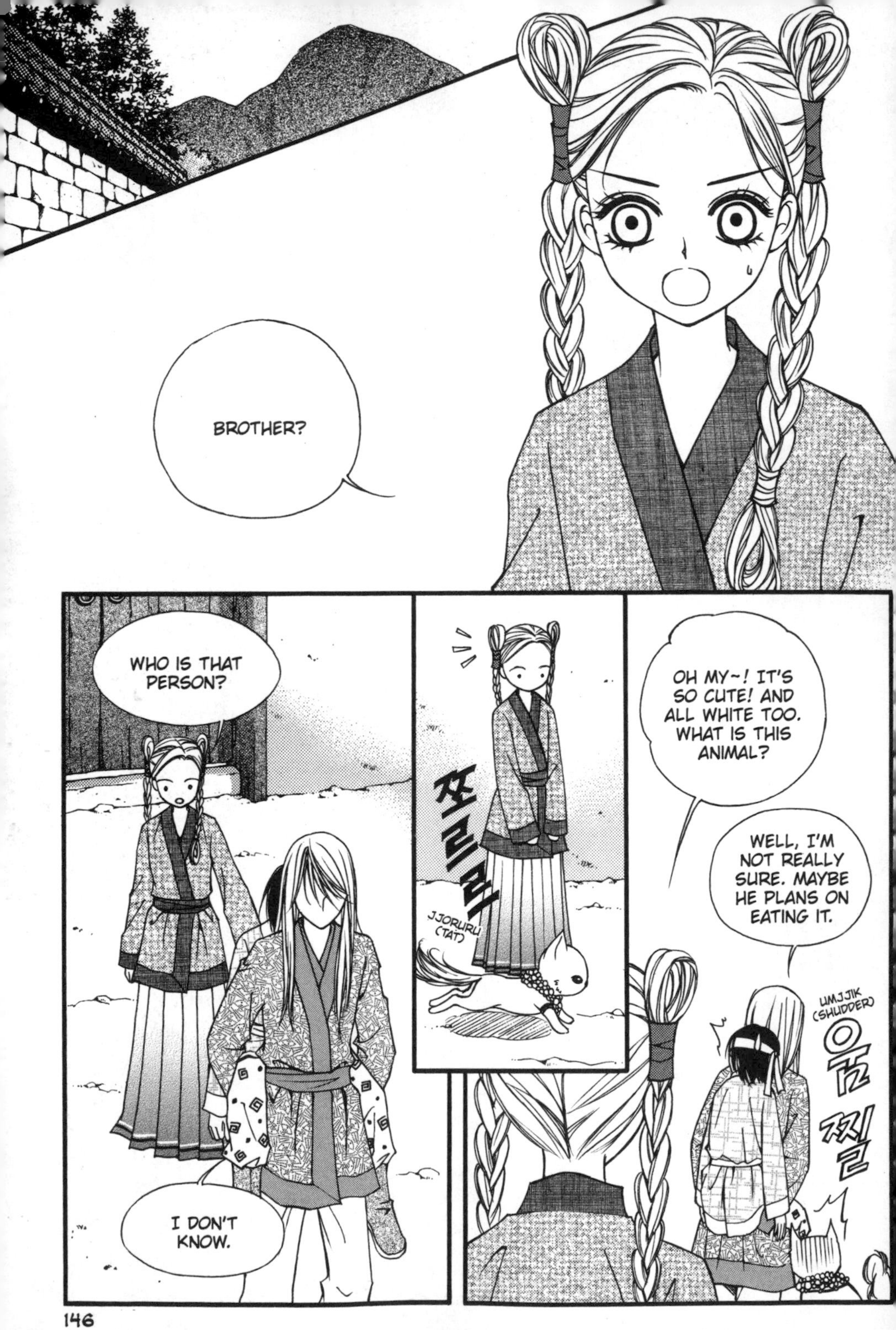
BROTHER?
WHO IS THAT PERSON?
I DON'T KNOW.
쪼르르
JJORURU (TAT)
OH MY~! IT'S SO CUTE! AND ALL WHITE TOO. WHAT IS THIS ANIMAL?
WELL, I'M NOT REALLY SURE. MAYBE HE PLANS ON EATING IT.
움찔
UMJJIK (SHUDDER)

TULSSUK
(FLOP)

IT'S RATHER SUSPICIOUS FOR HIM TO FAINT SO SUDDENLY, BUT...

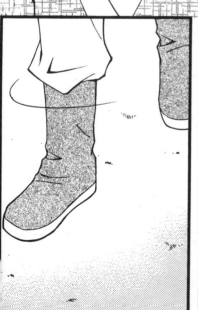

TAK
(CLACK)

BUNJJUK
(BLINK)

BULDDUK
(BOLT)

OH?

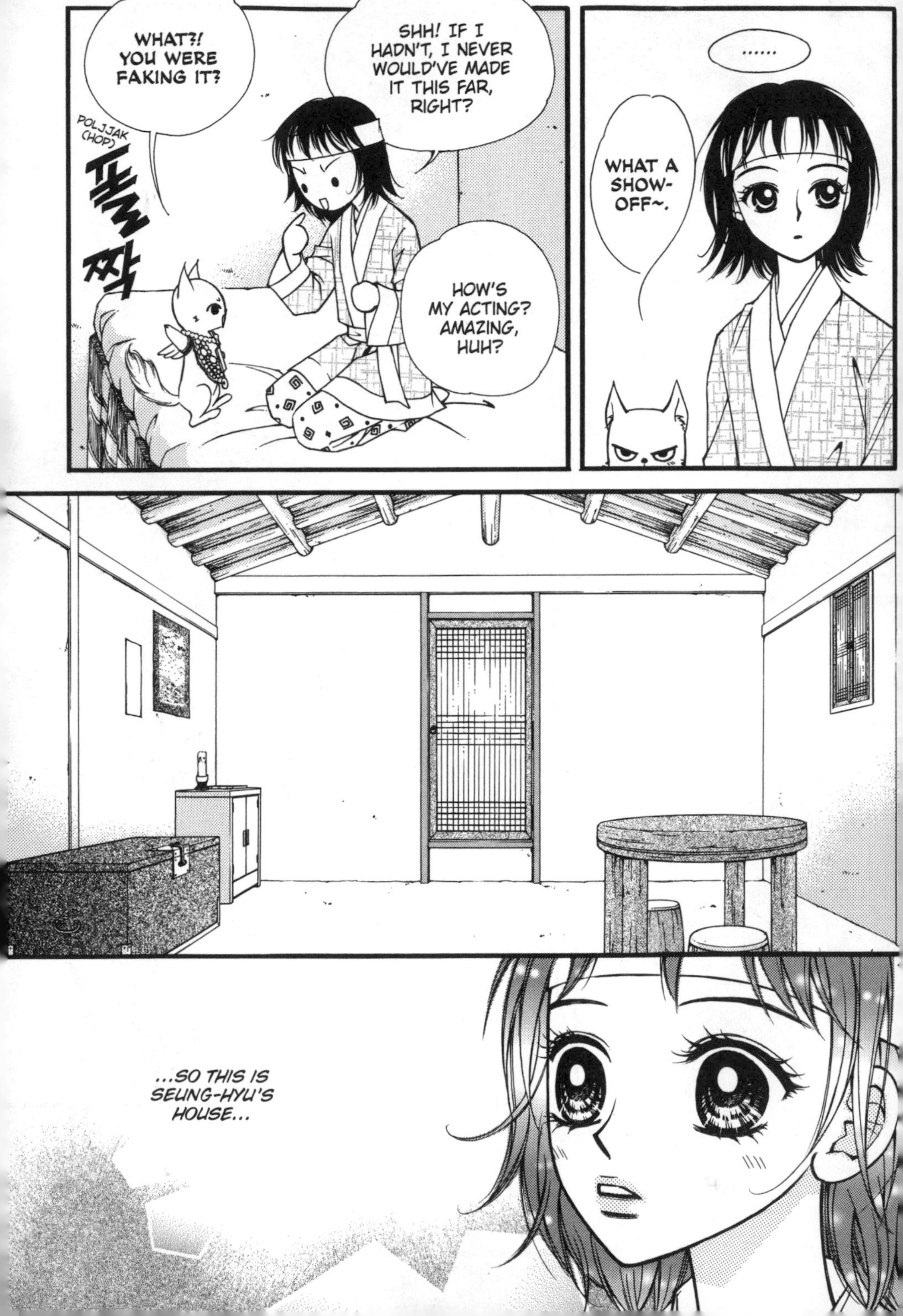
WHAT?! YOU WERE FAKING IT?
POLJJAK (HOP)
폴짝
SHH! IF I HADN'T, I NEVER WOULD'VE MADE IT THIS FAR, RIGHT?
HOW'S MY ACTING? AMAZING, HUH?
......
WHAT A SHOW-OFF~.
...SO THIS IS SEUNG-HYU'S HOUSE...

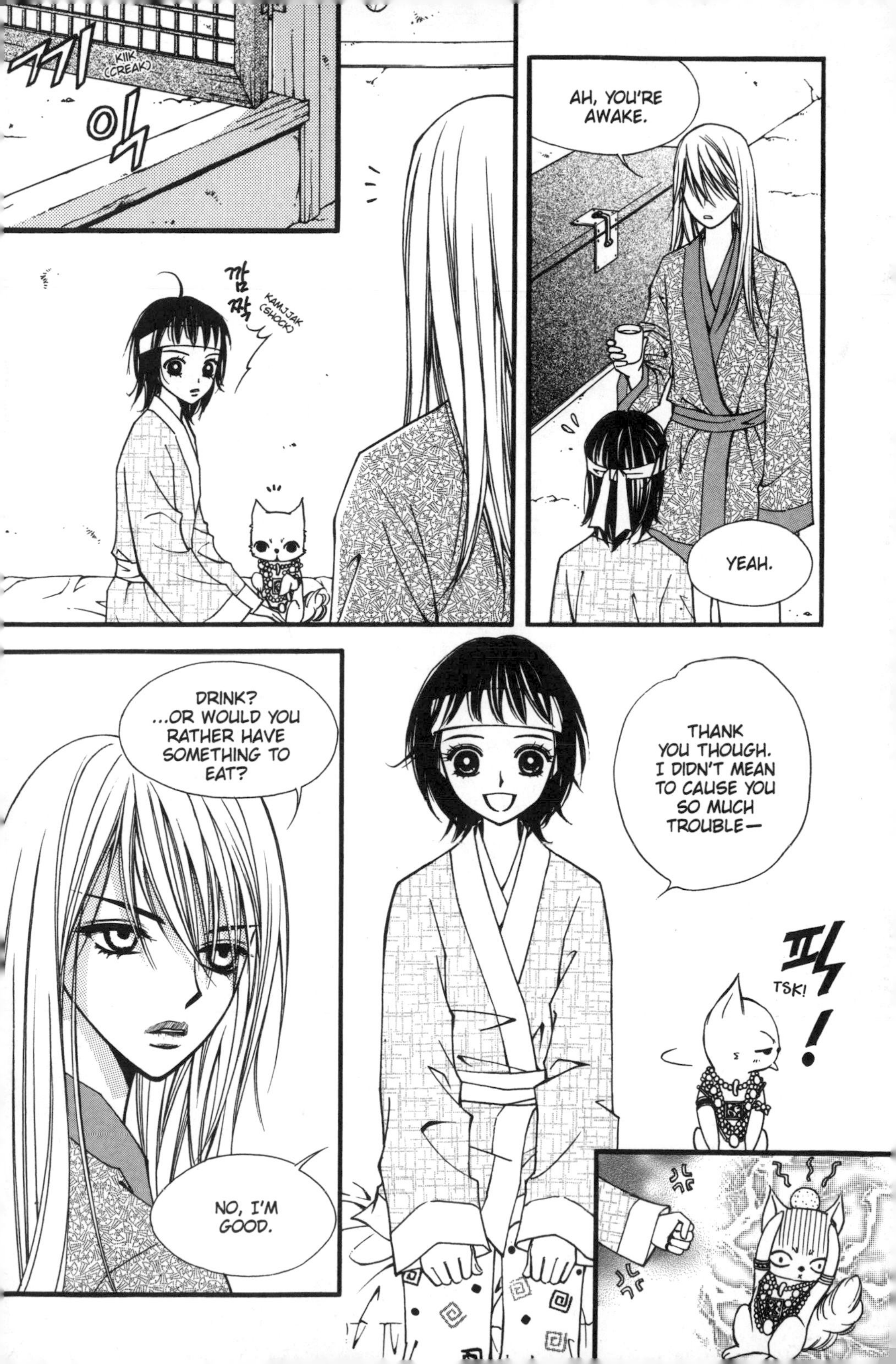
끼익
KIIK (CREAK)
깜짝
KAMJJAK (SHOCK)
AH, YOU'RE AWAKE.
YEAH.
DRINK? ...OR WOULD YOU RATHER HAVE SOMETHING TO EAT?
NO, I'M GOOD.
THANK YOU THOUGH. I DIDN'T MEAN TO CAUSE YOU SO MUCH TROUBLE—
피
TSK!

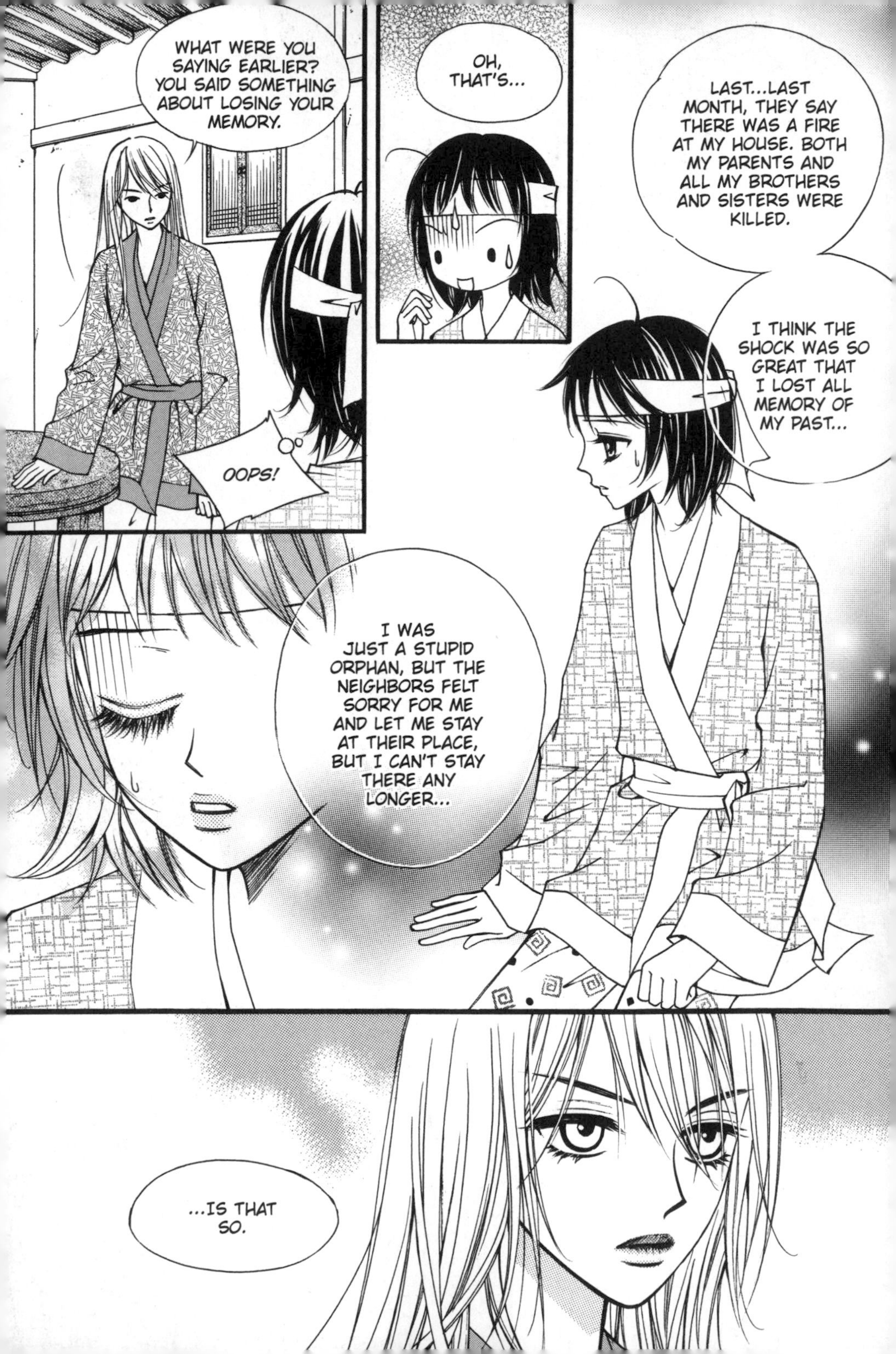
WHAT WERE YOU SAYING EARLIER? YOU SAID SOMETHING ABOUT LOSING YOUR MEMORY.
OOPS!
OH, THAT'S...
LAST...LAST MONTH, THEY SAY THERE WAS A FIRE AT MY HOUSE. BOTH MY PARENTS AND ALL MY BROTHERS AND SISTERS WERE KILLED.
I THINK THE SHOCK WAS SO GREAT THAT I LOST ALL MEMORY OF MY PAST...
I WAS JUST A STUPID ORPHAN, BUT THE NEIGHBORS FELT SORRY FOR ME AND LET ME STAY AT THEIR PLACE, BUT I CAN'T STAY THERE ANY LONGER...
...IS THAT SO.

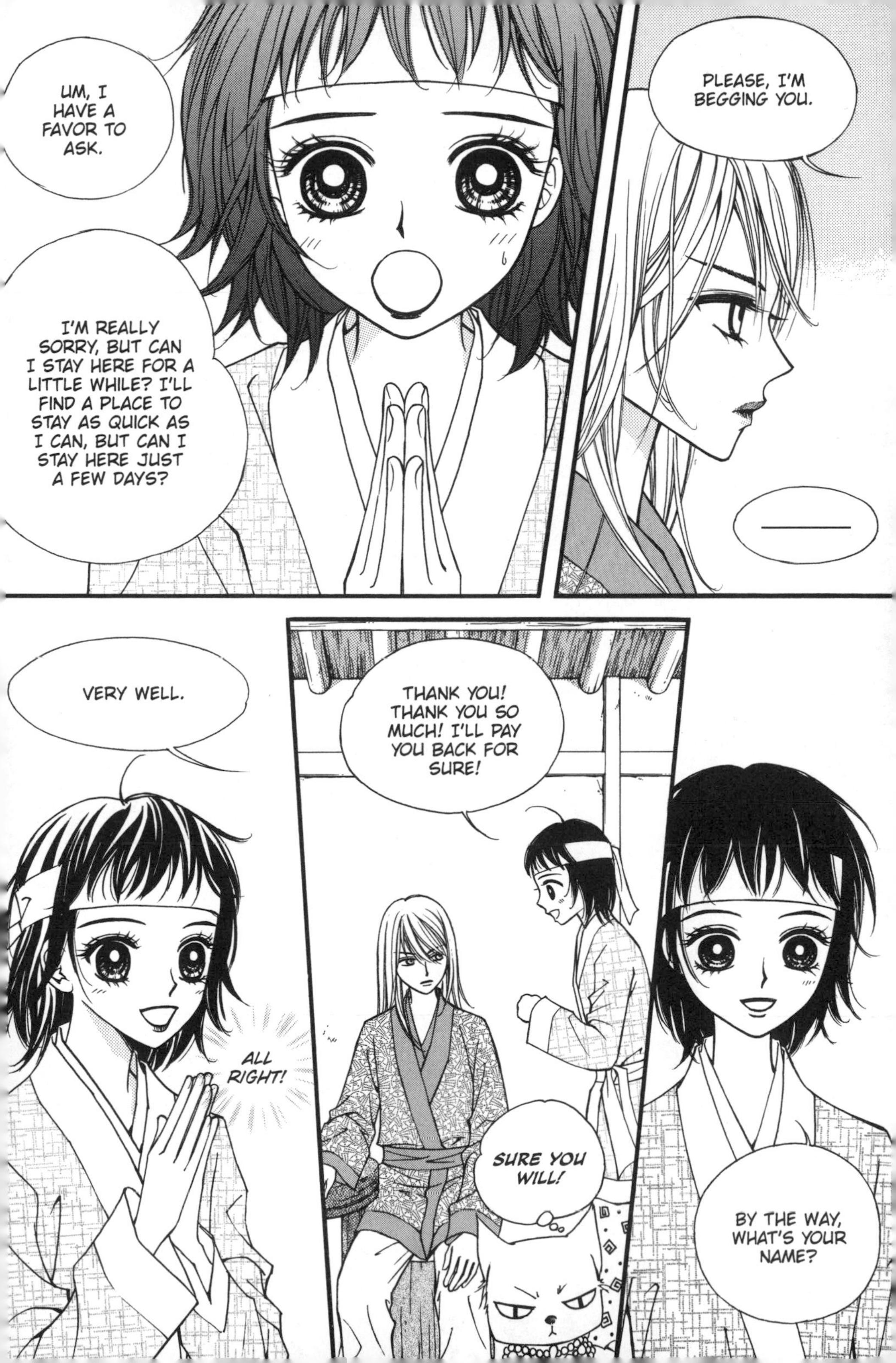
UM, I HAVE A FAVOR TO ASK.
I'M REALLY SORRY, BUT CAN I STAY HERE FOR A LITTLE WHILE? I'LL FIND A PLACE TO STAY AS QUICK AS I CAN, BUT CAN I STAY HERE JUST A FEW DAYS?
PLEASE, I'M BEGGING YOU.
———
VERY WELL.
ALL RIGHT!
THANK YOU! THANK YOU SO MUCH! I'LL PAY YOU BACK FOR SURE!
SURE YOU WILL!
BY THE WAY, WHAT'S YOUR NAME?

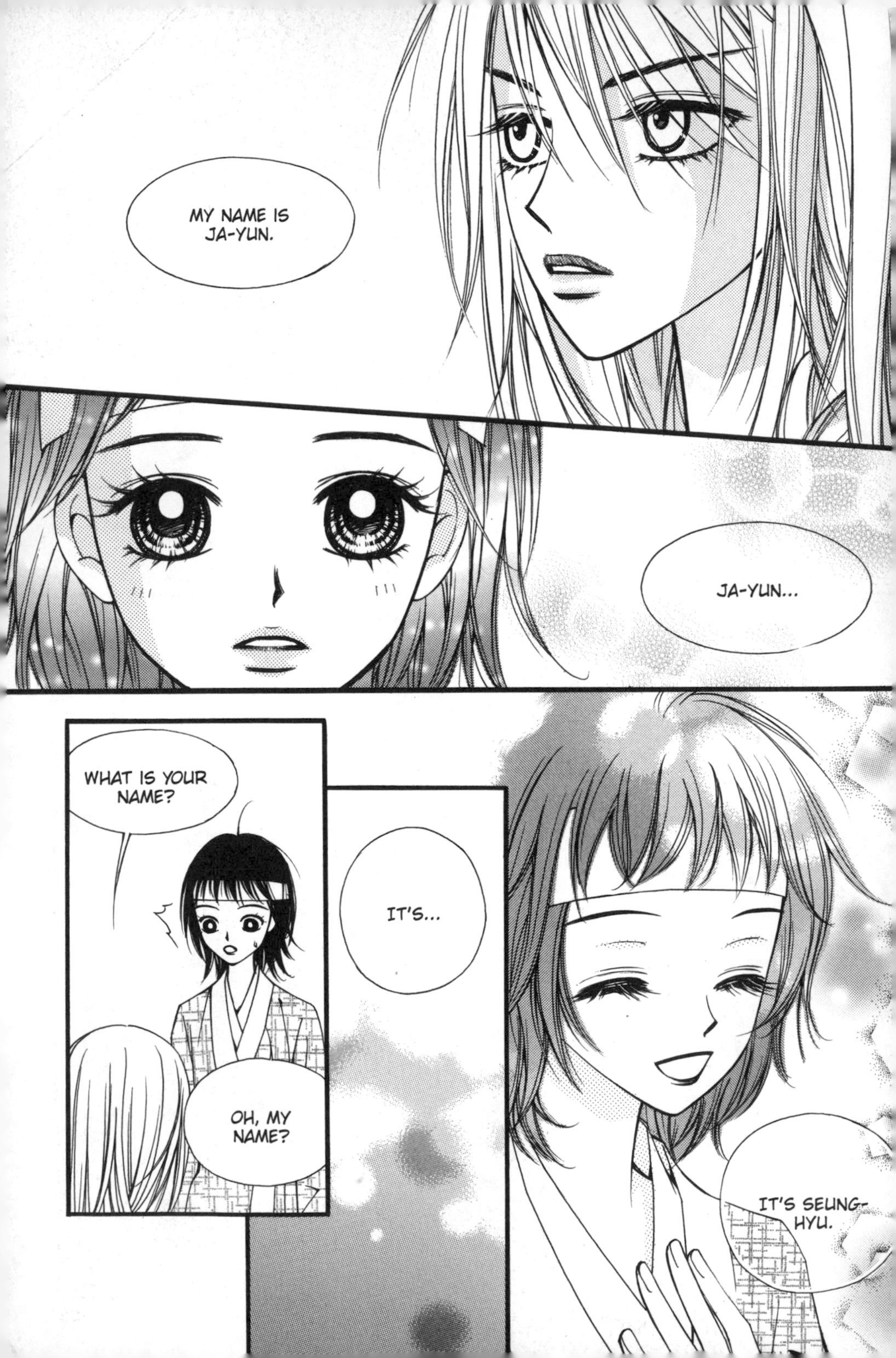
MY NAME IS JA-YUN.
JA-YUN...
WHAT IS YOUR NAME?
OH, MY NAME?
IT'S...
IT'S SEUNG-HYU.

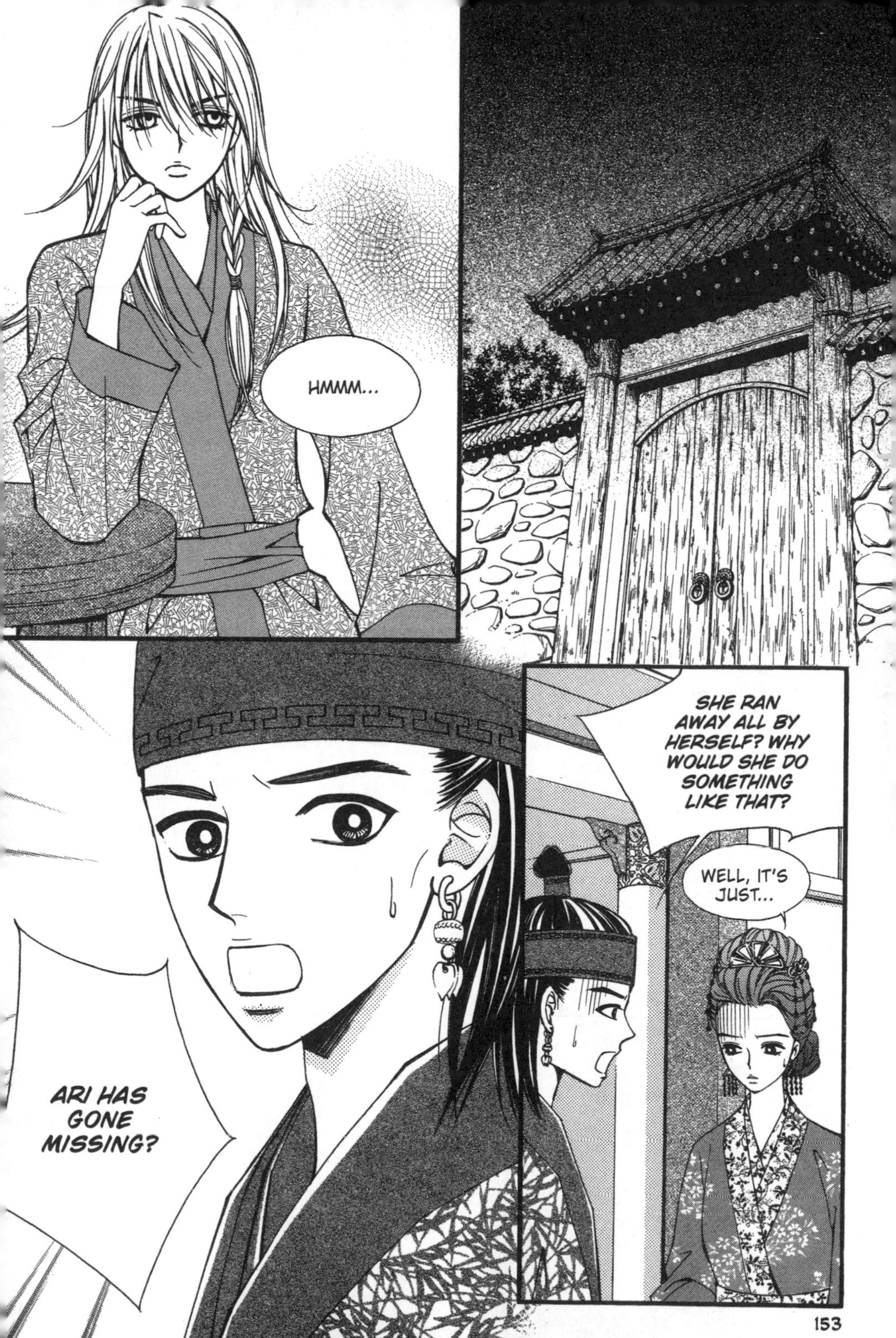
HMMM...
ARI HAS GONE MISSING?
SHE RAN AWAY ALL BY HERSELF? WHY WOULD SHE DO SOMETHING LIKE THAT?
WELL, IT'S JUST...

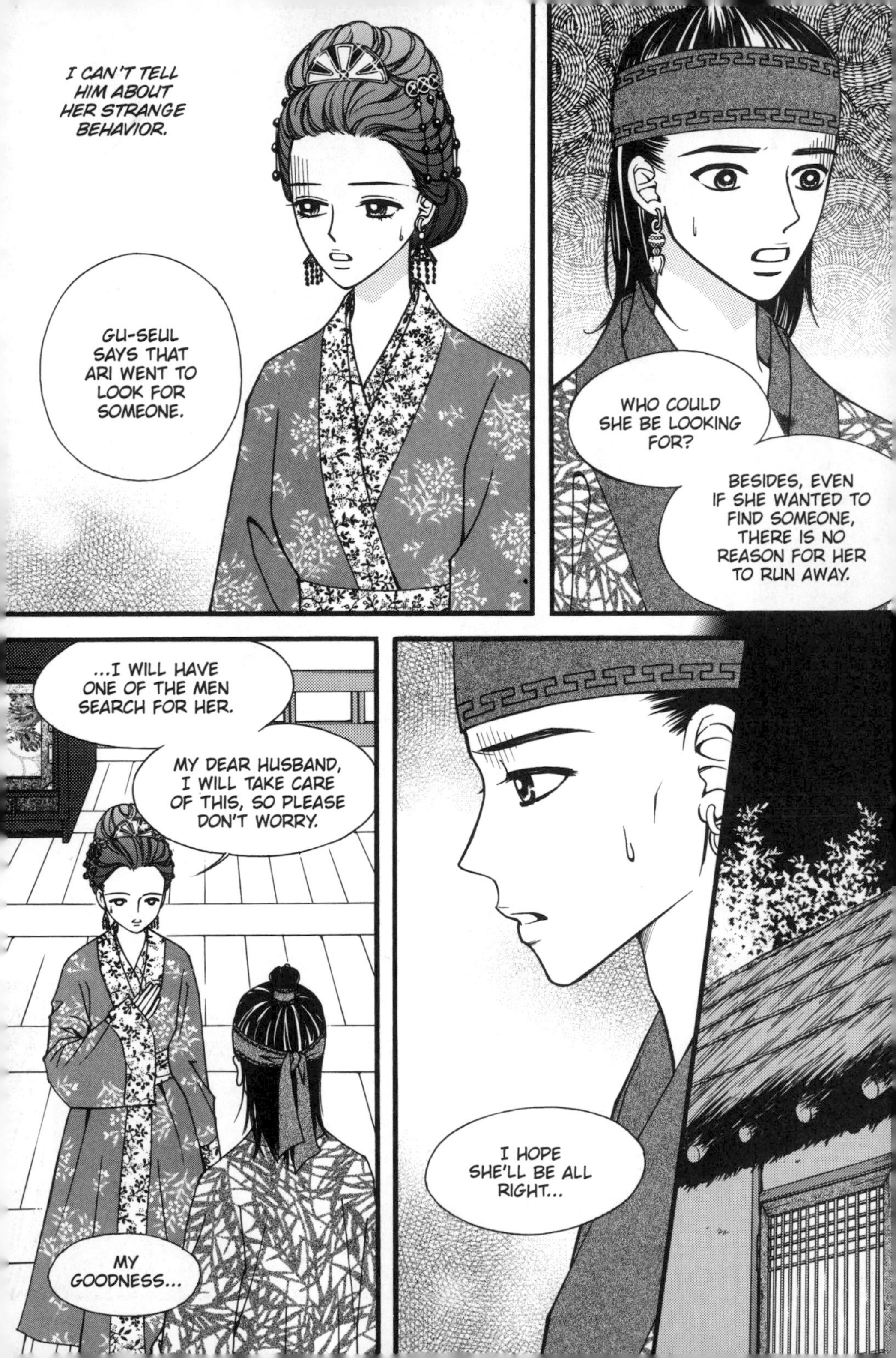
I CAN'T TELL HIM ABOUT HER STRANGE BEHAVIOR.
GU-SEUL SAYS THAT ARI WENT TO LOOK FOR SOMEONE.
WHO COULD SHE BE LOOKING FOR?
BESIDES, EVEN IF SHE WANTED TO FIND SOMEONE, THERE IS NO REASON FOR HER TO RUN AWAY.
...I WILL HAVE ONE OF THE MEN SEARCH FOR HER.
MY DEAR HUSBAND, I WILL TAKE CARE OF THIS, SO PLEASE DON'T WORRY.
MY GOODNESS...
I HOPE SHE'LL BE ALL RIGHT...

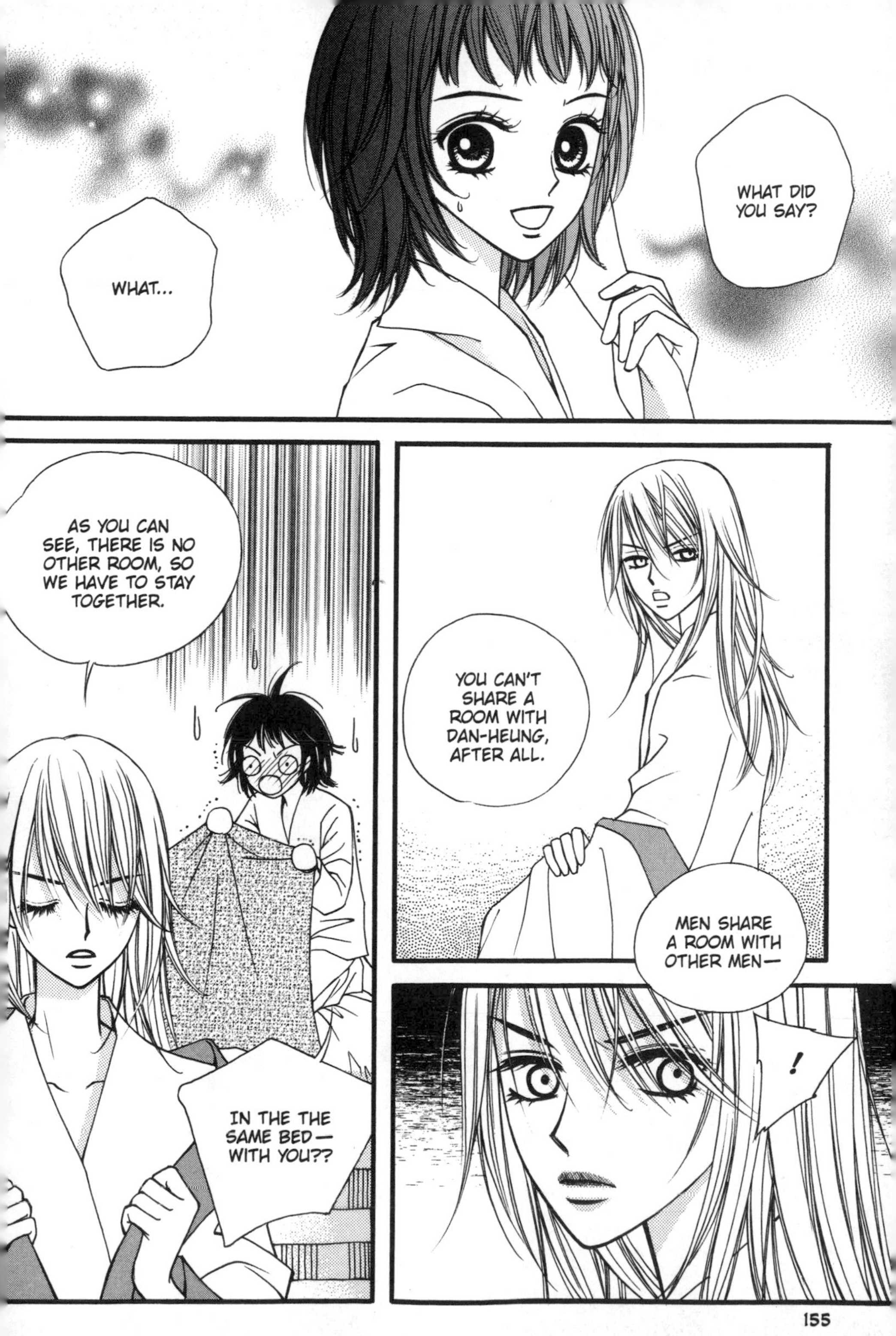
WHAT...
WHAT DID YOU SAY?
AS YOU CAN SEE, THERE IS NO OTHER ROOM, SO WE HAVE TO STAY TOGETHER.
IN THE THE SAME BED— WITH YOU??
YOU CAN'T SHARE A ROOM WITH DAN-HEUNG, AFTER ALL.
MEN SHARE A ROOM WITH OTHER MEN—
!

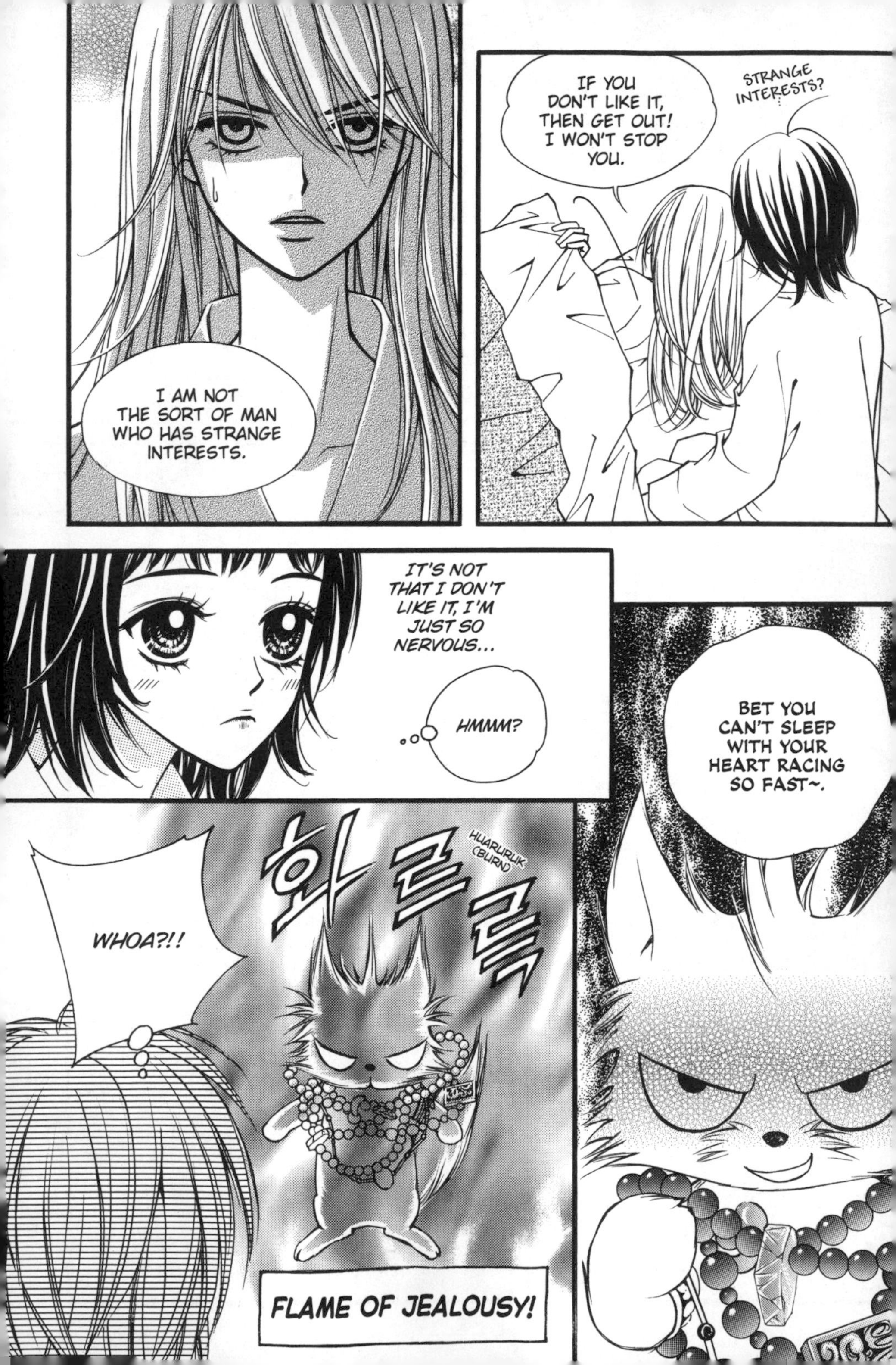
I AM NOT THE SORT OF MAN WHO HAS STRANGE INTERESTS.
IF YOU DON'T LIKE IT, THEN GET OUT! I WON'T STOP YOU.
STRANGE INTERESTS?
IT'S NOT THAT I DON'T LIKE IT, I'M JUST SO NERVOUS...
HMMM?
WHOA?!!
화르륵
HUARURUK (BURN)
FLAME OF JEALOUSY!
BET YOU CAN'T SLEEP WITH YOUR HEART RACING SO FAST~.

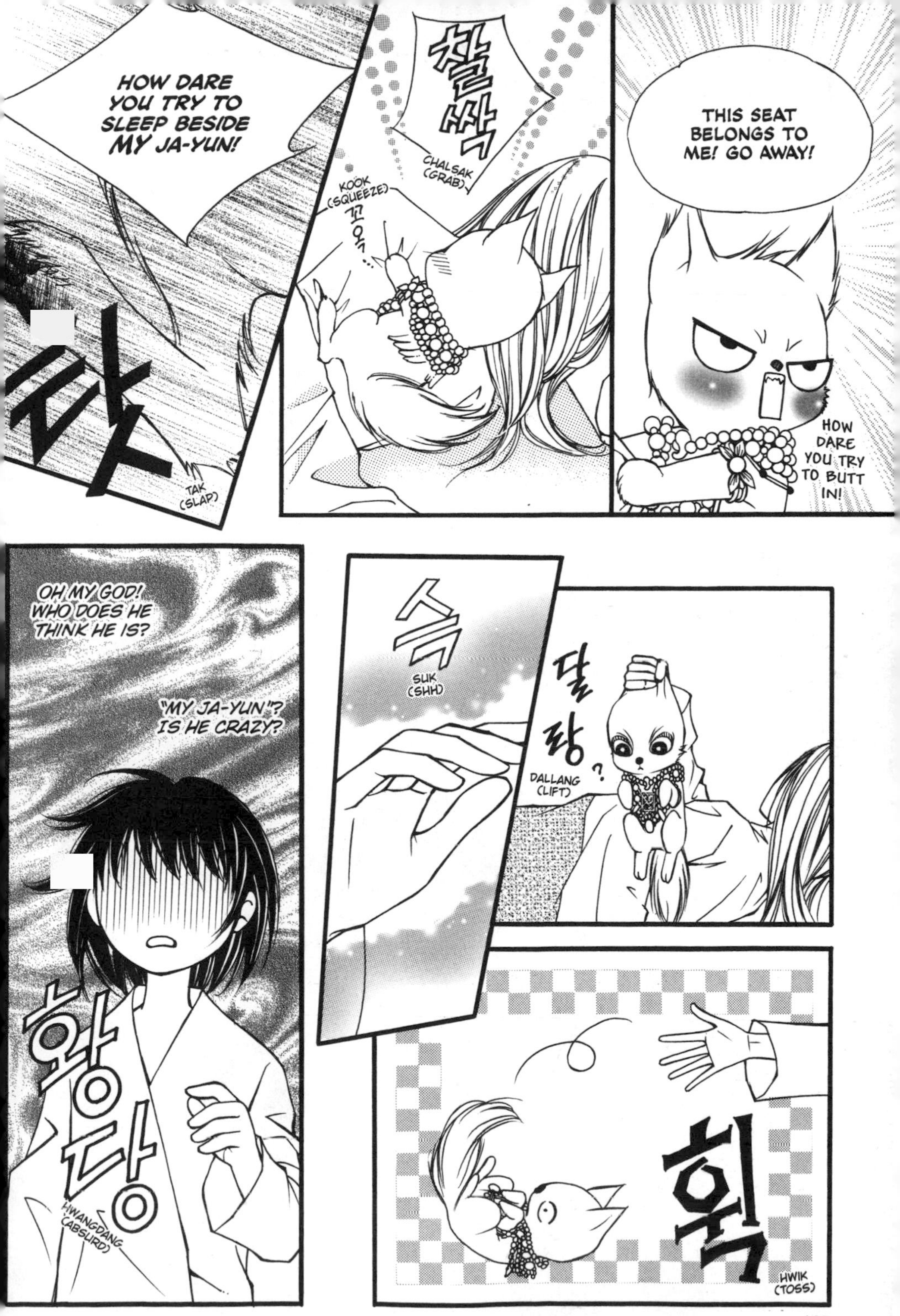
HOW DARE YOU TRY TO SLEEP BESIDE MY JA-YUN!
탁
TAK (SLAP)
찰싹
CHALSAK (GRAB)
꼬옥...
KOOK (SQUEEZE)
THIS SEAT BELONGS TO ME! GO AWAY!
HOW DARE YOU TRY TO BUTT IN!
OH MY GOD! WHO DOES HE THINK HE IS?
"MY JA-YUN"? IS HE CRAZY?
황당
HWANGDANG (ABSURD)
슥
SUK (SHH)
달랑
DALLANG (LIFT)
?
휙
HWIK (TOSS)

YOU WILL SLEEP ON THE FLOOR!

ㅍㅋ! POOB (PFFT)

OH, HE'S SHY.

GUESS HE'S JUST A SHY BOY~.

HEH. ♥

!

I GUESS I SHOULD TRY TO SLEEP.

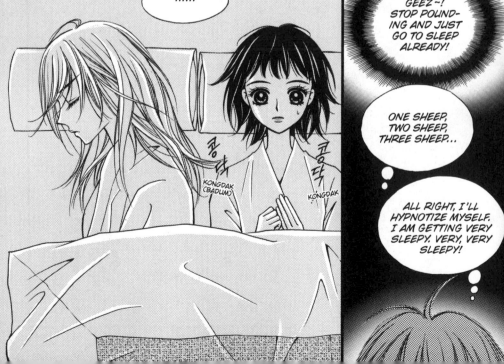

......

KONGDAK (BADUM)

KONGDAK

GEEZ~! STOP POUNDING AND JUST GO TO SLEEP ALREADY!

ONE SHEEP, TWO SHEEP, THREE SHEEP...

ALL RIGHT, I'LL HYPNOTIZE MYSELF. I AM GETTING VERY SLEEPY. VERY, VERY SLEEPY!

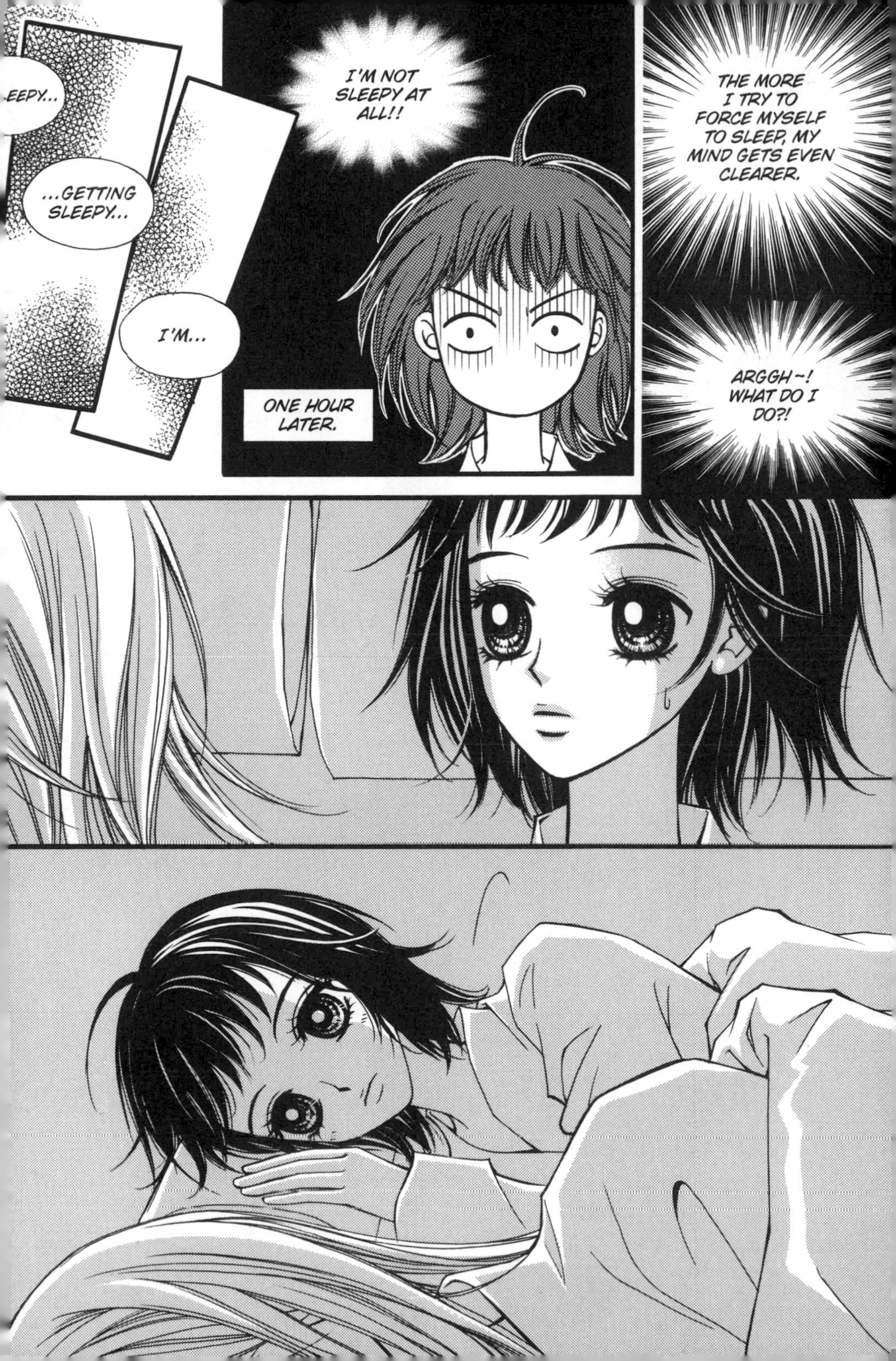
EEPY...
...GETTING SLEEPY...
I'M...
I'M NOT SLEEPY AT ALL!!
ONE HOUR LATER.
THE MORE I TRY TO FORCE MYSELF TO SLEEP, MY MIND GETS EVEN CLEARER.
ARGGH~! WHAT DO I DO?!

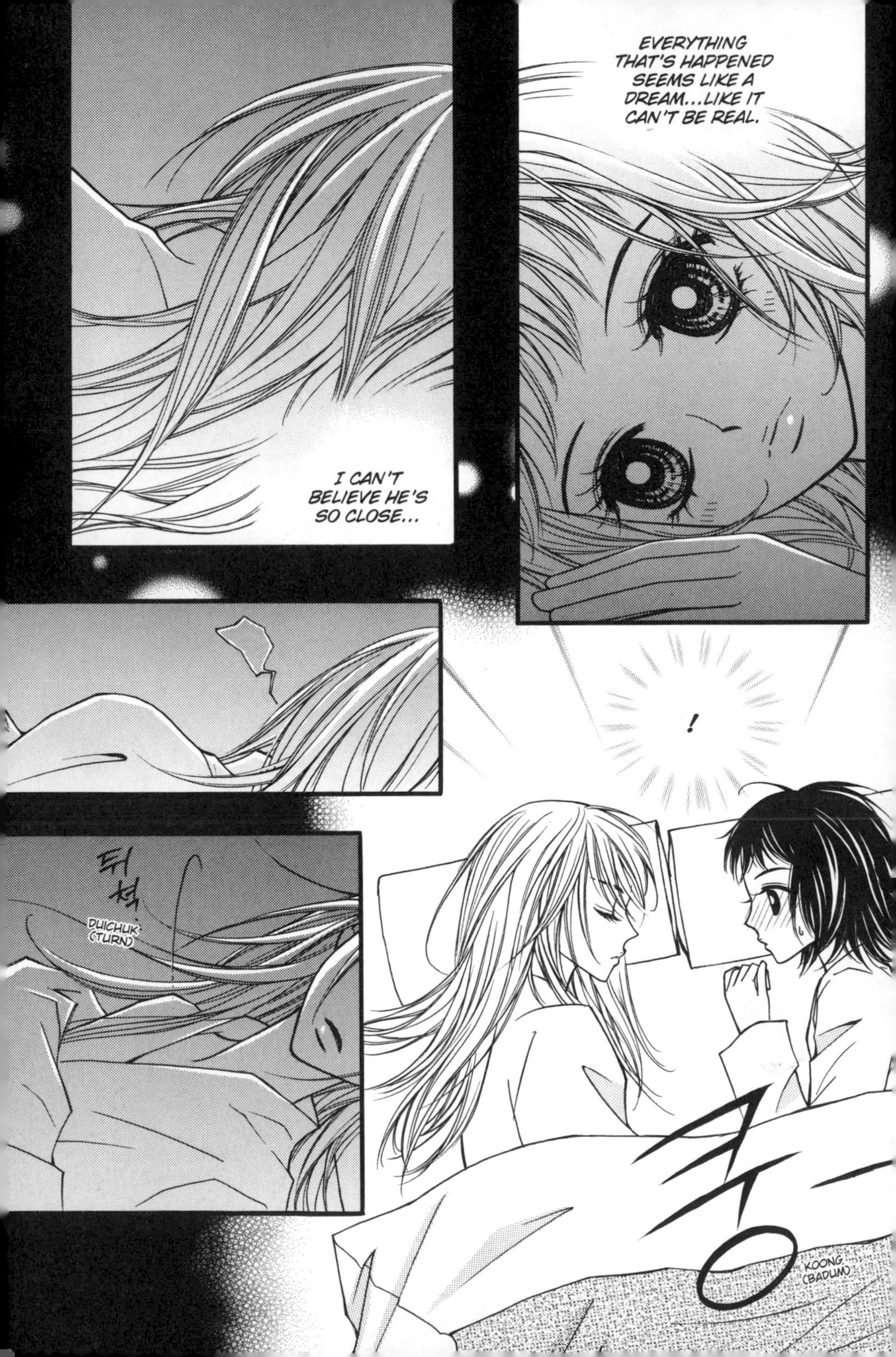
I CAN'T BELIEVE HE'S SO CLOSE...
EVERYTHING THAT'S HAPPENED SEEMS LIKE A DREAM...LIKE IT CAN'T BE REAL.
!
뒤척
DUICHUK (TURN)
KOONG (BADUM)

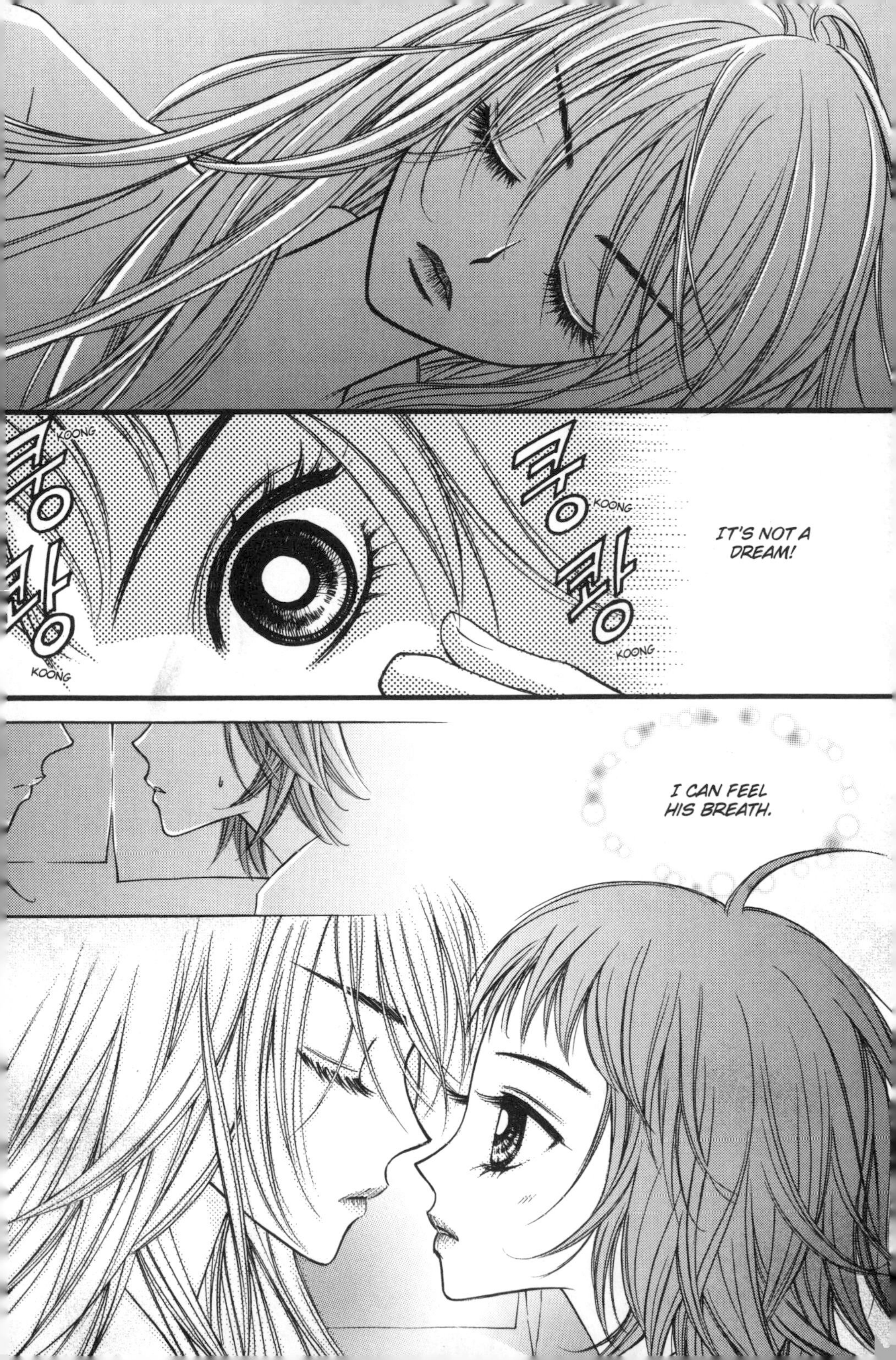
KOONG
KOONG
KOONG
KOONG
IT'S NOT A DREAM!
I CAN FEEL HIS BREATH.

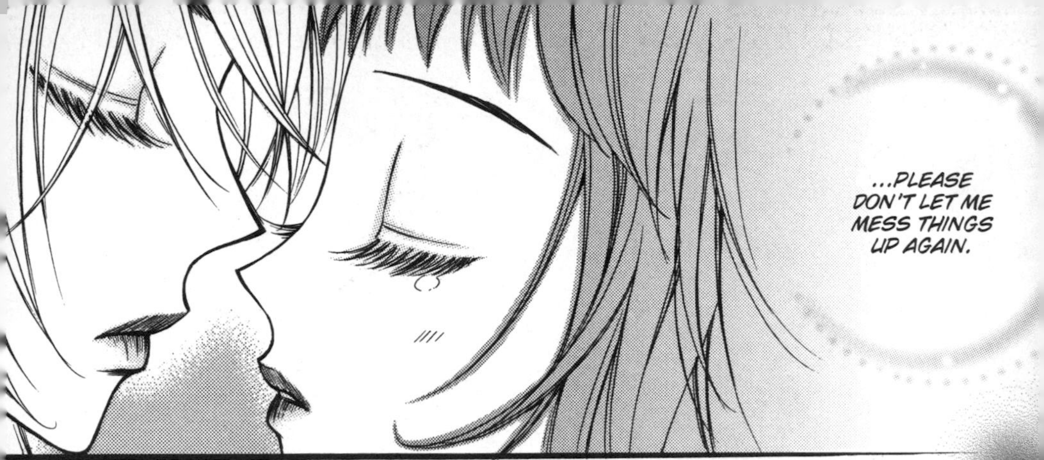
...PLEASE DON'T LET ME MESS THINGS UP AGAIN.
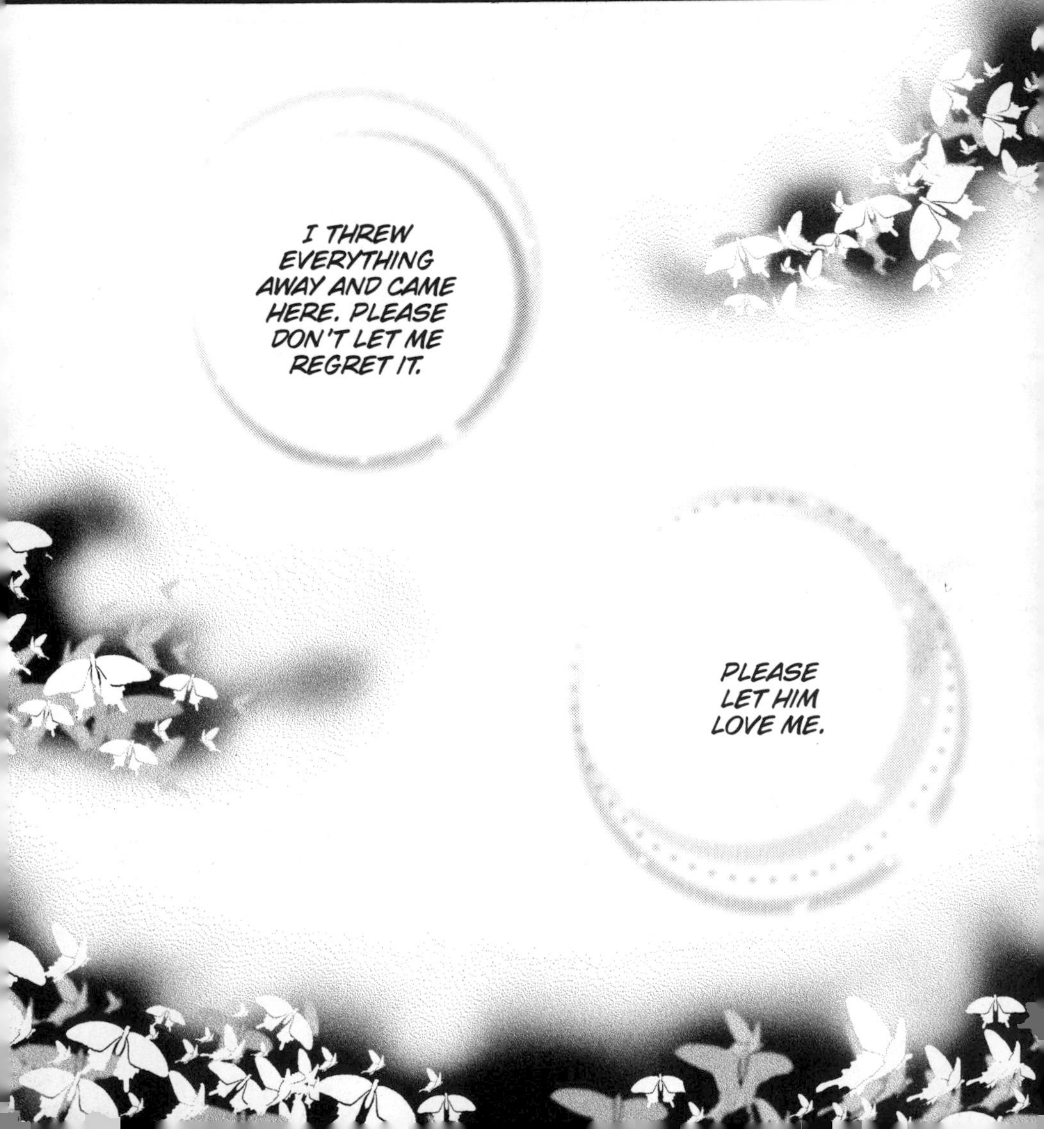
I THREW EVERYTHING AWAY AND CAME HERE. PLEASE DON'T LET ME REGRET IT.
PLEASE LET HIM LOVE ME.

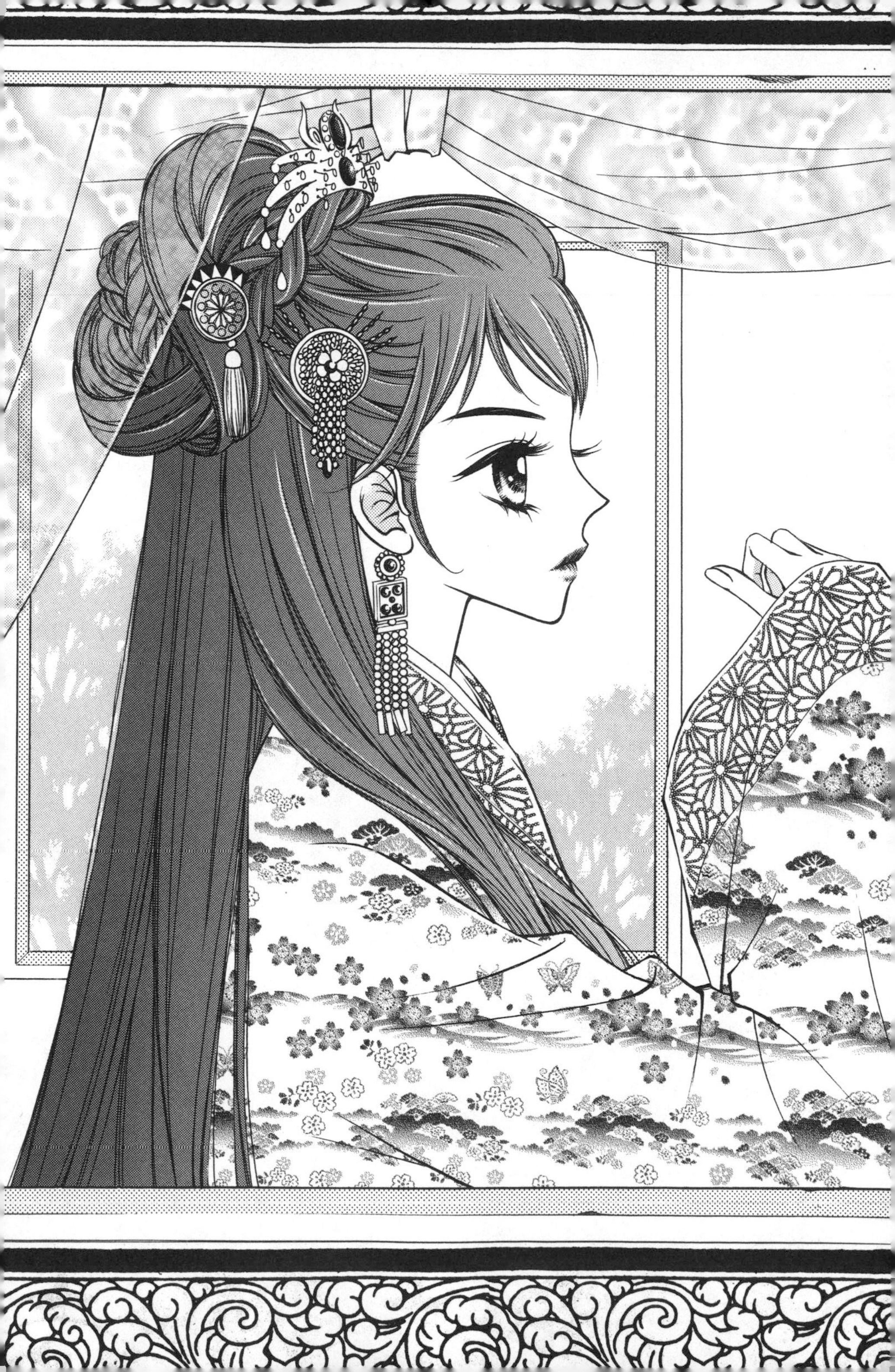

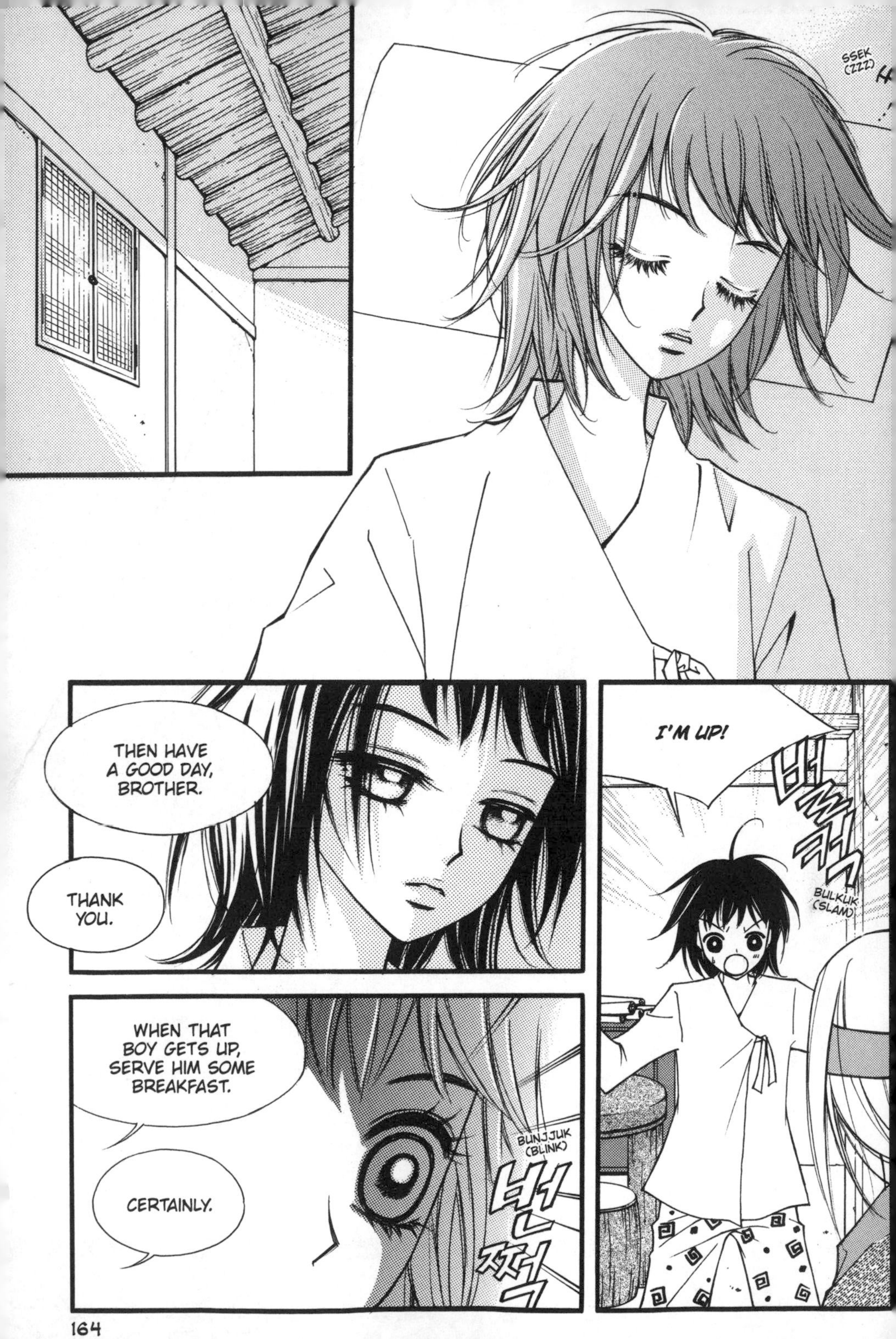

SSEK (ZZZ)
THEN HAVE A GOOD DAY, BROTHER.
THANK YOU.
WHEN THAT BOY GETS UP, SERVE HIM SOME BREAKFAST.
CERTAINLY.
BUNJJUK (BLINK)
I'M UP!
BULKUK (SLAM)

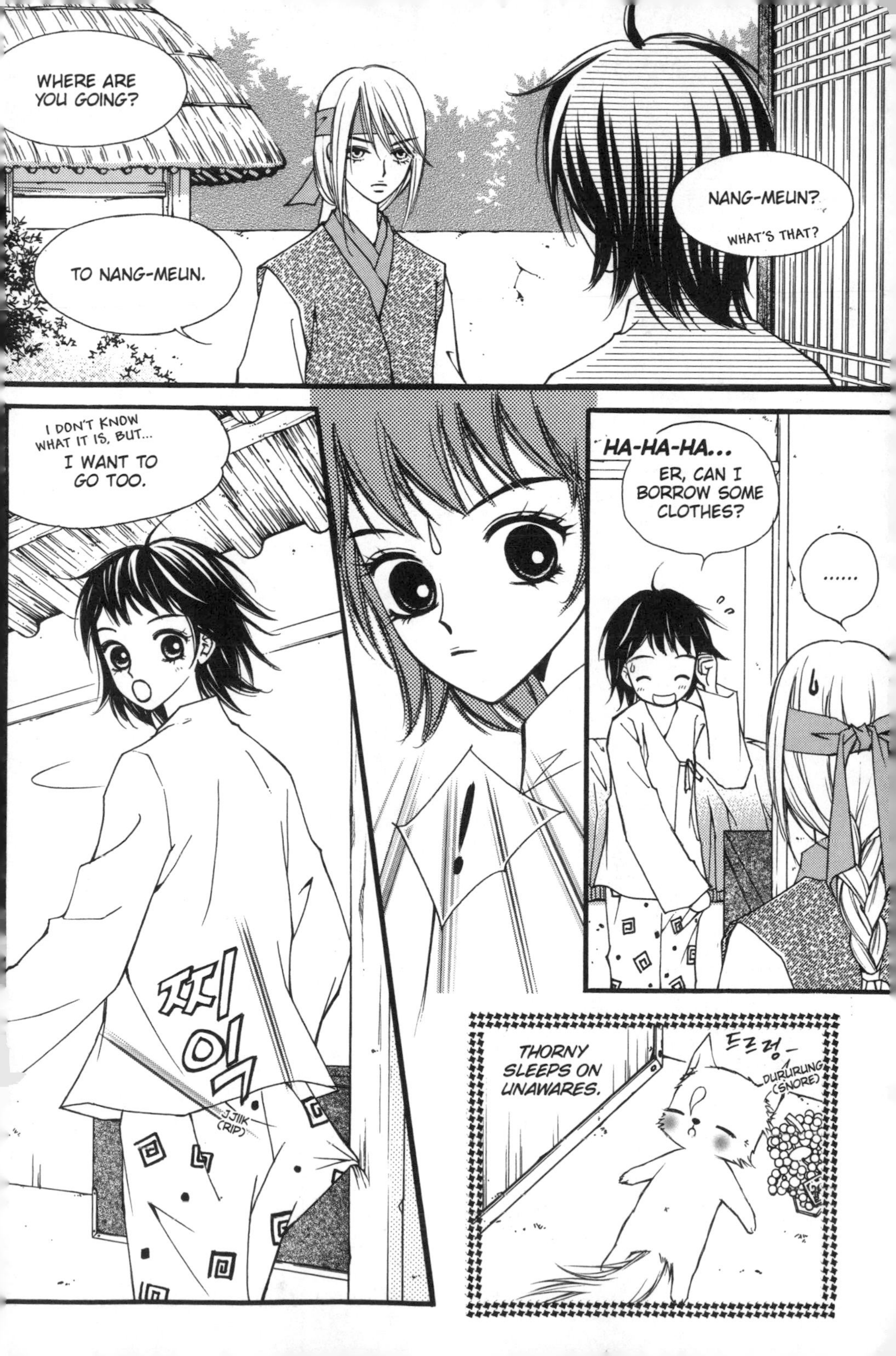

WHERE ARE YOU GOING?
TO NANG-MEUN.
NANG-MEUN? WHAT'S THAT?
I DON'T KNOW WHAT IT IS, BUT... I WANT TO GO TOO.
찌익
JJIIK (RIP)
!
HA-HA-HA...
ER, CAN I BORROW SOME CLOTHES?
......
THORNY SLEEPS ON UNAWARES.
드르렁
DURURUNG (SNORE)

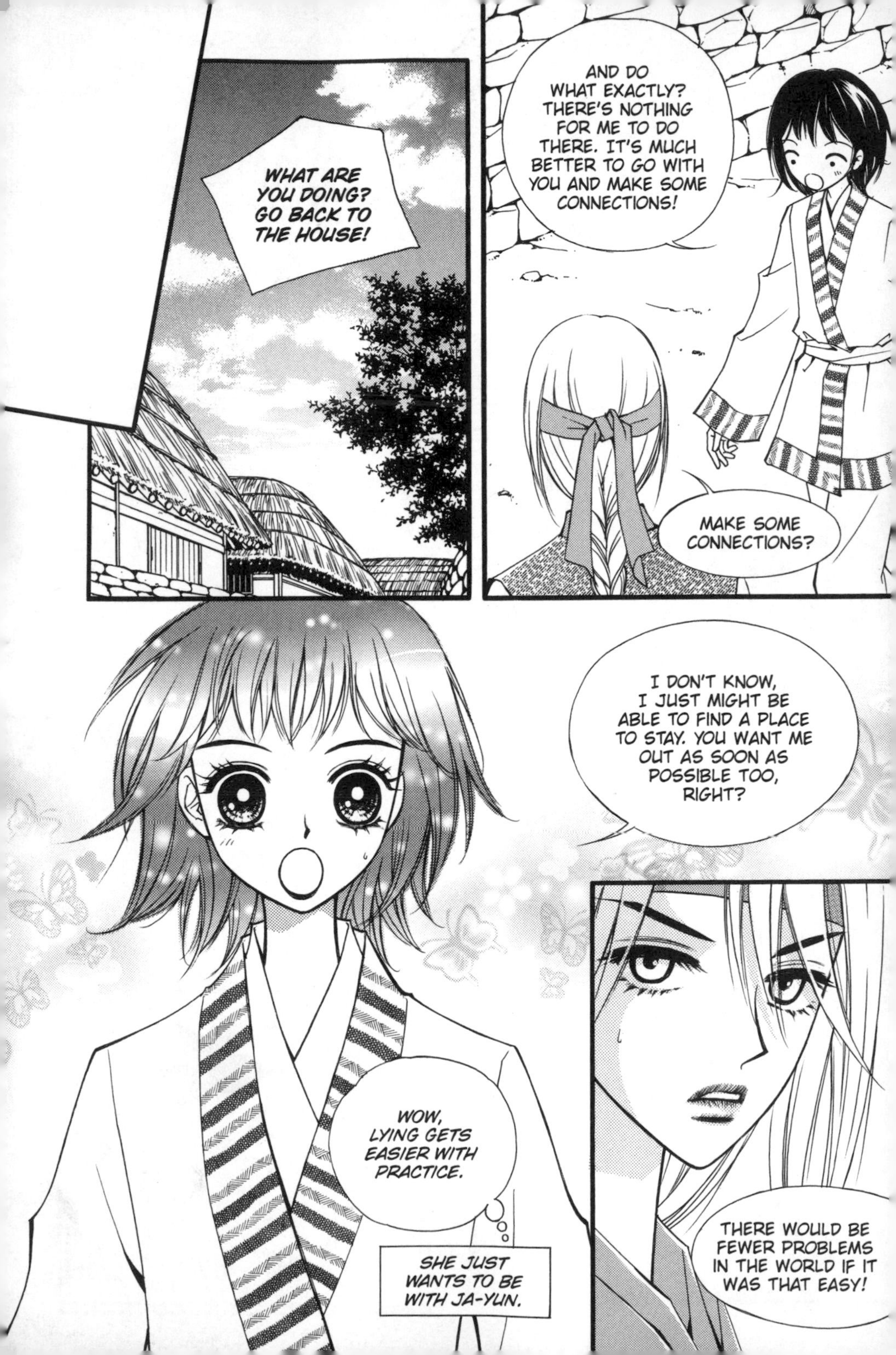
WHAT ARE YOU DOING? GO BACK TO THE HOUSE!
AND DO WHAT EXACTLY? THERE'S NOTHING FOR ME TO DO THERE. IT'S MUCH BETTER TO GO WITH YOU AND MAKE SOME CONNECTIONS!
MAKE SOME CONNECTIONS?
I DON'T KNOW, I JUST MIGHT BE ABLE TO FIND A PLACE TO STAY. YOU WANT ME OUT AS SOON AS POSSIBLE TOO, RIGHT?
WOW, LYING GETS EASIER WITH PRACTICE.
SHE JUST WANTS TO BE WITH JA-YUN.
THERE WOULD BE FEWER PROBLEMS IN THE WORLD IF IT WAS THAT EASY!

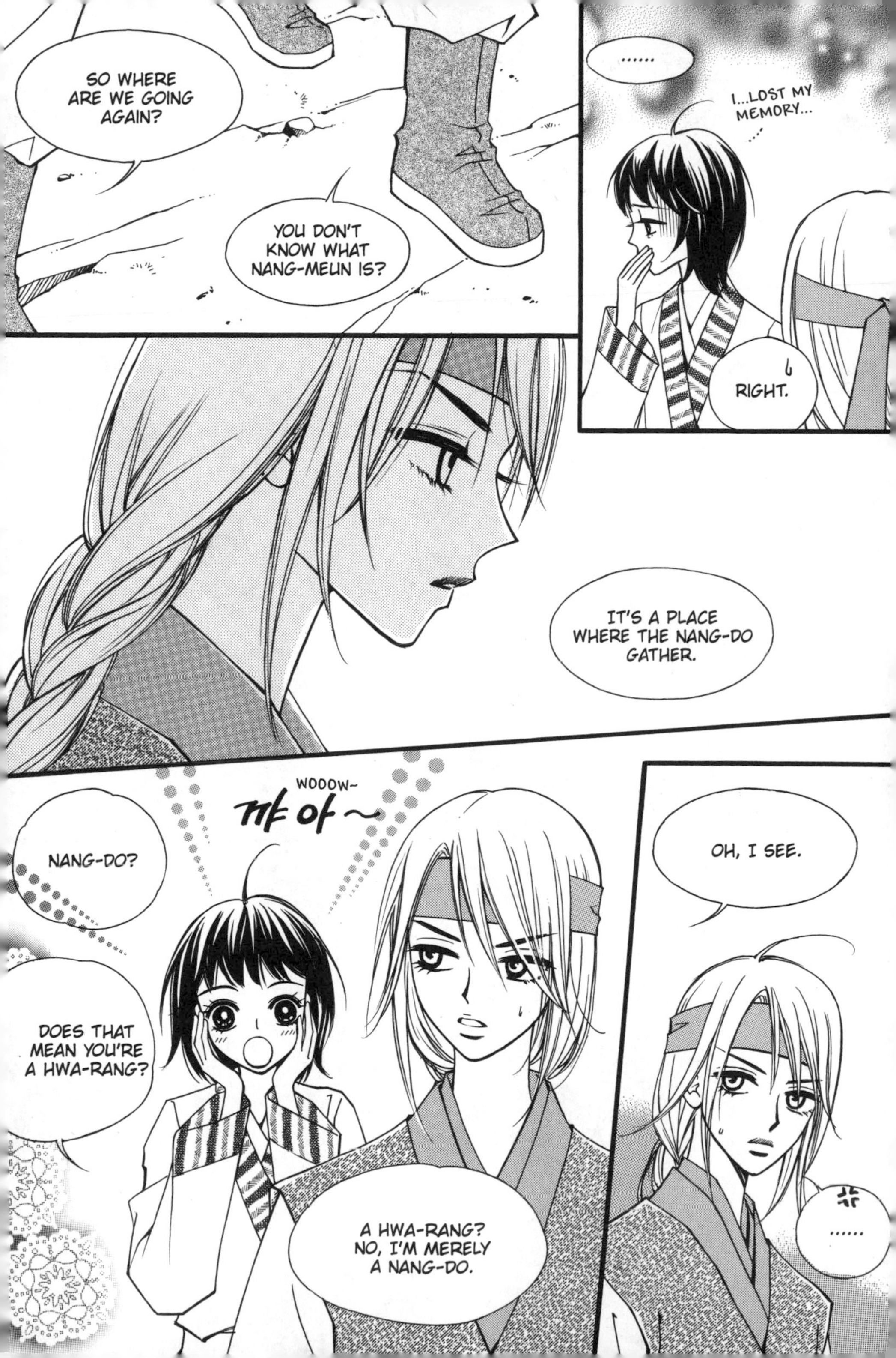
SO WHERE ARE WE GOING AGAIN?
YOU DON'T KNOW WHAT NANG-MEUN IS?
......
I...LOST MY MEMORY...
RIGHT.
IT'S A PLACE WHERE THE NANG-DO GATHER.
NANG-DO?
WOOOW-
꺄아~
DOES THAT MEAN YOU'RE A HWA-RANG?
A HWA-RANG? NO, I'M MERELY A NANG-DO.
OH, I SEE.
......

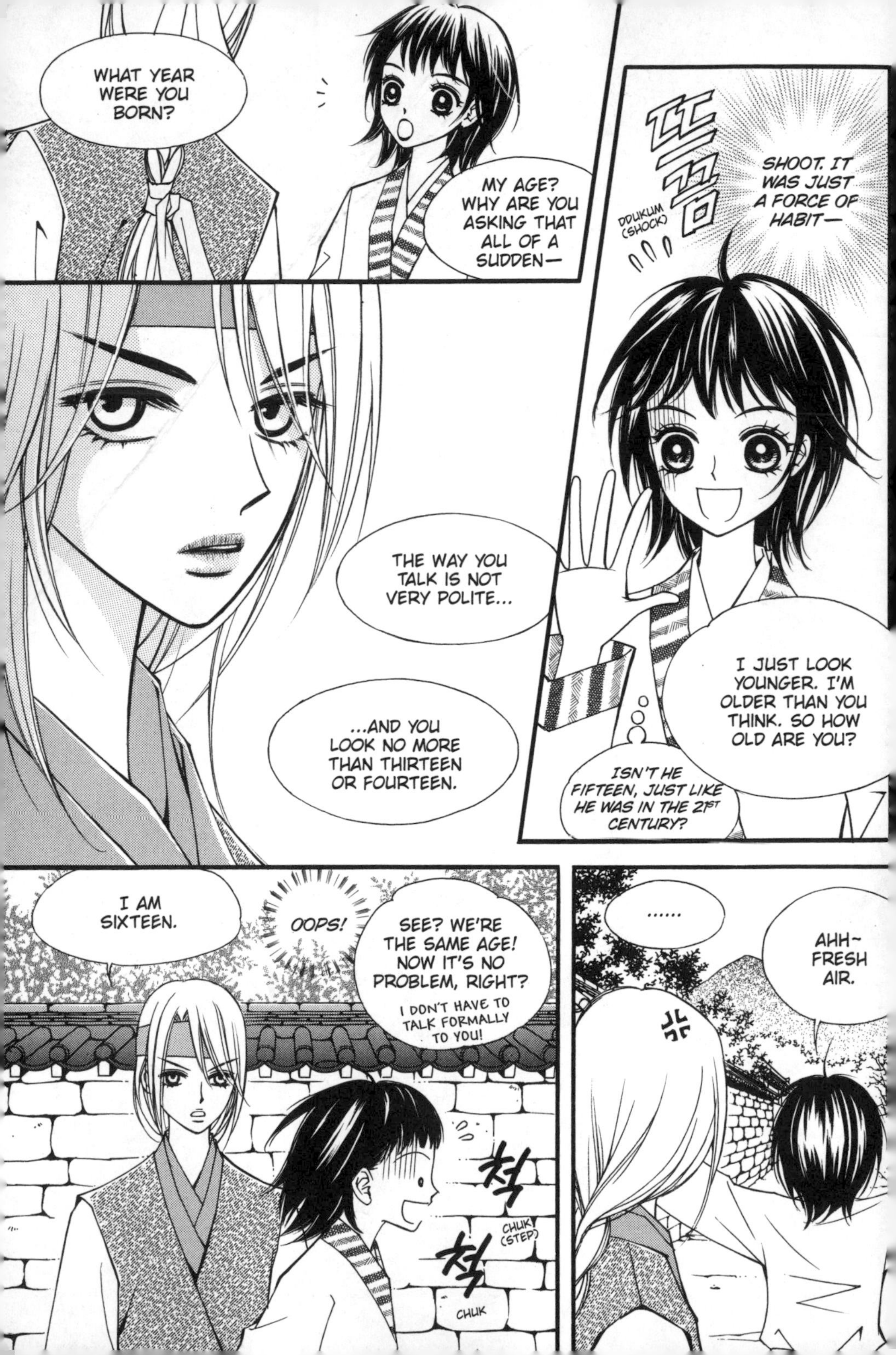
WHAT YEAR WERE YOU BORN?
MY AGE? WHY ARE YOU ASKING THAT ALL OF A SUDDEN—
THE WAY YOU TALK IS NOT VERY POLITE...
...AND YOU LOOK NO MORE THAN THIRTEEN OR FOURTEEN.
뜨끔
DDUKUM (SHOCK)
SHOOT. IT WAS JUST A FORCE OF HABIT—
I JUST LOOK YOUNGER. I'M OLDER THAN YOU THINK. SO HOW OLD ARE YOU?
ISN'T HE FIFTEEN, JUST LIKE HE WAS IN THE 21ST CENTURY?
I AM SIXTEEN.
OOPS!
SEE? WE'RE THE SAME AGE! NOW IT'S NO PROBLEM, RIGHT?
I DON'T HAVE TO TALK FORMALLY TO YOU!
척
CHUK (STEP)
척
CHUK
......
AHH~ FRESH AIR.

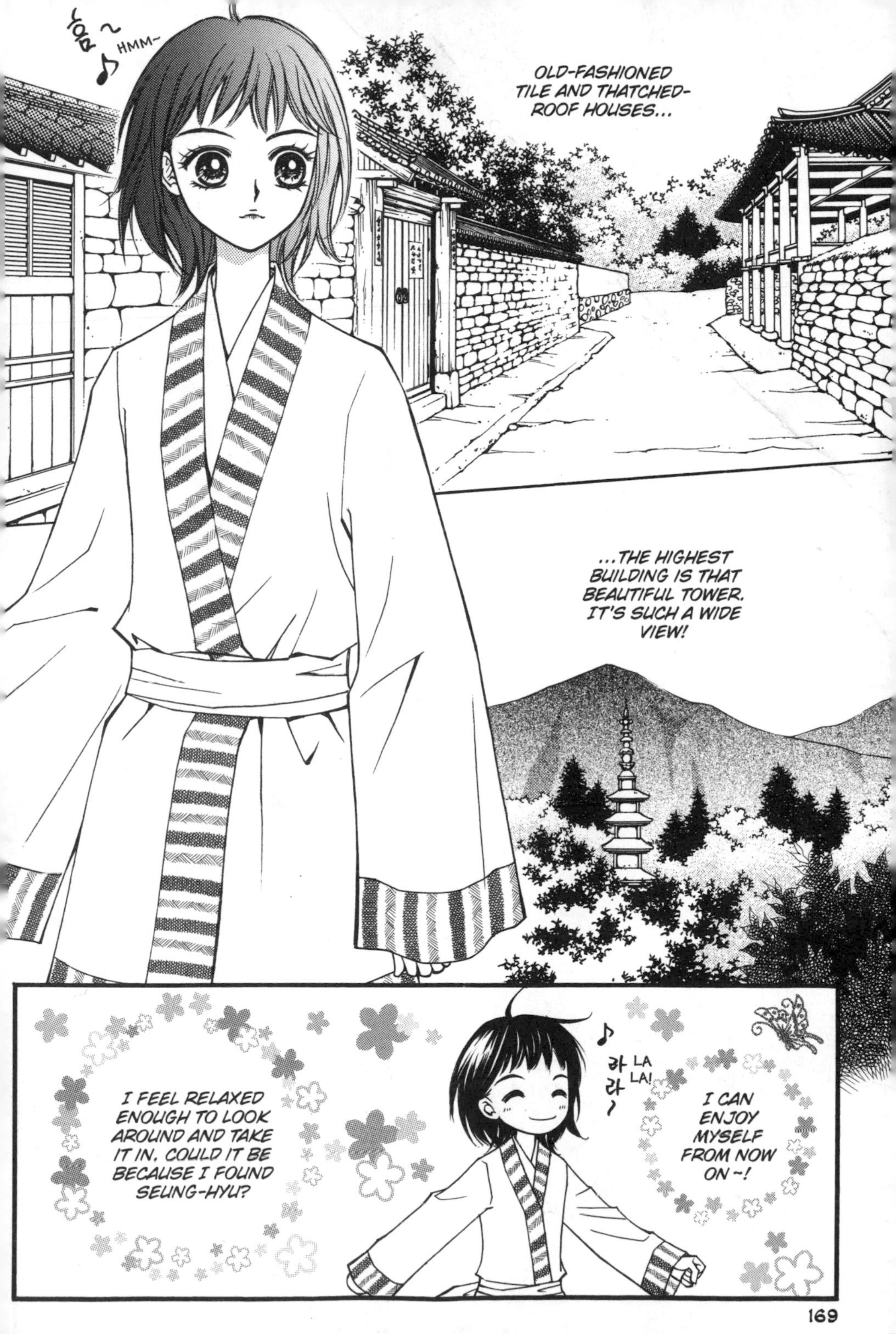

흠~ HMM-
OLD-FASHIONED TILE AND THATCHED-ROOF HOUSES...
...THE HIGHEST BUILDING IS THAT BEAUTIFUL TOWER. IT'S SUCH A WIDE VIEW!
I FEEL RELAXED ENOUGH TO LOOK AROUND AND TAKE IT IN. COULD IT BE BECAUSE I FOUND SEUNG-HYU?
라라~ LA LA!
I CAN ENJOY MYSELF FROM NOW ON~!

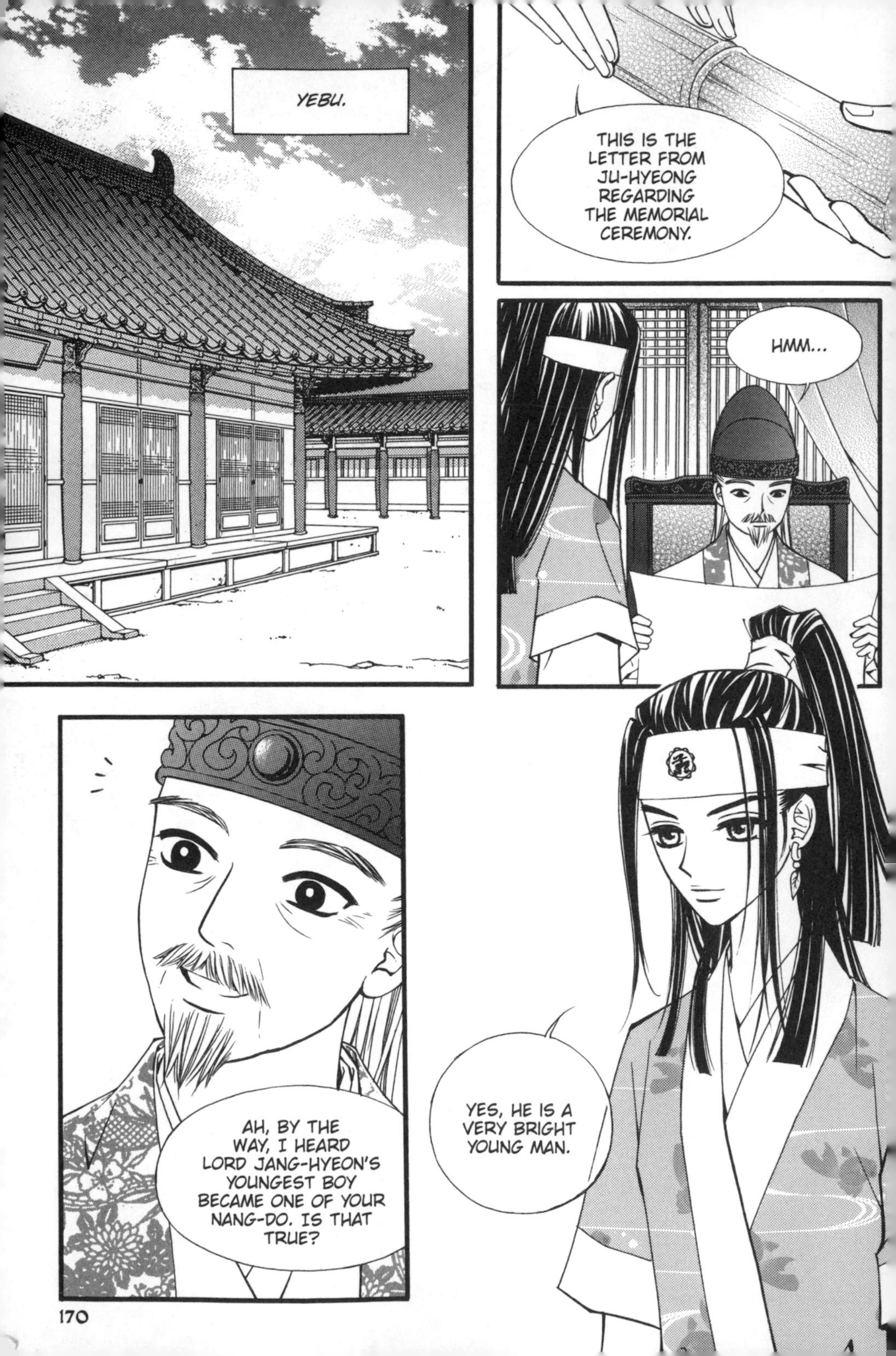
YEBU.
THIS IS THE LETTER FROM JU-HYEONG REGARDING THE MEMORIAL CEREMONY.
HMM...
AH, BY THE WAY, I HEARD LORD JANG-HYEON'S YOUNGEST BOY BECAME ONE OF YOUR NANG-DO. IS THAT TRUE?
YES, HE IS A VERY BRIGHT YOUNG MAN.

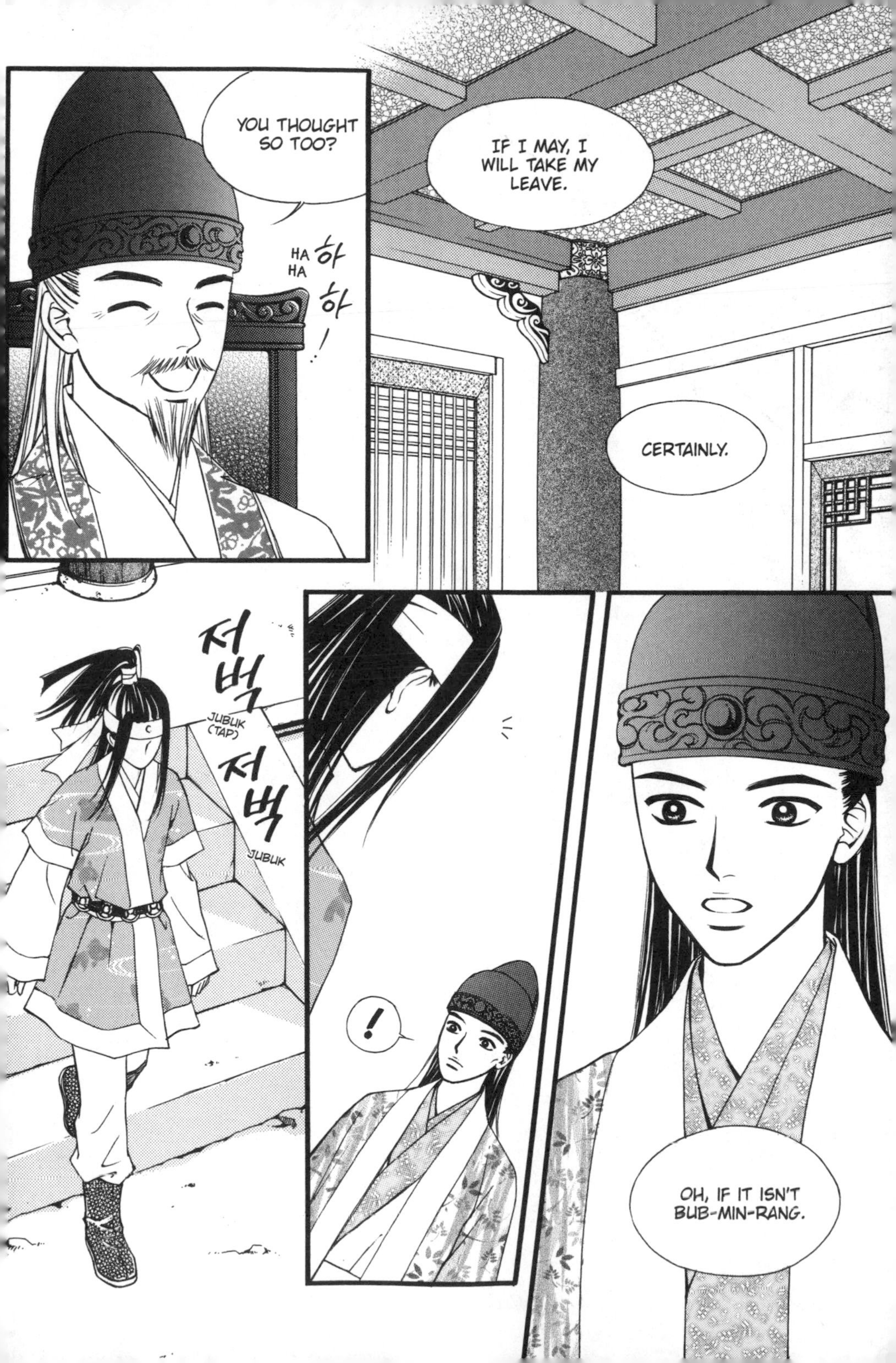
YOU THOUGHT SO TOO?
HA HA
하하!
IF I MAY, I WILL TAKE MY LEAVE.
CERTAINLY.
저벅
JUBUK (TAP)
저벅
JUBUK
!
OH, IF IT ISN'T BUB-MIN-RANG.

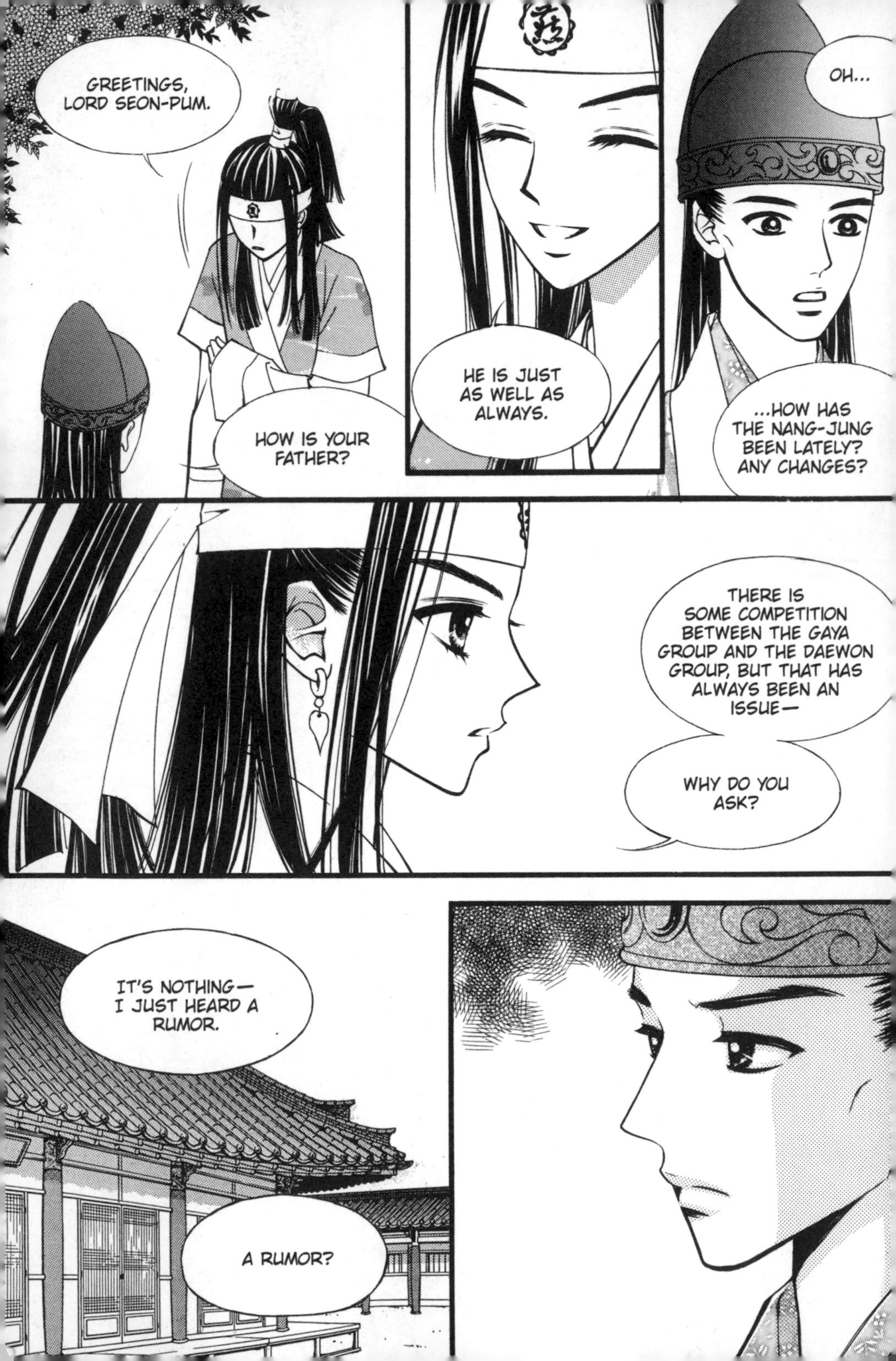
GREETINGS, LORD SEON-PUM.
HOW IS YOUR FATHER?
HE IS JUST AS WELL AS ALWAYS.
OH...
...HOW HAS THE NANG-JUNG BEEN LATELY? ANY CHANGES?
THERE IS SOME COMPETITION BETWEEN THE GAYA GROUP AND THE DAEWON GROUP, BUT THAT HAS ALWAYS BEEN AN ISSUE—
WHY DO YOU ASK?
IT'S NOTHING— I JUST HEARD A RUMOR.
A RUMOR?

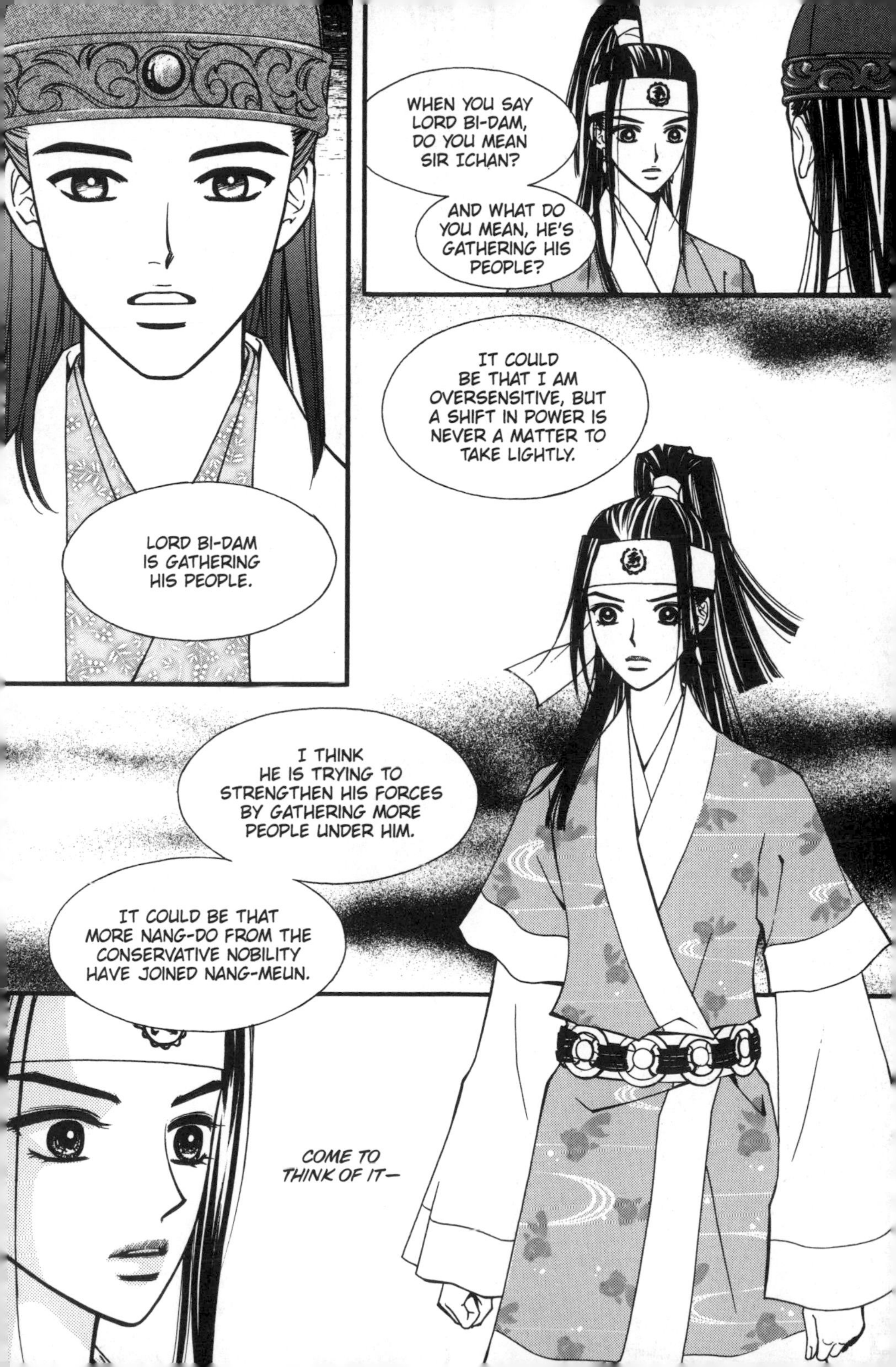
LORD BI-DAM IS GATHERING HIS PEOPLE.
WHEN YOU SAY LORD BI-DAM, DO YOU MEAN SIR ICHAN?
AND WHAT DO YOU MEAN, HE'S GATHERING HIS PEOPLE?
IT COULD BE THAT I AM OVERSENSITIVE, BUT A SHIFT IN POWER IS NEVER A MATTER TO TAKE LIGHTLY.
I THINK HE IS TRYING TO STRENGTHEN HIS FORCES BY GATHERING MORE PEOPLE UNDER HIM.
IT COULD BE THAT MORE NANG-DO FROM THE CONSERVATIVE NOBILITY HAVE JOINED NANG-MEUN.
COME TO THINK OF IT—

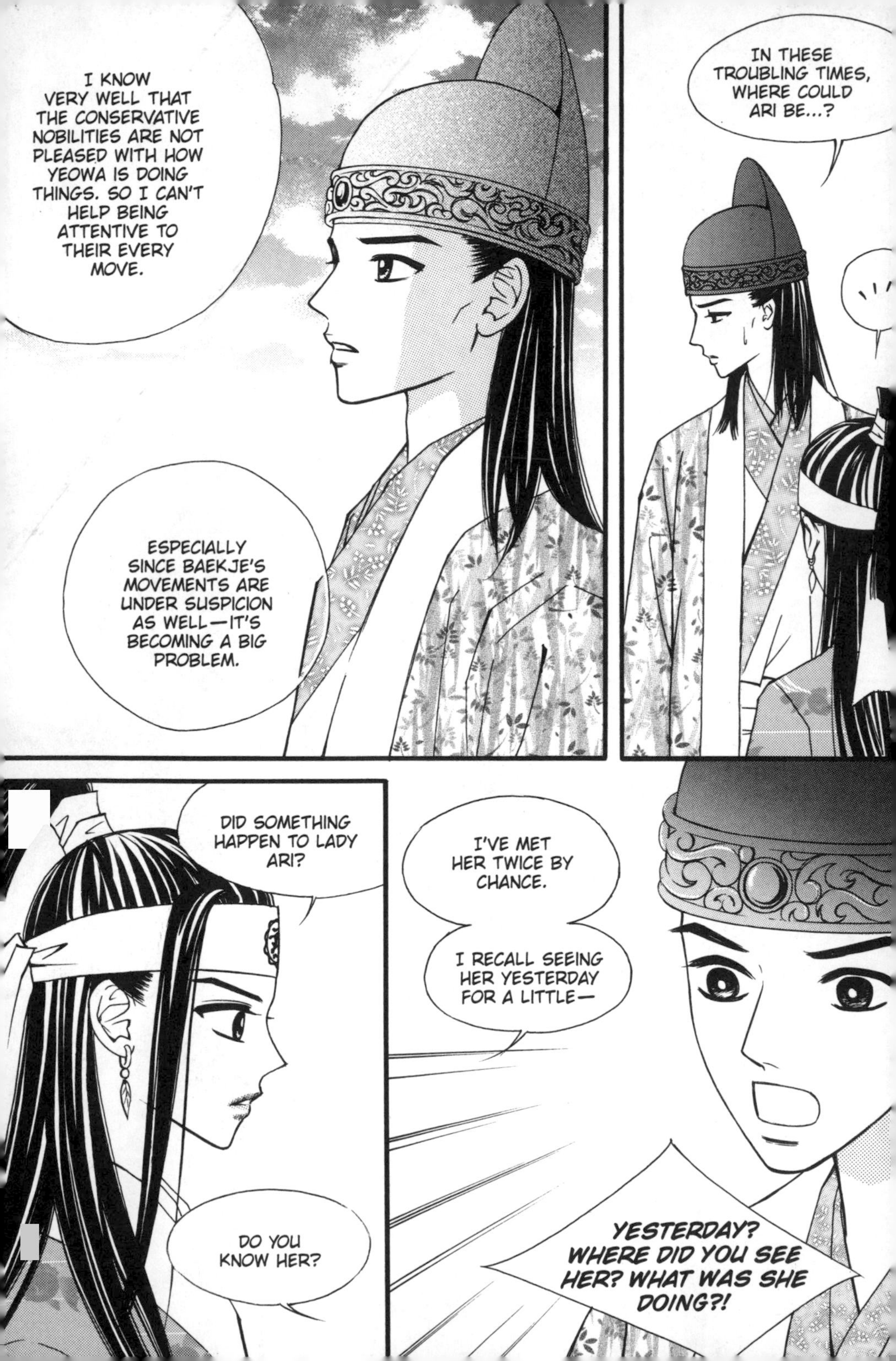

I KNOW VERY WELL THAT THE CONSERVATIVE NOBILITIES ARE NOT PLEASED WITH HOW YEOWA IS DOING THINGS. SO I CAN'T HELP BEING ATTENTIVE TO THEIR EVERY MOVE.
ESPECIALLY SINCE BAEKJE'S MOVEMENTS ARE UNDER SUSPICION AS WELL—IT'S BECOMING A BIG PROBLEM.
IN THESE TROUBLING TIMES, WHERE COULD ARI BE...?
...
DID SOMETHING HAPPEN TO LADY ARI?
DO YOU KNOW HER?
I'VE MET HER TWICE BY CHANCE.
I RECALL SEEING HER YESTERDAY FOR A LITTLE—
YESTERDAY? WHERE DID YOU SEE HER? WHAT WAS SHE DOING?!

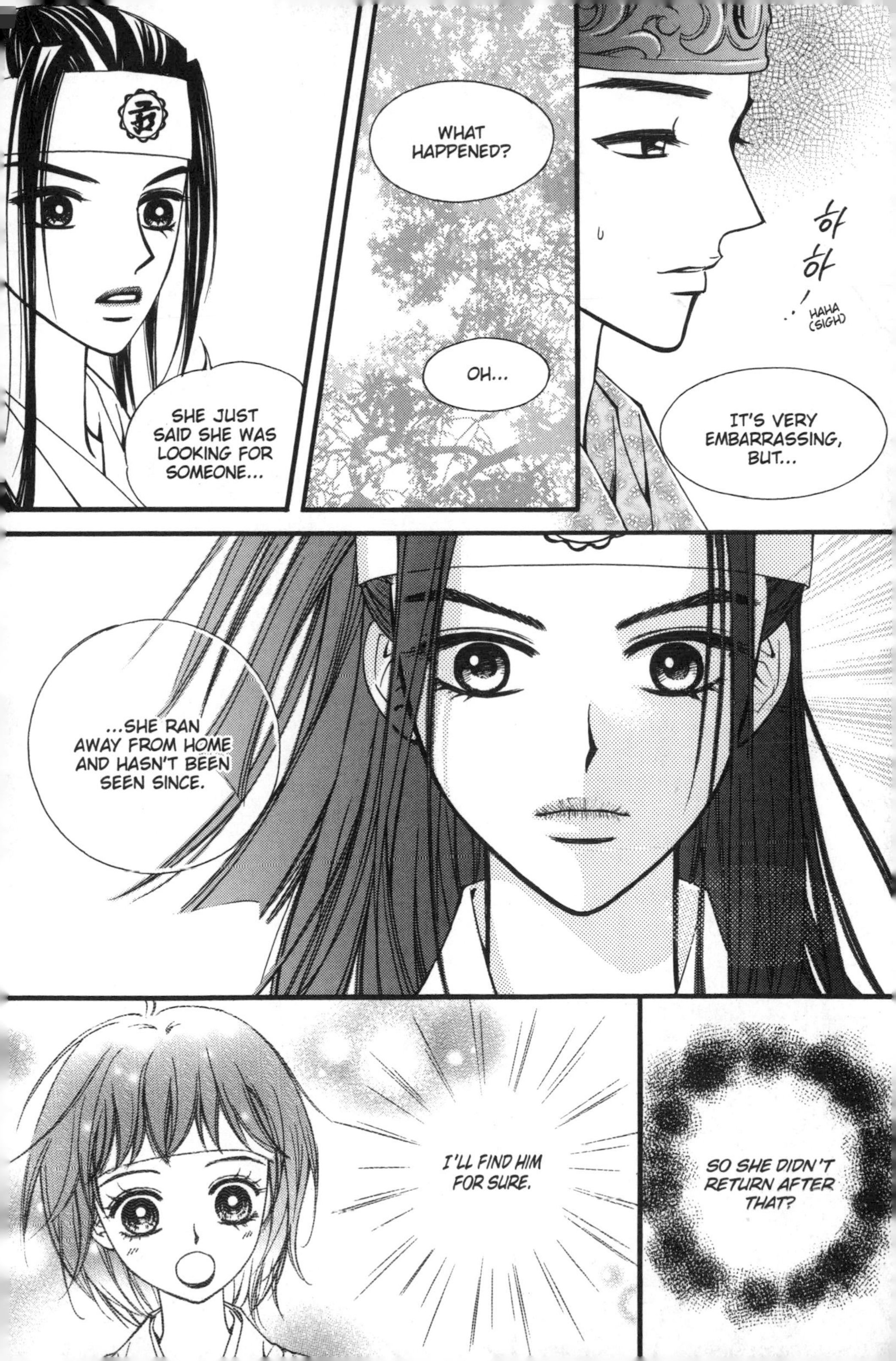
SHE JUST SAID SHE WAS LOOKING FOR SOMEONE...
WHAT HAPPENED?
OH...
하 하
HAHA (SIGH)
IT'S VERY EMBARRASSING, BUT...
...SHE RAN AWAY FROM HOME AND HASN'T BEEN SEEN SINCE.
I'LL FIND HIM FOR SURE.
SO SHE DIDN'T RETURN AFTER THAT?

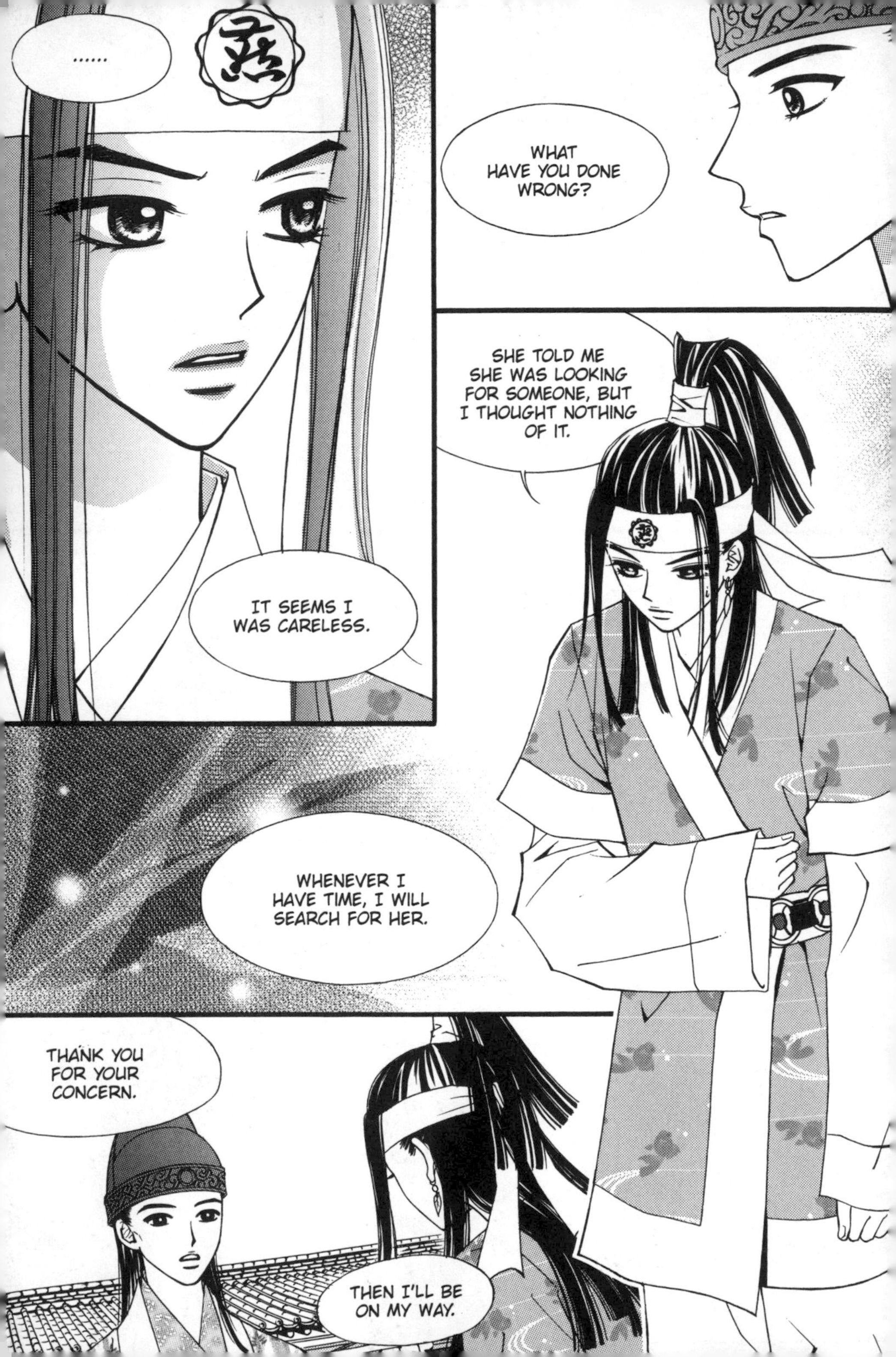
......
IT SEEMS I WAS CARELESS.
WHAT HAVE YOU DONE WRONG?
SHE TOLD ME SHE WAS LOOKING FOR SOMEONE, BUT I THOUGHT NOTHING OF IT.
WHENEVER I HAVE TIME, I WILL SEARCH FOR HER.
THANK YOU FOR YOUR CONCERN.
THEN I'LL BE ON MY WAY.

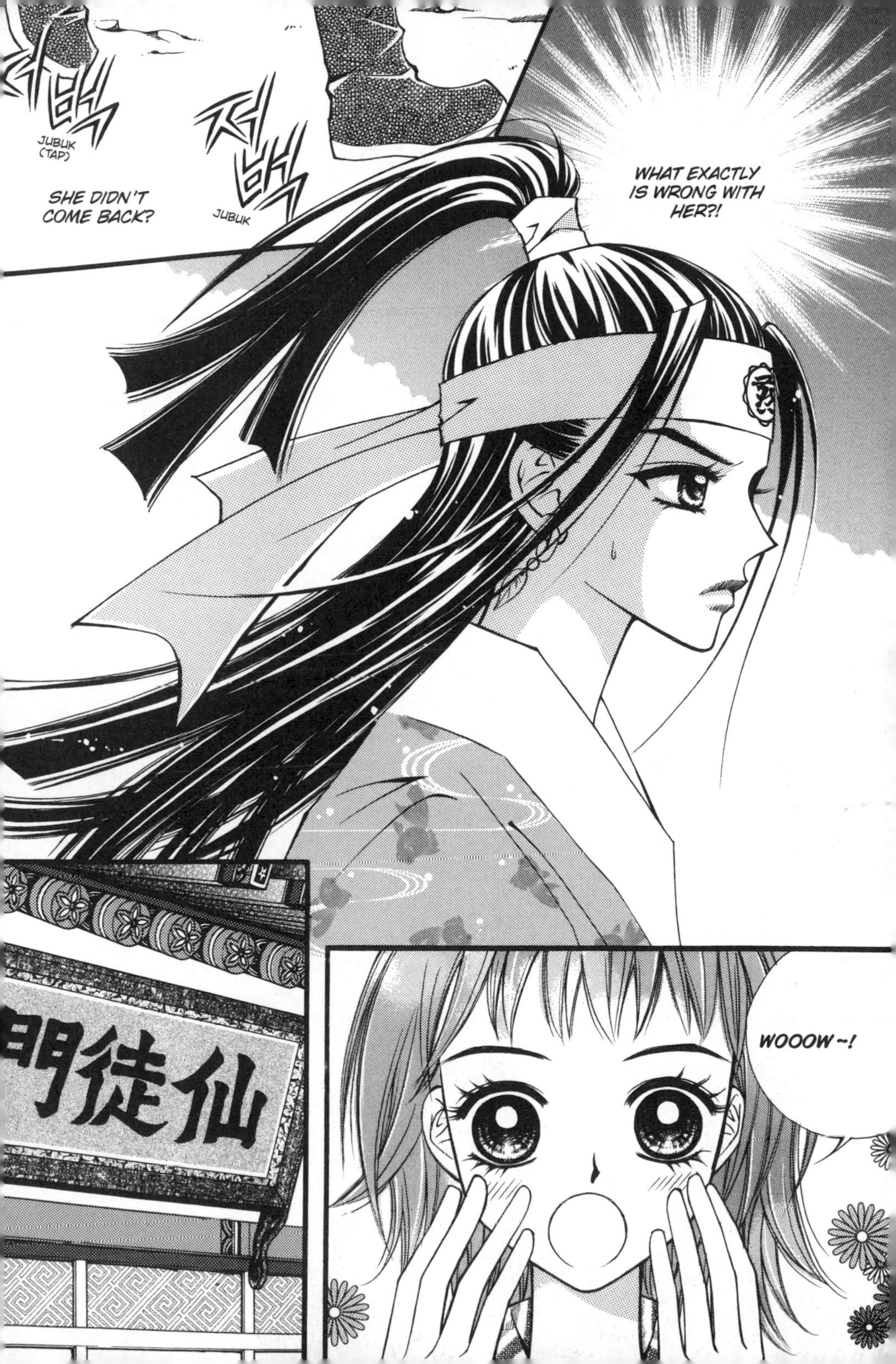

JUBUK (TAP)
SHE DIDN'T COME BACK?
저벅
JUBUK
WHAT EXACTLY IS WRONG WITH HER?!
WOOOW~!

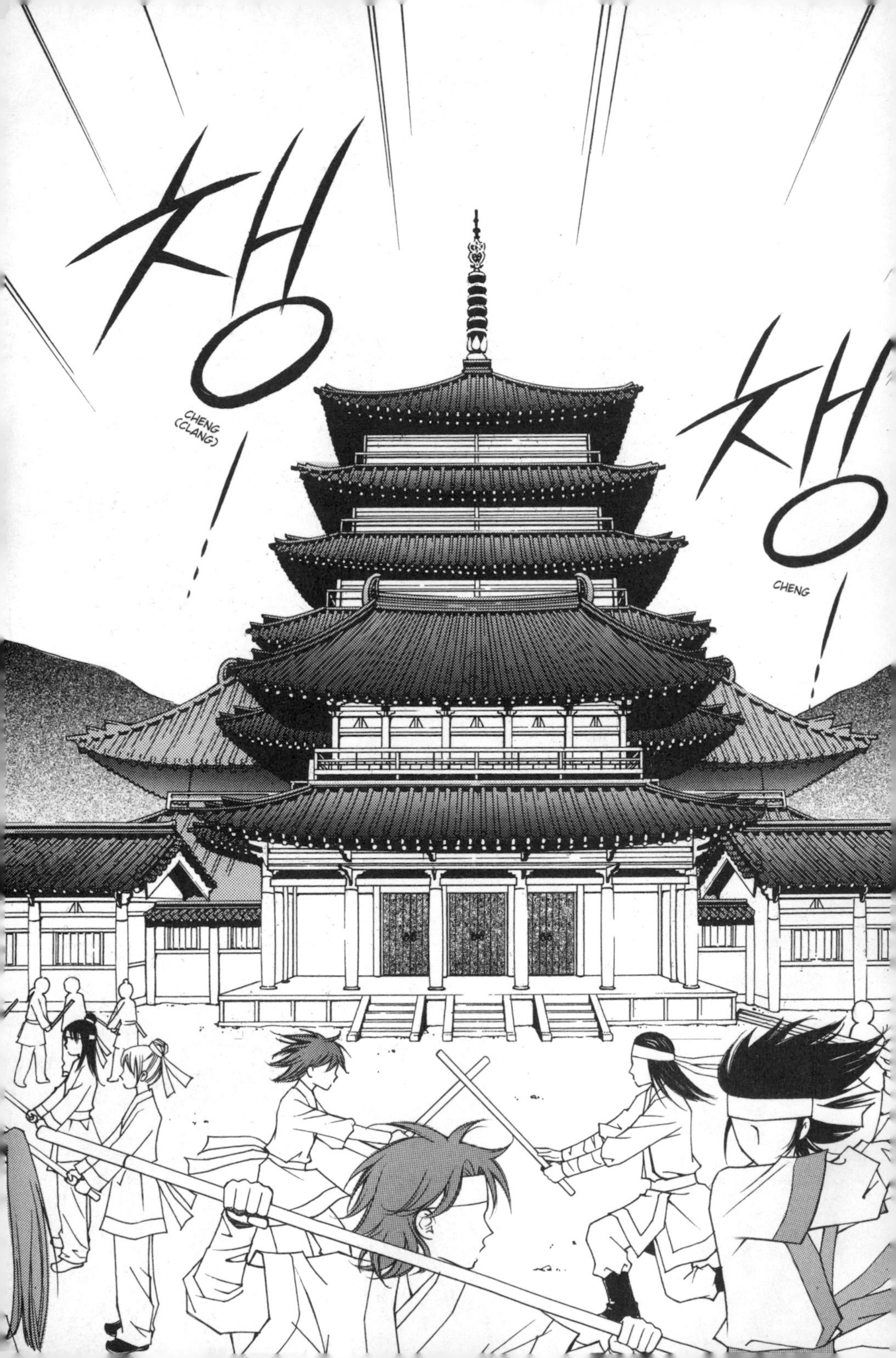
챙!
CHENG (CLANG)
챙!
CHENG

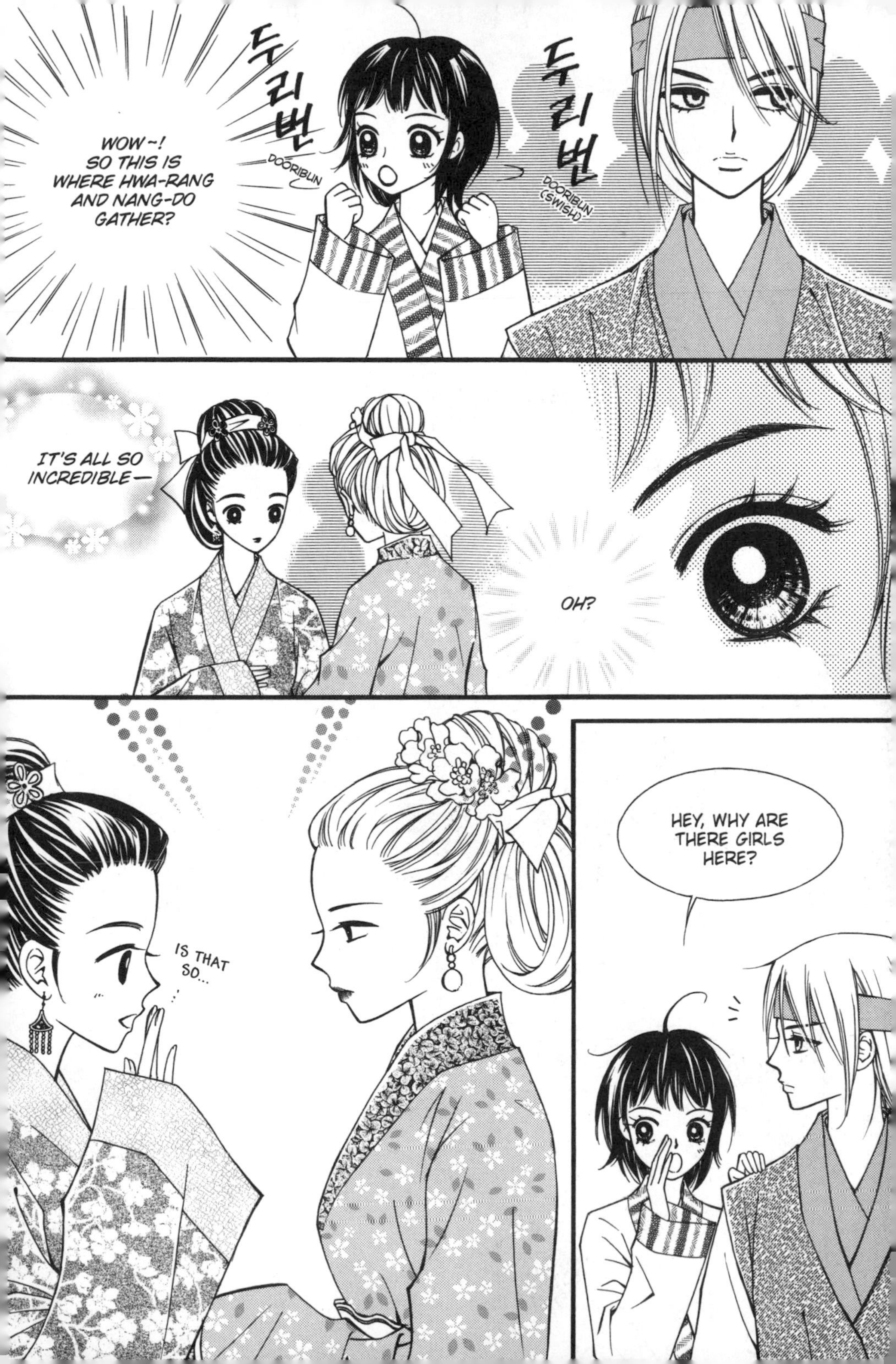
WOW~! SO THIS IS WHERE HWA-RANG AND NANG-DO GATHER?
두리번
DOORIBUN
두리번
DOORIBUN (SWISH)
IT'S ALL SO INCREDIBLE—
OH?
IS THAT SO...
HEY, WHY ARE THERE GIRLS HERE?

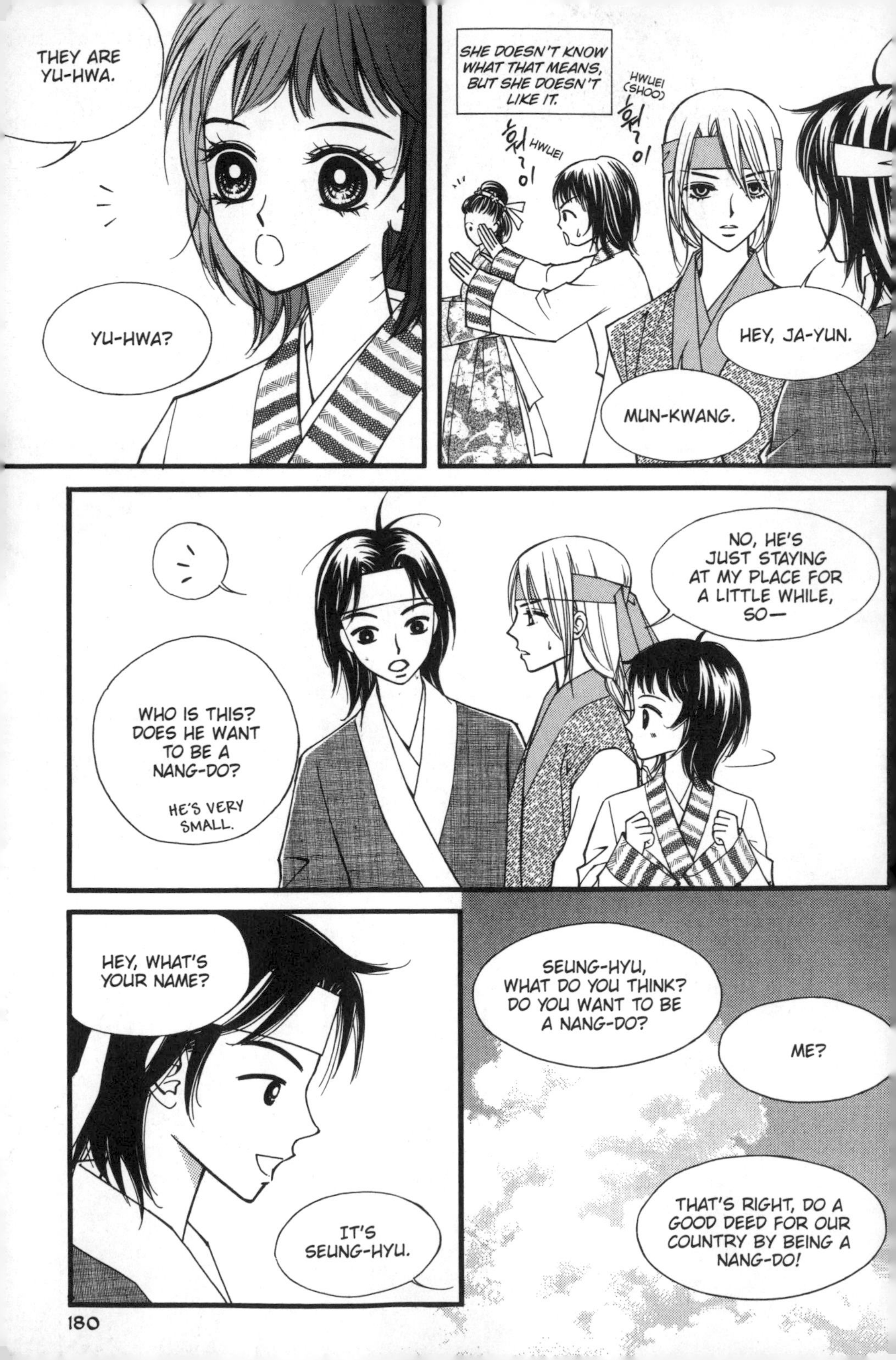
THEY ARE YU-HWA.
YU-HWA?
SHE DOESN'T KNOW WHAT THAT MEANS, BUT SHE DOESN'T LIKE IT.
HWUEI (SHOO)
HWUEI
HEY, JA-YUN.
MUN-KWANG.
...
WHO IS THIS? DOES HE WANT TO BE A NANG-DO?
HE'S VERY SMALL.
NO, HE'S JUST STAYING AT MY PLACE FOR A LITTLE WHILE, SO—
HEY, WHAT'S YOUR NAME?
IT'S SEUNG-HYU.
SEUNG-HYU, WHAT DO YOU THINK? DO YOU WANT TO BE A NANG-DO?
ME?
THAT'S RIGHT, DO A GOOD DEED FOR OUR COUNTRY BY BEING A NANG-DO!

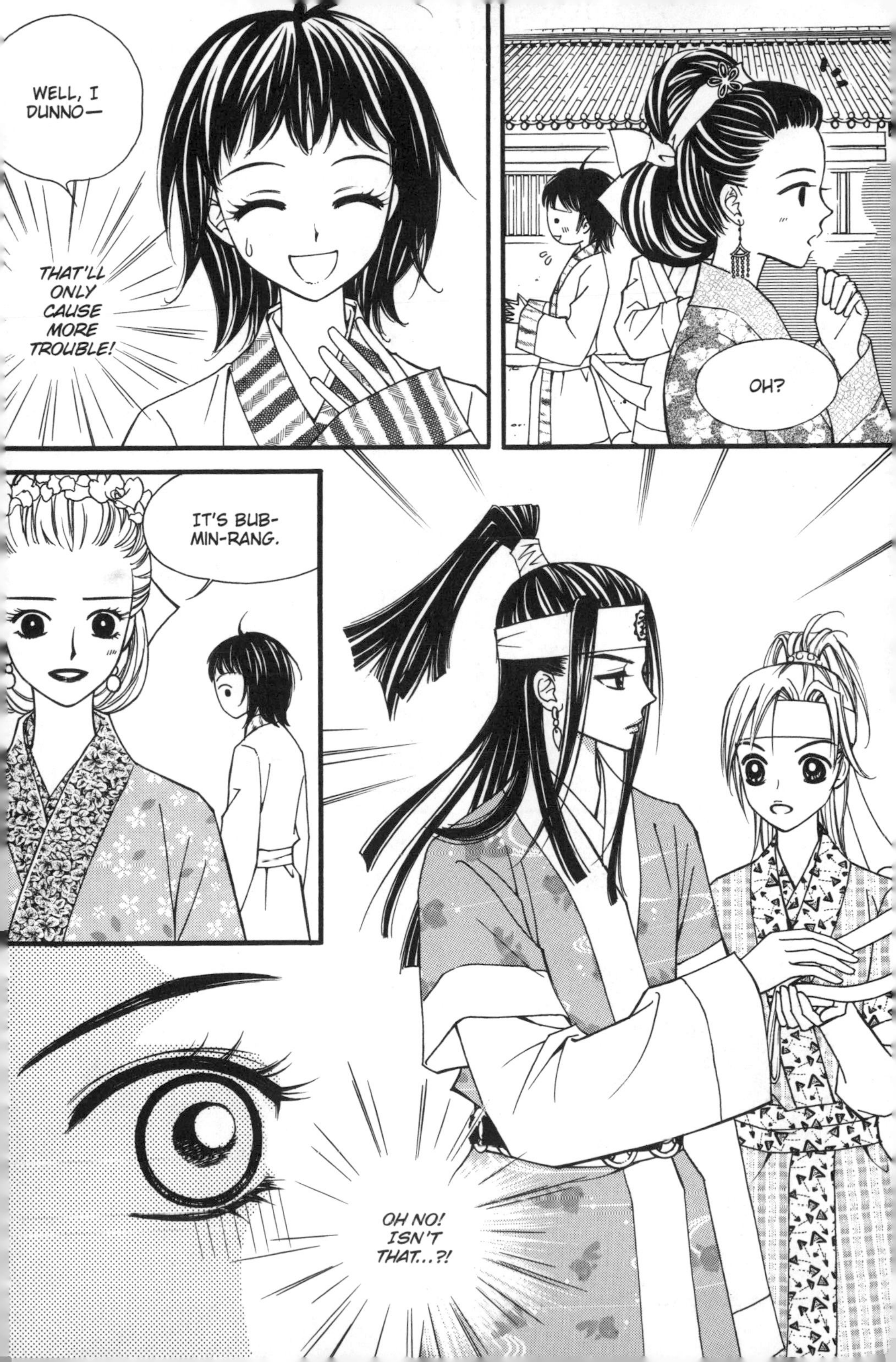
WELL, I DUNNO—
THAT'LL ONLY CAUSE MORE TROUBLE!
OH?
IT'S BUB-MIN-RANG.
OH NO! ISN'T THAT...?!

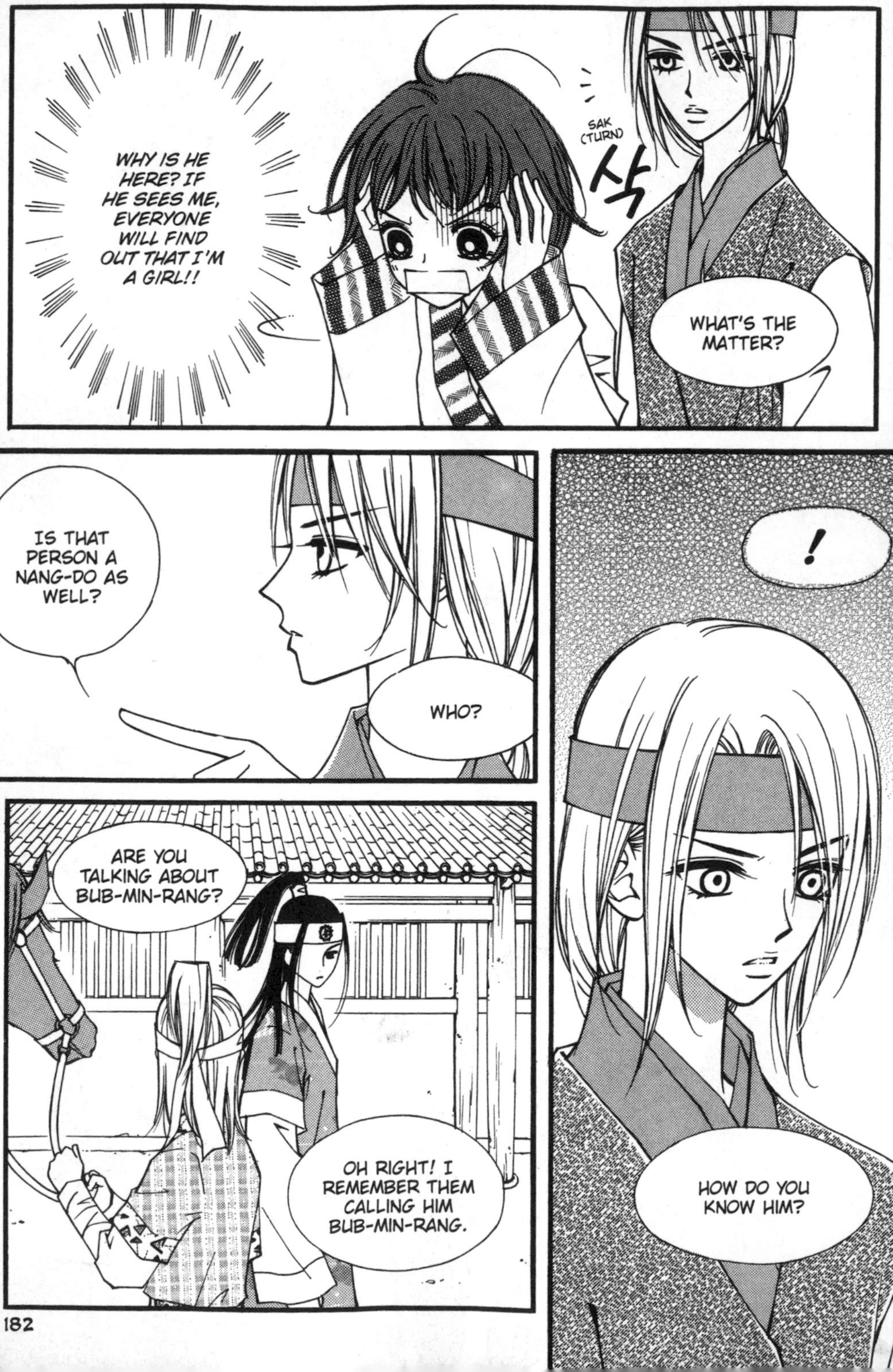
WHY IS HE HERE? IF HE SEES ME, EVERYONE WILL FIND OUT THAT I'M A GIRL!!
SAK (TURN)
삭
WHAT'S THE MATTER?
IS THAT PERSON A NANG-DO AS WELL?
WHO?
ARE YOU TALKING ABOUT BUB-MIN-RANG?
OH RIGHT! I REMEMBER THEM CALLING HIM BUB-MIN-RANG.
!
HOW DO YOU KNOW HIM?

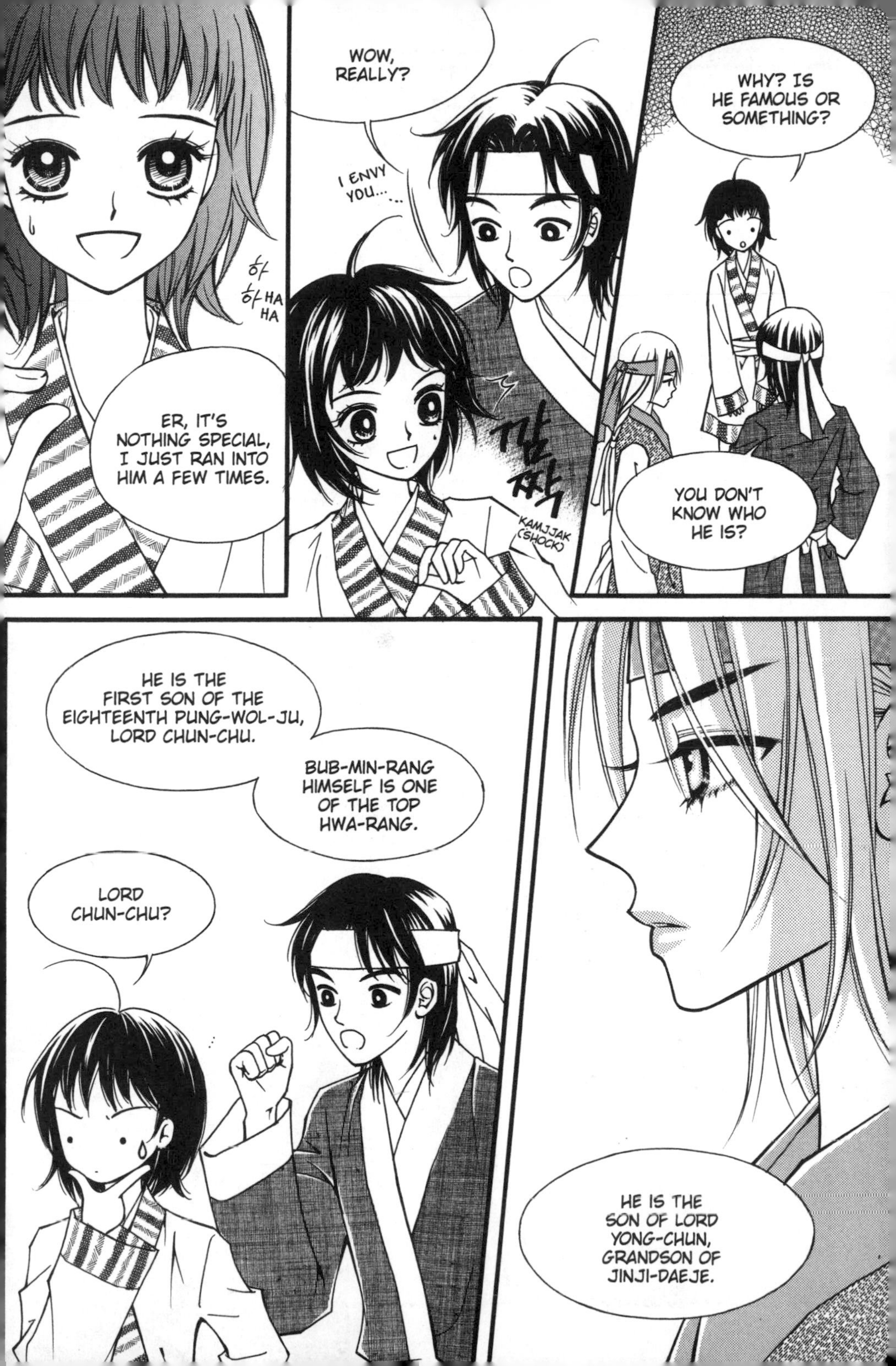
하
하 HA
HA
ER, IT'S NOTHING SPECIAL, I JUST RAN INTO HIM A FEW TIMES.
WOW, REALLY?
I ENVY YOU...
깜짝
KAMJJAK (SHOCK)
WHY? IS HE FAMOUS OR SOMETHING?
YOU DON'T KNOW WHO HE IS?
HE IS THE FIRST SON OF THE EIGHTEENTH PUNG-WOL-JU, LORD CHUN-CHU.
BUB-MIN-RANG HIMSELF IS ONE OF THE TOP HWA-RANG.
LORD CHUN-CHU?
HE IS THE SON OF LORD YONG-CHUN, GRANDSON OF JINJI-DAEJE.

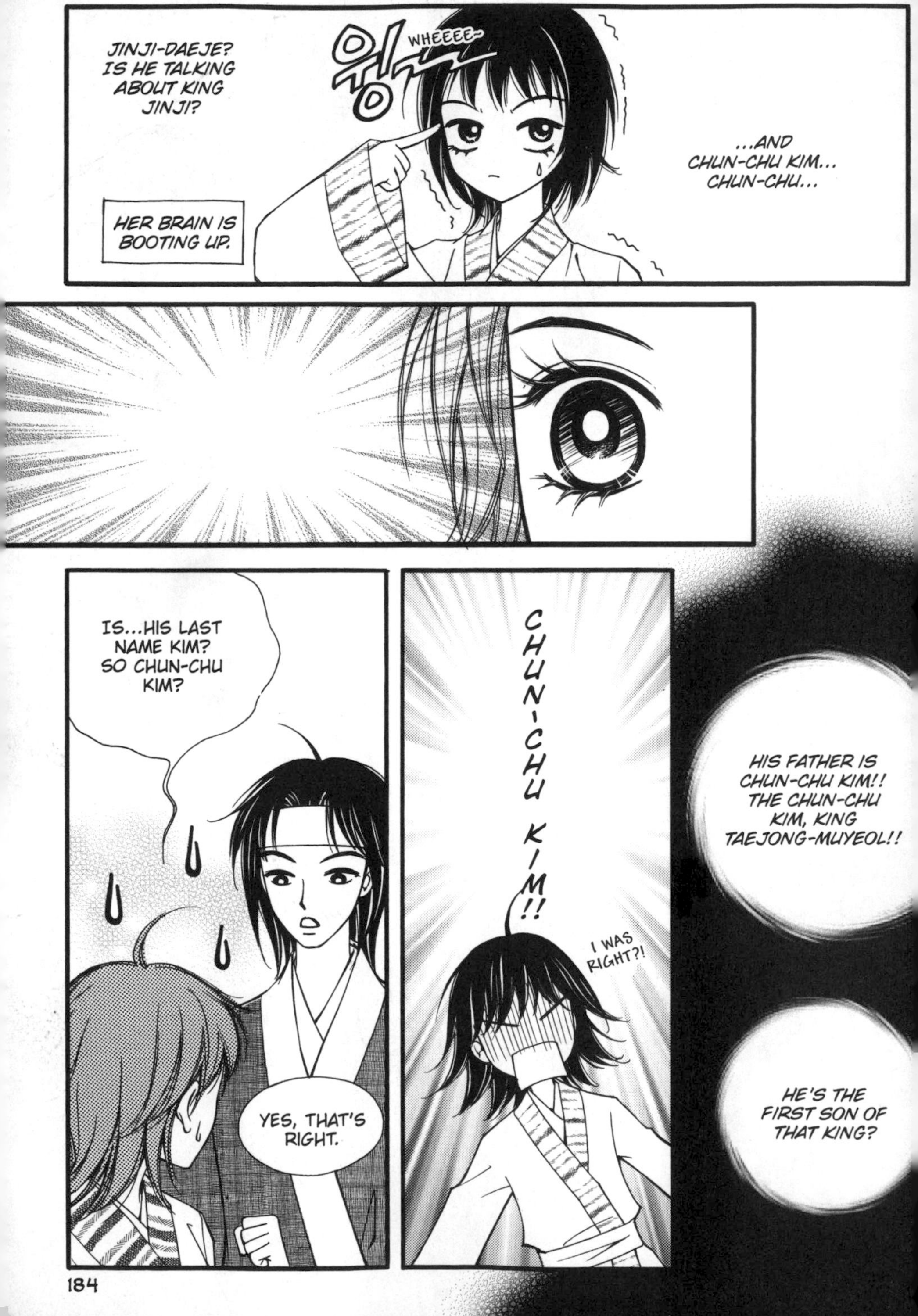
JINJI-DAEJE? IS HE TALKING ABOUT KING JINJI?
윙
WHEEEE-
HER BRAIN IS BOOTING UP.
...AND CHUN-CHU KIM... CHUN-CHU...
IS...HIS LAST NAME KIM? SO CHUN-CHU KIM?
YES, THAT'S RIGHT.
CHUN-CHU KIM!!
I WAS RIGHT?!
HIS FATHER IS CHUN-CHU KIM!! THE CHUN-CHU KIM, KING TAEJONG-MUYEOL!!
HE'S THE FIRST SON OF THAT KING?

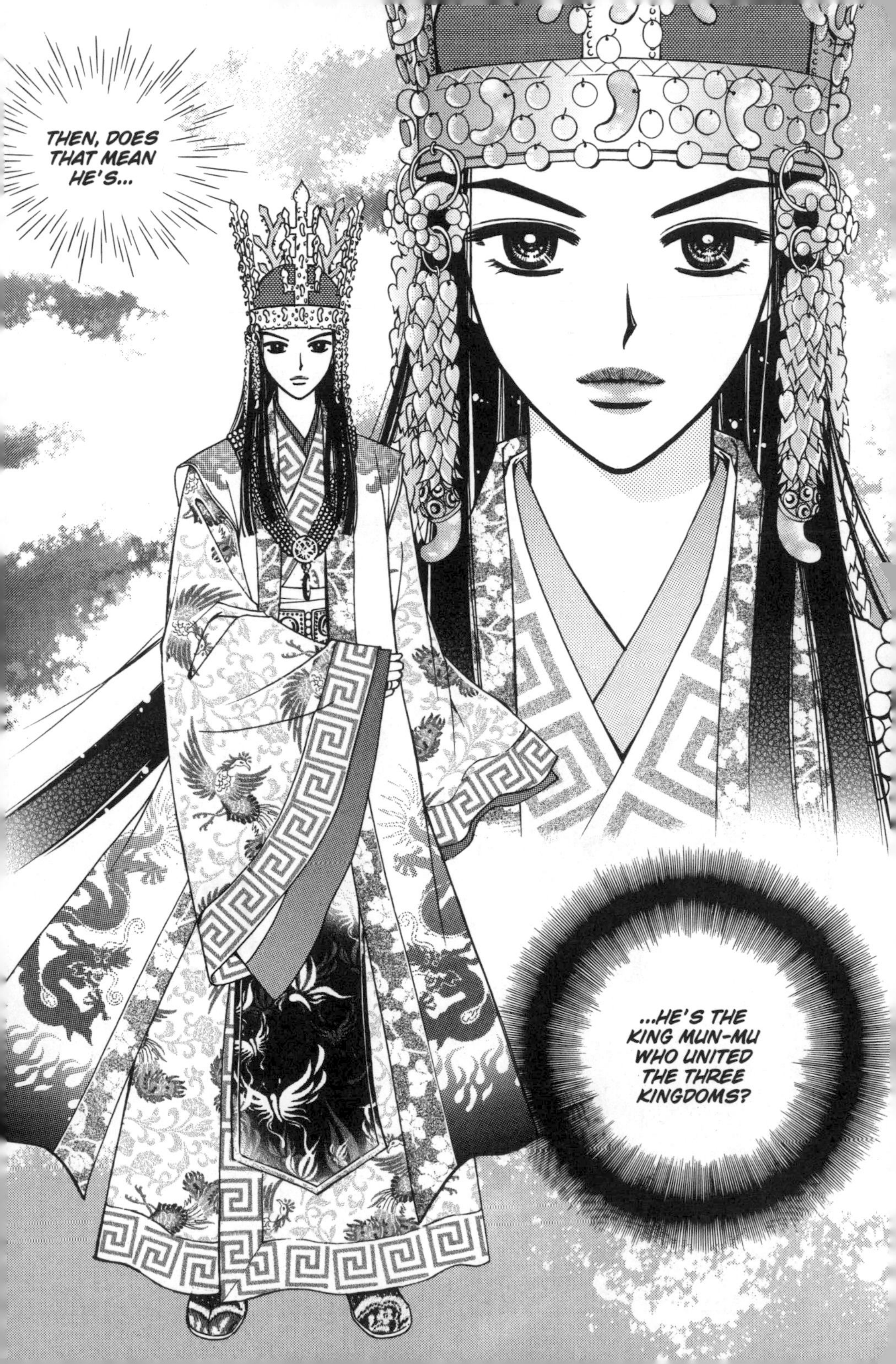
THEN, DOES THAT MEAN HE'S...
...HE'S THE KING MUN-MU WHO UNITED THE THREE KINGDOMS?

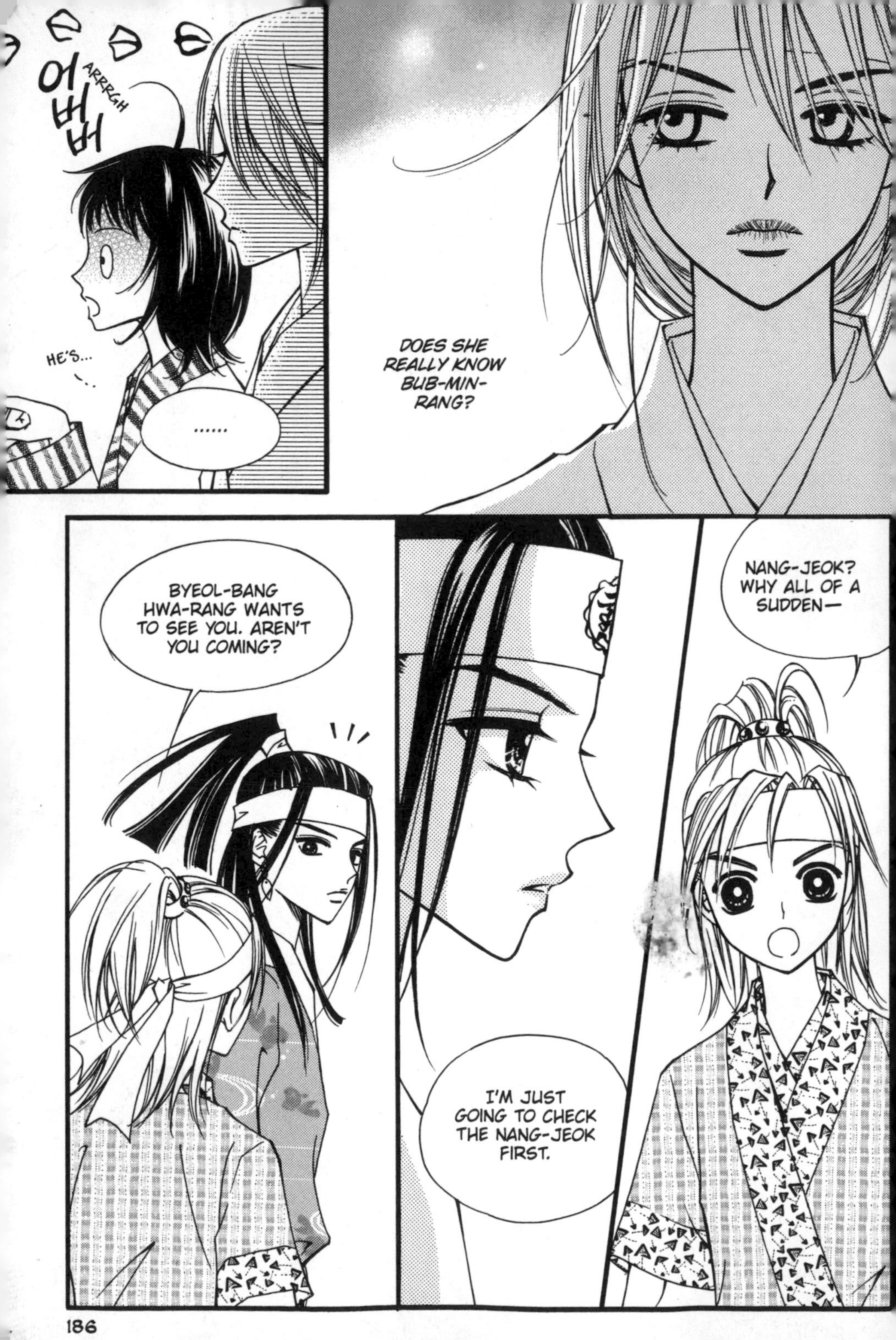
어버버
ARRRGH
HE'S...
......
DOES SHE REALLY KNOW BUB-MIN-RANG?
BYEOL-BANG HWA-RANG WANTS TO SEE YOU. AREN'T YOU COMING?
I'M JUST GOING TO CHECK THE NANG-JEOK FIRST.
NANG-JEOK? WHY ALL OF A SUDDEN—

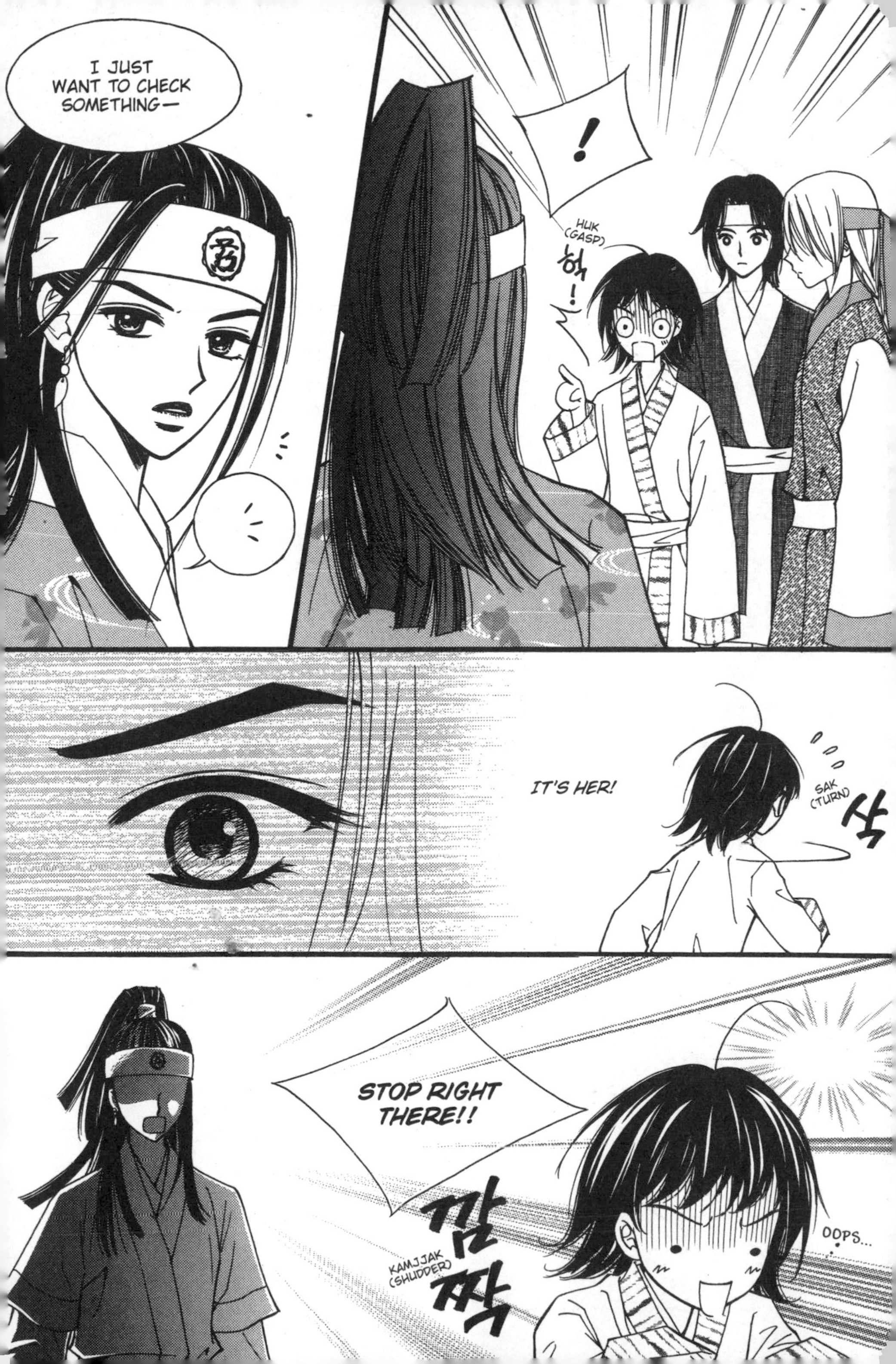
I JUST WANT TO CHECK SOMETHING—
!
HUK (GASP)
헉!
IT'S HER!
SAK (TURN)
삭
STOP RIGHT THERE!!
KAMJJAK (SHUDDER)
깜짝
OOPS...

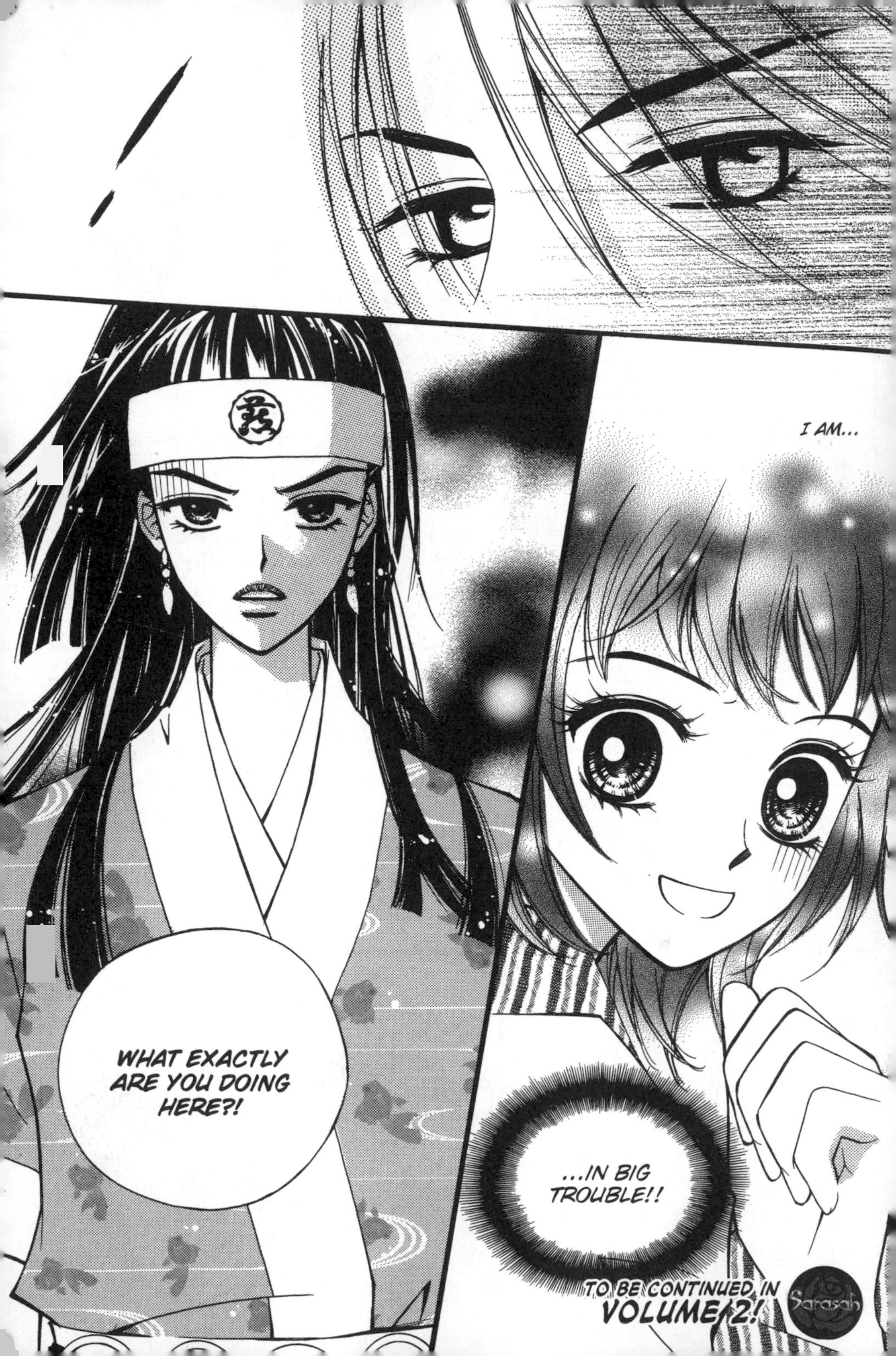
WHAT EXACTLY ARE YOU DOING HERE?!
I AM...
...IN BIG TROUBLE!!
TO BE CONTINUED IN VOLUME 2!

SARASAH BONUS STORY

THE UNTOLD STORY

I DECIDED TO HAVE JI-HAE GO TO THE SHILLA PERIOD IN THE FIRST CHAPTER...BUT THERE IS ONE SCENE THAT HAD TO BE CUT BECAUSE FIFTY PAGES JUST WEREN'T ENOUGH.

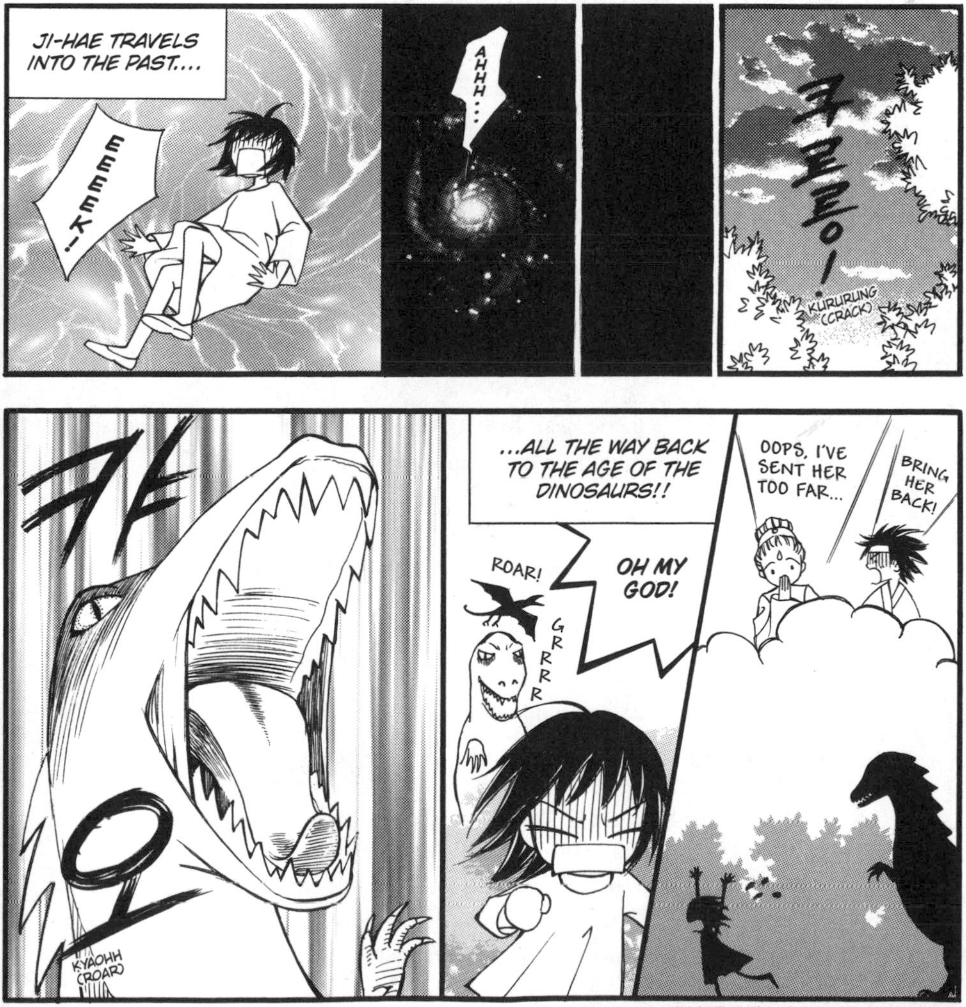
JI-HAE TRAVELS INTO THE PAST....
EEEEEK!!
AHHH...
쿠르릉!
KURURUNG (CRACK)
KYAOHH (ROAR)
...ALL THE WAY BACK TO THE AGE OF THE DINOSAURS!!
ROAR!
GRRRR
OH MY GOD!
OOPS, I'VE SENT HER TOO FAR...
BRING HER BACK!

WHAT? IT'S BETTER WITHOUT?

TRANSLATION AND HISTORICAL NOTES

Page 36
-nim is an honorific suffix, like "-san" or "-sama" in Japanese.

Page 81
Joseon Period: Joseon was an old dynasty of Korea founded around 1392 and lasted for approximately five centuries. Joseon was the last royal and the longest ruling dynasty of Korean history. After declaring the Korean Empire in 1897, the dynasty ended with Japanese annexation in 1910.

Goryeo: One of the old kingdoms of Korea established in 918 by uniting the Three Kingdoms (Goguryeo, Shilla, and Baekje) and ruled Korea until it was defeated by the Joseon dynasty in 1392.

Goguryeo: An ancient kingdom located in the northern and central parts of the Korean peninsula, southern Manchuria, and southern Russian Maritime province. Along with Baekje and Shilla, Goguryeo was one of the Three Kingdoms of Korea.

Page 87
Shilla: One of the Three Kingdoms of Korea. Allied with China, Shilla eventually conquered the other two kingdoms, Baekje and Goguryeo.

Page 118
Yaksajaeill: A day to give prayers to Buddha. It falls on the eighth day of every month in the Lunar calendar.

Page 167
Nang-Do: A term referring to a member of Hwa-Rang-Do.

Hwa-Rang: A leader within Hwa-Rang-Do. (-Rang is added as a suffix to one's name, i.e. Bub-Min-Rang.) Each Hwa-Rang has many Nang-Do beneath him. Hwa-Rang-Do was an elite group of youths in Shilla. It was an educational institution as well as a social club where members, who were mostly sons and daughters of nobility, gathered for all aspects of study. This group developed into a more military organization and was most famous for its members exceptional archery skills.

Page 168
I don't have to talk formally to you!: In Korea, one must use a respectful form of speech when addressing elders, even if the person being addressed is only a year older.

Page 170
Yebu: A government division of Shilla.

Ju-Hyeong: The head of Hwa-Rang-Do. Also known as Pung-Wol-Ju.

Page 172
Nang-Jung: Name or organization of different groups of Hwa-Rang-Do.

Page 183
Pung-Wol-Ju: The head of Hwa-Rang-Do.

Jinji-Daeje: The 25th monarch of the Shilla. Jinji reigned from August 576 to July 579.

Page 184
King Taejong-Muyeol: The 29th monarch of the Shilla who ruled from 654 to 661. He played a key role in developing the country's diplomatic links, which led to the unification of the Three Kingdoms of Korea in his son's period.

Page 185
King Mun-Mu: The 30th king of the Shilla, who united the Three Kingdoms of Korea. He is usually considered to have been the first ruler of the Unified Shilla period. Mun-Mu was the first son of King Muyeol. He was born Prince Bub-Min, and took the name Mun-Mu when he succeeded his father to the throne.

Page 186
Nang-Jeok: List of all the members of Hwa-Rang-Do.

Yen
Press
www.yenpress.com

Becoming the princess... Isn't that every girl's dream?!

Monarchy rule ended long ago in Korea, but there are still other countries with kings, queens, princes and princesses. What if Korea had continued monarchism? What if all the beautiful palaces, which are now only historical relics, were actually filled with people? What if the glamorous royal family still maintained the palace customs? Welcome to a world where Korea still has the royal family living in their everyday lives! Only for this one high school girl, Chae-Kyung, is this a tragedy, since she has to marry the prince — who apparently is a total bastard!

THE ROYAL PALACE
Goong
vol.1 ~ 5

Park SoHee

The newest title from the creators of <Demon Diary> and <Angel Diary>!

Once upon a time, a selfish king summoned the monstrous Bulkirin into the real world. The monster killed half of all human beings, leaving the rest helpless as to what to do. That is, until one day when a hero appeared and defeated the Bulkirin with the legendary "Seven Blade Sword." But···what does all this have to do with 8th grader Eun-Gyo Sung?! First, she gets suspended from school for fighting. Then, she runs away from home. The last thing she needed was to be kidnapped—and whisked into the past by a mysterious stranger named No-Ah!

Available at bookstores near you!

Legend 1-5

Kara · Woo SooJung

SARASAH ①

RYU RYANG

Translation: June Um

English Adaptation and Lettering: Abigail Blackman

Yen Press
Hachette Book Group
237 Park Avenue, New York, NY 10017

Visit our websites at www.HachetteBookGroup.com and www.YenPress.com.

Yen Press is an imprint of Hachette Book Group, Inc. The Yen Press name and logo are trademarks of Hachette Book Group, Inc.

First Yen Press Edition: July 2009

ISBN: 978-0-7595-3015-7

10 9 8 7 6 5 4 3 2 1

BVG

Printed in the United States of America